Soviet Policy in Eastern Europe

A COUNCIL ON FOREIGN RELATIONS BOOK

COUNCIL ON FOREIGN RELATIONS BOOKS

The Council on Foreign Relations, Inc., is a nonprofit and nonpartisan organization devoted to promoting improved understanding of international affairs through the free exchange of ideas. The Council does not take any position on questions of foreign policy and has no affiliation with, and receives no funding from, the United States government.

From time to time, books and monographs written by members of the Council's research staff or visiting fellows, or commissioned by the Council, or written by an independent author with critical review contributed by a Council study or working group are published with the designation "Council on Foreign Relations Book." Any book or monograph bearing that designation is, in the judgment of the Committee on Studies of the Council's board of directors, a responsible treatment of a significant international topic worthy of presentation to the public. All statements of fact and expressions of opinion contained in Council books are, however, the sole responsibility of the author.

SOVIET POLICY IN EASTERN EUROPE

Edited by Sarah Meiklejohn Terry

Yale University Press   New Haven and London

Set in Baskerville Roman type.
Printed in the United States of America by
Edwards Brothers, Inc., Ann Arbor, Michigan.

---

*The paper in this book meets the guidelines for permanence
and durability of the Committee on Production Guidelines
for Book Longevity of the Council on Library Resources.*

Library of Congress Cataloging in Publication Data
Main entry under title:

Soviet policy in Eastern Europe.

"A Council on Foreign Relations book."
Includes index.
1. Europe, Eastern—Foreign relations—Soviet Union—
Addresses, essays, lectures.   2. Soviet Union—Foreign
relations—Europe, Eastern—Addresses, essays, lectures.
3. Soviet Union—Foreign relations—1975–   —
Addresses, essays, lectures.   I. Terry, Sarah Meiklejohn, 1937–
II. Council on Foreign Relations.
DJK45S65S68   1984   327.47   83–21889
ISBN 0–300–03131-9

10 9 8 7 6 5 4 3 2 1

To my husband, Bob, with love and gratitude

Contents

List of Tables

Preface

The drama unfolding in Poland since August 1980 has served as a forceful reminder of the centrality of Eastern Europe in Moscow's foreign policy concerns—a centrality that had seemed to wane in the 1970s under the combined impact of détente and the globalization of Soviet power and policy. At the same time, the Soviet response to that drama—determined and rigid in rhetoric, yet prudent and vacillating in action—suggests not merely a greater sophistication on the Kremlin's part in the handling of alliance problems, but a growing level of tension among Soviet policy goals and requirements on several levels: first, between their global ambitions or domestic needs, on the one hand, and their regional interests, on the other; and second, among their political, economic, and ideological interests within Eastern Europe itself.

At the global level, the period since the late 1960s has witnessed a number of changes in the objective situation of the Soviet Union: its emergence as a superpower with far-reaching strategic capabilities, a festering China problem on its eastern flank, the post-Vietnam War decline in American prestige and power, vastly expanded opportunities for East-West trade, and the impact of the energy crisis on Soviet terms of trade, to mention only the most important. On the domestic front, the Soviet leadership is confronted by apparently intractable problems: a persistent decline in the economic growth rate, agricultural stagnation, a widening technological gap, the need for massive investments in resource development, and unfavorable demographic and labor distribution trends. These problems are all too familiar to require further elaboration here. For our purposes, the important point is that this combination of expanded global opportunities (and challenges) and constricted domestic capabilities has altered Moscow's perceptions of Eastern Europe's place in its political, economic, and strategic calculations—and in ways that accentuate the underlying tensions among the several dimensions of their policy toward the region.

These tensions are, of course, nothing new. But they have become more intense, and the options open to the Soviets, as well as to the East European regimes, for coping with these tensions are narrowing. At the most basic level, what is involved here is what James F. Brown has aptly called a conflict between "viability" and "cohesion":* that is, a conflict between Moscow's desire to see in Eastern Europe stable and productive societies that would gradually come to be regarded as legitimate by their populations, that would not require periodic propping up at Soviet expense, but would increasingly contribute to the collective well-being of the socialist commonwealth and to Soviet interests abroad; and, on the other hand, the requirement that these systems continue to conform in various ways to Soviet needs—particularly that they continue to serve as validation of the universality of the Soviet model of socialism.

While Khrushchev toward the end of his rule came to value viability (thus setting in motion the reformist tendencies of the 1960s), the Brezhnev period saw a shift back toward an emphasis on cohesion. Largely in reaction to the Prague Spring, as well as to the potential for ideological erosion in the face of expanded contacts with the West, Moscow reverted to a more rigid stance on the applicability of Soviet experience and policies even as it was becoming clear, to many East Europeans at least, that those policies were a major source of their chronic inefficiencies and instability. By the end of the 1970s, most of the economies of the region were experiencing sharply declining growth rates and dislocations, aggravated by heavy debt burdens.

Thus, well before Solidarity burst into the headlines, it was clear that Soviet-East European relations were entering a difficult and potentially volatile period. Unlike the 1970s, when the Soviet leadership was able to avoid the hard choices among competing interests—when détente and easy credits provided the illusion that Moscow had found the formula for achieving viability *with* cohesion—the problems and pressures already evident in the early 1980s, and certain to continue throughout the decade, will force a number of very difficult choices on the Soviet leadership concerning their economic, political, and strategic priorities not only in Eastern Europe but at home and beyond the bloc as well.

The design of the volume is intended to reflect both the diversity of Eastern Europe and the multiplicity of Soviet concerns in the region. Following a historical overview, which provides the substantive introduction and sets out the major themes of the volume, there are four country studies covering Soviet policy toward six of the eight East European communist states (chapters 2–5). These chapters are not meant to be strictly parallel in either format or coverage. Rather, each focuses on the specific set of issues and problems posed by the country or countries in question,

---

*J. F. Brown, "Détente and Soviet Policy in Eastern Europe," *Survey*, 20 (Spring/Summer 1974), 46–58, or idem, "Relations Between the Soviet Union and Its Eastern European Allies: A Survey," Report R-1742-PR (Santa Monica: The Rand Corporation, 1975).

thereby pointing up the disparities as well as the similarities in Soviet-East European relations. Thus the chapter on Soviet policy toward the German Democratic Republic focuses not only on bilateral relations and the GDR's growing importance within the bloc but also on the complex triangular Moscow-Berlin-Bonn relationship; while the chapter on Poland—on the one hand the largest of the Soviet Union's East European allies and the strategic linchpin of the bloc, but at the same time the most troublesome and least stable member of the alliance—provides a test case of Soviet tolerance for domestic deviation and of their skills in crisis management short of military intervention. The remaining two country-focused chapters each cover Soviet policy toward two East European countries: Czechoslovakia and Hungary, and Romania and Yugoslavia. These pairings are not meant to imply that the countries in question are either less important or less interesting than the GDR and Poland, and certainly not that Soviet policy toward the paired countries has been identical. Rather, they are paired because they have posed broadly comparable challenges—of internal systemic reform in the one case and of national autonomy in the second—and because the differences as well as the similarities in Moscow's response to those challenges are best understood in a comparative context.

Of the two East European communist states omitted from these country studies, one, Albania, has had no meaningful relations with the USSR for two decades and was viewed as of only marginal relevance to the basic concerns of this volume. Omission of Bulgaria, on the other hand, was a compromise solution that provoked some disagreement among the contributors. Although the widely accepted view of Bulgaria as the most conformist, loyal, and passive of Moscow's client states is generally accurate, it remains an important and from the Soviet viewpoint highly useful (if not always politically interesting) member of the bloc. In the final analysis, space considerations militated against including a separate chapter on Soviet policy toward Bulgaria, although it has of course been treated elsewhere in the volume.

The next four chapters are topical in nature, each addressing some dimension of Soviet policy as it affects the entire region. Chapters 6 and 7 are concerned with different aspects of the economic relationship: the former with the institutions and functions of the Council for Mutual Economic Assistance (CMEA) as instruments of Soviet policy, the latter with the increasingly critical role that energy plays as a source of Soviet leverage over the region. Chapter 8 focuses on questions of ideology and systemic change and on the role that the theory of "socialist development" plays in regulating the broader Soviet-East European relationship. Finally, chapter 9 analyzes relations within the Warsaw Pact from the point of view both of its utility as an instrument of Soviet military policy and of the tensions generated within the alliance by a growing asymmetry of interests and needs.

In the last two chapters, the focus shifts away from the Soviet-East European relationship per se to the question of how that relationship influences or is influenced by East-West relations. Chapter 10 explores the complex dilemmas facing the Soviets as they attempt to expand their influence in Western Europe without sacrificing control over its Eastern half, while chapter 11 examines the interplay between the bilateral U.S.-Soviet relationship and the policy of each superpower toward Eastern Europe and sets forth the likely choices that will face U.S. policymakers in the unpredictable and potentially volatile conditions of the mid-to-late 1980s. Finally, the brief concluding essay addresses the dilemmas that succession politics and economic stringency will pose for Moscow in the 1980s.

One final note: References to Yuri Andropov are in the present tense, his death having been announced just as the book was going to press.

Acknowledgments

In any undertaking of this scope, there are more people to whom authors and editor are indebted than there is space to thank them. The authors have acknowledged their separate debts in their individual chapters. It is my pleasure to acknowledge our collective debt to the Council on Foreign Relations, to Project Director Robert Legvold, and to the many other members and associates of the Council who contributed to the volume in various ways. In particular, our special thanks go to Project Administrator Andrea Zwiebel, whose meticulous coordination and editorial skills were instrumental in its production.

1

Soviet Policy in Eastern Europe: An Overview

JOHN C. CAMPBELL

The Polish nation, so often throughout European history a victim and a symbol of oppression and of tragedy, has directed the eyes of the world once more to the explosives lying beneath the surface of the Soviet empire in Eastern Europe, as the Czechs did in 1968 and the Hungarians in 1956. The succession of crises has confirmed two inescapable propositions: first, that the Soviet Union, the dominant power in the region since the Second World War, has not been able to stabilize the situation there, to find answers to the pressing problems, or to win the consent of the governed; second, that when those peoples, in attempting to deal with their own problems or to realize their aspirations to greater freedom, reach the point where the Soviet Union sees its vital interests at stake, it will act to assert control by whatever means are deemed necessary.

Those two propositions, put in that stark and simplified form, illustrate the basic Soviet dilemma. The main purpose of policy is to have the East European states serve as assets, not as burdens or points of vulnerability, in the strategy of the USSR as a global power. But the capacity to intervene and suppress dissent does not in itself achieve that purpose. When matters come to the point of military intervention or forcible suppression, it means that Soviet policy has already failed, that the chosen instruments, primarily the local Communist parties, have proved unequal to their task. Indeed, the real story lies not just in the climactic moment of a decision to use force but in the many decisions made over the years when the storms are gathering, or after an intervention takes place and "socialist order" is restored: decisions on the nature of a reliable political structure and on what guidance to give the local Communists; on what economic relations to build among the states of the bloc; on what openings to the West to permit or deny; on how to balance the economic benefits of reform against prospective threats to the political system; or on how to deal with one East European state in the light of the likely or possible impact on the others.

For the Soviets, every choice has its risks and its costs. They want the East European states to be viable and productive, with the necessary minimum of cooperation and tolerance on the part of the people. They also want to be sure of maintaining control. Yet these two aims may be in conflict. Reforms that relax economic or political restrictions in the interest of viability can fuel popular currents that could threaten the structure of control. Conversely, the rigid maintenance of control can lead to economic stagnation, passive resistance, and violence. One can describe the course of Soviet policy as a quest for the right balance between viability and control. Where the point of balance may be in dynamic situations of great complexity, or whether such a point exists at all, has never been easy to determine.

A study of Soviet policy, accordingly, calls for an investigation of many factors, varying from one state to another and changing over time. It involves a continuing reassessment of Soviet aims, as the East European countries, and in some respects the USSR itself, have become quite different societies from what they were in 1945.

The Soviet leaders themselves have not been particularly helpful in providing enlightenment on the subject. At no time have they deigned to present to the world a candid exposition of their aims, interests, and policies in Eastern Europe. They reiterate, of course, the familiar dogma according to which these states have their natural and appointed place as members of the socialist camp or commonwealth. They are all marching forward to "scientific socialism." On particular occasions—as in the midst of the crises of 1956 and 1968—the Soviet leadership has issued pronunciamentos on the nature of relations with Eastern Europe, but they have reflected the political purposes and circumstances of the time, both in content and in the fact of their publication. Like the programs of party congresses and thousands of official statements, they are but partial evidence of policy and may indeed misrepresent it instead of providing accurate definition.

Soviet aims and interests are best deduced from the record of Soviet conduct, with whatever help the arts of Kremlinology can provide. What is especially necessary for an understanding of recent Soviet policy—and that is the major task of this book—is to assess in dual perspective (a) the Soviet Union's perceptions of its stake in the region in the light of its own strategic, political, and economic position, and (b) the evolving East European context in which Soviet policy must operate.

The dominant fact of Soviet physical power, present or nearby, has always been in the forefront of thinking in both Moscow and Eastern Europe. But power has not been a substitute for good intelligence, judgment, and diplomacy. As the Soviet Union moves through the 1980s, the task of maintaining its position and interests in the region bids fair to become more complex and more difficult than at any time since Soviet dominance was established there in the wake of the Second World War. Most of the East European states face economic problems beyond their ability to solve, and some are weighed down with a huge burden of foreign debt. Can the Soviet Union, with its own economy under pressure, furnish the resources these states will need, help pay their debts, supply energy at prices they can afford? Will one or another East European regime, unable to give its people either more bread or more freedom, strain harder at Moscow's leash or try to edge its way to independence, or perhaps simply fall apart?

Finally, what of the broader international aspects? Soviet policies elsewhere in the world have been handicapped by the continuing challenge in Poland. Will the Soviets conduct a more vigorous or riskier political strategy in Western Europe to compensate for weakness in the east? Will the deterioration in Eastern Europe reach the point where the West may have to be brought into joint rescue operations, and if so, how will Soviet security and political interests be affected? East-West relations will inevitably be influenced by developments in the Soviet half of Europe. May they also provide a channel for dealing safely with them? These are questions to be explored in this book. They should also be, sooner or later, on the agenda of the Soviet Union's post-Brezhnev leadership.

HISTORICAL BACKGROUND

To gain perspective, to see how the Soviets got there and why they stayed, it is necessary to go back to the time of Stalin. Not that he was the source of all policies or that little has changed since then. Stalin might not easily have recognized all of Khrushchev's and Brezhnev's policies as lineal descendants of his own. Yet the pattern of change has been one of evolution and adjustment rather than of sharp and unpredictable zigzags and reversals. Policy in action, in any event, begins with Stalin.

The establishment of Soviet power in Eastern Europe can be seen, historically, as a continuation, perhaps the culmination, of a process of westward expansion begun long ago under the czars. Stalin's bargain with Hitler and their subsequent disputes left no doubt about the Soviet Union's interest and ambitions in Eastern Europe—whether for security, for imperial expansion, or for the cause of revolution—and those ambitions were not abandoned even when the Soviet state was fighting for its life and needed Western help. With the defeat of Hitler's armies and the creation of a vacuum in the region, it was inevitable that the Soviets would move in. The Western powers were not there; they were not able or prepared to contest Soviet moves except by ineffective protest.

It was not entirely clear, in 1944 and 1945, how much of the area the Soviets would insist on dominating, or whether they would be satisfied in some cases with influence short of domination.[1] Stalin's ambitions may

1. Vojtech Mastny, *Russia's Road to the Cold War: Diplomacy, Warfare, and the Politics of Communism, 1941–1945* (New York: Columbia University Press, 1979), pp. 183–228.

have been extensive but his policies probably did not become fixed at an early date except perhaps in the case of Poland, which he was resolved to control; the record of his dealings with the Polish government-in-exile and with the Western allies leaves no doubt on that point. He knew, moreover, that control of Poland would give the Soviet Union access to Germany and decisive leverage over Czechoslovakia, where President Beneš himself, sensing that what independence his country would be allowed to enjoy depended primarily on Moscow, had already during the war made the decisions that mortgaged Czechoslovakia's future both internationally and internally. As for Hungary and the Balkans, Stalin's famous percentage deal with Churchill in 1944 documented his insistence on Soviet primacy in Romania and Bulgaria (in return for British primacy in Greece), while in Yugoslavia and Hungary, where he agreed to a more even division of influence with the West, he must have had confidence that the cards were stacked in the Soviet Union's favor.

It is often said that the boundaries of empire were set by the lines reached by the Soviet armies in World War II and that their presence made possible the imposition of satellite regimes in Eastern Europe. Both propositions are generally but not precisely true. The pattern of the presence or absence of Soviet forces was a checkered one. The lines of occupation in Germany and Austria were set by international agreement, not by the circumstance of military positions at the end of the war (and Khrushchev later gave up the Soviet zone in Austria in exchange for neutralization of the whole country); Soviet forces did not occupy all of Czechoslovakia (and withdrew very soon, in 1945), passed through only part of Yugoslavia and did not stay, and did not enter Albania at all.

The decisive events that established Soviet dominance in Eastern Europe were those that marked the seizure of political power by Communist parties. The pace, pattern, and degree of Soviet involvement varied from country to country, taking account of local conditions. The Soviets were always prepared, however, to make their own conditions when necessary in order to bring about the desired result. The chosen instruments were the leaders of the local Communist parties, some of whom returned to their countries in the baggage train of the Soviet armies, while others emerged from the anti-Nazi resistance. These leaders were helped from the start to gain a share of power, then to take full control by suppressing or coopting their erstwhile non-Communist allies. They were also helped to carry through a directed political and social revolution in which the transition stage of "people's democracy" would presumably lead, in time, to the form of socialism in effect in the USSR. The local Communist parties and the new governing structures were watched and supervised by Soviet officials and, just to make sure, thoroughly penetrated by Soviet agents.

Neither in political strategy nor in military dispositions, however, was the Stalinization of Eastern Europe as planned, thoroughgoing, or monolithic as it has generally been pictured. In Yugoslavia and Albania the national Communist parties gained power on their own, and the absence of Soviet forces made it easier for them, some years later, to throw off the Soviet connection. Whereas in Bulgaria and Romania the Soviets had imposed Communist regimes by the spring of 1945, in Hungary they followed a strategy of gradualism, even permitted a free election (in which the Communists got but 17% of the vote), and did not establish full Communist control until 1947.[2] In Czechoslovakia they gave up a powerful lever by withdrawing their forces, counting on President Beneš's mixed regime, with Communists in key positions, to secure their interests; as it turned out, the timing and circumstances of the Communist takeover in February 1948 were determined more by internal factors, including a perceptible decline in Communist popularity, than by Moscow, although Moscow made sure of the outcome.[3] Throughout the area the Communist parties were torn by factionalism that even Moscow's recognized authority could not entirely suppress. And the issues that were beginning to sour Yugoslavia's relations with the Kremlin were present, in milder form, in the other states.

In any event, by the spring of 1948 Stalin had succeeded in his primary purpose, which was to seal off the entire area from the Arctic to the borders of Greece from the military power and effective political influence of the West. In Finland, a nation with a peripheral location and a demonstrated will to independence, he had settled for a compromise that met Soviet security interests through limitations on Finland's foreign policy without insisting on Communist domination in domestic affairs. In Greece, where indirect support of the Communists in a civil war failed to bring them to power, he had accepted the fait accompli of Western intervention, which was part of what he saw as a bargain keeping the West out of the other Balkan states. In between was a bloc of states led by Communists and tied to the USSR by formal security treaties, by political and party ties, and by the inability of the West to challenge Soviet dominance.

Was it necessary to go so far? Once the process gained momentum, apparently, there was no reason to risk reliance on less drastic ways to ensure Soviet security, not to mention other benefits. During the forma-

2. Stephen D. Kertesz, ed., *The Fate of East Central Europe: Hopes and Failures of American Foreign Policy* (Notre Dame: University of Notre Dame Press, 1956), pp. 228–31. See also Charles Gati, "Seven Themes in Search of Reality: Political Life in Postwar Hungary (1944–1947)," paper delivered at the 1982 National Convention of the American Association for the Advancement of Slavic Studies.

3. Paul E. Zinner, *Communist Strategy and Tactics in Czechoslovakia, 1918–1948* (London: Pall Mall, 1963), pp. 186–218.

tive period 1945–48, the Soviets had the option of applying the Finnish model to the other countries of Eastern Europe. There is no evidence that Stalin ever contemplated doing so. His judgment was that non-Communist governments there would be anti-Soviet governments. Security required control.

The intensification of the cold war confirmed the Soviet leadership in this view. The United States, largely as a result of Soviet policy in Eastern Europe, was protesting and contesting what it saw as Soviet expansion and had embarked on a strategy that looked, in Moscow, very much like military and political encirclement. As American power took on a global role, in effect organizing the non-Soviet world into an anti-Soviet world, Soviet control of Eastern Europe appeared all the more necessary. The Soviet empire in Eastern Europe had become a fact of world politics. Although no master plan to reach that point may have existed, policies and events had unfolded as if there had been such a plan. No retreat was contemplated.

The same year that marked the completion of the system by the coup in Prague, however, produced a new kind of challenge in Yugoslavia, a revolt from within on the part of a ruling Communist party. By its novelty and its boldness Tito's defiance was a surprise to the Soviets and to the world, although in its essence it should not have been, since nationalism is an elemental force to which even Communists are not immune. In the interwar period the Soviet leadership and the Comintern had had to cope with it in many Communist parties, including those of Eastern Europe, often resorting to drastic purges to keep matters in hand. "Nationalist deviation" had always been a cardinal sin in the world communist movement, for it threatened the ideological and political authority of Moscow, on which the whole edifice rested. In postwar Eastern Europe the conflict between "Muscovite" and "indigenous" Communist leaders, sometimes suppressed or muted as they fought common enemies, was always there. For the first time in the history of world communism, the Soviets had to work through parties and leaders who, although they might owe their positions to Moscow, were at least nominally in charge of sovereign states and had the responsibility of carrying on the functions of government and of serving national interests.

In serving those interests, both domestic and international, they looked to Moscow for support, and generally got it. But in neither respect was it unthinkable that there would be differences with the USSR. The myths that had grown up and been carefully cultivated—that Stalin was always right; that by Marxist law a natural harmony must exist among communist states; that East European Communists would never go against the Kremlin because that would serve the common capitalist enemy, or could not do so because they were obedient Soviet agents—died hard. But they were all disproved in the case of Yugoslavia.

We are concerned here with how the dispute with Tito and the fact of an independent Yugoslavia affected Soviet views and policies toward Eastern Europe as a whole. First, the empire became more vulnerable through the loss of strategically valuable territory. The Yugoslavs had moved the iron curtain from the Alps and the Adriatic to the center of the Balkan peninsula. Second, Stalin had to cope with the effect on all Communist parties, particularly in Eastern Europe, of a Yugoslavia flaunting its independence and claiming to be true to Marx and Lenin even as it defied Stalin.

Stalin did not find these prospects tolerable. He intended to deal with Tito as he had dealt with others, at home or in the international movement, who had defied him or deviated from the line. As Khrushchev reported later, he thought he had only to lift his little finger, and Tito would fall.[4] He tried methods he apparently felt sure would bring about that result: condemnation by loyal Communist states and parties, armed threats and incursions across Yugoslavia's borders, breaking of alliance treaties, economic boycotts and pressures, intrigue with Cominformists within Yugoslavia, and constant propaganda. If he had taken direct military action at once, in mid-1948, he might have been able to impose a puppet regime in Belgrade.[5] By 1949 and 1950, as Western aid and commitments to Yugoslavia increased and world tensions rose with the fighting in Korea, the risks of war were greater. In any case, Stalin stayed his hand, and Tito withstood all the other pressures.

Stalin was never reconciled with Tito, but it is significant that for nearly five years he lived with Tito's "intolerable" deviation. Meanwhile, he had to adjust Soviet military strategy to the loss, and tried to contain Titoism in Eastern Europe by a series of purges of the leadership, complete with show trials. It was left for Khrushchev, two years after Stalin's death, to make the grand gesture of reconciliation with Yugoslavia, a confession of Stalin's errors and his failure, and the beginning of a new Soviet approach to Eastern Europe.

The new Soviet policy toward Yugoslavia was adopted primarily because the old one had not worked. Restoration of state and party ties, however insincere, offered a better chance to restore Soviet influence in Yugoslavia than continued ostracism and threats. Undoubtedly Khrushchev and his colleagues were aware of the risk that the new relationship with Yugoslavia would contribute to the destabilization of the bloc. In

4. In his "secret speech" to the 20th Congress of the CPSU, published in Dan N. Jacobs, ed., *The New Communist Manifesto and Related Documents* (New York: Harper & Brothers, 1962), p. 114.

5. Khrushchev, in his memoirs, says that he is absolutely sure that Stalin would have intervened militarily if the USSR had had a common border with Yugoslavia. See Strobe Talbott, ed., *Khrushchev Remembers: The Last Testament* (Boston and Toronto: Little, Brown, 1974), p. 181.

reestablishing normal relations they conferred a certain legitimacy on Tito's heresy. The Yugoslavs, half inside and half outside the movement, could provide a more dangerous example and have more influence when recognized as proper socialists than when denounced as fascists. But choices had to be made, and Khrushchev was not a man to shrink from risks.

Actually, the process of change had already started before the reconciliation with Tito. The end of the Stalin era brought decompression and new departures both in the USSR itself and, as if by reflex action, in Eastern Europe. The new Soviet rulers, as they sorted out the distribution of power among themselves and debated what should be done at home, called into question the state of affairs in the satellites as well. The New Course of liberalization and reform begun in Hungary in 1953, putting Imre Nagy at the head of the government and clipping the wings of Mátyás Rákosi, the old Stalinist, could not have originated in Budapest alone. It emerged from decisions made in Moscow. Comparable manifestations of the thaw took place in East Germany, Poland, and other states of the bloc, although in some the change was negligible.

In seeking to maintain a reliable political base in Eastern Europe, Stalin's successors groped their way toward new relationships, acting to ease tension and to dissociate themselves from failed and unpopular leaders but uncertain of their course, wavering between past practice and reform, and underestimating the extent of disaffection. The fact that individual Soviet leaders had differences with one another, and that their relations were linked to those between leaders and factions in the satellite states, contributed to the Soviet Union's surprise and unpreparedness when events began to spin out of control in Poland and Hungary in 1956.

Because those events shook the foundations of the system, the Soviets took the necessary decisions to protect their vital interest in military control and in the maintenance of Communist rule. In Poland they made sure of their minimum terms through tough negotiations with Władysław Gomułka, the new party leader. In Hungary negotiations were overtaken by revolution, whereupon decisions were taken for military intervention and the imposition of a new leader, János Kádár, and a reconstituted Communist party. In neither country, however, were the causes of the upheaval exorcised. The thinness of the Communist veneer had been exposed in Hungary, and in both countries the appeal of nationalism among both Communists and non-Communists had been demonstrated.

The events of 1956 showed how the system had changed in basic respects. The Kremlin was no longer totally in charge of designating the local leadership. The new leaders in Poland and Hungary had been imprisoned during the Stalinist era and had the taint of nationalism. Gomułka was the choice of the Polish party, not of the Soviets; they accepted him because there was no easy alternative. Kádár was chosen by the Soviets partly because of his record; he was not a discredited Stalinist like Rákosi. In both cases they had to take account of the standing of the leadership with its own people.

Khrushchev's regime was innovative, in Eastern Europe as in other aspects of his policy. He knew he had to find substitutes for Stalinist terror and coercion. Thus, an indeterminate gray area was allowed to develop around the old Stalinist standards of conformity. Within that area the Soviet Union permitted the East European regimes considerable leeway in coping with their own problems, responding to domestic pressures, stressing national interests, or even quarreling with each other (as Hungary and Romania did over minority rights in Transylvania).

Khrushchev introduced the concept of the socialist commonwealth (*sodruzhestvo*), conceding that national conditions could differ on the road to socialism as long as essential Leninist principles were preserved. The idea was not purely propaganda, although ultimate power remained in the hands of only one member of the commonwealth. The Soviet Union never accepted the concept of multiple centers of authority on ideology and doctrine, and asserted the right to determine which policies were correct and which were revisionist. The arcane discussions at the world conferences of Communist parties held in Moscow in 1957 and 1960 reflected a determined effort to discipline institutional diversity with ideological conformity, leaving no doubt that the leading role of the Soviet Union was the primary principle that all, including Gomułka's Poland, would have to accept.[6] This was the issue that sealed Yugoslavia's exclusion from the socialist camp or, expressed differently, its choice for independence.

To support the necessary unity of the bloc the Soviet Union attempted to strengthen the network of military and economic ties, in the Warsaw Pact and the Council for Mutual Economic Assistance (CMEA), but with less than complete success. The remarkable thing about Soviet policy in the Khrushchev period was not its striving for unity and control, almost instinctive with Soviet leaders, but its unexpected flexibility in tolerating changes that escaped or even challenged Soviet control. Gomułka kept the gains of the Polish October (except those such as intellectual freedom, for which he had no liking anyway). Kádár took the road of "goulash communism" and conciliation with non-Communists, and Khrushchev endorsed it. Albania left the bloc and got away with it. Gheorghiu-Dej of Romania rejected Khrushchev's plan for integrated development through CMEA and embarked on a series of independent moves in for-

---

6. Zbigniew K. Brzezinski, *The Soviet Bloc: Unity and Conflict,* 2d ed. (Cambridge: Harvard University Press, 1967), pp. 292–308, 410–14.

eign policy. By the time Khrushchev was ousted in 1964, these extraordinary changes had become more or less institutionalized.

The transition to Brezhnev and Kosygin brought no indications of new departures in policy toward Eastern Europe. Again, however, the uncertainty of where power resided in Moscow in a transitional period raised questions in the minds of East Europeans. In the first years Brezhnev's primacy was not clearly established, nor were his positions known. Kosygin's prominence and the encouragement of new thought on industrial management pointed to the possibility of economic reform throughout the Soviet bloc. A muted tug-of-war was going on in Moscow among individuals and factions, not with a clear division between neo-Stalinists and reformers but with tendencies in both directions.[7] It was natural that Czech and Hungarian reformers would find signs of encouragement in the reports from Moscow.[8]

Meanwhile, the growing Sino-Soviet conflict, by shattering carefully cultivated myths of political and ideological solidarity in the communist world, had its effects in Eastern Europe. The Chinese were contesting Soviet hegemony not only in Asia but in the USSR's European backyard. The Soviets naturally intensified their efforts to maintain primacy and ideological discipline, but one practical effect of the dispute was to give East European states a chance to turn it to advantage at Soviet expense. Thus, Albania could make the break with Moscow, having China as a haven, and Romania could seek a diplomatic middle ground between the two giants.

The main challenge of the late 1960s came from Czechoslovakia, hitherto a relatively docile member of the bloc. A change in leadership in January 1968, the result of internal pressures for economic reform and political renovation, brought the untried Alexander Dubček to the top post in the Czechoslovak Communist party. He and his colleagues did not intend to destroy the system of one-party rule or to break the connection with the USSR, but the Soviet leaders became increasingly alarmed by the prospect of threats to those fundamentals: by the relaxation of censorship and discipline, the democratization of the Communist party, and the momentum of liberalizing forces that Dubček, riding a wave of popularity, could not or would not control. The limits of tolerance were eventually reached and Moscow acted to invade and occupy the country, restoring control through subservient Czech and Slovak leaders.[9] That decision, not easily made but ruthlessly executed, was not seriously chal-

7. Michel Tatu, *Le Pouvoir en U.R.S.S.: Du déclin de Khrouchtchev à la direction collective* (Paris: Bernard Grasset, 1967), pp. 463–566.

8. Zdeněk Mlynář, *Nachtfrost: Erfahrungen auf dem Weg vom realen zum menschlichen Sozialismus* (Cologne/Frankfurt: Europäische Verlagsanstalt, 1978), pp. 108–10.

9. Jiri Valenta, *Soviet Intervention in Czechoslovakia, 1968: Anatomy of a Decision* (Baltimore: Johns Hopkins University Press, 1979), pp. 25–26.

lenged. The quiet of resignation settled over Czechoslovakia. But the attempt to give socialism "a human face" was not forgotten there or elsewhere.

THE NATURE OF SOVIET INTERESTS

The crackdown in Czechoslovakia in 1968 provides a convenient point for analysis of the essentials of Soviet policy in Eastern Europe in the quarter century following World War II, before we turn to the problems of the 1970s and of the present day. The dilemmas and decisions of that period, illustrated by the events outlined above, illustrate basic concepts having contemporary as well as historical significance. Soviet interests were of three kinds: strategic, political-ideological, and economic. In each case the evidence allows more than one interpretation of Soviet purposes, but on essentials there is an iron consistency.

From the very beginning it was made clear that Eastern Europe, won at a high cost in Soviet lives, is vital to the security of the USSR. Stalin saw the territory as a glacis providing defensive depth and protecting the Soviet Union from invasion not just by some future Hitler but by a present and powerful America. Obviously it could not serve that purpose, at least not so well, if the East European states were free to ally themselves with the West or to choose nonalignment, Yugoslav-style. Soviet leaders never modified that basic view. Although Soviet military thinking and planning may have changed with the advent of new weapons and types of warfare, the conviction of the importance of Eastern Europe for Soviet defense did not. The Soviet Union never considered compromising its overall military position there or weakening the Warsaw Pact. On the contrary, it strengthened the pact organization, kept it under Soviet control, and resisted attempts to water it down.

Was the territory of Eastern Europe also intended for possible offensive purposes, a springboard for military action against Western Europe? We have no evidence of serious Soviet intentions, at any time since World War II, to launch such an attack, although that contingency has certainly been a part of Soviet military planning. The capability for attack, however, adds tremendously to the influence the Soviet Union can exert in European and world affairs. Use of the territory of Eastern Europe contributes to that capability and keeps it before the eyes of the nations of Western Europe. It is an advantage no Soviet government has contemplated giving up, in whole or in part.

Of the Warsaw Pact members, Poland and the German Democratic Republic (GDR) have had the highest priority for reasons of location, population, and political and economic weight. Together with Czechoslovakia they constitute a kind of special security bloc within the pact. There the Soviet Union faces the West at the point of high political stakes and of concentrated power on both sides.

The priority has not been the same for the Balkans, where the defections of Yugoslavia and Albania were reluctantly accepted. The case of Romania is somewhat puzzling in that its location on the border of the USSR does not permit indifference, yet its straying from the fold on foreign policy and other questions was tolerated by Khrushchev, and Brezhnev did not react differently. Perhaps it was because Romania could be brought to heel at any time the Kremlin should deem it necessary, perhaps because internally the communist system was rigidly maintained. The Romanians have been cautious enough not to leave the Warsaw Pact and assert genuine nonalignment like Yugoslavia's, for they could hardly have expected any other Soviet response than intervention.

As Soviet foreign policy took on global dimensions in the 1960s, the military position in the Balkans acquired added importance beyond use as pressure on Yugoslavia and NATO's southeastern flank. The Soviet naval buildup in the Mediterranean, involvement in the Arab-Israeli conflict, and efforts to acquire and support clients in the Middle East and Africa all depended on routes of access and supply that ran through the Balkans. If there had been any prior disposition to consider the Balkan satellites as marginal, to allow Bulgaria to be cut off territorially from the rest of the bloc, or to ignore the desirability of someday bringing Yugoslavia back into it, the demands of Soviet global strategy must have dispelled such ideas.

While the bedrock military reasons for the control and use of Eastern Europe's territory by Soviet forces have been obvious, the Warsaw Pact and East European forces have a broader, and less clearly defined, place in Soviet thinking and strategy. Satellite forces have constituted roughly half the conventional forces of the Warsaw Pact in the European theater, which offset and outnumber those of NATO arrayed on the other side.[10] How effective the East Europeans would be in a war is a question much debated in the West, probably in the East as well, and which no one wishes to test in actuality. But that is not the main point. The existence of more than half a million East European soldiers trained by the Soviets, equipped with Soviet weapons, and integrated into combined forces under Soviet command is an ineluctable fact of the military balance in Europe. It contributes to Soviet security and also to the "correlation of forces" in the world, which the Soviets see, or have always professed to see, as shifting in their favor.

As the Soviet Union moved into military confrontation with China in

10. Thomas W. Wolfe, "Soviet Military Capabilities and Intentions in Europe"; John Erickson, "Soviet Military Posture and Policy in Europe," in Richard Pipes, ed., *Soviet Strategy in Europe* (New York: Crane, Russak, 1976), pp. 133–42, 176–81.

the 1960s and engaged in far-flung adventures in the Third World, the significance of the Warsaw Pact forces was enhanced. It was important not to weaken the main front, even as new friends and allies were being won—some, like Cuba, deemed worthy of inclusion in the socialist camp. But with none of them were the ties so close, or deemed so vital, as those with the allies in the Warsaw Pact. In general, the East European governments were unenthusiastic about the new global reach. They were alarmed at the prospect of a Sino-Soviet war and did not contemplate use of their own forces as proxies for the USSR in Asia or Africa. Nevertheless, they accepted the reasoning that, with the spreading of Soviet responsibilities, they had to do their full part in maintaining the balance in Europe. All of them, including a reluctant Romania, knew that in the existing superpower balance and the division of Europe they had no choice. They were quite aware of the correlation of forces between themselves and the Soviet Union.

Defensive or offensive, the security factor was in the forefront of Soviet thinking about Eastern Europe. Every negotiation or agreement with the West on arms or other matters, every political change in Eastern Europe itself, had to be scrutinized from the standpoint of the maintenance of the Soviet military position. The presence of military forces, of course, helped to maintain the necessary political control, but reciprocally, political influence and control were seen as necessary to the military position.

Creation and preservation of the political base for Soviet power in Eastern Europe constituted more than just a security requirement. It became an end in itself, an integral part of the Soviet leaders' conception of the USSR as a new global power. It was not enough to be a superpower in size and military strength. An essential element of the new status was having other states, making up a large part of Europe, in the socialist camp. Power was wed to ideology in the constant advertisement of the extension of the Soviet system to Eastern Europe as a giant step in the advance of socialism toward its eventual triumph over capitalism on a world scale. No time was set for the achievement of the ultimate goal, but what could not be lost was the sense of momentum in that direction.

Ideology is woven into policy, especially into its public expression, but has to be seen in relation to politics and power. That Eastern Europe is a testing ground where the world will witness the success of Moscow-defined Marxism-Leninism in lands beyond its country of origin is a proposition in which Soviet confidence must have eroded in the light of experience with Yugoslavia and China (both having set up countermodels), and with Hungary, Poland, and others. Such an experience might make the nations of Eastern Europe seem more like an indigestible mass than a vision of the bright socialist future, and even a danger to the stability of the USSR itself, as was evident in Soviet concern over the Prague Spring. Yet even if the Soviets harbored grave doubts about trends in Eastern Europe, they could not admit that socialism is not firmly grounded there or that the ties with the USSR are not organic and immutable. Whatever shape the political and economic structure might assume in a given state, socialism in the sense of Communist party (and ultimate Soviet) control had to be made to work, however nasty the political consequences or however high the economic cost. Retreat would represent a failure of huge proportions, an unacceptable loss of prestige, and perhaps a threat to the Soviet regime in its home country.

The decline of ideological unity among communist states, however, was a fact of international life, to which changes in the Soviet Union itself contributed. The issue of de-Stalinization—how far to go in relaxing the constraints of the internal system, and how much to pull back when relaxation seemed to invite dangers—created uncertainty in both the USSR and Eastern Europe as to which lines of action were properly Leninist and which were not. Mikhail Suslov, the late guardian of ideological purity, might lay down "universal laws of building socialism," as he did in 1956 and on later occasions. But separate governments and parties were applying those laws in their own fashion. Orthodoxy, in fact, was what the Soviet leadership determined it to be at a given time, but the Soviets always had the problem of deciding how to enforce a particular principle, and whether it was worth the effort. "National communism" was heresy, condemned both by Moscow and by the East European parties, but national communism in one form or another, pronounced in some cases and faint in others, existed in every member state of the bloc.

The economic side of Soviet policy, from the start, was primarily a means of maintaining the system of military security and political subordination, with whatever beneficial economic side effects there might be. Original Soviet aims did not go much beyond taking East European assets as war reparation and on other grounds, using economic pressures to advance Soviet political purposes, and setting in train in each country the nationalization of industry, collectivization of agriculture, and expansion of trade with the USSR at the expense of traditional ties with the West. In the early years the new regimes, with Soviet guidance and the enthusiastic cooperation of the local Communist parties, concentrated on building new industries, particularly basic heavy industries, trying to make their countries small-scale models of the USSR. Much of this development was uneconomic, given the limited resource base of the individual states, and the problems were intensified by the general confusion of social revolution, neglect of agriculture, and the exactions of the Soviet Union.

The cult of autarky throughout Eastern Europe and Moscow's insistence on dealing with each state separately made impossible a rational economic approach in the region as a whole, either by Moscow or by the local regimes. Formation of CMEA in 1949 was little more than a political response to the West's Marshall Plan, and it was not until years after Stalin's death that a rudimentary regional economic system began to take shape.

The legacy of the Stalin era proved to be a heavy burden for the satellite economies and eventually for the Soviet Union itself. As Paul Marer points out (chap. 6), the outcome was a grossly inefficient allocation of resources, declining living standards after 1950, and a terrorized, resentful population—problems that eventually led to political upheavals in several countries. Stalin's successors saw the need for a redefinition of interests and for different policies.

After the shocks of 1956 they found that they had to put in resources as well as take them out in order to shore up regimes in which they had already invested political capital. They made foreign aid an accepted tool of policy, primarily in the form of credits and of ostentatious deliveries of food and other goods in emergency situations. They recast trade relations to put them on a more commercial basis, looking to long-term mutual benefit as well as their own immediate needs. They began to put life into CMEA, in the direction of a more rational international division of labor, as a means of improving the performance of the East European economies and developing resources on a blocwide basis. It was not an easy process, since the basic investments and patterns had been set in the Stalin period. Each country had its own command economy, and each still wanted an impressive iron and steel industry.

It is a matter of controversy among Western economists whether Eastern Europe has represented a benefit or a burden to the USSR. Soviet publications, as might be expected, have praised and magnified the aid so generously provided. Not aid, however, but trade and the pricing of traded goods are the main part of the story, and here the question is how much the USSR has in fact subsidized Eastern Europe in this way. On balance, Eastern Europe has been, since the 1950s, a drain on Soviet resources, although the size of the burden seems impossible to measure.[11] The Soviets probably did not make any fine calculations on that point. They could reduce the burden at will. They had the economic bargaining power, as the biggest trading partner, as well as political and military dominance. Yet they knew they could not exploit Eastern Europe without paying a price for it in their political and security interests. If Eastern Europe was a burden, it was not one that could be cast off.

The critical questions on the economic side had to do less with where

11. Morris Bornstein, "Soviet-East European Economic Relations," in Morris Bornstein, Zvi Gitelman, and William Zimmerman, eds., *East-West Relations and the Future of Eastern Europe: Politics and Economics* (London: Allen & Unwin, 1981), pp. 106–10. Cf. chap. 6.

the balance of exploitation or of aid lies than with how the economies of Eastern Europe, and indeed the economy of the USSR, could be rescued from their structural problems. The dilemmas would grow sharper in the 1970s for both parties. The economic interests of the USSR in Eastern Europe might not be vital ones, but economic problems to which the Soviets had no solution held serious possibilities of jeopardizing interests they did consider vital.

PROBLEMS OF THE 1970s AND TODAY: VIABILITY, COORDINATION, AND CONTROL

Looked at in a simplified way—an ideal way from the Kremlin's standpoint—all the military, political, and economic interests of the USSR in Eastern Europe tend to support one another. Soviet policymakers, however, have had to act in a world not of clear and simple choices but of complexity and contradictions. The invasion and occupation of Czechoslovakia in 1968, for example, may have served important security interests, but it stifled the chances for a Communist regime to gain legitimacy in the eyes of its own people and to revive the Czechoslovak economy. Traditional Russian-Czech friendship suffered a mortal blow when Czechoslovakia became an involuntary host to Soviet armed forces, stationed there on an apparently permanent basis. Furthermore, the fate of Czechoslovakia sharpened divisions within the bloc, for where the leaders of Poland and the GDR urged and supported the crackdown, Kádár of Hungary—his own economic reform thrown into question— was unhappy about it, and Ceauşescu of Romania shouted his opposition from the housetops. Time and again the Soviets have a choice only of evils. Action taken to strengthen or save the empire can deepen its existing fissures. Action avoided—giving the local leaders their head—carries the risk that in their rush to pursue their own interests they will ignore those of the USSR.

In the contemporary period these complexities have remained, and have been joined by others stemming from new developments in East-West relations and from the global ambitions and activities of the Soviet Union. Eastern Europe, without any fundamental change in its position within the Soviet alliance system and sphere of influence, has moved gradually into a more active and prominent place in world affairs, with inevitable repercussions on Soviet interests.

The foreign policy of the Soviet Union in the 1970s was determined, above all, by the strategic decision to play the part of a global superpower, and in doing so to combine steadily increasing military and economic strength with a policy of "peaceful coexistence" with the West. The Brezhnev leadership, in other words, saw the Soviet Union's security best served by pursuing the inevitable competitive struggle with rival powers in ways that would enable it to increase its relative strength and bargaining power and make political gains without incurring dangerous risks of nuclear war. The marked turn to a foreign policy of coexistence and détente with the West at the end of the 1960s, sanctified at the 24th Congress of the Communist Party of the Soviet Union (CPSU) in 1971, was rooted in that broad global strategy, sharpened by the perceived threat from China and by the immediate needs of the Soviet economy, including advanced technology available only in the West. Its timing was affected by the readiness of the West to accept the fait accompli in Czechoslovakia, reduce tensions, negotiate on arms limitation, expand trade, and settle outstanding political questions in Europe.

In Eastern Europe itself, after the Czechoslovak crisis, Soviet policy was to reemphasize ideological orthodoxy, tighten discipline, and strengthen the institutions in which there was no question about the leading role of the Soviet Union. Those institutions included the Warsaw Pact military structure, its Political Consultative Committee, and CMEA. Some of the bilateral security treaties with individual East European states were renegotiated and renewed. Brezhnev began the practice of receiving the top leaders of the East European Communist parties, one after another, each summer while enjoying the climate and repose of the Crimea. The term *socialist commonwealth* popularized by Khrushchev was heard less and the term *socialist community* (*obshchina*), without the same connotation of equality, was heard more.[12] All this was a defensive reaction to the Czechoslovak affair, but it was also a preparation for new relations with the West and for the European security conference the Warsaw Pact countries were proposing.

The building of more normal and cooperative relations with the West required a settlement of long-standing East-West differences over Eastern Europe, just as such a settlement, which Moscow wanted in order to confirm its position there, required a new relationship with the West. The appearance of a government in the Federal Republic of Germany, under Willy Brandt, prepared to negotiate normalization of relations with its eastern neighbors, recognize the Oder–Neisse line, and put aside the issue of German reunification made it possible to place Eastern Europe at the center of the new policy of détente. It is well to remember, however, that Eastern Europe was not the Kremlin's sole concern. While it had vital objectives there and would bargain hard for them, the strategy was global, and stabilization of the situation in Eastern Europe had as a major pur-

---

12. Peter A. Toma, ed., *The Changing Face of Communism in Eastern Europe* (Tucson: University of Arizona Press, 1970), p. 8.

pose reducing vulnerabilities, enabling the Soviet Union to pursue with greater assurance and success its broader aims, and making it possible to mobilize East European as well as Soviet resources on behalf of those aims.

Détente registered spectacular progress in the early 1970s, including Bonn's treaties with Moscow, Warsaw, Prague, and East Berlin, a new four-power accord on the status of West Berlin, and a rapid expansion of trade and financial relations between East and West. The climactic point was President Nixon's celebrated visit to Moscow in 1972 to sign the SALT treaty and other accords. The formal internationalization of détente in Europe, however, required three more years of tortuous negotiation among 35 governments, concluding in the signing of the Final Act of Helsinki on August 1, 1975.

For the Soviet Union the most important part of the "peace settlement" that the complex of agreements on Europe could be said to represent was the confirmation of the political and territorial status quo in Eastern Europe. The GDR attained international legitimacy, even though Bonn maintained its position on the eventual reunification of the German nation, and the facts of Soviet hegemony and Communist rule in Eastern Europe received implicit acceptance. Détente and the formulations of Helsinki, however, meant not only the abandonment by the West, at least for the foreseeable future, of political claims against the status quo in the East, but also, partly as a price for it, an opening of doors and windows between East and West; and the obligations in the Final Act regarding human rights gave the Western powers (and dissidents in communist countries) a handle to challenge the existing system.

How did these prospects conform to long-term Soviet interests in Eastern Europe? The West's signing of the agreements seemed to hold great significance for Brezhnev, judging from his persistence in seeking it and willingness to make major concessions to get it. Presumably it would remove all doubt in the minds of East Europeans concerning the permanence of their Communist regimes and of Soviet dominance. Actually it represented no great change, as the West had long come to the conclusion that these were facts of international life that could be altered only by evolution within Eastern Europe and within the USSR, which the West might influence marginally but could not direct.

Execution of the Helsinki agreements would, in any case, remain within the control of the governments of the Soviet Union and the East European states, as would the nature and tempo of economic cooperation. They recognized elements of danger in the human rights clauses of the Helsinki accords and in the increased contacts with the West, and prepared to meet them with adequate measures of control and with heightened ideological vigilance. Détente, they never ceased to remind themselves and the world, meant peaceful coexistence between different political and social systems, not relaxation of the ideological struggle.

With all their vigilance, however, the Soviet leaders were entering areas not wholly charted and predictable. They might keep a tight grip on developments within the USSR itself but in Eastern Europe it was more difficult. Although they had considerable leverage on the local regimes, to a large extent they had to depend on those regimes to find the right balance between dealings with the West and fealty to the Soviet Union, between reform and orthodoxy, between national interests and those of socialist internationalism. Most East European states, being heavily dependent on foreign trade, had to increase ties with the West if they were to be useful, and not just a growing burden, to the Soviet economy. Increased integration within CMEA, given formal sanction at its Bucharest meeting in 1971, offered possibilities of enhancing efficiency and control, both desirable from Moscow's standpoint, but autarky for the bloc was no answer to the economic needs of either the USSR or Eastern Europe.

The East European countries were under pressure from the Soviet Union to produce higher quality goods for the Soviet market and to contribute to the development of Soviet raw materials they needed in order to keep their industries going. They needed capital goods and technology from the West but could not compete strongly enough in world markets to earn the necessary foreign exchange, and some borrowed heavily in hard currencies. They had to face these pressures on their international economic position, from which political overtones were never absent, as well as domestic pressures for higher living standards, which they had made a criterion of the success of socialism.

With the advance from "people's democracy" to socialism, proudly proclaimed in public pronouncements and in the changed official names of several East European states, the regimes had presumably arrived at a new, more advanced stage on the road to the promised land. Yet just at this point, reached in the 1960s in most cases, the limits of extensive growth in simple basic industries became apparent, and the system did not have the resiliency, the resources, or the leadership to adapt to new requirements. The problems were largely structural but were compounded by deficiencies in planning, management, and social policy. Remedies were not readily apparent. Inevitably the question of reform was posed—a test for economists, planners, and high officials in each country as they tried to decide how much, if any, decentralization of decisions, use of incentives, and freeing of prices would be compatible with the system. Not least among the obstacles and constraints was the fear of party moguls that experimentation and change might eat into the base of their political power, get out of control, or provoke the Soviet Union. Hungary's New Economic Mechanism, a reform begun in 1968, while successful in introducing greater flexibility and showing encouraging results, had to proceed carefully, with some tactical retreats, so as not to disturb the political balance at home or cause unpleasant reactions beyond the frontiers.

Almost unnoticed, economic change had brought social change, with political consequences. Except for the GDR and Czechoslovakia, which had long had substantial industries, Eastern Europe had since the war undergone a transformation from a peasant to an industrial society. Industrialization created a new managerial group or middle class, a new working class, and a new intelligentsia. These groups grew with the system and in many respects owed their existence and status to the economic growth and social mobility it fostered; they had, presumably, a stake in its success. Yet, with the passage of time and the knowledge of their own importance to economic progress, they had their own aims and concerns and did not fit so easily into a system that reserved all power to the party *apparat*. New kinds of relations developed among social groups and between party and populace, as well as new kinds of industrial relations, including strikes, which governments often had to deal with by compromise, not simply by coercion.[13] Occasional open dissent and violence were only the most spectacular manifestation of the unanticipated effects of economic and social change. A more persistent result was the transformation of the nature of the problems, which became less easy to define and prescribe for, quite beyond the nostrums of the official ideology.

As tensions appeared in East European societies, the governmental and party structures inevitably felt the strain. The state of affairs differed considerably from one country to another. In Hungary, party leaders were able to ease pressures by relatively successful economic reforms, by concessions to nonparty people, and by relaxation of censorship. In Poland, on the other hand, the problems were more severe, the leadership was less adroit, and elements outside the party were more demanding.

Poland was a special case in that, first, the Communist party had to live in uneasy coexistence with a powerful Catholic church; second, Polish workers demonstrated three times (in 1970, 1976, and 1980) that by strikes and opposition to government policies they could force concessions from, and even changes in, the party leadership; and third, these strong forces had links with major elements of the intelligentsia, both Catholic and Marxist. Here, accordingly, was a potentially formidable opposition that could, at a time of crisis, coalesce against the official establishment.[14]

13. Walter D. Connor, "Social Change and Stability in Eastern Europe," *Problems of Communism*, 26 (Nov.–Dec. 1977), 16–32.

14. Jacques Rupnik, "Dissent in Poland, 1968–78," in Rudolf L. Tőkés, ed., *Opposition in Eastern Europe* (Baltimore: Johns Hopkins University Press, 1979), pp. 60–112.

The key, in the case of Poland, was an increasingly self-conscious working class. The workers who stood up to the Warsaw regime in 1980 were not carbon copies of those who were there at the establishment of the regime in the mid-1940s, or even those who rioted in 1956. They represented decades of additional experience in a communist system and the advent of a younger generation of new workers not bound by old habits. They had acquired the power to organize, to find their own leaders, to take the measure of the regime, and to act. The official ideology had no hold on them. Socialism in a general sense they accepted, but socialism as the rallying cry of the existing Communist party, socialism Soviet-style, no. The most powerful ideology for them, it became clear by 1980, was their Catholic faith. Thus a massive workers' protest became, inevitably, a challenge to the system and to the Soviet Union.

The experience of the 1970s brought home to the East European regimes the narrow range of their choices. Under growing economic and social pressures, they could not find panaceas either in halfhearted reform or in the credits and industrial cooperation available from the West, although both could be helpful in postponing fundamental decisions. Under such handicaps, the East European countries could hardly be the models of stability and bastions of security the Kremlin wanted them to be.

Fundamental Soviet interests, of course, remain as before. The first is control, and the ultimate means of control is still physical power, military forces stationed in most of the East European countries and backed by the might of the entire Soviet military machine. That Soviet leaders are prepared to use this power has been demonstrated. The commitment has been defined by a number of public statements to the effect that whenever socialism is in mortal peril in an East European state (in fact, more generally, in any socialist state), the socialist community has the right of intervention to remove the danger. No doubt has existed that a decision to intervene would be made by the Soviet Union itself, although other members of the bloc, as in 1968, might choose or be directed to participate in the action.

When events might be entering the zone in which the Kremlin would judge socialism to be in danger is not defined. The circumstances of the interventions of 1956 and 1968, of the decisions against intervention in Poland in 1956, 1970, and 1980–81, plus statements issuing from Moscow on those occasions, give some indications. The conclusions many observers draw from such evidence are that the Soviet Union would not find it tolerable that a member state should leave the Warsaw Pact or should dismantle the system in which effective political control is in the hands of a leadership and organization, presumably a Soviet-type Communist party, whose loyalty to the Kremlin can be relied upon; that such a party cannot be permitted to share real power with other parties (as the Hungarian was ready to do in 1956), to change its own character through liberalization (as the Czechoslovak did in 1968), or to drift into ineffectiveness and lose control of events. That is why the revolutionary developments that began in Poland in 1980 immediately raised the question of possible Soviet intervention.

The Brezhnev doctrine of intervention (a name bestowed by the Western press) tells only that the sanction of force exists and may be used. In that general sense it could as easily and accurately be given the name of Stalin or of Khrushchev, for the principle has remained the same since the takeover of Eastern Europe in the 1940s. The intervention in Czechoslovakia seemed to require a specific rationale, which was worked out as the crisis developed in 1968 and then, after the invasion, given formal expression in an authoritative article in *Pravda* and in statements by Brezhnev himself.[15] The doctrine does not call for automatic intervention in a given objective situation. The crucial question is whether Moscow decides intervention is necessary: if it does, the danger to socialism provides the pretext.

Because the sanction of force exists, it rarely has to be used, for it exerts a restraining hand on East European governments, both in how they deal with Moscow and in what they allow to happen in their own countries. The Soviets have also at their disposal less drastic means than military action. Obviously, they do not have the same instruments of direct control they had 30 years ago. They do not have Soviet officials in all key places, and they cannot at will change governments or dictate their policies. But they do have available persuasive means of military, political, and economic pressure. They can mobilize armed forces along the frontiers. They can be accommodating, or tough, in the granting of credits or in setting the prices of oil and other products. They can provide, or withhold, support for specific national aims of East European states. They can decide, for example, on how much backing to give the GDR or Czechoslovakia on questions at issue with the Federal Republic, or manipulate disputes within the bloc, holding out to each side the hope of support against the other.

Soviet purposes, to be sure, go beyond merely holding these countries in thrall. If the connection is to have tensile strength, if this is to be commonwealth rather than empire, then all its members should play their full part in working for common objectives. Hence Soviet efforts to give a positive content to relations with Eastern Europe. By Soviet definition,

15. *Pravda*, Sept. 26, Nov. 13, and Dec. 4, 1968. See also the discussion by Karen Dawisha and Peter Summerscale in Karen Dawisha and Philip Hanson, eds., *Soviet-East European Dilemmas: Coercion, Competition, and Consent* (London: Heinemann for the Royal Institute of International Affairs, 1981), pp. 9–40.

however, common objectives are Soviet objectives, and vice versa. In practice the question has been how the East European allies—through the Warsaw Pact, CMEA, or individually—can help to advance Soviet policies. There are many ways. It may be useful to list some of them and to indicate the measure of Soviet success as well as the effects on Soviet-East European relations.

1. The East European states enhance the military position of the USSR, in Europe and in the global balance, by making available their territory, their armed forces, and their military industry. Their governments may differ in the degree to which they see their own security served thereby and in the measure of their cooperation, but Soviet power is so dominant and the Warsaw Pact system so firmly established that this military role is an accepted fact of their international position.

2. The East European states stand together with the USSR in the United Nations and other international forums, adding their supporting speeches and their votes to Soviet positions. While Romania goes its own way, spoiling the solid front, the others find such nonconformity insufficient compensation for the trouble it would bring to their relations with Moscow.

3. The East European states take part, with varying degrees of enthusiasm, in Soviet strategy toward the Third World, providing military and technical advice, trade and credits, diplomatic contacts, and intelligence, helping to implant Soviet influence and to buttress it when established. Not least important is the image of a "socialist world" in natural alliance with socialist-oriented developing nations, not just a single superpower looking for clients and camp followers. Sometimes it has been camouflage useful for Soviet purposes, as in the famous "Czech arms deal," which signaled Egypt's turn to Moscow in 1955; sometimes it has been a substantial contribution in its own right, conveniently supplementing Moscow's own, as with the GDR's role in building internal security systems in Asian and African states.

4. As long as there is an international communist movement run from Moscow, the willingness of the parties of Eastern Europe to play Moscow's game with other ruling and nonruling parties has helped its efforts to preserve the movement as an instrument of Soviet policy. In mobilizing the parties to meet the challenges from Yugoslavia, China, and the Eurocommunist parties of Western Europe, the Kremlin has relied heavily on the East European parties. Without them it could hardly maintain the pretense that there is in fact a truly international movement. Most have played their assigned parts but the record has not been entirely satisfactory to the Soviets. The Berlin conference of European Communist parties in 1976 produced the spectacle of the Romanians lining up with the

Yugoslavs and the Eurocommunist Italian and Spanish parties, all holding firmly to the principle of independence. Eurocommunism has had echoes in Eastern Europe (it had had some antecedents there, like Imre Nagy and Alexander Dubček) without being a tangible threat to the status quo.[16]

5. Finally, Eastern Europe has made its contribution to the Soviet economy, although this has been a two-way process. The difficulty is that, either for the benefit of the Soviet economy or for the furtherance of Soviet global policies, Eastern Europe has little to offer. Some products, such as Polish coal, could earn hard currency, but not enough to pay for Eastern Europe's needed imports. In unexpected ways, however, as a result of their weakness, the East European economies served Soviet policy. Their growing trade with Western Europe and resulting indebtedness increased Western Europe's stake in Eastern supplies and markets and also in the viability of the Eastern economies. The interdependence fostered by détente, which in West European nations meant industrial orders and jobs and new sources of energy, had a limiting effect on their ability and willingness to oppose Soviet policies in regions like the Middle East or Asia and thus put strains on the Western alliance.

The total picture is a complex one in which elements of common interest, cooperation, coercion, and conflict exist side by side. Insofar as there is a balancing of Soviet and East European interests, what kind of bargain is it? In other words, what is the real nature of the socialist commonwealth?

The Soviet practice has been to maintain the general facade of sovereign equality and socialist solidarity, and behind it to make sure of Eastern Europe's cooperation, to be maximized as may be possible but in no case to fall below an essential minimum. If it is understood in Eastern Europe—by the Communist leadership and by others—that there is no other way, then they may be expected to seek to fulfill their own aims only within the framework of association with the Soviet Union. They may, in theory anyway, find rewards for their loyalty and benefits from the general success of the global Soviet enterprise. In reality, the Soviet Union has never been able to enlist the vital forces of the East European societies in that enterprise.

The key position is occupied by the local governing regimes. Moscow, since it decided not to rule directly, is dependent on them to perform the

16. On the impact of Eurocommunism in Eastern Europe, see Rudolf L. Tőkés, ed., *Eurocommunism and Détente* (New York: New York University Press for the Council on Foreign Relations, 1978), pp. 437–511, and Vernon V. Aspaturian, Jiri Valenta, and Daniel P. Burke, eds., *Eurocommunism between East and West* (Bloomington: Indiana University Press, 1980), pp. 103–270.

tasks of keeping order and mobilizing the people and the resources; to make sure that the workers and peasants produce, the managers manage, and the party functionaries keep the system going. They are the men in the middle, subject to pressures from above and from below. Inevitably their position has elements of stability and uncertainty. The stability comes from Moscow's support and from the nature of the system through which they govern. The uncertainty comes from intractable domestic problems and the need to adjust to them, from the unpredictability of events and of Moscow's reactions to them, and from the incompatibility of nationalism and subordinate status.

Some leaders were handpicked by Moscow; their dependence may be all the greater because of their lack of support at home. Others, having risen to the top on their own, may have a broader base and more independence. It is a mistake to see the East European regimes as mere puppets of the USSR, at one extreme, or as striving incessantly for the greatest possible national independence, at the other. The more subservient leaders, such as Todor Zhivkov and Gustáv Husák, gain certain concessions for their countries (e.g., loans or diplomatic support) in return for their loyalty. The more independent ones, such as János Kádár or Nicolae Ceauşescu, are not always straining at the leash; they may assert national interests in one field but then compensate for it by staying well within bounds in others.

None of the East European regimes is without bargaining power, for the Soviet Union has a stake in their durability and their success. Even weakness can provide leverage. The Soviets have the capability, of course, if the situation demands it, to replace a satellite leader in whom they have lost confidence. They may do it by supporting a rival leader or faction, as when they helped remove Walter Ulbricht in favor of Erich Honecker in the GDR in 1971. The mere threat of intervention may put sufficient pressure on a local Communist party to compel it to change its own leaders; or unwillingness to intervene to save a leader caught in a crisis may spell his downfall, as happened with Gomułka's ouster in Poland in 1970. To most East European leaders today the fate of Dubček must seem more instructive than the example of Tito. Still, a decision to get rid of an East European regime by forceful intervention is not an easy one to make, for the use of force carries risks and always has a price.

Thus, a rather wide range of varying and uncertain relations exists between the Kremlin and individual East European regimes. Both sides are under constraints in dealing with each other; both must fear that events will push them into situations of crisis desired by neither. The central problem for both, as we have noted, is how to have control and viability at the same time. The Soviets wish to be sure of their control over the regimes, and the latter, of their control over their own societies. Both have need of a viable system with effective government and a productive economy. Such viability cannot be automatically attained by command and control. It requires a minimum of willing cooperation on the part of key elements of the population. When that is lacking, local regimes and the Soviet overlords face agonizing choices.

The conclusion is inescapable that the Soviets have failed, over more than three decades, to develop a stable, dependable, and viable system in Eastern Europe. True, they succeeded in the sense that, except for Yugoslavia and Albania, they have retained their empire. They have developed blocwide institutions, the Warsaw Pact, and CMEA and engage in periodic political consultation. But they have not created a true community or commonwealth. Nor have they, for obvious reasons, allowed the East European states to form combinations among themselves in which the USSR is not included. Thus, instead of a uniform system there is a series of bilateral relationships between Moscow and the governmental and party leaders of the individual states. Each of these relationships has its own balance and its own variables, depending on Soviet priorities (which can change) and on conditions in the respective country, such as the quality of leadership, authority of the party, relevance of ideology, growth or stagnation of the economy, social tensions, morale of the labor force, strength of national traditions, and relations with the West.

Despite the fact of overall Soviet predominance, the East European regimes are largely on their own in attempting to steer their way through these currents. The Soviet Union can help them but its power to help is limited. The Soviet Union can impose its will on them, but its power to intervene is no answer to the problems of viability or even to the long-term problem of control.

PROSPECTS

As we look ahead, we must put the analysis largely in the form of questions the Soviet Union will face in this decade. While the record of the past tells us something about what the alternatives will be, it provides no unfailing guide to the future. The succeeding chapters of this book, as they explore Soviet relations with individual countries, with the region as a whole, and with the world outside the bloc, throw light on what the policy choices will be and how the Soviet leadership will make them. Here, I do no more than draw a general picture and point to crises to come.

The Soviets must be especially concerned about three problem areas in relations with Eastern Europe: the differences in approach to international issues, the failure of ideology, and the specter of economic stagnation or decline.

We have mentioned how the Soviet Union's global position and policies have changed, making Eastern Europe less central in the totality of its grand strategy. For what the Soviets hope to achieve in changing the global balance—making advances in the Third World, removing the threat from China, gaining greater influence in Western Europe, or bargaining with America—they will rely above all on the military power, economic strength, and political weight of the USSR itself. While East European states contribute marginally to those ends, the differences of priority and of approach may complicate their attainment. They have shown, for example, greater concern for international stability and more reluctance to jeopardize economic cooperation with the West, as negotiations in the Helsinki-Belgrade-Madrid process indicate, and have been less than enthusiastic about such Soviet ventures as the invasion of Afghanistan. Furthermore, when there are troubles in Eastern Europe, as in Poland, the Soviets are handicapped in their ability to act forcefully elsewhere.

The ideological problem is a related one. Ideology and common institutions were to bind the socialist community together, so that control and viability would not have to rest on physical force alone or on state-to-state bargaining based on national interests. Socialism, however, has not proved to be a binding cement, a fact that Soviet leaders may admit to themselves although they cannot admit it publicly, for it is the only legitimation of their power. One reason for the problem is the attenuation of the concept itself and the appearance of rival interpreters and interpretations of socialist truth. In the ebb and flow of Soviet experience in international politics some countries left Moscow's camp of socialism without ceasing to proclaim their faithfulness to Marx and Lenin (e.g., Yugoslavia and China), others remote from Eastern Europe were added (e.g., Cuba, Vietnam, and Cambodia), and still others were in and out as dictated by Soviet tactics. The socialist label was applied by Moscow to backward states like Ethiopia and the People's Democratic Republic of Yemen, and bloc resources were diverted to them for alleged reasons of socialist solidarity but in fact having nothing to do with Eastern Europe's interests.

A second and more potent reason is that for the most part the peoples of Eastern Europe find the ideology empty at best. It is associated with failure, with privation, with the denial of freedom. As for the governments, they have come to think of their own requirements and of relations with the USSR in terms of national interest. From that standpoint, socialist solidarity is fine in principle but may be interpreted in practice by each nation in the commonwealth as that nation sees fit. And if socialism, as defined by Moscow, is deformed or discarded in Eastern Europe, what is left but domination based on superior power?

The most serious problems of all are economic. Although the Soviet leaders have regularly asserted and practiced the primacy of politics over economics, the Marxist principle of economic determinism may return to haunt them in Eastern Europe and in their own country.

The economic forecast for the Soviet Union in the 1980s is not a hopeful one. The prospect is for declining growth, slow technological progress, serious labor problems, a heavy military drain on resources, and stagnation or decline in production of a vital commodity: oil. In the absence of drastic reform of the system and of a great expansion of trade with the West—neither very likely—the Soviet economy may be forced back on itself, squeezing the most out of its own resources and living standards. In such a situation, what would be the effect on relations with the countries of Eastern Europe? The USSR cannot count on making up for its own deficiencies by drawing on them. They will have similar problems, many of them in more acute form, for they are smaller economies, more dependent on international trade and credits, and hobbled by the same rigidity of the political and economic system that blocks reform. Eastern Europe's continuing need for Soviet oil and gas, moreover, creates an obligation to continue the supply at bearable cost or else face the near certainty of economic crisis and potential political explosion.

Is economic salvation to be found in détente and increased economic cooperation with the West? That was a primary motive for the Soviet policies of the 1970s, which opened doors to a broader participation in the world economy both for the USSR itself and for Eastern Europe. The latter, indeed, given heavy dependence on foreign trade and the inability of the USSR to meet its needs, had little choice but to turn to the West. For their own reasons the Soviets encouraged and approved that trend, hoping to contain the threat of political infection that might come with it.

Where political advantage from burgeoning East-West economic ties may lie is by no means certain, for they are not easily subject to manipulation. The Soviet Union, with its schemes for "all-European cooperation," could try to make them serve a strategy of weakening the Atlantic alliance and "Finlandizing" Western Europe, especially if Western Europe's growing stake in trade with the East should increase its reluctance to ruffle the surface of détente by opposing the Soviets on political issues. On the other hand, both Western and Eastern Europe might see advantage in a growing network of cooperation that would loosen the latter's ties with the Soviet Union—good reason for the Soviets to set limits to it. All parties may speculate on these possibilities and make the most of them. What seems most likely is that these economic connections will not be decisive either in meeting Eastern Europe's economic needs or in resolving the Soviet Union's political dilemmas.

Does an inevitable series of crises lie ahead? Must the Soviet leaders face continuing unsolved problems, unrest, and possible explosions in Eastern Europe, controllable only by force and repression? Or can they move toward a relationship that offers the chance of relative stability based on acceptance?

Developments in Poland since the summer of 1980 have given no definitive answers, although they have sharpened the questions. They have torn away some myths and established some hard truths. It was apparent, during the months of relative freedom from August 1980 to December 1981, that the political monopoly of the established Communist party had crumbled under the pressure for change and reform; that various sectors of society (workers, peasants, the religious establishment) were engaging in the political process on their own; that the independent union, Solidarity, not the party or the tame official unions, represented the working class. The key questions were whether these diverse forces representing the Polish nation could find some agreed basis with the still functioning government for saving Poland from civil conflict and economic chaos, and whether, agreement or no agreement, the Soviet Union would continue to tolerate a situation in which it was not exercising command and control either directly or through a reliable Polish leadership.

On this latter point the Soviets apparently reached a negative conclusion some time in the latter part of 1981. The cost of direct intervention being high, they sought and finally found what was both a Soviet and a Polish answer to the problem: government by a military council applying martial law and headed by General Wojciech Jaruzelski, who was already both prime minister and first secretary of the United Workers' Party. From Moscow's standpoint it was a master stroke, breaking the power of Solidarity and doing it without civil war and without the use of Soviet forces. In the months that followed, the Polish people were not able to mount a serious challenge to the military regime, the nominal termination of martial law in 1983 brought no basic change, and much of the hope and enthusiasm that marked the pre-December period faded. The story is unfinished, however, and it would be unwise to draw cosmic conclusions from the state of affairs at any given time.

What has happened and will happen in Poland cannot fail to influence developments elsewhere in Eastern Europe. We can assume the Soviets know that in their decisions on the destiny of Poland, the largest and most important satellite, they are dealing with the destiny of their East European empire. The alarm expressed by their satraps in East Berlin and Prague during the heyday of Solidarity was genuine and deep, and the regimes in Hungary and Romania also looked for ways to ward off pernicious influences on their restive workers. The success of Jaruzelski in suppressing the movement for reform and freedom in Poland, whatever interpretation be placed on his own motivation, has had a very salutary effect from the Soviet standpoint, both there and elsewhere. Nevertheless, the Polish events are historical facts that cannot be blotted out of people's minds, and the problems remain. Rule by the military may not be a happy precedent, and the Kremlin will have to make new appraisals and new decisions affecting Eastern Europe in the years ahead. The salient issues can be briefly and generally stated in a few paragraphs.

First, can the Soviet Union find effective instruments by which the East European states can be governed in ways that do not endanger Soviet interests? The Communist parties, created to serve that purpose, have failed in critical instances. The Soviet corrective, in the past, has been to purge or reconstruct them to make them reliable. But the Polish case exposed the plight of a ruling Communist party that could no longer rule, having lost all credibility in the eyes of the people; and it is questionable whether it can be rebuilt. Meanwhile, the Jaruzelski experiment—rule by force without any pretense of government by the classic Soviet-type institutional system—can scarcely be regarded as an enduring solution for Poland or as a model for the rest of Eastern Europe.

Second, Soviet dilemmas in coping with Eastern Europe's dubious economic prospects, glaringly evident in Poland, may be summed up in two words: rescue and reform. Are the Soviets prepared to bail out faltering economies with massive aid in grants and loans, cheap energy, and concessionary terms of trade? Will they be willing to pump in funds so that they can be pumped out again to service and repay Western loans? It seems doubtful, but what are the alternatives? Economic reforms might make these economies more productive and thus lighten the Soviet burden, but not without providing incentives to workers and peasants and concessions to private initiative that would compromise elements of socialism Moscow has deemed essential. In theory the New Economic Mechanism, which the Soviets have tolerated in Hungary, might be applied elsewhere, but Hungary's was a step-by-step process suitable to the peculiar conditions of Kádárism, the relations of accommodation worked out between party leaders and people, and between party leaders and Moscow. Such conditions will not easily be repeated in the rest of Eastern Europe. It is not even certain that in Hungary itself Kádárism will survive Kádár.

Third, can the demands of workers for independent unions and a share in economic decisions be indefinitely ignored? Poland's Solidarity was clearly too formidable a challenge to the very basis of a Communist regime for the Soviets to tolerate, but they have to face the issue of gaining workers' cooperation. The demand for workers' councils has arisen in Eastern Europe whenever the least chance for self-expression has appeared. Yugoslavia's particular institutions may not be suitable for other states; they may be far from ideal for Yugoslavia itself. But the Yugoslav example of self-management, tied to the fact of Yugoslav independence, remains highly significant.

Fourth, a vital point, and a constraining influence, for the Soviets in dealing with every one of these key questions is the potential impact on the USSR itself. They cannot experiment with political freedom and economic reform in Eastern Europe without raising the specter of freedom and reform at home. It is often said that no fundamental change in the status of Eastern Europe can take place until the Soviet Union itself has changed. Will Eastern Europe, through its own experience or by serving as a transmission line for ideas from outside, help speed a process of change in the USSR? Perhaps, but the time when the Kremlin will find room in the Soviet system for free labor unions or for "socialism with a human face" seems far away. For the foreseeable future the signs are that the peril such heresies represent in the USSR continues to make them intolerable anywhere in the socialist commonwealth.

Fifth, in the links between their position in Eastern Europe and their approach to East-West relations, the Soviets will have important choices to make. They can, of course, simply batten down the hatches and pay whatever the costs may be in economic drain, periodic crises, and risks of war. There are, however, conceivable alternatives to the current dictates bearing the labels of security and the defense of socialism. Closer ties with Western Europe and participation in the world economy might in time be teamed with new international security arrangements reducing tensions and giving substance to the invertebrate Helsinki system. Security and economic interests, in turn, might foster a greater flexibility and tolerance on the part of the Soviet Union toward Eastern Europe. The present agony of Poland and the looming economic crisis in Eastern Europe point logically to international rescue operations and to broad discussion of security questions between East and West.

Is there a possibility that this road may be taken? It would require a bold and imaginative gamble that there is more to be gained by Finlandizing Eastern Europe than by holding on grimly there while trying to Finlandize Western Europe. The choice is primarily Moscow's, not the West's or Eastern Europe's, although both may have some influence on it. The post-Brezhnev leadership, at a later stage if not now, conceivably could see matters in a new light. But will accommodation to opposition and to difficult situations, even to clear portents of failure, be anything more than tactics? At the present time we have no signs that the guiding principles of Soviet thought on what is fundamental in Eastern Europe will be any less absolute in the future than in the past.

2

Soviet Policy toward the German Democratic Republic

ANGELA E. STENT

Germany has for centuries exerted a major influence on Russian society and politics, both attracting and repelling Russian politicians and alternately presenting both opportunities and threats. This ambivalent historical legacy has had a profound impact on Russian political culture, an impact that continues to affect the definition of Soviet interests in Germany. The Russian anarchist Mikhail Bakunin captured one aspect of this contradictory love–hate relationship when he wrote,

> I say, as Voltaire said of God, that if there were no Germans we should have to invent them, since nothing so successfully unites the Slavs as a rooted hatred of Germans.[1]

Yet Germany, the common enemy, the repeated security threat to the Russian heartland, is only one side of the tradition; the other side is the Russian admiration for Germany's technological prowess, for its cultural achievements, attitudes that prompted successive czars to invite Germans to come to Russia and develop its economy.

Russia's ambivalent relationship with Germany has also been reflected, since the Bolshevik revolution, in alternating periods of cooperation and confrontation between the two states. For the Western world, the ultimate symbol of Russo-German collusion and perfidy in the twentieth century remains the Rapallo Treaty of 1922, the "unholy alliance" between Chicherin and the reluctant Rathenau, a treaty that the Soviets continue to praise as an example of mutually advantageous cooperation. Likewise, the Molotov–Ribbentrop Pact revealed that for Stalin the dictates of *Realpolitik* overrode all ideological exigencies. The historical legacy of Russo-German relations suggests a complex mixture of enmity and entente.

The USSR's relationship with East Germany is unique among Soviet ties with Eastern Europe because of the unusual degree of East German dependence. The German Democratic Republic (GDR) was created by the USSR and owes its existence entirely to Moscow. It has traditionally

1. Cited in Walter Laqueur, *Russia and Germany* (Boston: Little, Brown, 1965), p. 13.

33

served three main functions for the USSR. Strategically it is the most important buffer state, the politicomilitary bulwark guaranteeing the Soviet security system in Eastern Europe. Second, it is a vital source of economic assistance to the USSR and provides advanced technology and manufactured goods unavailable in other East European countries. Third, it is one of the most loyal replicas of the Soviet political system and offers both ideological and institutional legitimacy for the Soviet Marxist-Leninist model.

Moscow has pursued two major goals toward East Germany in the postwar era, one connected to its policy toward Eastern Europe (*Blokpolitik*) and the other to its policy toward the Western alliance (*Westpolitik*). The GDR's role in Soviet *Blokpolitik* remains predominant, although its significance for Soviet *Westpolitik* has grown in the last decade. The control of the GDR and the containment of the Federal Republic of Germany (FRG) have been the chief goals of Soviet policy toward Germany. Constant Soviet reminders of the threat of West German revanchism have provided one of the main rationales for Soviet control over Eastern Europe. Nevertheless, East Germany continues to present opportunities for the Kremlin's *Westpolitik*. Although it is doubtful that the USSR would permit German reunification under any circumstances, Moscow has been able to dangle the possibility of closer intra-German ties both to manipulate the GDR and to entice the FRG into developing a special relationship with the Soviet Union that might distance Bonn from the United States. The danger of this dual policy is that the Soviet offer of concessions to both Germanys might lead to an intra-German rapprochement that destabilizes the GDR. Soviet relations with East Germany must, therefore, be analyzed both in bilateral terms and as part of the triangular relationship of the USSR with both Germanys.

There are a number of asymmetries in the Soviet stakes in this complex triangle. The GDR, because of its crucial role in the Warsaw Pact system, is more important for Soviet security than is the FRG. However, the USSR is far more important for the GDR's survival than vice versa. The USSR could survive without the GDR, although its global role would be diminished without East German technology and logistical support in the Third World. The GDR as a state could probably not survive without the USSR, unlike Hungary or Czechoslovakia, because it lacks a consensus on national legitimacy. Its relationship with the Soviet Union is its central relationship, and its key source of stability is the maintenance of its position in the Soviet alliance system. The continued division of Germany is the vital issue, the *Existenzfrage,* for the GDR, and it depends on the USSR to guarantee this division. The FRG, on the other hand, could survive without the USSR, yet Moscow holds the key to the future viability of West Berlin and to the continuing intra-German relationship. The

USSR, therefore, has more to offer the two Germanys than either Germany has to offer the Soviet Union.

The opportunities for the USSR in its triangular German policy have, however, been tempered by the USSR's worries about the legitimacy of the GDR. This is a twofold problem for the Kremlin. Given the inherent instability of the GDR, the Soviets have always been concerned to strengthen the domestic legitimacy of the East German regime, to promote a socialist German national identity. They have also realized that any strengthening of the GDR's international legitimacy might reinforce domestic legitimacy, and have therefore sought to gain international recognition of the GDR and promote the foreign role of East Berlin. Since the normalization of Soviet-West German and intra-German relations, the GDR has expanded its role outside Eastern Europe as a means of reasserting its importance to Moscow following the demise of West German revanchism as a central rationale for the GDR's role in the Warsaw Pact.

The USSR's choices in formulating and implementing its policy toward the GDR have thus been determined by the role of the GDR in both *Blokpolitik* and *Westpolitik*. The prime Soviet goal toward the GDR in the context of Soviet *Blokpolitik* is defensive: the maintenance of the GDR as the bulwark of a stable Eastern Europe and as a dependable ally. Prior to 1970 the GDR played a significant role in reinforcing the negative strategic importance of the FRG for the USSR. Moscow demanded West German recognition of East Germany as the precondition for a European settlement. As long as the FRG refused to recognize the GDR, the USSR could invoke the West German threat as a means of maintaining cohesion within the Warsaw Pact. However, Moscow has also utilized the GDR more assertively in its *Westpolitik*. The promise of better intra-German relations is the main reason why Bonn seeks closer ties with the USSR, and this policy causes problems in U.S.-West German relations. Nevertheless, the Kremlin does realize that the promise of closer intra-German ties as a bargaining lever with both Germanys must be balanced against the overriding goal of stabilizing the GDR. These contradictions have been inherent in Soviet policy since Stalin's time.

After reviewing briefly Soviet policy toward the GDR under Stalin and Khrushchev, I shall examine in greater detail the nature of political, economic, and military bilateral relations in the last decade. I shall analyze the political and economic aspects of trilateral Soviet ties with both Germanys and shall discuss the implications of current developments for Soviet-GDR relations in the 1980s.

SOVIET-GDR RELATIONS PRIOR TO 1969

Stalin's preoccupation with preventing Germany from ever again being in a position to attack the USSR determined his goals toward his defeated enemy after 1945. He may initially have been undecided about Germany's fate, but ultimately the imposition of Soviet-controlled governments in Eastern Europe, creating a ring of loyal buffer states between Germany and the USSR, took precedence over experimentation with a reunified Germany whose future political orientation would be uncertain.

Apart from a few episodes in the Stalin and Khrushchev eras, Soviet behavior on the German question has been remarkably consistent since 1949; but the few deviations from this consistency suggest residual Soviet flexibility on the German issue that lasted until Khrushchev's fall. In particular, Stalin's 1952 note proposing a reunited, neutralized Germany remains a subject of speculation as to whether it represented a genuine Soviet offer of reunification or was only a tactic intended to forestall the FRG's integration into the Western alliance.[2] Stalin used this proposal to fuel opposition within the FRG to Germany's incorporation into NATO, the first of a series of such tactics showing the assertive nature of Soviet policy.

With Stalin's death, Soviet policy toward the GDR became an issue in the 1953 power struggle that led to Lavrentii Beria's demise. Indeed, both Soviet and East German sources subsequently claimed that Beria had planned to "give up" the GDR and permit reunification.[3] With the June 1953 East German uprising, however, Moscow had little choice but to keep the loyal though unpopular Walter Ulbricht in power to prevent the disintegration of the GDR. Although the USSR continued to discuss the prospect of German reunification with the Western powers until the FRG's entry into NATO in 1954, the emphasis of Soviet policy had shifted: until the building of the Berlin Wall in August 1961, it was the preservation of East Germany and not the wooing of West Germany that would determine Soviet policy.

In the meantime, Khrushchev adopted a more aggressive policy toward the West, this time using Berlin as the pressure point. With its open borders providing an easy means of escape for the rising tide of refugees from East to West, the city dramatically symbolized the GDR's instability. Thus, in an attempt to solve the question of the GDR's domestic and international legitimacy, Moscow's 1958 Berlin ultimatum demanded that West Berlin become an independent demilitarized city. With the resumption in January 1960 of the forced collectivization drive abandoned in 1953, the emigration situation took on catastrophic proportions,

2. See Thomas W. Wolfe, *Soviet Power and Europe, 1945–1970* (Baltimore: Johns Hopkins Press, 1970), pp. 27–31, and Victor Baras, "Stalin's German Policy After Stalin," *Slavic Review*, 37 (June 1978), 259–67.

3. For a discussion of these revelations, see Ilse Spittmann, "Wollte Moskau die DDR wirklich aufgeben?" *Süddeutsche Zeitung*, May 19, 1963.

reaching a peak of about 2,000 refugees a day. Because this spelled near-term economic and ultimate political disaster for the GDR regime, the Soviets opted, as they had in 1953, for supporting Ulbricht and built the Wall.[4]

The Wall marked an important turning point in Soviet-German relations. By helping to consolidate the Ulbricht regime and, thereby, secure the stability of the GDR, it ultimately enabled the USSR to pursue a more flexible policy toward both Germanys. Nevertheless, when Khrushchev announced his plan to visit the FRG in 1964, it was clear that opposition to this initiative both in the GDR and within the Kremlin provided the occasion, although not the cause, of his downfall.[5] Another attempt to take advantage of the new-found flexibility would not be made until after the Warsaw Pact invasion of Czechoslovakia in 1968.

In the intervening four years, Soviet and East German determination to resist West German *Ostpolitik* became increasingly aligned—this despite (or perhaps because of) the reinforcement of contradictory pressures on Moscow with the beginnings of a more flexible West German *Ostpolitik*. As long as Bonn refused to accept the postwar territorial and political settlement, the threat of West German revanchism could be used to legitimize Soviet control over Eastern Europe; by the same token, any softening of the revanchist threat would remove much of the rationale for such control. Small wonder, then, that the formation in December 1966 of Bonn's Grand Coalition, and the inauguration under Foreign Minister Willy Brandt of a more active and differentiated *Ostpolitik*, were initially viewed by the Soviets as more inimical to their interests than Konrad Adenauer's former rigidity. The new *Ostpolitik* yielded some results: the establishment of diplomatic relations between Bonn and Bucharest in January 1967 and the resumption of relations with Belgrade. These moves represented a significant setback for both the USSR and the GDR as the first major break in East European solidarity on the German question and prompted the GDR, no doubt with Moscow's support, to announce the Ulbricht doctrine (a counterpart to West Germany's Hallstein doctrine), stipulating that no East European country should establish diplomatic relations with the FRG without prior West German diplomatic recognition of the GDR.

Confronted the following year with the Czechoslovak crisis, the USSR again found the GDR one of its staunchest supporters. From Ulbricht's perspective, not only did the domestic model of reform socialism provide a destabilizing alternative to the GDR system, but Dubček's willingness to

4. Ulbricht played a major role in persuading Khrushchev to build the Wall. See Philip Windsor, *City on Leave: A History of Berlin, 1945–1962* (London: Chatto & Windus, 1963), p. 239.

5. For the best discussion of this episode, see Wolfe, *Soviet Power*, pp. 117–27.

deal with "realistic" forces in the FRG posed the danger that yet a second East European country might normalize relations with Bonn without the latter's prior recognition of the GDR, further weakening its already tenuous legitimacy and influence.[6] The Soviets and East Germans thus shared an interest in containing the Prague infection, and the invasion of Czechoslovakia represented both a setback for West German *Ostpolitik* and a reinforcement of Ulbricht's usefulness to the more hard-line elements in Moscow.

In the period between the end of the war and the invasion of Czechoslovakia, then, the USSR had achieved its main goals toward the GDR. It had created a loyal, dependent buffer state, whose economy was a constant source of support for the USSR, whose army played an important role in the Warsaw Pact and which identified itself ideologically with the USSR. On the other hand, the Soviet Union had been less able prior to 1969 to utilize its leverage over the FRG. After the invasion of Czechoslovakia, however, the USSR's interests increasingly diverged from those of the GDR. Having asserted its power both to veto any West German *Ostpolitik* that did not meet Soviet requirements and to control the pace of political development in Eastern Europe, Moscow now felt able to pursue its broader global interests and to seek an accommodation with the West on its terms—policies that ultimately threatened Ulbricht's position.

SOVIET *WESTPOLITIK* AND ULBRICHT'S DEMISE, 1969–71

The Soviet decision to respond favorably to West German initiatives for normalizing relations in 1969 precipitated a two-year crisis in USSR-GDR relations. The GDR, despite its dependence on the USSR, refused to play the role of compliant client. Ulbricht was the USSR's most loyal ally during the Czech crisis, and he assumed that he could continue to exercise a veto power over any rapprochement between the FRG and Eastern Europe that fell short of his maximalist goal: full diplomatic recognition of the GDR. Moscow's view was somewhat different. While Western ratification of the postwar division of Europe and of Germany had been a consistent Soviet goal since 1955, Moscow was ultimately willing to compromise on the issue of the de facto as opposed to de jure recognition by the FRG of the GDR, since this still involved Western acceptance of existing boundaries and of Soviet hegemony in Eastern Europe.

The origin of Soviet-GDR tensions lay in their differing objectives in Europe following the Czech invasion. The Soviet Union now felt able to

6. For a detailed discussion of the GDR's fears of West German-Czechoslovak economic contacts in this period and of Bonn's use of economic diplomacy in general, see Michael J. Sodaro, "Ulbricht's Grand Design: Economics, Ideology and the GDR's Response to Détente, 1967–1971," *World Affairs*, 142 (Winter 1980), 147–68.

pursue its longer term goal of promoting détente in Europe and convening a European Security Conference. Even before the election of Willy Brandt as chancellor of the FRG in September 1969, the Kremlin had put out feelers toward West Germany. This was linked to other major Soviet concerns: the desire to revitalize a dialogue with the United States, including the move to begin arms control talks; the growing fear of China; and the attempt to loosen ties between Washington and Bonn. Soviet-GDR tensions first began to surface at the March 1969 Warsaw Pact Consultative Committee meeting in Budapest, where the USSR revived its proposal for a European Security Conference and where the final communiqué was notable for its mild language toward Bonn.[7] Later that month, at the conference celebrating the fiftieth anniversary of the founding of the Comintern, Politburo members Mikhail Suslov and Boris Ponomarev refuted the Stalinist theory that social democracy was the chief enemy of communism, an obvious signal to the West German Social Democratic Party (SPD), which had begun informal contacts with the Communist Party of the Soviet Union (CPSU). Ulbricht, however, defended the Comintern's 1928 equation of social democracy with "social fascism."[8] Clearly, this exchange represented something more than an esoteric dialogue about the theoretical nature of social democracy.

The USSR pursued its dialogue with the new Bonn government partly in response to changes in West German policy. After Brandt was elected chancellor in 1969, the FRG ceased to pursue a revisionist policy toward Eastern Europe: instead of seeking to alter the postwar status quo, Bonn agreed to accept it, as the USSR had demanded. Moreover, Brandt explicitly declared his desire to reach a modus vivendi with the GDR, acknowledging the existence of "two German states in one nation" and indicating a willingness to recognize East Germany. This, plus Bonn's agreement to sign the nuclear nonproliferation treaty and the assent to ratify the postwar European boundaries, induced Moscow to respond favorably to Brandt's initiatives. The USSR, on balance, considered that the benefits of rapprochement with West Germany outweighed the risks of undermining the GDR's security. It initially expected that détente would be beneficial for East Germany because the FRG's de facto recognition would bring the GDR international legitimacy.

In negotiations leading up to the signing of the Soviet-FRG Renunciation of Force Treaty, the USSR sought to gain West Germany's de jure recognition of the GDR, but after a difficult series of negotiations be-

7. *Pravda*, Mar. 12, 1969; F. Stephen Larrabee, "The Politics of Reconciliation: Soviet Policy Towards West Germany, 1961–1972" (Ph.D. diss., Columbia University, 1977).

8. For details of the SPD–CPSU contacts, see Heinz Timmerman, "Im Vorfeld der neuen Ostpolitik," *Osteuropa*, no. 6, 1971, pp. 388–99. For Ulbricht's position, see *Kommunist*, no. 5, 1969, pp. 9, 24, and *Neues Deutschland*, Mar. 26, 1969.

tween Soviet Foreign Minister Andrei Gromyko and West German State Secretary Egon Bahr, Moscow made two concessions. It settled for de facto recognition and permitted Bonn to append a letter to the treaty claiming that "this treaty does not conflict with the political objective of the Federal Republic of Germany to work for a state of peace in Europe in which the German nation will recover its unity in free self-determination."[9] After the Soviet-West German treaty was signed in August 1970, Ulbricht made known his opposition to the Soviet compromise on the recognition question, although Foreign Minister Gromyko had consulted with the East German leaders in advance.[10] Moreover, Brandt had made it clear to the Soviet leaders that the ratification of the Moscow and Warsaw treaties in the German Bundestag was dependent on a satisfactory solution to the Berlin problem. Gromyko made several trips to East Berlin to prod Ulbricht into greater cooperation on the intra-German negotiations and the Berlin problem, on which quadripartite talks had begun in December 1969.[11] Despite two meetings between Chancellor Brandt and GDR Prime Minister Willi Stoph, the East Germans were reluctant to intensify the intra-German dialogue or to allow a continuation of West German links with West Berlin.[12]

Ulbricht was not only recalcitrant about supporting the Soviet position on Berlin; he sought to ally himself with opponents of Brezhnev's *Westpolitik* in the USSR, particularly the Politburo member Pyotr Shelest. Hints of this opposition began to filter out during the Berlin negotiations.[13] Ulbricht ultimately challenged not only Moscow's right to dictate the course of East German foreign policy, but also the supremacy of the USSR's domestic political model. At the 24th Congress of the CPSU in March 1971, he invoked his personal acquaintance with Lenin, pointing out that his "Soviet comrades also had things to learn." He also announced his intention to unveil a comprehensive program for "the developed social system of socialism," throwing down his gauntlet to the Soviet leadership by claiming that the GDR was an advanced socialist society, perhaps more advanced than the USSR.[14]

9. See William E. Griffith, *The Ostpolitik of the Federal Republic of Germany* (Cambridge: MIT Press, 1978), pp. 190–91.

10. "Kommunike o Vizite Ministra Inostrannykh Del SSSR A. Gromyko v Germanskuyu Demokraticheskuyu Respubliku," *Pravda*, Feb. 28, 1970.

11. Griffith, *Ostpolitik,* p. 198.

12. "Russians Seen Prodding Ulbricht," *International Herald Tribune,* Oct. 30, 1970; "Gromyko's Besuch in Ost Berlin," *Neue Zürcher Zeitung,* Oct. 31, 1970; "Gromyko Said to Prod East Germans on Berlin," *International Herald Tribune,* Nov. 26, 1970.

13. Larrabee, "Politics of Reconciliation," chap. 4. Evidence is, however, scanty on this issue.

14. Melvin Croan, *East Germany: The Soviet Connection,* The Washington Papers 36 (Beverly Hills: Sage Publications, 1976), p. 28.

In his unrelenting opposition to Soviet *Westpolitik* and to any intra-German rapprochement, Ulbricht was isolated from other East European leaders, who shared the Soviet desire for improved relations with the FRG. His ultimate goal was to liquidate the four-power status of Berlin, and the Soviet willingness to begin quadripartite negotiations on Berlin threatened his central policy goal.[15] While the USSR may well have shared this ultimate aim vis-à-vis Berlin, in the short term Ulbricht was obstructing Moscow's rapprochement with Bonn. Indeed, both the Berlin and the intra-German negotiations made progress only after his resignation in May 1971. When the situation became critical, the USSR could still control events within the GDR and give priority to its policy toward the FRG.

SOVIET-GDR BILATERAL RELATIONS IN THE DÉTENTE ERA

Political Ties

Brezhnev's *Westpolitik* increased the complexity of Soviet-GDR relations, multiplying the sources both of agreement and disagreement, of control and interdependence between the USSR and its most dependent and dependable ally. Détente has highlighted some differences of interest between the Soviet Union and East Germany, although the GDR shares Moscow's view of détente—namely, that it is regional and divisible, applying to Europe but not to the Third World. Soviet pursuit of a more active global policy in the last decade has somewhat diminished East Berlin's overall role in Soviet foreign policy concerns, although the GDR has gained in international legitimacy since détente. Moreover, the relationship with the GDR is only one factor in a much broader spectrum of Soviet foreign policy goals. Hence Moscow was less disturbed about the impact of the invasion of Afghanistan on relations between Eastern and Western Europe than was the GDR, with its more limited, regional concerns.

Apart from these potential divergencies over foreign policy issues, the Soviet-GDR relationship remains stable and cooperative. The essence of the bilateral Soviet-GDR relationship has not altered since 1949: Moscow has final decision-making power on all critical issues affecting GDR-Soviet relations. However, in nondecisive, more marginal issues, the GDR since the early 1970s has gained more room for maneuvering and has acquired some veto power over Soviet decisions. It cannot induce the Soviet Union to initiate policies that Moscow does not favor or change key policy decisions, but it can question certain noncrucial policies.

The bilateral agreement regulating relations between the USSR and

15. Christian Deuvel, "Some Thoughts on Ulbricht's Dispute with the Kremlin on 'Westpolitik,'" *Radio Liberty Research CRD IS/71*, Munich, Jan. 18, 1971.

the GDR is the 25-year Treaty of Friendship, Cooperation and Mutual Assistance of October 7, 1975, which replaced the two previous GDR-Soviet treaties of 1955 and 1964. The treaty institutionalizes a high degree of integration between the two states and contains some omissions and additions to previous treaties. It envisages a closer degree of bilateral political, economic, and military cooperation than that between the USSR and other East European states. Its preamble also states that "the close fraternal alliance (is) based on the fundament of Marxist-Leninism and socialist internationalism," the last phrase referring to the so-called Brezhnev doctrine.[16]

Unlike the two previous treaties, this one no longer mentions the commitment to German reunification but speaks instead of the "inviolability of borders," omitting entirely the "peaceful change" formula of the Helsinki Final Act. Whereas the previous treaties had pledged the GDR to come to the military aid of the USSR if it were attacked "in Europe," the 1975 treaty promises GDR military assistance in case of an attack on the USSR by "any state or group of states," an indication that the Soviet Union may perceive the main threat to its security to be from China rather than from the Federal Republic. The treaty also claims that "West Berlin is not a constituent part of the FRG," the conventional Soviet formula for depicting political ties between West Berlin and Bonn, and obliges the GDR and USSR to cooperate more closely than before in military and economic matters.[17]

The GDR's domestic political system is a close replica of the USSR's. Since its creation in 1946, through the forced merger of the SPD and the German Communist Party (KPD), the SED (Socialist Unity Party) as a "party of the new type" has fashioned itself on the CPSU. Although four noncommunist parties exist in the GDR, their presence in no way diminishes the similarity of the GDR's political system to that of the USSR. Moreover, there are close institutional ties between the SED and the CPSU, ranging from annual summits between the two party leaders to contacts at every level of the party. These contacts reinforce, through a

16. For the text of the treaty, see "Dogovor o Druzhbe, Sotrudnichestve i Vzaimnoi Pomoshchi mezhdu Soyuzom Sovetskikh Sotsialisticheskikh Respublik i Germanskoi Demokraticheskoi Respublikoi, *Novoye Vremya*, no. 41 (1975), p. 12; for a West German interpretation, see Theodor Schweisfurth, "Die neue vertragliche Bindung der DDR an die Sowjetunion," *Europa Archiv*, no. 24 (1975), pp. 753–64; Hans Heinrich Mahnke, "Die neuen Freundschafts- und Beistandsverträge der DDR," *Deutschland Archiv*, 10, no. 11 (1977), 116–84. For an East German interpretation, see Herbert Kroeger, "Der Freundschaftsvertrag mit der UdSSR—ein Vertrag von historischer Bedeutung," *Deutsche Aussenpolitik*, 26, no. 1 (1976), 18–32.

17. See Fred Oldenburg and Christian Meier, "Zum Verhältnis UdSSR/DDR nach dem XXV Parteitag der KPdSU," (Cologne: Bundesinstitut fur ostwissenschaftliche und internationale Studien, Report no. 43, 1976).

complex and cross-cutting network of ties, the relationship between the two parties, in which the CPSU takes the leading role.

Although institutional and structural party ties provide the long-term framework for Soviet control over the GDR, individuals are sometimes important in the exercise of influence. The primary channel of Soviet influence in the 1970s was the close personal relationship between GDR leader Erich Honecker and Leonid Brezhnev. There was uncertainty in the GDR after Brezhnev's death because the Honecker–Brezhnev relationship would presumably be hard to duplicate with Yuri Andropov, and yet the CPSU has a closer relationship with the SED than with any other party.[18] One element of continuity was Pyotr Abrassimov, Soviet Central Committee member and ambassador to the GDR from 1962 to 1971, who played a role in ousting Ulbricht and was renamed ambassador to East Berlin from 1975 to 1983. Known as a hard-liner on issues such as German reunification, Abrassimov was a major actor in links between the CPSU and the SED, and he supervised the day-to-day operations of Soviet control over the GDR. He also had considerable control over SED Politburo decisions. In 1983, he was replaced by Vyacheslav Kochemasov, a member of the Central Committee with reportedly close ties to both Honecker and Andropov.

East Germany also plays a central role in the ideological aspect of Moscow's *Blokpolitik* and its ideological significance for the USSR has increased since the 1970s. The Soviet Union has tended to demand greater domestic and foreign policy conformity from the GDR since détente, to protect it from the infectious bacilli of greater Western influence. Since the beginning of the crisis in Poland, the GDR has been a vociferous defender of Soviet-type socialism. The SED reinforces the legitimacy of the Soviet system as one of the staunchest supporters (together with Bulgaria) of Soviet ideological pronouncements except at the end of the Ulbricht regime. It therefore performs an important function in endorsing the correctness both of the domestic Soviet system and of its ideological claim to be the leading model for all its socialist allies.

The GDR's ideological reliability and significance for Soviet foreign policy have emerged in numerous multilateral Communist gatherings—most notably in the choice of the GDR to organize the June 1976 conference of Communist parties in East Berlin, at which the SED played a conspicuous role in combating the various Eurocommunist heresies.[19] The SED has consistently criticized both Eurocommunist and Chinese deviations from the Soviet line and continues to stress the "ideological

18. Karl Wilhelm Fricke, "Die SED und der Moskauer Führungswechsel," *Deutschland Archiv*, 16, no. 12 (1983), 1238.

19. Kevin Devlin, "The Challenge of Eurocommunism," *Problems of Communism*, 26 (Jan.–Feb. 1977), 14–20.

unity and political uniformity of the CPSU and the SED."[20] The unswerving loyalty of the SED is a vital asset for the CPSU.

Economic Relations

The USSR's economic relations with the GDR exist on a number of overlapping levels. Bilateral Soviet-GDR economic relations, embodied in a series of trade and cooperation agreements, are the cornerstone of the relationship. They are reinforced by the multilateral role of the GDR and the USSR in the Council for Mutual Economic Assistance (CMEA), which has grown in the last decade. The economic relationship is important for both countries.

Soviet economic relations with the GDR have undergone a series of modifications since the end of the war. Initially, East Germany's main function was to provide the USSR with large-scale reparations, including transportation to the USSR of much of what was left of East German industry. The division of Germany cut off the eastern part from its former sources of supplies in the western part of Germany and forced East Germany to reorient its economy completely. After Stalin's death and the 1953 uprisings in the GDR, the USSR placed its economic relations with East Germany on a less exploitative basis and granted it credits in order to improve the economic situation. By the mid-1950s, East Germany, under Soviet orders, had begun to intensify its industrial development, and it experienced its own "economic miracle." In 1963 Ulbricht introduced his New Economic System, implementing reforms comparable to those introduced in the Soviet Union in 1965,[21] but in both countries these failed because they threatened to create a class of independent managers who challenged vested party interests. The East Germans have always been limited in the extent to which they can introduce decentralizing reforms by their need both to promote an economic system similar to that of the Soviet Union and by their fear of the potentially destabilizing political consequences of large-scale economic reform.

From the Soviet point of view, the complementary economic relationship with the GDR, its foremost trading partner, involving the exchange of East German industrial goods for Soviet raw materials, is both an asset

20. I. J. Andronov and K. I. Savinov, "Das Kampfbündnis der KPdSU und der SED—Herzstück der engen Zusammenarbeit zwischen der UdSSR und der DDR," *Einheit*, 34, no. 21 (1979), 145–57.

21. For the GDR reforms, see Michael Keren, "The Rise and Fall of the New Economic System," in Lyman Letgers, ed., *The German Democratic Republic* (Boulder: Westview Press, 1978), chap. 3. For the Soviet reforms, see Roger Munting, *The Economic Development of the USSR* (New York: St. Martin's Press, 1982), pp. 152–54.

and a liability. The GDR's almost total dependence on Soviet raw material imports represents a drain on Soviet resources and is particularly problematic in the energy field. In 1970, 7% of all GDR exports to the Soviet Union went toward paying for oil. In 1980 the figure was 25%, with a predicted 35% by 1985.[22] Not only does the USSR have to supply the GDR with almost all its energy, it is also concerned about East Germany's hard-currency debt, which rose to $12.8 billion in 1981. However, by 1983 East Germany had cut that debt to $1.6 billion.[23] On the other hand, East German machinery exports have greatly contributed to the development of the Soviet industrial infrastructure. East Germany is the most important supplier of advanced technology to the Soviet Union, thus contributing an essential ingredient to Soviet economic growth. For instance, after President Reagan imposed extraterritorial sanctions on compressor components for the West Siberian pipeline, Moscow charged the GDR with developing substitute rotors.

Between 1960 and 1980, Soviet-GDR trade rose by an annual average of 8.8%. In 1982 it rose by 10%. While the share of Soviet goods in GDR total foreign trade rose in the 1970s, the GDR's share in total Soviet foreign trade has fallen. The primary East German exports to the Soviet Union are machinery, machine tools, and equipment for the chemical industry. The GDR supplies 44% of the USSR's imports of agricultural machinery, 36% of its rail vehicles, and 23% of its ships. The USSR supplies the GDR with 89% of its oil, 100% of its natural gas, 66% of its coal, 80% of its sheet metal, 85% of its cotton, and 99% of its cut timber. The 1975 Soviet-GDR Friendship Treaty stipulated that economic contacts between the two nations would be intensified, and bilateral trade was supposed to increase 40% between 1970 and 1980.[24] However, in 1975 the USSR increased the prices charged for its raw materials, creating problems in GDR–Soviet relations. As raw material prices, especially those for energy, have risen in the last seven years, the terms of trade have shifted increasingly in the USSR's favor. The GDR's negative balance of trade with the USSR has grown, and in 1978 East Germany agreed to supply the Soviet Union with technical expertise in return for extra supplies of Soviet oil and gas, while Moscow granted East Berlin extra credits.[25]

The USSR and GDR signed a specialization and cooperation agree-

22. *Economist,* Mar. 22, 1980.

23. "Weiterhin Anspannung aller Ressourcen: Die Lage der DDR-Wirtschaft zur Jahreswende 1982/83," *DIW Wochenbericht,* no. 5 (1983) (Berlin: Deutsches Institut für Wirtschaftsforschung), p. 57.

24. *Sotsialisticheskaya Industriya,* Aug. 2, 1975, p. 3.

25. Leslie Collitt, "Soviet Oil Buys East German Skills," *Financial Times,* June 23, 1978.

ment on the GDR's thirtieth anniversary in 1979, which runs until 1990 and stresses technological cooperation.[26] They have since 1950 collaborated in scientific and technical branches of industry, and they engage in common research and development projects.

The most problematic economic issue in Soviet-GDR relations in the 1980s will be the GDR's energy situation. The GDR, whose only indigenous source of energy is lignite, has become increasingly dependent on imports of energy over the last decade. Energy consumption rose from 48.7 to 119.3 million tons of coal equivalent between 1950 and 1978, while energy production rose from 44.6 to 83.5 million tons.[27] As the GDR economy has become more modernized, it has consumed liquid fuels at a faster rate than solid fuels, and it is considerably less efficient in its use of energy than is either the United States or the FRG. The prospects for conservation in the GDR are not good, although it has the lowest rate of energy-use growth within CMEA.[28] It appears that East Germany will become more dependent on oil in the next decade. However, the USSR cut its oil deliveries to the GDR by 10% in 1982, forcing East Germany to look elsewhere for oil supplies.

The USSR has recently become more concerned about domestic economic problems within East Germany. Although the GDR remains the most highly developed socialist country, with the tenth-highest per capita GNP in the world, its economic situation has deteriorated in the last few years. The GDR's 1980 economic plan indicated growing economic problems. The plan lowered the rate of increase for industrial production and called for increases in energy imports from the Soviet Union and for increased exports, but these targets have already been revised, especially the oil figures. In 1982 the GDR's economic position—particularly its need to cut the hard-currency debt—was only improved through a drastic reduction in imports, increased exports, and forced saving. Although East Germans enjoy a higher standard of living than their Soviet counterparts, the USSR is aware that economic problems in the GDR can be more destabilizing politically than those in the USSR because of the fragile political situation.

The energy problems of the GDR are one manifestation of a far wider series of difficult choices facing the USSR in its economic relations with the GDR. Both Moscow and East Berlin are especially concerned about the economic health of the GDR because its government seeks to sub-

26. N. Tikhonov, "Novy Etap Ekonomicheskogo Sotrudnichestva," *Izvestiya*, Nov. 14, 1979.

27. Cam Hudson, "Eastern Europe and the Energy Crisis: An Overview," *Radio Free Europe Research RAD Background Report*, no. 136 (June 10, 1980).

28. "Energiewirtschaft der DDR vor schwierigen Aufgaben," *DIW Wochenbericht*, no. 5 (1981), p. 58.

stitute consumer communism for a sense of legitimate national identity. It is in the Soviet Union's economic and political interest that the GDR continue to stress its industrial development and a higher standard of living for its population, which compares its standard of living with that of its West German counterparts. This places extra pressure on the East German government to stress consumption. At the same time, the relative affluence of East German citizens is obvious not only to Soviet and East European tourists but also to the 400,000 Soviet troops in the GDR, who may well question why they are worse off than the population of the country they are occupying.

The USSR faces a potential conflict between economic and political goals in its economic relations with the GDR. Although it is in its economic interest to raise the prices for raw material exports to the GDR and cut back on supplies, it is in its political interest to maintain domestic stability in East Germany, which a sudden price increase would threaten, and to encourage consumerism. Moreover, it is in the USSR's political interest to intensify its economic integration with the GDR to maintain a constant source of control and influence.

Military Contacts

One of the principal mechanisms of Soviet control over the GDR is the presence of 19 Soviet divisions in East Germany and the close links between the Soviet and GDR armies. Soviet forces serve both defensive and offensive military and political functions. As the westernmost projection of Soviet military power in Eastern Europe, their main stated purpose is to counter NATO troops in the FRG. Soviet troops also perform a useful offensive function as a source of Soviet foreign policy leverage in the USSR's dealings with the West. From time to time since 1958 the USSR has publicized the withdrawal of some of its forces from the GDR as a means of demonstrating to the West its peaceful intentions and possibly inducing NATO to cut its troops or causing conflicts between the FRG and NATO.[29]

The primary task of these Soviet troops in reality is defensive—to perform domestic control functions in the GDR, Poland and Czechoslovakia—and the Soviets bear the brunt of troop stationing costs. Soviet troops in the GDR also serve to check domestic developments within East Germany by reminding the East German population of the potential costs to the GDR of any significant challenge to Soviet policy. In this sense the

29. For the last Soviet troop withdrawal offer, see "Rech Tovarishcha L. I. Brezhneva," *Pravda*, Oct. 7, 1979, p. 1. The Soviet Union offered to withdraw 20,000 troops and 1,000 tanks from the GDR in 1979.

GDR government presumably welcomes the presence of Soviet troops as a deterrent to internal unrest.[30]

The GDR National People's Army (NVA) is also an important asset to the USSR. It is the only East European military establishment wholly subordinated to the Warsaw Pact Command in peacetime. Although party control over the military is firmly established, one might question the fundamental morale of the NVA. If a war were to break out in Europe, would East German soldiers be willing to take up arms against their West German brethren? While the efficiency and effectiveness of the NVA are no doubt a military asset to the Soviet Union, Moscow must be careful to couple this military prowess with a large dose of political control and to maintain the firm integration of the NVA into the Warsaw Pact.

The USSR has in the last decade increasingly relied on the NVA and on other East German logistical services to support Soviet expansion in the Third World. Since the GDR gained international recognition, its foreign policy activities have greatly increased. The Soviet Union to a large degree encourages these developments both because they raise the international prestige of the GDR and because East Germany can augment Soviet foreign policy activity. Moreover, East Germany can engage directly in activities that might be inappropriate for the USSR, given the latter's broader international concerns and responsibilities.

East Germany has assumed an active role in promoting Soviet goals in the Third World. The GDR has four main reasons for undertaking these military and economic activities: They reinforce East Berlin's importance to Moscow as an indispensable supporter of the USSR's global policy; they enhance the GDR's international legitimacy; they provide the GDR with raw material imports and export markets; and they enable it to compete with the FRG in a non-European area, although the two Germanys are active in different African countries. East German activities include training certain national liberation groups, such as the Angolan Movimento Popular de Libertaçao de Angola (MPLA), the Mozambique Frelimo, Mengistu followers in Ethiopia, Nkomo's Zimbabwe African People's Union (ZAPU), the Namibian South-West African People's Organization (SWAPO) and the South African African National Congress (ANC), and providing military assistance and logistical support in Yemen and Afghanistan, and to the Palestine Liberation Organization (PLO). In addition, the GDR's aid to the Third World, especially to Africa, has been growing in the last decade, presumably at Soviet bidding. Currently the GDR is dispensing an estimated $20 million annually in military aid and an additional $300 million in economic assistance in the Third World.[31]

---

30. Croan, *East Germany*, p. 48.
31. "Here Come Europe's Cubans," *Time,* Apr. 15, 1980.

The GDR trains both party cadres and intelligence services (the *Staatssicherheitsdienst* has trained the Angolan and South Yemen secret police), and youth exchanges between the *Freie Deutsche Jugend* and African groups are growing.[32] The most controversial aspect of the GDR's role in Africa is its military assistance. Indeed, all Western suggestions that there is a new Afrika Korps are strongly denied by East German officials. By some Western accounts there are at least 3,000 East German military advisers operating in more than a dozen Third World countries, with 1,500 in Africa alone.

East German Defense Minister Heinz Hoffmann, who regularly visits GDR army installations in Africa, has claimed that "in reality, there are no and never have been any units of our National People's Army in any African country."[33] It is generally accepted that, rather than sending entire battalions or regiments of the NVA to Africa, East Germany instead tends to send smaller groups of troops, trainers, and organizers to work with African groups. Nevertheless, apart from a few failures, such as the backing of Joshua Nkomo's ZAPU prior to Zimbabwe's independence, the GDR has generally enjoyed growing success and influence in Africa.

From the Kremlin's point of view, the bilateral relationship with East Germany must be a source of considerable satisfaction. The GDR is one of Moscow's most faithful allies, upholder of Soviet orthodoxy in domestic and foreign policy issues, uncritical of Soviet actions in public. It has promoted Soviet policy in the Third World and has zealously supported the USSR in the United Nations since it became a member in 1973. Its technology fuels Soviet economic development. East German dependence on Soviet raw materials is a continuing liability for Moscow, but these economic problems are far outweighed by the political, military, and economic benefits that the GDR brings the USSR.

TRILATERAL RELATIONS

Annäherung (rapprochement) vs. *Abgrenzung* (demarcation): Soviet and East German Choices

Moscow's evaluation of the triangular aspects of Soviet-GDR relations is more mixed than its estimation of bilateral ties. It encourages the intra-German dialogue partly to promote disunity within the Atlantic alliance,

---

32. For an extensive discussion of the GDR's activities, see Bernard von Plate, "Afrika südlich der Sahara," in Hans-Adolf Jacobsen, Gert Leptin, Ulrich Scheuner, and Eberhard Schulz, eds., *Drei Jahrzehnte Aussenpolitik der DDR* (Munich: Oldenbourg Verlag, 1979), pp. 657–72. See also Melvin Croan, "A New Afrika Korps?" *Washington Quarterly*, 3 (Winter 1980), 21–37.

33. General Hoffmann, writing in the SED party journal *Einheit*, cited in "DDR: In Afrika keine Einheiten stationiert," *Frankfurter Allgemeine Zeitung*, Apr. 30, 1980.

although the Kremlin is also aware of the drawbacks of these contacts. Although bilateral GDR-USSR ties are the key relationship for Moscow, the trilateral relationship with both Germanys has increased Moscow's leverage over the GDR and East Berlin's over Moscow. In forcing the GDR to accept its *Westpolitik*, Moscow anticipated that the benefits of an intra-German rapprochement would outweigh the dangers of increased West German ties with East Germany. However, it appears that although the GDR's international legitimacy has increased as a result of détente, the intra-German rapprochement has in some ways eroded the stability of the East German regime. In other ways, intra-German détente has made the East Germans more aware of how different they are from the West Germans as they become more familiar with the FRG. Moscow's interest in the intra-German rapprochement is limited by its concern that this dialogue may in the long run develop an independent momentum that the USSR will find it more difficult to control. Moreover, while the USSR's optimal scenario may be the development of a partially Finlandized West Germany, this might represent a greater threat to the GDR than the current FRG, which can now be portrayed as a military menace to the GDR.

The USSR has so far had little reason to be displeased with the GDR government's reaction to the intra-German rapprochement, although its impact on the population is worrying. The GDR's response to Soviet pressure to improve relations with the FRG was to intensify Ulbricht's policy of *Abgrenzung* (demarcation) against the FRG, especially during the 1973–76 period. This policy seeks to differentiate the GDR from the FRG and to insulate the East German population from the potentially destabilizing effects of détente with West Germany. For instance, before détente about 2.5 million West Germans and West Berliners used to visit the GDR every year. The 1982 figure was 5.75 million, down from 8 million in 1979 (to a country with a population of 17 million), with 1.6 million (largely senior-citizen) East Germans going the other way. These closer human contacts are the main reason for the FRG's pursuit of a policy of *Annäherung* (rapprochement) with the GDR, and the main reason for the GDR's *Annäherung* with the USSR, since East Berlin fears these contacts. The GDR responded to the influx of West Germans by trying to limit contacts between West Germans and East Germans in sensitive positions, including those in the NVA. East Berlin, however, has benefited from other human aspects of intra-German relations. It has partially dealt with its dissident problem by literally selling its troublemakers to the FRG for hard currency. This *Menschenhandel* (human trade) has curious results—for instance, the voluntary imprisonment of hundreds of GDR citizens hoping to be sold to the West.[34] While both the USSR and the

34. For a discussion, see Norman Naimark, "Is It True What They're Saying About East Germany?" *Orbis*, 23 (Fall 1979), 572–75.

from other financial flows from the FRG, particularly the private money transfers between citizens of the FRG and GDR, transit fees for visitors to the GDR, and West German payments for the autobahns constructed between Berlin and Mannheim and Berlin and Hamburg. However, the East Germans gain far more financially, both indirectly and directly, from the FRG than trade statistics alone would indicate.[39] Between 1970 and 1977, the total of swing credits, visa charges, minimum foreign-exchange requirements for visitors, road tolls, and other fees amounted to a cumulative DM 7.5 billion paid by the FRG to the GDR.[40]

The USSR gains economically from the intra-German relationship in two ways. First, the FRG's willingness to supply the GDR with hard currency and oil somewhat eases the burden of East German dependence on Soviet financial and material resources. Second, intra-German technology transfer benefits the USSR. Moscow gains access to West German products and it imports East German goods that often embody West German technology. The USSR also benefits politically from intra-German trade inasmuch as consumer goods from the FRG improve the standard of living of East German citizens and diminish disaffection. The potential disadvantage is that the GDR has had to make political concessions—involving closer intra-German human ties—in return for trade.

Trilateral economic relations have not been without tension, especially when Soviet and East German goals conflict. For instance, in 1974 the USSR and West Germany had prepared the plans for West German construction of a $600 million, 1,200-megawatt nuclear power plant in Kaliningrad, from which the Soviets would supply West Berlin and West Germany with electric current. This project was particularly important for West Germany because of West Berlin's acute energy shortages. The USSR suggested that instead of the power going directly through to West Berlin, a branch line be built from the GDR city of Magdeburg to West Berlin. In 1976 the GDR strongly objected to being used as a transit route from which the USSR would supply West Berlin with electricity. As one Soviet spokesman said when it was announced that the project had been abandoned, "Just as America must sometimes take notice of West Germany, we must sometimes listen to what the GDR says."

Nevertheless, in 1981 the GDR agreed to allow 750,000 billion cubic meters of natural gas to be delivered annually to West Berlin, beginning in 1984, as part of the Soviet-West German agreement on the West Sibe-

39. Jochen Bethkenhagen, Siegfried Kupper, and Horst Lambrecht, "Ueber den Zusammenhang von aussenwirtschaftlichen Interessen und Entspannung," unpublished paper, 1980.

40. Michael J. Sodaro, "Foreign and Domestic Policy Linkages in the GDR," in Michael J. Sodaro and Sharon L. Wolchik, eds., *Eastern Europe in the 1980's: Aspects of Domestic and Foreign Policy* (New York: St. Martin's Press, 1983).

rian natural gas pipeline. The November 1981 Soviet-West German communiqué for Brezhnev's visit to Bonn announced that the GDR would
permit a branch line to cross its territory in order to deliver the gas to West
Berlin, although the pipeline itself will run from western Siberia to Germany through Czechoslovakia. This represented a departure from previous GDR policy and signified the importance of Berlin as an intra-
German and Soviet-German lever.[41]

Berlin

The status of Berlin has been both a major problem and a source of
leverage in Soviet relations with East and West Germany. As the key issue
on which Soviet policy toward both Germanys converges, Berlin is also
one of the main sources of tension between the two Germanys. It is of
particular symbolic importance not only to Moscow and East Berlin, but
to Bonn and Washington, and has become a bellwether of the state of
East-West relations.

During the four-power negotiations from December 1969 to September 1971 there were serious conflicts between the USSR and GDR over
the Soviet position on West Berlin, as discussed earlier in this chapter.
The USSR was willing to make concessions to the West, as part of its more
flexible *Westpolitik,* and this time it opted for *Westpolitik* over *Blokpolitik.*

The 1971 Four-Power Agreement embodied consensus on the need to
normalize and regularize the situation of Berlin. The main points of the
agreement were that (1) in the interests of striving for reduced tensions in
Berlin, the USSR would ensure unimpeded access to Berlin from West
Germany, and (2) West Berlin, although not a constituent part of West
Germany, could maintain special ties with the FRG.[42] The four powers
agreed to disagree on whether the agreement applied to the whole of
Berlin or just to West Berlin. The West gained on the question of ties
between the FRG and West Berlin because West Berliners could now visit
the GDR on the same basis as FRG citizens. Despite the restriction on
Bonn's symbolic presence in Berlin, the West was probably the net winner
from this agreement because the FRG gained more secure travel access to
and from West Berlin and from West Germany to East Germany. The
GDR was the loser because its role was legally circumscribed.[43]

41. For further details on these negotiations, see Angela Stent, *Soviet Energy and Western Europe,* The Washington Papers, no. 90 (New York: Praeger, 1982), pp. 65–74.

42. For the text of the treaty, see Presse- und Informationsamt der Bundesregierung, *Die Berlin Regelung* (Bonn: 1971); for a Soviet discussion, see V. Vysotsky, *Zapadny Berlin* (Moscow: Progress Publishers, 1974), pp. 208–18.

43. Griffith, *Ostpolitik,* p. 209; Renata Fritsch-Bournazel, *Die Sowjetunion und die deutsche Teilung* (Opladen: Westdeutscher Verlag, 1979), pp. 121–22.

Since 1971, other problems have arisen, particularly in interpreting the kind of ties which Bonn can have with West Berlin. The West claims that the FRG is entitled to closer ties with West Berlin than Moscow is willing to concede. Whenever the West Germans attempt to strengthen their presence in West Berlin, the Soviet Union and the GDR object. Moreover, the USSR has refused to sign a number of scientific and technical cooperation agreements with the FRG, which would be of economic benefit to the USSR, because they contain Berlin clauses stipulating that the agreement applies to West Berlin too. It has so far signed only trade agreements containing Berlin clauses because of the overriding importance of regularized economic relations with the FRG.

Nevertheless, the position of Berlin is infinitely better today than in 1970, when there was no regulation of civilian access to the city recognized by all four powers, and any official West German presence in West Berlin was the occasion of Soviet and GDR protests and harassment. The situation has improved even further since the invasion of Afghanistan, showing that both the GDR and the USSR realize the value of Berlin as an "oasis of détente," after being a major trouble spot for so long. Berlin serves to remind West Germany of the value of improved relations with the USSR and GDR particularly when U.S.-Soviet relations deteriorate.

The USSR retains decisive control over all Berlin questions that it defines as important. Although the GDR only reluctantly accepted the limited sovereignty that the Four-Power Agreement bestows on it, the GDR and USSR share common goals toward Berlin. They both want to minimize the FRG's political links with West Berlin, yet they derive economic benefits from the FRG-West Berlin relationship: The GDR profits from the FRG's willingness to finance a variety of municipal projects that benefit West Berlin but are located largely in the GDR.

Despite formal Soviet commitment to the ultimate desirability of incorporating the whole of Berlin into the GDR, it is likely that Moscow prefers to keep Berlin divided. It can use its control over Berlin as a lever with both East and West Germany: reminding the East Germans of their need to comply with Soviet wishes on all key matters, and reminding West Germans of their dependence on Soviet goodwill for the viability of West Berlin. As long as Moscow can manage this delicate balancing act, it can maximize its position in Berlin and control the intra-German relationship.

SOVIET-GDR RELATIONS IN THE 1980s

The Soviet Union will continue its dual German policy in the next decade, pursuing both the defensive and assertive sides of the German triangle. Andropov's accession to power has not produced a change in Soviet policy toward the GDR, although the initial signals stressed the *Westpolitik* side of the triangle. At Brezhnev's funeral, Andropov did not hold talks with Honecker, although he spoke with West German President Carstens and Foreign Minister Genscher for an hour. However, there is no sign that the GDR has been downgraded in Soviet foreign policy, although Andropov's ties to *Staatssicherheitsdienst* chief Erich Mielke are presumably closer than those with Honecker.

Since August 1980, events in Poland have played an increasingly important role in Soviet relations with the two German states and in intra-German relations. They have reemphasized stability in the GDR, as well as the wooing of West Germany, as the twin cornerstones of Soviet German policy. Indeed, Honecker's role from August 1980 to December 1981 resembled that of Ulbricht during the Czech crisis—the upholder of Soviet orthodoxy. The GDR consistently supported Soviet criticism of Solidarity and warnings to the Polish leadership about the need to combat anti-Soviet and antisocialist trends in Poland, and it reacted approvingly to the imposition of martial law. Although there is little evidence that the Polish trade-union movement found much sympathy in the GDR, the East German government nevertheless feared possible infection by the Polish bacillus (despite the apparently widespread derision of Poland's economy and population in the GDR).[44] The East German population is excellently informed about the events in Poland through West German television. The nationalist aspects of the Polish experiment were potentially more threatening to East Germany than to the Soviet Union, and domestically more destabilizing than the Czech reform movement.[45] Consequently GDR Prime Minister Willi Stoph announced the need for "tighter state discipline and party vigilance—to safeguard the protection of our socialist state" from external threats.[46]

While the Polish crisis reinforced the GDR's importance in Soviet *Blokpolitik,* the Soviet invasion of Afghanistan challenged the intra-German relationship and became a source of tension between the USSR and the GDR. Although the GDR officially supported the Soviet position, privately East German leaders expressed their discontent at the lack of consultation and information prior to the invasion. It became increasingly evident after December 1979 that the GDR wished to maintain the intra-German dialogue and insulate it from the harmful effects of Soviet actions in Afghanistan on Soviet *Westpolitik.* Indeed, subsequent moves prompted a high Soviet official to complain to a high West German offi-

44. *Der Spiegel,* Oct. 20, 1980, p. 21, carried an interview with GDR citizens about their attitudes toward Poland, in which they described Poles as "too lazy to work," "they are pulling us into their mess," and so forth.

45. Peter Jochen Winters, "Zur Reaktion der DDR auf die Ereignisse in Polen," *Deutschland Archiv,* 14, no. 11 (1981), 4–8.

46. *New York Times,* Apr. 15, 1981.

cial that the pace of intra-German relations was "zu viel, zu schnell" (too much, too quickly).

This remark, however, might equally have come from an East German official. There have been increasing signs that the GDR too is concerned about the unwelcome domestic effects of détente. Indeed, the government launched a frontal attack on intra-German relations as a result of the Polish crisis. The escalation of *Abgrenzung* and the GDR's *Annäherung* to the USSR since October 1980 reflect the conflicting demands of *Westpolitik* and *Blokpolitik*. Less than a week after Helmut Schmidt's reelection, Honecker instigated a series of actions that threatened to set back intra-German relations further than at any time since the 1972 Basic Treaty (*Grundvertrag*) normalizing relations between the FRG and GDR. On October 9 the GDR raised the minimum exchange fee for visitors from West to East Germany from DM 12 to DM 25, thereby reducing the flow of visitors.[47] Four days later, in a major speech to party workers at Gera, Honecker demanded that the FRG recognize East German citizenship and cease giving West German citizenship automatically to refugees from the GDR.[48] This demand, which has subsequently been reiterated, is counter to the agreement in the Basic Treaty. Since then, the GDR has added more demands that the FRG recognize GDR sovereignty. The Soviet Union has supported all these moves and has echoed Honecker's demands for FRG recognition of GDR statehood.[49]

Nevertheless, intra-German relations have not deteriorated so much as might initially have been expected. The GDR, presumably with Moscow's endorsement, has continued to pursue its dialogue with the FRG. Indeed, in 1981 Honecker suddenly raised the specter of reunification. "Be careful," he warned the West Germans, "socialism will one day also knock on your door—and then the question of the unification of both German states will be posed completely anew." This remark may have been as much a warning to Moscow as an offer to Bonn. The dual GDR policy was evident during the December 1981 visit of Helmut Schmidt to the GDR. The meeting occurred during the weekend on which martial law was imposed in Poland—a source of embarrassment to Schmidt, if not to Honecker. During the talks, the two leaders spent a number of hours alone, without advisers, and both men praised the meeting, although little substantive emerged from the talks.[50]

Honecker was to have made a return visit to the FRG in 1983 but

47. *Neues Deutschland,* Oct. 10, 1980.

48. Ibid., Oct. 13, 1980.

49. Honecker has explicitly denied that these measures against the FRG are in any way connected with the Polish crisis. See Honecker's interview with Robert Maxwell, *Neues Deutschland,* Feb. 13, 1981.

50. For documentation of the meeting, see Bundesministerium für innerdeutsche Beziehungen, *Das Deutsch-Deutsche Treffen am Werbellinsee* (Bonn, 1982).

canceled it ostensibly because of a series of intra-German clashes over the deaths of three West German citizens in the GDR. It is also possible that the USSR encouraged the cancellation of the visit to remind the new West German government that problems may arise in intra-German relations if Bonn complies with U.S. foreign policy too closely. Although the GDR would have preferred the Social Democrats to return to power in Bonn in March 1983, it was willing to deal with the Christian Democrats, particularly since Chancellor Helmut Kohl has stressed continuity in the intra-German relationship.

Indeed the Christian Democrats and their Christian Socialist (CSU) partners went out of their way to elicit political concessions in return for substantial economic benefits. In June 1983 Franz-Josef Strauss, leader of the CSU and conservative critic of the GDR, announced that a consortium of German banks had awarded the GDR an unprecedented DM 1 billion credit, not tied to any specific projects. In September, East Germany rescinded the minimum exchange fee for children under 15 visiting the country, who account for about 15% of West German visitors. The new Bonn government indicated that it would continue to pursue closer ties with East Berlin. As long as the FRG pursues the intra-German dialogue, irrespective of who is in power, the GDR will respond, and the USSR will encourage these ties because they ultimately reinforce West German and American conflicts over the East-West relationship.

The future Soviet-German and intra-German relationships largely depend on the outcome of U.S.-Soviet negotiations over intermediate-range nuclear forces (INF). It is this issue, more than any other, that has highlighted the dilemmas of the intra-German dialogue for both the USSR and the GDR. East Germany has supported Soviet efforts to prevent the stationing of Pershing II and cruise missiles in West Germany, and both the USSR and GDR have given material and moral support to the West German peace movement that opposes INF deployment. Nevertheless, East German and Soviet interests may not entirely coincide here. Although the GDR would prefer not to have new U.S. missiles deployed, its economic problems necessitate a continuing relationship with the FRG, regardless of other political developments. The USSR, in an attempt to influence West German government policy, may well threaten the FRG with a deterioration in intra-German relations if the missiles are deployed or may take measures that disturb the relationship once the first missiles are stationed, in order to prevent further deployment. This would hardly be in the GDR's economic interest, yet there is little that the GDR can do to prevent this.[51]

51. Peter Jochen Winters, "Die DDR in Moskau's Doppelstrategie," *Deutschland Archiv*, 16, no. 2 (1983), 113–115.

The NATO two-track decision has also affected Soviet-GDR relations because it has led to the growth of a peace movement in the GDR. The West German peace movement has spilled over into the GDR, where the Protestant church has been active in opposing paramilitary education in schools, in advocating the NVA's acceptance of the legitimacy of conscientious objection as an alternative to military service, and in criticizing both the U.S. military buildup and calling for a reduction in the Soviet SS-20s. Various East German peace groups, echoing their West German counterparts, have called for an end to the U.S. and Soviet presence in Germany, and for a demilitarized, possibly neutral, Germany.[52] Thousands of young people have begun to wear "swords into ploughshares" buttons, which the government has banned. The authorities have counterattacked with the slogan, "Der Friede muss bewaffnet sein" (Peace must be armed). Although the East German Protestant church has 8 million members, its leadership is well aware of the limits of its power in a highly controlled, militarized society, and its members are by no means politically homogeneous.[53] Thus, one should not exaggerate the extent of the East German peace movement. The USSR and GDR are aware that the more successful the peace movement in the FRG becomes, the more likely it is to have an undesirable impact in East Germany because of the close links between the West and East German Protestant churches. The USSR promotes the West German peace movement as part of its *Westpolitik,* but it must also be aware that it unwittingly has contributed to the development of an East German movement that seeks equidistance between the two superpowers.

The peace movement highlights Moscow's delicate triangular balancing act in policy toward Germany. The irony is that neither the USSR nor the GDR can ultimately want an unambiguous resolution of the German question, because this would remove a major bargaining lever with the West Germans and would limit Moscow's ability to promote tensions within the Western alliance. If the FRG were to recognize the GDR and end its special relationship with it, the GDR would suffer economically (it could no longer be the eleventh member of the EEC) and it could not utilize its relationship with the FRG in dealing with the USSR. More importantly, if the FRG were no longer interested in closer intra-German ties, the Soviet Union would have lost its major card in pursuing a more assertive *Westpolitik.*

Soviet policy toward Germany has come full cycle in 1983. Since the removal of Ulbricht, Moscow has focused more on the assertive *Westpolitik*

52. *New York Times,* July 6, 1982. For the West German view, see Wolfgang Venohr, ed., *Die Deutsche Einheit Kommt Bestimmt* (Bergisch-Gladbach: Gustav Lübbe Verlag, 1982).

53. Peter Wensierski, "Zwischen Pazifismus und Militarismus," *Deutschland Archiv,* 15, no. 5 (1982), 449–52.

side of its German triangle: the wooing of West Germany as growing U.S.-West German differences over East-West relations have brought benefits to the USSR. The Polish events reasserted the primacy of the defensive *Blokpolitik* aspect of Soviet policy: the need to maintain stability in East Germany. Yet the missile question has reaffirmed the benefits of courting the FRG. The security of Eastern Europe ultimately takes precedence over opportunities in Western Europe, although the USSR will always attempt to have its German cake and eat it—and is doing so at the moment. Moscow's dual German policy is ultimately the product of the unresolved German question. As long as reunification remains a live issue in both East and West Germany, this must be of deep concern to the USSR.

3

Soviet Policy toward Poland

ANDRZEJ KORBONSKI

By virtue of its physical characteristics—area, population, resource base, and geographical location—Poland has since 1945 been the most important member of the bloc next to the Soviet Union itself. Whether measured by its military or its economic strength, it is the largest contributor among the East European countries both to the Warsaw Pact (WTO) and, at least until recently, to the Council for Mutual Economic Assistance (CMEA). For these reasons alone, Poland has long been perceived as the geopolitical linchpin of Moscow's hegemonic system in Eastern Europe and, contrarily, as a potential catalyst of change in the region. Any shift in Soviet policy toward its largest ally could be expected to have a powerful, even domino, effect on the rest of the area. The most recent crisis, culminating in the imposition of martial law in December 1981, underscores once again Poland's vital importance to the Soviet Union.

At the same time, Poland has long been the most problematic of the East European countries. As Russia's immediate neighbor to the west—indeed as a quintessentially Western country in its intellectual traditions and Roman Catholic faith—Poland has served for centuries as a conduit for alien (and generally unwanted) influences. In return, its own history has repeatedly been impacted and for more than a century overwhelmed by czarist and later Soviet expansionism. As a result of this process of mutual interaction, Poland emerged as one of Russia's traditional adversaries—characterized also by a long history of opposition to authority, both foreign and domestic, and a tenacious attachment to its own national identity. It is this combination of geopolitical confrontation and historical-cultural antipathy that has made the Soviet Union's relationship with Poland more complex, more unpredictable, and frequently more intense than that with its other Warsaw Pact allies.

The USSR's basic stakes in Poland—whether strategic, political, or economic—do not differ greatly from its interests in the rest of the region. Nonetheless, to a greater extent than in any other country, they reflect the ambiguities and conflicts inherent in Soviet policy toward the region. Moreover, the combination of Poland's geopolitical salience and turbulent historical legacy has clearly had an impact on the relative weight

61

assigned to the several factors. On balance Moscow appears to have attached greatest significance to its strategic interests, while showing some willingness to make limited concessions to Polish idiosyncrasies in the ideological and economic realms.

Although it may be argued that the missile age has reduced the strategic value of geography, there is little doubt that the Kremlin continues to view Poland, the traditional invasion route and gateway to Russia, as a key component of its East European buffer zone. The fact that Poland lies astride the lines of transportation and communication linking the Soviet homeland with the Group of Soviet Forces in East Germany adds a vital dimension to Moscow's relationship with Warsaw. It is, ostensibly, to protect these lines that two Soviet divisions have been permanently stationed in Poland since 1945, except for East Germany the longest time that any Soviet troops have been stationed outside the borders of the USSR.

Poland's armed forces, the largest in the region, remain the mainstay of the WTO's so-called Northern Tier. Except for a brief confrontation in October 1956, Soviet military leaders have had little reason to complain about their Polish counterparts. In contrast to Romania and to some extent Czechoslovakia, the Polish military has never challenged total Soviet domination of the alliance; on the contrary, next to East Germany, Poland was the strongest supporter of the military intervention against Czechoslovakia in 1968, providing also the largest troop contingent from among WTO's junior partners. Its strategic importance to the Soviet Union is further enhanced by its control of about 300 miles of the Baltic coast. Indeed, according to the WTO's *ordre de bataille* of the mid-1960s, in the event of war with NATO the Polish military was to participate in a westward thrust along the Baltic coast and occupy Denmark.[1] In addition, Poland plays a crucial role in the aerial defense of Soviet territory, the importance of which cannot be underestimated in the age of cruise missiles and other theater nuclear weapons.[2]

Moscow's main political-ideological objective in Poland, as elsewhere in Eastern Europe, has been to safeguard the existing communist political system. The seizure of power in the wake of World War II, as well as the subsequent Stalinization of the country, did not deviate markedly from the norm. Yet the illusion that Poland could serve as a relatively successful model of a faithful Soviet satellite did not long outlast Stalin himself. Since 1956, recurrent crises have forced successive Soviet leaderships to trim their expectations to Polish realities. Compared for instance with the Soviet view of the GDR or Bulgaria, which are routinely trotted out as exemplary models of socialist development in the Soviet mold, Moscow's

    1. Personal interviews, Los Angeles, California, Summer 1978.
    2. Peer H. Lange, "Poland as a Problem of Soviet Security Policy," *Aussenpolitik* (English ed.), 32, no. 4 (1981), 332–43.

approach to the Warsaw regime has often appeared aimed as much at containing Polish heresies within manageable limits as at imposing the prescribed orthodoxy. The difficulties of dealing with Warsaw have been further compounded by the remarkable ineptness of Polish Communist leaders, whose repeated and dismal failure to generate popular support for the regime has necessitated periodic propping up by the Kremlin.

Economically as well, Soviet interests present a mixed picture. Together with the rest of the region, Poland was heavily exploited in the Stalinist period—the size of its contribution to Soviet economic recovery illustrated by the amount of the "debt" owed by Poland to the USSR and canceled by Moscow in November 1956.[3] Since then, Poland has represented less of an economic asset to Moscow than East Germany and Czechoslovakia, the principal suppliers of technologically advanced machinery and equipment; still, as the most populous and generously endowed East European country, it has been far from unimportant. As part of the "international socialist division of labor" within CMEA, the Poles, in addition to being major suppliers of coal and other raw materials, have specialized in the production of ships and rolling stock as well as other specialized industrial equipment; moreover, and especially during the 1960s, they were an indirect source of Western technology otherwise unavailable to the USSR.[4] On the other hand, recurrent crises have not only threatened Poland's political stability but have imposed an increasingly onerous burden on Soviet resources and disrupted overall CMEA activities.

Following a brief review of the pre-1970 period, I discuss the Gierek period and then address the challenge posed by the emergence of Solidarity between August 1980 and the declaration of martial law in December 1981. Finally, I deal with the dilemmas posed by the fact that, having decided against direct interference in Poland, Moscow must attempt to exercise its influence through the existing regime.

TWILIGHT OF THE GOMUŁKA ERA, 1968–70

Although the return to power in October 1956 of Poland's postwar Communist leader, Władysław Gomułka, had all the earmarks of a dramatic

3. The total amount canceled was $626 million, which reportedly represented less than 50% of Poland's claim against the Soviet Union on the German reparations account. See Paul Marer, "Soviet Economic Policy in Eastern Europe," in John P. Hardt, ed., *Reorientation and Commercial Relations of the Economies of Eastern Europe*, compendium of papers submitted to the Joint Economic Committee, Congress of the United States (Washington, D.C.: U.S. Government Printing Office [hereafter GPO], 1974), pp. 139–40.

4. For a discussion of Poland's participation in CMEA, see Andrzej Korbonski, "Poland and the CMEA: Problems and Prospects," in Paul Marer and J. M. Montias, eds., *East European Integration and East-West Trade* (Bloomington: Indiana University Press, 1980), pp. 355–81.

confrontation with the Kremlin, the next several years witnessed the emergence of a "special relationship" between Gomułka and Nikita Khrushchev. For his part, the Polish leader was compelled to acknowledge the USSR's leadership of the bloc; at the same time, the Soviet leader allowed Poland to maintain more room for maneuver than that granted most other East European countries: an expansion of economic, cultural, and even political contacts with the West; maintenance of a large private sector in agriculture; a modus vivendi with the Catholic church; and a rather impressive, if gradually diminishing, degree of artistic and intellectual freedom.

Moscow's tolerance of these limited heresies was due to the fact that they were precisely that—limited. As soon became clear, Gomułka was essentially an orthodox Communist leader, unlikely to stray far from the straight and narrow path of loyalty to the Soviet Union's systemic and foreign policy goals. His initial relatively benign attitude toward the peasants, the church, and the intellectuals never posed a serious challenge to overall party hegemony; furthermore, in contrast to several of Poland's neighbors, he did not introduce major economic reforms that threatened to spill over into the political arena. In his foreign policy as well, Gomułka showed little inclination to emulate Romania's independent stance, instead generally supporting Moscow in its quarrels with Beijing and rejecting Bonn's initial attempts at *Ostpolitik* in 1966–67. All this must have convinced the Kremlin not only that he could be trusted but that, despite growing popular dissatisfaction with the lack of material improvement and what had come to be called the *mała stabilizacja* (or small-scale stabilization), his domestic position was secure.

The three-year period between 1968 and 1970, however, proved the stability of the Gomułka regime to be illusory. In the face of both domestic and external challenges, it became evident that in the course of the preceding decade he had antagonized not only the workers, students, and intellectuals but also various elements within his own party. While the March 1968 student riots represented a powerful domestic challenge to Gomułka's position (one from which he would not fully recover despite Soviet support), it was ironically the signing of the long-sought treaty with West Germany that provided the occasion for his removal less than three years later.

Faced with the options of maintaining Gomułka in power in the wake of the March riots or letting him fall, the Kremlin chose the former course, at least for the time being. The progressive deterioration of the Czechoslovak situation put a premium on preserving relative tranquility in the rest of the bloc. Gomułka's ouster, however peaceful and orderly, was bound to be destabilizing at a time when Moscow needed Warsaw's explicit support against Prague, especially in light of Hungary's reluctance to participate in armed intervention. (According to one source, Gomułka also remained undecided regarding the use of force against Alexander Dubček as late as July 1968.)[5] Moreover, Gomułka was infinitely preferable to his immediate challenger, Interior Minister Mieczysław Moczar, who must have seemed from the Soviet perspective too much like a Polish Ceaușescu.

Thus Gomułka survived the crisis of 1968 but it was clearly a Pyrrhic victory. Despite the praise heaped upon him by Brezhnev at the 5th Congress of the Polish United Workers' Party (PUWP) in November, he was unable to heal the rifts within the party. Indeed, in order to outflank one group of challengers, Moczar's Partisans, he had to promote members of another, the so-called technocrats led by Silesian party leader Edward Gierek, unwittingly setting the stage for his own succession.

In his fight for survival, Gomułka was initially helped by developments on the international scene, in particular by the emergence of the Brandt coalition in Bonn and by Moscow's resumption of the policy of rapprochement with the West that had been interrupted by the Czechoslovak crisis.[6] Both these events provided Gomułka with an opportunity to rebuild his prestige within the Polish party and society at large, and there is no doubt that the change in the official Soviet reaction to West German overtures provided the incentive for his unexpected receptivity to Bonn's new approaches. Thus, in a major speech on May 17, 1969, Gomułka proclaimed his readiness to engage in a dialogue with the Federal Republic with a view toward normalizing Polish-West German relations.

The Kremlin must have watched the ensuing negotiations with mixed feelings. Having initiated the process of rapprochement with Bonn, Moscow could not easily veto a similar rapprochement sought by its most important partner in the WTO. At the same time, a Warsaw-Bonn agreement, providing for official West German recognition of Poland's western frontier, would certainly affect relations between Warsaw and Moscow, which since 1945 had been the sole guarantor of Poland's territorial integrity. Settlement of the border issue could be seen as reducing Poland's dependence on the USSR and as granting Warsaw greater room for maneuver vis-à-vis the West.

Having concluded a treaty with Bonn, signed during Chancellor Willy Brandt's memorable visit to Warsaw in early December 1970, Gomułka failed to see that the German bogey had become an indispensable crutch for his power and, in a serious miscalculation, embarked on a major reform of retail prices as a first step toward reform of Poland's ailing

5. Erwin Weit, *Eyewitness* (London: André Deutsch, 1973), pp. 196–210.
6. See chap. 2.

economy. The resulting riots on the Baltic coast brought to a sudden end an important chapter in Poland's postwar history that had begun so auspiciously fourteen years earlier.[7]

THE YEARS OF HOPE AND RISING EXPECTATIONS, 1971–75

From the Soviet point of view, the speedy restoration of political and economic stability in Poland was a matter of paramount importance, and Gierek, widely touted as a pragmatist and modernizer and highly regarded for his effective administration of the key industrial district of Silesia, must have seemed a welcome choice to lead the country out of stagnation and discontent. At the same time, the selection of Piotr Jaroszewicz as prime minister suggested that the new first secretary's authority was to be somewhat circumscribed in both the party and government. Whether rightly or wrongly, Jaroszewicz was popularly identified from the beginning as "Moscow's man" in the Polish oligarchy, instructed by the Kremlin to keep an eye on Gierek, who, despite his otherwise impeccable credentials, was not well known to the Soviet leaders and whose "Western" background may have aroused lingering reservations. Especially in light of the rapid progress of détente, which carried with it a risk of Western penetration of Eastern Europe, it is likely that Moscow saw Jaroszewicz as a reliable guardian of orthodoxy in Warsaw.[8]

The strategy of the new Gierek leadership has been widely discussed in the literature and need only be briefly summarized.[9] At the domestic level, Gierek embarked on an ambitious and comprehensive program of industrial modernization and resource development that, initially at least, appeared to be a resounding success. In the first three to four years Poland enjoyed a high rate of economic growth, second only to that of

7. It was widely reported in Warsaw that Gomułka had made a desperate appeal to Brezhnev to keep him in office and that Brezhnev's dislike of Gomułka, who tended to bore his Soviet counterparts with ideological diatribes at international Communist meetings, was partly responsible for Moscow's lack of interest in him (Adam Bromke, "Poland under Gierek: A New Political Style," *Problems of Communism*, 21 [Sept.–Oct. 1972], 14).

8. Possibly to reinforce Moscow's supervision of the Gierek regime, a new Soviet ambassador, Stanislav Pilotovich, arrived in Warsaw in March 1971, replacing Averkii Aristov, who had served in Poland for ten years and was reported to have been close to Gomułka and opposed to Gierek. A Polish-speaking member of the Soviet Central Committee, Pilotovich had a reputation as a hard-liner. See *Radio Free Europe Research [RFER]*, Polish Situation Report/17, May 3, 1971.

9. For a more comprehensive treatment, see Zbigniew M. Fallenbuchl, "The Polish Economy in the 1970s," in John P. Hardt, ed., *East European Economies Post-Helsinki*, compendium of papers submitted to the Joint Economic Committee, Congress of the United States (Washington, D.C.: GPO, 1977), pp. 816–64, and Central Intelligence Agency, National Foreign Assessment Center, *The Scope of Poland's Economic Dilemma*, ER78-10340U (Washington, D.C., July 1978).

Bulgaria and Romania, with rapid increases in industrial production in both the producer and consumer goods areas. This expansion program was accompanied by tentative (if only vaguely defined) moves in the direction of structural economic reform, a reduction of centralized controls over the private agricultural sector, as well as hints of the shirt-sleeve populism characteristic of János Kádár's Hungary.

At the international level, Gierek's policy was based on exploiting the new turn in East-West relations. Possibly borrowing a leaf from Romania's experience, he declared Poland's readiness to seek Western credits and technology for his modernization program. Moreover, this economic "opening to the West" was accompanied by equally dynamic diplomatic initiatives. In sharp contrast to his predecessor, Gierek became a frequent visitor to Western capitals, soon rivaling Nicolae Ceauşescu as the most peripatetic East European leader. He also hosted a number of Western leaders: two successive American presidents, the president of France, and other heads of government. Such contacts paid off handsomely, in the short run at least, in the form of a steady flow of government-guaranteed loans during the first half of the 1970s; also, there can be no doubt that it was this infusion of Western credits and technology that allowed Gierek to boost real incomes at the same time as he was pursuing an excessively ambitious investment program, in effect temporarily buying off Poland's volatile working class.

On the basis of the evidence available, Moscow's response to these new departures in Polish policy can best be described as ambivalent. That is, while some aspects were entirely compatible with—indeed, supportive of—Soviet *Westpolitik*, others at least implicitly challenged Leonid Brezhnev's emerging strategy of bloc management and appear to have evoked subtle countermeasures from Moscow.

On the plus side, the Soviet Union could expect to benefit from Gierek's opening to the West in several respects. To the extent that Poland's poor economic performance in the 1960s had contributed to the 1970 crisis, almost any measure designed to revitalize the economy was likely to be welcomed by the Soviets, if only because it would relieve them of the need to provide an embattled Polish regime with substantial economic aid. (The USSR is thought to have supplied approximately $100 million in hard currency and ruble credits following the 1970 crisis, an amount that was quickly overshadowed by Western loans.) Moreover, in view of the role that Poland had played in the 1960s as a conduit for Western technology, Moscow could expect that the additional injection of Western credits would result in further technological spillover in the form of higher quality industrial and consumer exports to the USSR.

Along more political lines, the Soviets most likely endorsed Gierek's diplomatic initiatives and growing international visibility, which supplemented their own efforts to promote a rapprochement with France and West Germany and in general to draw the two halves of Europe closer together at the expense of Western Europe's ties with the United States. Throughout his rule, Gierek never deviated from his unceasing support of Soviet foreign policy—as evidenced, for instance, by his lack of interest in cultivating relations with China or the Eurocommunist parties, and by his careful support of the Soviet line at the 1975 Helsinki Conference. Furthermore, his support tended to assume a more sophisticated and less strident form than that of the Czechoslovak and East German leaders, who were universally recognized as Soviet puppets with little international standing of their own. In contrast, Poland perhaps even more than Romania was increasingly perceived as a serious international actor whose views deserved attention, despite its close affiliation with the USSR. A good deal of credit for this highly favorable (and essentially false) image was due to the Polish leader himself, who played the role of bridge-builder between East and West to the hilt.

At the same time, these and other aspects of Gierek's program must have appeared as mixed blessings at best, or even as potential threats to Moscow's interests in (and control over) Poland. The first was the very ambitiousness of Gierek's economic development program. Although in view of their own economic opening to the West the Soviets could hardly prohibit Poland from following suit—and despite the obvious benefits to themselves—the prospect of a Polish economy progressively dependent on Western markets had worrisome implications for bloc cohesion and CMEA integration. In particular, a rapid expansion of trade with the West implied a diversion of Poland's most salable commodities and manufactures to non-CMEA markets. Similarly, plans drawn up in the early 1970s to expand direct oil imports from the Middle East, while easing the burden on Soviet energy resources, would also deprive Moscow of an important source of leverage over the Warsaw regime.

Second, several elements of Gierek's domestic program were distressingly reminiscent of Gomułka's policies in 1956–57: the concessions to the private agricultural sector (elimination of compulsory deliveries, promises of better access to machinery and supplies, as well as improved land availability); a renewed modus vivendi with the Catholic church; relaxation of the cultural and intellectual climate; promises of a more prominent role in policymaking for representative institutions, especially for the Sejm (or national parliament); and a revival of discussions of far-reaching economic reforms. Although all these proposals taken together fell far short of the threat posed by Dubček's "socialism with a human face"—and although it soon became clear that Gierek himself had little stomach for the genuine economic reforms favored by some of his advisers—the overall direction of Polish domestic developments was nonetheless out of step with the new definition of socialist orthodoxy that was gradually taking shape in Moscow and, under the tutelage of the Communist Party of the Soviet Union (CPSU), being adopted in most other East European capitals as a kind of insurance policy against any repetition of the Czechoslovak experience.[10]

At the time, official pronouncements from Moscow gave no hint of Soviet dissatisfaction. Indeed, Gierek's three-day visit to the USSR in December 1973 ended with glowing reports of a "complete identity of views." In retrospect, however, it seems likely that Brezhnev used the occasion to put pressure on the Polish leader to bring his domestic policies more into line with bloc norms. The evidence, although almost entirely circumstantial, is highly suggestive:

- In February 1974 a new Institute for Fundamental Problems of Marxism-Leninism was established under the Central Committee of the PUWP to study questions of "socialist construction" in Poland; the same year also saw the establishment of a joint Polish-Soviet Commission in Economic Sciences under the respective Academies of Sciences. While the first published product of this commission appeared (ironically) only in 1980, it held annual working sessions from 1976 on, and among its assigned tasks was "the development of the socialist agricultural structure."
- After Gierek's visit, the Soviet press began to lavish attention on Polish agriculture, especially on its alleged "socialist transformation." It has now been admitted widely that, despite numerous official statements to the contrary, an unwritten policy of discrimination against the private peasant sector in Poland was resumed in 1974.
- The uncensored Polish press has also revealed that 1974 was the year in which discussion of the promised economic reforms petered out. While noting the antireform bias of the Gierek leadership, at least one dissident writer has hinted at Soviet pressure.
- Finally, 1974 was the year in which Moscow recognized Poland as one of the countries that had embarked on the new stage of building "developed socialism," whereas others had been so designated in 1971 or 1972. It was also at this point that the Poles themselves began discussing the new orthodoxy—and in decidedly Soviet-style terms.[11]

Soviet pressure appears to have come to a head around the time of the 7th Congress of the PUWP in December 1975. Both Brezhnev's speech

10. See chap. 8.

11. The following points are summarized from a preliminary draft of Sarah M. Terry's analysis of the events leading up to the 1976 crisis for *Poland's Six Crises,* Jane L. Curry, ed. (forthcoming, 1984).

and Gierek's main address to the congress reaffirmed the tougher line on agriculture. Shortly thereafter, and with little advance notice, the Polish regime announced a series of amendments to the constitution, bringing its provisions concerning the "leading role" of the party and Poland's fraternal alliance with the USSR into line with amendments already incorporated into the constitutions of the other East European states. The proposed revisions provoked an outcry from some of Poland's leading intellectuals as well as the Catholic church, resulting in a softening of the language of the amendments but not without lasting damage to Gierek's relations with those two important constituencies.

It may or may not have been coincidental that Gierek's visit and the subsequent pressures from Moscow took place in the immediate wake of the Arab oil embargo and the quadrupling of world oil prices. But there can be little doubt that the effect was to deliver the coup de grace to his development strategy and to greatly enhance Moscow's leverage over Warsaw. On the one hand, the combination of recession and inflation brought on by the energy crisis in Western economies both raised the cost of Poland's hard-currency imports and reduced demand for its exports, resulting in a progressive deterioration of its balance of payments and a rapid increase in its hard-currency debt. On the other hand, soaring world prices threw the Poles back into Moscow's lap for satisfaction of their growing oil needs by rendering totally unrealistic Gierek's plans for large-scale imports from world market sources.

Precisely how the Soviets exercised their enhanced leverage is another question, and one that cannot be answered with any certainty. Again, oil was the most obvious vehicle, and here announced changes in projected deliveries of Soviet oil for the 1976–80 plan period pose intriguing, if unanswerable, questions. According to the original trade protocol, announced in September 1975, Poland was to receive 50 million metric tons (MMT) of crude plus 6.5 MMT of petroleum products over the five-year period—that is, slightly less than the 58 MMT delivered in the 1971–75 period and, on an annual basis, more than 8% less than Soviet oil deliveries in 1975. By the start of the new plan period, however, the total had been raised by one-third to 75 MMT.[12] We can only wonder what concessions Brezhnev managed to wring out of Gierek for an increase of that magnitude, or what Moscow's original purpose was in trying to cut deliveries to Poland.

In light of the above, and in the absence of any clear evidence of concern over Poland's mounting debt burden, we are left to conclude that Moscow shared complicity in that country's economic plight. For, whatever the truth of Gierek's much rumored susceptibility to flattery and

---

12. *Trybuna Ludu,* Sept. 29, 1975; John R. Haberstroh, "Eastern Europe: Growing Energy Problems," in Hardt, ed., *East European Economies Post-Helsinki,* pp. 384–86.

eagerness to ingratiate himself with his patrons in the Kremlin—in particular, his ambition to recoup Poland's position as the second-ranking power in the alliance, a position that was increasingly being eroded by the GDR—it was still the Soviets who set the standards and who appear to have seen Poland's tightened straits not as signaling the need for genuine reform but as an opportunity to rein in one of their less orthodox allies.

CRISIS RENEWED AND THE UNSTABLE BALANCE, 1976–80

By mid-decade it had become clear to everyone in Poland, if not in Moscow, that radical measures were necessary to overcome lagging economic performance. Among the most serious obstacles to improved efficiency was an irrational price structure according to which retail prices, especially for basic food items, were held artificially low while state subsidies imposed an intolerable burden on the national budget but still not enough to offer the peasant a reasonable return on produce. Although comprehensive price reform was a necessary condition of further systemic change, it was also politically the riskiest measure, if only in light of the abject failure of the previous attempt to reform retail prices, which had ended in Gomułka's downfall in December 1970.

Yet, instead of proceeding with utmost caution in the preparation of the reform, Gierek incredibly disregarded the lessons of that earlier experience and, with little warning, announced a radical increase in food prices at the end of June 1976. Although it is true that some rise in food prices to counter growing shortages had been rumored for more than a year—indeed, that Gierek himself had warned of the need for such an increase at the 7th Congress the previous December—the unexpectedly sharp jump in prices of sensitive items (such as meats and sugar) combined with the marked absence of the oft-promised "consultations" led to predictable results. Workers in several industrial centers rioted, forcing the regime to call off the price increases within 24 hours. That the incident occurred on the eve of the long-awaited Conference of European Communist Parties in East Berlin made it all the more embarrassing, for both Warsaw and Moscow, and testified to the Gierek leadership's overconfidence and growing isolation from the population.[13]

Despite the apparent restoration of order—aided by the regime's hasty retreat and renewed pledge of consultations on the price question—

13. Former U.S. ambassador to Poland, Richard T. Davies, has suggested that the timing of the price increases may have been related to the CMEA meeting scheduled for early July, at which the member countries were to coordinate their 1976–80 economic plans. According to Davies, "The other member-governments had published various materials in preparation for this meeting, but the Polish government had published very little. It later developed that the planning documents had been drawn up using the new, higher prices for food and consumer goods that Jaroszewicz announced to the Sejm on June 24. Before documents based on these figures could be published or used as the basis for the discussions to be held

Poland's domestic stability proved short-lived and superficial. It soon became clear that various constituencies, mostly outside but also within the party, were only too eager to exploit any signs of weakness on Gierek's part to reopen unresolved questions from the past. Thus a crisis, which for all intents and purposes was over in less than two days, set in motion the events that led to the full-dress challenge to Polish Communist rule four years later.

The intellectuals, their ire already aroused by the fight over the constitution the previous winter, moved quickly to correct the mistakes of 1968 and 1970, when, in the first instance, the workers refused to side with the students and intellectuals and, in the second, the intellectuals failed to come to the defense of the workers. The formation of KOR (Committee for the Defense of the Workers) in the summer of 1976, whose initial purpose was to defend workers arrested or dismissed in the aftermath of the June riots and to provide for their families, proved to be only the opening wedge in a wide-ranging opposition movement, which, in addition to the emerging worker–intellectual alliance, included the so-called Flying University (providing uncensored and unauthorized courses on contemporary and historical topics) as well as an "underground" (but surprisingly visible) press of unprecedented proportions for a Soviet-bloc country.

Although the church adopted a more cautious position, in line with its traditional role of opposing any action that might place the Polish nation at risk, it too had been stung by the constitutional crisis. Thus its willingness to support the regime's appeal for calm in the wake of the June riots was less a sign of accommodation than a stance from which to push for resolution of long-standing grievances in church-state relations: most importantly, the church's legal status, its right to build new churches, and access to adequate paper for its publications. Moreover, while its undisputed leader, Stefan Cardinal Wyszyński, was as yet unwilling to challenge the regime openly, the lower ranks of the clergy as well as some groups of Catholic intellectuals were showing signs of impatience with the cautious policy of the episcopate and a growing readiness to cooperate with other elements of the opposition. Meanwhile, the authority and prestige of the church received an unexpected boost from the election in October 1978 of Karol Cardinal Wojtyła, Archbishop of Cracow, as Pope John Paul II, and from his visit to Poland in June 1979.

---

by the Comecon Council, Jaroszewicz apparently insisted that the price rise be put into effect." See R. T. Davies, "Politico-Economic Dynamics of Eastern Europe: The Polish Case," in John P. Hardt, ed., *East European Economic Assessment,* pt. 1: *Country Studies, 1980,* compendium of papers submitted to the Joint Economic Committee, Congress of the United States (Washington, D.C.: GPO, 1981), pp. 23–24.

Even within the party, the "June events" provided an opening for the reemergénce of reform tendencies that had been suppressed after 1973. Although far less extensive than the opposition press, and generally couched in more veiled language, critical party writings (both published and privately circulated) expressed with varying degrees of urgency many of the same concerns over the implications of the deteriorating socioeconomic situation for Poland's political stability. Most radical among establishment critics was Experience and the Future (DiP for short), a discussion group of party and nonparty intellectuals whose analyses of the dire state of the Polish polity and economy circulated widely in 1979 and 1980.[14]

Gierek's initial response to the June crisis was modestly encouraging. Avoiding an open confrontation with the nascent opposition (very likely for fear of enhancing its popular credibility and support), he made a few tentative gestures suggesting a return to the more open and quasi-populist policies of the early 1970s. The "economic maneuver" announced in December 1976 promised substantial changes in the pace and direction of the country's development strategy: investment was to be slowed, and priorities were to be shifted in favor of agriculture, housing, and other neglected consumer industries; concessions were again to be made to private farmers and artisans to spur production. The following spring, a top-level panel of experts was appointed to advise the Polish leadership on social and economic problems, while Gierek himself again promised a more prominent policymaking role for elected representative bodies.

As it became apparent, however, that Gierek was unable or unwilling to follow through on his promises—either to rein in the runaway economy or to restore some semblance of political order—rifts within the party widened, progressively weakening his position. By mid-1977 the ruling oligarchy was divided into roughly three groups: the conservative faction led by the so-called Gang of Four, four Central Committee secretaries allied on some (but not all) issues with Prime Minister Jaroszewicz; the centrist group clustered around Gierek and his immediate entourage; and the reformist (albeit not liberal) group headed by Stefan Olszowski, referred to by some as "enlightened despots" and supported by a number of younger pragmatically oriented regional party secretaries who were increasingly appalled by the blatant corruption and incompetence that pervaded the economy.

Faced with renewed crisis on their western doorstep, the Soviets had

14. See chap. 8, n. 43, for a selected listing of published articles. The first two DiP reports, compiled and circulated in 1979 and 1980, respectively, are translated in *Poland Today: The State of the Republic*, ed. Jack Bielasiak (Armonk, N.Y.: M. E. Sharpe, 1981). For an overall view of dissent within Poland in this period, see George Schopflin, "Poland: A Society in Crisis," *Conflict Studies*, no. 112 (London, Oct. 1979).

deceptively simple options: to replace Gierek, or to keep him in power and, at least for the time being, to shore him up. That they should have chosen the latter option in the summer and fall of 1976 is not particularly surprising. It mirrored the Kremlin's confidence in its ability to maintain control over its junior allies by indirect means, as well as its willingness to tolerate some departures from the general line in order to preserve over-all stability in the region. In this sense, Soviet policy toward Poland was consistent with its tolerance of Romania's repeated assertions of independence and the absence of overt interference with Hungary's economic experiments in the same time period.

On the other hand, that Moscow should have continued to back Gierek over the next several years, in the face of his patent ineffectiveness in coping with Poland's rambunctious opposition and multiple economic ills, is less easily explained. It may well be that Brezhnev was inclined for a time to accept Gierek's pleas that he had the domestic situation in hand and that the way to handle the dissidents was to squeeze them out gradually, as had been done with some success after 1956 and 1970, rather than risk turning what seemed like a marginal group into a mass movement. But this is at best a partial explanation. What is more likely is that, in a complex and changing international environment, Moscow's competing expectations and interests forced it to seek compromises and trade-offs in its relations with Warsaw, and that, however ineffective Gierek might be at home, he was useful to the Soviets in other ways and was at least susceptible to their control—the more so in view of his domestic difficulties. Besides, with the Czech experience freshest in their minds, the Soviet leaders may have believed that the key to stability in Eastern Europe was control over top levels of the Communist party in question. (After all, wasn't it the removal of the unpopular and ineffective Novotný that had opened the floodgates to the Prague Spring in 1968?)

Moscow's immediate reaction to the June riots was to shore up the Gierek regime economically, but already there were nuances in Soviet policy suggesting less than total confidence in the Polish leader. In November 1976 a blue-ribbon Polish delegation returned from Moscow with promises of increased deliveries of Soviet oil and grain, as well as a low-interest loan in both rubles and hard currency. (While the amount of the loan was never announced, it was rumored to be in the range of $1.3 billion.) At the same time, the economic aid was apparently not without its political price. According to a joint communiqué, the two parties declared that the "staunch defense and consolidation of the achievements of socialism . . . are the internationalist duty of the socialist states." That this represented something more than a routine repetition of standard formulas was confirmed by the stepped-up schedule of supervisory visits by high-ranking CPSU functionaries in the fall of 1976: in October by a delegation from the Organizational Department of the Central Committee Secretariat; and in December by Central Committee Secretary Mikhail Zimyanin, the former editor of *Pravda* and a reputed hard-liner, accompanied by two department heads in charge of propaganda and education. The latter visit in particular reflected Soviet determination to ward off unwanted political changes and ended, according to the official Polish press, with "acceptance" of a "document defining the main directions of cooperation of the PUWP and CPSU in the ideological and educational fields in the years 1977–1978" and stressing the need for a "further diffusion of the universal regularities of Marxism-Leninism and the popularization of the experiences of communist and socialist construction in the two fraternal countries."[15]

One of the more difficult aspects of Polish-Soviet relations in this period to fathom is the Soviet attitude toward Poland's faltering economy and burgeoning hard-currency debt. Did the Soviets appreciate the seriousness of the economic crisis? Did they in any way attempt to curtail Warsaw's borrowings? Logic would tell us yes, but there is no hard evidence to that effect. Moreover, although the popular belief that Moscow was largely responsible for Poland's economic excesses was oversimplified and unsupported,[16] what evidence does exist suggests that, in the face of stagnating production and mounting shortages, Moscow took advantage of Gierek's domestic vulnerability to induce Poland to assume a greater share of the burden of Soviet Third World goals. For instance, a cursory survey of Polish trade with four Soviet client states (Cuba, Vietnam, Syria, and Angola) shows both substantial increases in total trade turnover in the late 1970s (especially 1979 and 1980) and, more importantly, dramatic increases in Poland's trade surpluses with each of them. Since none of these countries was likely able to cover its deficit in hard currency, Poland's surplus exports amounted to a subsidy. In view of the precipitous deterioration of their own economy, it is inconceivable that the Poles would voluntarily begin shipping to Cuba in 1978 or 1979 such items in short supply at home as pharmaceuticals, powdered milk, meat products, textiles and knit goods, as well as a wide variety of metallurgical and electrical machine products. Exports to the other countries as well included a wide range of industrial goods, again including some deficit

15. *RFER*, Polish Situation Report/37 (Nov. 8, 1976) and 1 (Jan. 14, 1977); see also Roman Stefanowski, "Polish-Soviet Trade: Specialization, Co-operation, and Integration," *RFER*, RAD Background Report/20 (Jan. 27, 1977).

16. For an extreme statement of this view, see John Van Meer [pseudonym], "Banks, Tanks, and Freedom," *Commentary*, 73 (Dec. 1982), 17–24; for the opposing view, see Davies, "Politico-Economic Dynamics," p. 28.

items. In return, the Poles imported goods of marginal to moderate importance—or important goods (e.g., phosphorus) but in such small quantities that they could not possibly justify the trade surpluses.[17]

The 1978 election of a Polish pope and his triumphal return visit to Poland the following year also presented the Kremlin with a serious dilemma. On the one hand, the second half of the 1970s witnessed a number of visits to the Vatican by high-ranking Soviet and East European officials, eager to build bridges between the Holy See and the European Communist regimes (including Gierek himself in December 1977). Vetoing the pope's visit would not only have put a damper on this policy of rapprochement but might have pushed the Polish church into open confrontation with the party. On the other hand, the Soviet leadership could not have helped being apprehensive about the impact of the visit on a badly weakened Gierek regime and the boost that it would give to the dissident movement, as well as about the possible effect on the rest of Eastern Europe. Those apprehensions were not misplaced. Although it was possible to gauge the full impact only by hindsight, John Paul's visit proved to be a major catalyst to the birth of Solidarity a year later. In particular, his enthusiastic reception by Polish youth was widely perceived as a telling sign of the bankruptcy of communism in Poland and as a warning that, if the existing system were to survive, it had to undergo fundamental change.

In the period between the end of 1976 and the 8th Congress of the PUWP in February 1980, Moscow may well have reassessed its support of Gierek at least once, in the end deciding in his favor perhaps more for reasons of Soviet state interest than Poland's stability. By 1978 widening rifts within the Polish leadership, especially Gierek's tendency to waver between the tough stance favored by Moscow and conciliatory gestures toward the opposition, appear to have caused Brezhnev to toy briefly with the idea of throwing his support to Olszowski, Poland's foreign minister from 1971 to December 1976, when he was reappointed to the Central Committee Secretariat to oversee economic policy. After Gierek's April 1978 trip to Moscow, a visit that was reported to have ended in something less than total harmony, political circles in Warsaw were rife with rumors to the effect that Brezhnev's personal meeting with Olszowski the pre-

17. From Terry draft on the 1976 crisis (n. 11 above). See the Polish foreign trade handbooks, *Rocznik Statystyczny Handlu Zagranicznego* (Warsaw: Główny Urząd Statystyczny), for the years 1976 to 1980, and the *Mały Rocznik Statystyczny 1981* (Warsaw: GUS, 1982); see also Lawrence H. Theriot, "Cuba Faces the Economic Realities of the 1980s," in *East-West Trade: The Prospects to 1985*, studies prepared for the use of the Joint Economic Committee, Congress of the United States (Washington, D.C.: GPO, 1982), pp. 104–35.

vious year had been an ostentatious display of Soviet favoritism.[18] What-ever the truth of the rumors, the message was not lost on the remaining two factions in the Polish leadership, who promptly papered over their differences. By 1979, Olszowski's star was on the wane, his decline culminating at the 8th Congress, when he was removed from the Polit-buro and subsequently appointed ambassador to East Germany.

Having removed Olszowski as a potential contender, Gierek turned to the task of neutralizing the conservative faction. In this he was helped by the lengthy illness of Prime Minister Jaroszewicz, which kept the latter absent from the political arena for a good part of 1978 and 1979. During that period Gierek managed to weaken the Gang of Four by persuading one of its members (and his future immediate successor), Stanisław Kania, to move closer to the center. This made it possible for Gierek to get rid of Jaroszewicz, also at the 8th Congress, when he was replaced as prime minister by the somewhat less conservative Central Committee Secretary, Edward Babiuch.

Whether the Soviets ever seriously considered Olszowski as a replace-ment for Gierek, or whether their brief flirtation with him was merely a way of keeping the Polish leader in line—or whether the whole affair was a figment of Warsaw rumor mills—it is inconceivable that Gierek could have executed this double-edged surgical operation without Moscow's imprimatur. In turn Moscow's decision finally to settle on Gierek as the undisputed leader of the Polish party appears to have turned largely on international considerations—in particular, on Brezhnev's intention to salvage what he could of détente, especially with Western Europe. Despite mounting problems at home, Gierek's stature as a statesman and an inter-mediary between East and West had continued to grow throughout the second half of the 1970s, boosted not only by President Carter's visit in December 1977 but also by his success in developing a "special relation-ship" with both French President Valéry Giscard d'Estaing and West German Chancellor Helmut Schmidt. These contacts proved invaluable when the Soviets began looking for channels for resuming the East-West dialogue interrupted by the invasion of Afghanistan in December 1979. Although Warsaw was apparently taken by surprise by the invasion and, initially at least, gave it a rather chilly endorsement,[19] nonetheless it was Gierek who in February 1980 was chosen by Moscow to propose the convening of a European disarmament conference, and who was then

18. Personal interviews, Warsaw, Summer 1978. For a report of Gierek's trip, see *RFER*, Polish Situation Report/10 (May 2, 1978); for coverage of Olszowski's trip, see *Trybuna Ludu* and *Pravda*, Mar. 18–20, 1977.

19. See "Polen im Sog der Afghanistankrise," *Neue Zürcher Zeitung*, Feb. 6, 1980.

asked to host the meeting between Brezhnev and Giscard in May. (His role as intermediary was to be further enhanced by a forthcoming trip to West Germany in August and by Giscard's return visit to Warsaw in September but, as a result of the summer 1980 events in Poland, neither visit took place.)

Having settled accounts (or so he thought) with his domestic rivals, Gierek could turn his attention back to the economy. Nineteen seventy-nine had been a difficult year, with national income falling 2% below the 1978 level. But this figure fails to convey the true dimensions of Poland's pending economic collapse. Following the unusually harsh winter of 1978–79—the "recipe for catastrophe in Warsaw" was said to be "half a meter of snow and 30 years of socialism"—key services such as rail transportation and power production never returned to normal levels, generating "bottleneck multipliers" that rippled through the economy as shortages and delays in one sector caused more shortages and delays in others. After years of inaction and evasion in which it appeared that the Polish system had lost the will to reform itself, some of the speeches delivered to the 8th Congress suggested that the Gierek regime, its political flanks shored up, was at last prepared to tackle the question of economic reform. This resolve undoubtedly received an additional boost from a group of Western bankers—by the end of 1979 Poland's debt to the West exceeded $20 billion—who visited Poland in April 1980, reaffirming their demand for reforms.[20]

As it was generally agreed that one of the first steps in that direction had to be a rationalization of the price system, to bring prices into line with real costs and to ease the burden of food subsidies on the state budget, a partial revision of retail meat prices was announced on July 1, 1980. By announcing partial rather than across-the-board increases in food prices, the Polish leaders were obviously hoping to avoid a repetition of the 1970 and 1976 experiences. History has recorded their error.

AUGUST 1980: THE CHALLENGE OF SOLIDARITY

Initially confident that it could control the strikes that broke out in early July by settling wage demands individually with each industrial plant, the government was utterly unprepared for what happened when the strike wave reached the port city of Gdańsk, where memories of December 1970 were still fresh and bitter. Faced with the refusal of the workers of the giant Lenin Shipyard to bargain separately, it was eventually forced to negotiate with an Inter-Factory Strike Committee over a set of 21 demands, which, in addition to the standard economic issues such as higher

20. *New York Times*, Apr. 17, 1980.

wages, shorter working hours, and better health care, included a number of demands aimed at the core of the political system: the establishment of free and independent trade unions, a guaranteed right to strike, and the abolition of censorship. On August 31, a "social compact" was signed in which the only major concession to the Communist regime was the workers' grudging last-minute acknowledgment of the "leading role of the party" in the Polish political system.

From the palpable tension of the days preceding the signing it was clear that the agreements—the one at Gdańsk together with similar ones signed in Szczecin and, three days later, with striking miners in Silesia—reflected less a consensus within the party on the concessions agreed to than a realization that the regime did not have the power to end the strikes by any other means. With hundreds of thousands of workers already on strike, their number growing daily as the movement spread to industrial centers around the country—and, in a final blow to Gierek's personal prestige, the Silesian coal miners joining their ranks—any attempt to quell the strikes by force would almost certainly have ended in failure, with the ever-present danger that the ensuing chaos would result in Soviet military intervention. Thus, Solidarity was born not out of genuine compromise but in a desperate move by Poland's Communist leadership to buy time to regroup and regain the upper hand.[21]

The Kremlin too had been caught off guard by the suddenness and depth of the crisis, misled no doubt by Gierek himself, who was on his annual summer pilgrimage to the Soviet Union and, presumably convinced that the strikes would soon be settled, did not bother to return to Poland until the middle of August. This may help to explain the lack of a Soviet reaction to the Polish events during July and most of August (the first article of any substance appeared in *Pravda* on August 20 reporting on Gierek's speech of the eighteenth), as well as their initial confusion over the meaning of the strikes and the proper way to report them. Nonetheless, even this early coverage provided a clear indication of the Soviets' displeasure and set the themes that would dominate their approach to Solidarity during the sixteen months of its existence. Largely ignoring Gierek's admissions of mistakes, *Pravda* emphasized the alleged role of "anti-socialist elements." A week later, a lengthy TASS commentary elaborated on this theme, linking the strikes to Western subversion and "reactionary" emigré circles, and ominously hinting that the sanctity of Poland's western border was being questioned by a "revanchist" West

21. For a detailed day-by-day account of events, see *RFER, Poland: A Chronology of Events July–November 1980*, Mar. 31, 1981; subsequent chronologies were issued to cover the periods: *November 1980–February 1981* (Sept. 11, 1981), *February–July 1981* (Mar. 5, 1982), and *July–December 1981* (July 16, 1982) [cited hereafter as *Chronology 1, 2, 3,* or *4*].

German press. Irritation over the concessions made to the workers was particularly evident in the failure of the Soviet media to report the Gdańsk agreement for fully a day after it was signed, during which period TASS distributed another especially bitter attack on the strike leaders; even when the agreement was acknowledged, none of the particulars— most importantly the right to form an independent trade union—was mentioned.[22]

Having failed to forestall an agreement, Moscow appeared to temper its tone and tactics. On August 31, *Pravda* for the first time criticized, albeit indirectly, "the weaknesses" of the Polish leadership, whose "distortions of socialist methods and approach" were responsible for the crisis— a formulation implying that the Soviets would not object to Gierek's removal. The effusive praise heaped on his successor by Brezhnev a few days later confirmed their genuine relief at the changeover.[23] Indeed, by contrast with the ousted Gierek, whose ineffectual behavior in the critical days of August must have persuaded the Kremlin that he had lost all credibility within the Polish party and society at large, Kania's credentials were impressive. By virtue of his responsibilities in the Central Committee Secretariat, which included supervision of military-security affairs and church-state relations, as well as his generally conservative reputation, he must have seemed the best available choice to stabilize the Polish situation. Perhaps for this reason, and in order to give him time to restore some semblance of normalcy to the country, the Soviet media campaign vis-à-vis Poland over the next two months was relatively subdued. This is not to say that the Soviets fell entirely silent in this period. Indeed, one of the most important statements signaling the attitude they expected the new Polish leadership to take was a September 25 article in *Pravda* concerning the role of trade unions under socialism; without mentioning Poland (the article was a review of a book on Lenin's views on the subject), the message was clear enough: there is no place in a socialist society for trade unions independent of the Communist party.

A second reason to deescalate the polemics was the growing concern over Poland in the West. From the viewpoint of the USSR's broader international interests, the new difficulties within the bloc could hardly have come at a more inopportune time. Bogged down in Afghanistan, with a wary eye on China's rapprochement with the West, economically

22. For extensive coverage of the Soviet press reaction to the events in Poland in late August and early September, see *August 1980: The Strikes in Poland* (Munich: RFER, Oct. 1980), pp. 237–52.

23. The August 31 criticism came in a reprint of an undated article by U.S. Communist party leader Gus Hall; for details of the Soviet reaction to the replacement of Gierek by Kania, see Jan B. de Weydenthal, "Moscow Supports the Polish Party," *RFER*, RAD Background Report/266 (Nov. 10, 1980).

more and more overextended, and bent on pursuing détente with West-
ern Europe in the face of the U.S. grain embargo and Olympic boycott,
Moscow's room for maneuver was severely circumscribed. Most pertinent
in the early autumn of 1980 were the election campaigns in the United
States and West Germany, in which, despite repeated assurances from the
Kremlin, the threat of Soviet intervention in Poland figured prominently.
Moreover, the Soviet Union was participating in two major international
conferences—the Helsinki Review Conference in Madrid and the U.S.-
Soviet talks in Geneva on limiting theater nuclear weapons in Europe—
both of which could be adversely affected by events in Poland.[24] Possibly
for these reasons, it was Czechoslovakia and East Germany that took the
lead in criticizing Polish developments, partly as Moscow's proxies and
partly in order to forestall potential spillover of labor unrest into their
respective countries.

Moscow rejoined the anti-Polish campaign in the second half of
November after resolution of the crisis over formal registration of Solidarity, which had begun in late October with a court ruling arbitrarily
altering the new union's proposed statute by deleting the right to strike
and inserting a paragraph on the "leading role of the party" and the
sanctity of Poland's alliances. In response, Solidarity appealed the ruling
and called a general strike alert for November 12. The crisis was defused
two days before the deadline when, in a retreat obviously orchestrated by
the party leadership, Poland's Supreme Court upheld the Solidarity appeal. The Soviets' initial reaction was reminiscent of their response to the
Gdańsk agreement at the end of August: they ignored it, reprinting
instead carefully selected excerpts from an article in the Polish party
daily, *Trybuna Ludu*, reiterating *Pravda*'s earlier stance on the unaccept-
ability of independent unions under socialism.[25]

It was only a full two weeks after Solidarity's legalization that its existence was first mentioned in the Soviet media, accompanied by dark hints
that a strike by Polish railroad workers, potentially involving supply links
with the GDR, threatened Soviet security interests. Over the next several
weeks, tensions reached a fever pitch as a continuous flow of criticism
from Moscow, together with an extensive buildup of Warsaw Pact forces
around Poland, seemed to presage imminent military intervention. The
tension was temporarily dissipated on December 5 by a sudden summit
meeting of Warsaw Pact leaders, who issued a declaration expressing the
hope that Poland would be able to overcome its difficulties alone.[26]

At the time, the tone of near hysteria in the Soviet media (including at

24. For an interesting analysis, see Bruce Porter, "Poland and European Détente: The
View from Moscow," *Radio Liberty Research* [*RLR*], no. 413/80, Nov. 5, 1980.
25. *Pravda*, Nov. 17, 1980; from *Trybuna Ludu*, Nov. 15–16, 1980.
26. R. W. Apple, Jr., in *New York Times*, Dec. 6, 1980.

least one false report of industrial sabotage)[27] seemed oddly out of place as lingering strike actions were being resolved and a general atmosphere of calm was restored in Poland itself. In retrospect, however, it is clear that this was only the opening gambit in a pattern of Soviet behavior that was to be repeated, with slight variations to suit changing circumstances, over the next year. This pattern stemmed both from the lessons of the Prague Spring (hence their intense concern to keep the reform movement from gaining a firm foothold within the PUWP) and from the unique aspects of the Polish situation (the spontaneous and mass character of the movement, which dictated a more gradual and indirect resolution to the crisis than if it had been limited and more easily contained).

Having decided at the outset that direct intervention should be absolutely the last resort (although there may have been some disagreement in the military and perhaps in the Politburo itself as to what constituted that "last resort," especially in December 1980[28]), the Soviets adopted a strategy as straightforward in purpose as it was manipulative in tactics: never permit the Polish party to strike a genuine compromise with Solidarity, disrupt even temporary lulls that might allow the union to consolidate its legal and political status, and ultimately force the Poles themselves to end the threat to one-party rule. Thus, at each point at which confrontation between party and union seemed about to give way to compromise (usually because the party had reneged on one of its promises only to be forced into retreat in the face of a strike threat it could not effectively counter), the Soviets would step up their polemics and pressure tactics, which in turn would stiffen the regime's resistance to Solidarity's demands. The stage would then be set for renewed confrontation, in some cases sparked by acts of provocation by hard-line elements reassured that the Kremlin was in their corner. Moreover, with each cycle of confrontation-compromise-provocation leading to renewed confrontation, the two sides became increasingly polarized, not only suspicious of the other's motives but rent by internal splits between moderates convinced of the need for compromise and radicals (in the case of Solidarity) or hard-liners (in the party) equally convinced of its impossibility or undesirability.

A review of some of the most salient events will suffice to illustrate the pattern of action and reaction: In response to the buildup of tensions following Solidarity's registration, the Polish regime toughened its stance on such volatile issues as free Saturdays, the removal of corrupt officials,

27. *Chronology 2*, pp. 28–29.

28. According to information originating from Western Communist sources, in early December the Soviet Politburo split 6 to 6 on the issue of intervention, with Brezhnev casting the deciding vote against (Robert C. Toth in *Los Angeles Times*, Apr. 4, 1981). See also Richard D. Anderson, Jr., "Soviet Decision-Making and Poland," *Problems of Communism*, 31 (Mar.–Apr. 1982), 22–36.

and the establishment of a farmers' union (Rural Solidarity); by early February of 1981 the ensuing wave of labor strife had prompted the third change of governmental leadership within a year. In one of his first acts as prime minister, General Wojciech Jaruzelski (who retained his post as Poland's defense minister) appealed for a 90-day strike moratorium in order to allow his government to move toward economic stabilization and "wide-ranging reforms of the economy." Despite the swift resolution of most outstanding labor disputes (largely on Solidarity's terms), the lull was unexpectedly broken on March 4, at the conclusion of the 26th Congress of the Soviet Communist Party, by the announcement of a Polish-Soviet summit meeting in Moscow. The tone of the communiqué was ominous: in addition to giving the Jaruzelski–Kania leadership a lukewarm vote of confidence, the Kremlin resurrected the thirteen-year-old Brezhnev doctrine by declaring that the unity of the socialist camp was "indissoluble" and that its defense was a matter of great concern not only for a single state but also for the entire camp. Moscow also reiterated its readiness to help the Polish party in a "radical healing of the situation in the country."[29]

The specter of a reinvocation of the Brezhnev doctrine was made more credible by the simultaneous announcement of joint military maneuvers, code-named *Soyuz '81,* to be held in the second half of March with the participation of forces from the USSR, Czechoslovakia, East Germany, and Poland; the actual number of troops to be involved was not disclosed, but the fact that the maneuvers were to take place on the territory of four countries suggested they would be extensive. At the same time, the political signal given by the Moscow communiqué in all probability contributed to a renewed escalation of tensions within Poland caused by the March 19 police beating of three Solidarity activists in the provincial capital of Bydgoszcz. The outrage evoked by this incident, widely interpreted as a deliberate provocation by hard-line elements in the party and security forces, led to yet another general strike threat that was defused only by a last-minute agreement on March 30 (the strike had been called for March 31), in which the party once again made significant concessions to Solidarity.

The agreement was ratified only after a stormy session of the party's Central Committee and despite the opposition of two conservative members of the Politburo—Olszowski and Tadeusz Grabski—who were apparently saved from being ousted only by the direct intervention of Brezhnev himself.[30] Moscow's displeasure at the concessions, and at the

29. John Darnton, in the *New York Times,* Mar. 5, 24, 1981; according to Darnton, the meeting was a "humiliating encounter" for the Poles.

30. Ibid., Apr. 14, 1981.

decision also taken by the Central Committee to set a July 20 deadline for the long-postponed Extraordinary Party Congress, was evident in the unexpected continuation of military exercises into the first week of April and a renewal of Soviet press criticism of the PUWP. Although tensions again eased with the end of the maneuvers and with Brezhnev's speech to the Czechoslovak Party Congress on April 7—in which the Soviet leader expressed his confidence that "Polish Communists" themselves would be capable of rebuffing the enemies of socialism—his failure to endorse the Polish leadership was seen as a warning to Kania and Jaruzelski.

The cycles of confrontation-compromise-polemic varied in a number of respects. For instance, the Soviet reaction to Jaruzelski's call for a three-month strike truce was probably delayed by the timing of the 26th Congress (no doubt because Brezhnev did not want anything to mar the atmosphere for the congress), whereas after the post-Bydgoszcz compromise the reaction was very swift. The focus of Soviet anxieties also shifted with circumstances: in November and December of 1980, it was on Solidarity and remained largely there through the winter. With Bydgoszcz, however, it began to shift to developments within the party, where the so-called horizontal links movement and preparations for the now-scheduled Extraordinary Congress raised fears of a repetition of what had been pending in Czechoslovakia in 1968: internal democratization of the Communist party and a clean sweep of conservatives from leading party offices. Hence, from April on, Moscow's first order of priority had to be to delay the congress or, if it could not be further delayed, to ensure that it was not a genuinely reform congress.

The opening salvo in this effort was the surprise one-day visit to Warsaw by Mikhail Suslov, the Soviet Central Committee's late senior secretary for ideological and international affairs and well known as a guardian of orthodoxy. The visit, on April 23, proved inconclusive and was immediately followed by a sharp official attack on the Polish party, accusing it of "revisionism," one of the gravest heresies in the communist vocabulary.[31]

By far the sharpest and most intimidating attack on the leadership of the Polish party was contained in the June 5 letter of the Soviet Central Committee addressed to its Polish counterpart. The letter recalled the warnings issued by the Kremlin at the Moscow Summit in December 1980, at the 26th Congress of the Soviet Communist Party in March, and during Suslov's visit to Warsaw in April, stating that despite promises to deal with the crisis, the Polish leaders had let the situation deteriorate still further.[32] The Soviet message provided an opportunity for the last des-

31. Anthony Austin, in ibid., Apr. 26, 1981.
32. The full text of the letter can be found in ibid., June 11, 1981.

perate effort by the conservative faction within the Polish leadership to unseat Kania, an attempt that failed and that, in fact, appeared to solidify Kania's position.

Although the Kremlin letter did not prevent the Extraordinary 9th Congress of the Polish Party from taking place as scheduled, it achieved Moscow's second, or fallback, goal by influencing the election of delegates to the congress and averting its being dominated by "reform" candidates. Moscow then made another attempt to influence the outcome by sending Foreign Minister Andrei Gromyko to Warsaw on July 3, eleven days before the opening of the congress, to discuss the agenda. The joint communiqué issued after the visit reaffirmed Moscow's decision to allow the congress to proceed, at the same time restating once again the Brezhnev doctrine, claiming that the defense of communism in Poland was a legitimate concern of all members of the Warsaw Pact.[33]

The congress itself, which met on July 14, was, in a sense, an anticlimax. The delegates elected a new Central Committee and Politburo, reaffirming, at least on the surface, their support of the middle-of-the-road policy pursued by Kania and Jaruzelski by defeating both the conservative and liberal candidates. In addition the congress approved a series of party reforms that included elections by secret ballot, limitation on tenure in party offices, and greater participation by the rank and file in decision-making.

Moscow must have greeted the results of the congress with mixed feelings. On the one hand, the endorsement of the moderate line represented by Kania and Jaruzelski, as well as the overwhelming approval of the reforms that made the Polish party truly unique in the annals of international communism, could only further displease the Soviet leadership. On the other hand, the congress not only endorsed Poland's close ties to the Soviet Union but also kept the liberal faction in check. In other words, things could have been worse, and the official Soviet reaction following the congress indicated continued ambivalence toward developments within the Polish party.

The next four months witnessed a rapid deterioration in Poland's political and economic situation. It soon became clear that the expectations of further democratization and economic reforms raised by the congress were not being fulfilled and that both the party and the government were neither able to cope with the escalating crisis nor willing to negotiate with Solidarity. At the same time, the latter appeared to grow stronger and bolder, and began to confront the regime with a series of radical political demands that reached their height at the Solidarity Congress, held in two stages in September and October. The demands in-

33. John F. Burns, in ibid., July 6, 1981.

cluded a call for free elections, economic self-management, free access to media, and final legalization of free labor unions.

The Soviet reaction was not long in coming. On September 10 the Soviet ambassador delivered a message from Moscow complaining about the "mounting wave of anti-Sovietism in Poland" and warning that "further leniency shown to any manifestation of anti-Sovietism does immense harm to Polish-Soviet relations and is in direct contradiction to Poland's allied obligations and the vital interests of the Polish nation."[34] The sharply worded statement was considerably harsher than the Kremlin letter of June 5, which criticized Solidarity as a counterrevolutionary force without, however, invoking the specter of anti-Sovietism. The September message was followed by a barrage of attacks on virtually every aspect of Polish "renewal," which continued unabated for the next two months.

The pressure from Moscow succeeded in intimidating the moderate faction within the Polish party and in strengthening the conservative wing, long dissatisfied with Kania's inability or unwillingness to suppress Solidarity and other opposition groups. Most likely with the encouragement of the Kremlin, the newly elected Central Committee ousted Kania on October 17, replacing him with General Jaruzelski, who thus became the most powerful leader in the communist world, combining party leadership with premiership and command of Poland's armed forces.

Those who expected the new party leader to deal with the crisis in a resolute manner were soon disappointed. Like his predecessor, Jaruzelski was unable or unwilling to reach an agreement with the opposition for the purpose of stabilizing the country and initiating the process of economic recovery. His feeble attempt to bring Solidarity and the Catholic church into some kind of "united front" proved abortive when it became obvious that both the union and the church were to play a highly subordinate role in the new arrangement. Presumably on Moscow's insistence Jaruzelski subsequently declined to negotiate with Solidarity and also refused to proceed with the legislation on self-management, censorship, and independent labor unions that were of particular interest to Solidarity. The latter responded with a threat of a general strike, a call for a referendum

34. The text of the message can be found in ibid., Sept. 13, 1981. The Soviets were using other not-so-subtle pressure tactics in this period, including crude innuendos concerning Poland's postwar borders. Among the more bizarre scenarios was one that had Brezhnev, presumably during his trip to West Germany in November 1981, offering Chancellor Schmidt a reunification of the two Germanys *plus* generous corrections in the Polish-German frontier in Pomerania and Silesia; in addition, Czechoslovakia was to get some territory in southern Silesia, while the USSR would gain in the northeast. (These reports are derived from personal interviews in Warsaw, Sept. 1982.) While this author views such a scenario as wholly improbable, it was widely believed by usually well-informed people in high places in Poland at that time.

concerning the future Polish political system, and a demand for the ouster of the party from industrial enterprises. Solidarity designated December 17 as the day of national protest to coincide with the anniversary of the
1970 Baltic coast riots. Shortly before that date, on December 13, General
Jaruzelski proclaimed the state of emergency, imposed martial law, and
established a military council to rule the country until further notice.

The coup, which was executed with admirable precision, managed to
decapitate Solidarity, which put up a surprisingly mild resistance. Justifying the imposition of martial law as a last-ditch effort to prevent a national
catastrophe, the military regime arrested more than 6,000 opposition
members and abolished several concessions granted to Solidarity in the
course of the previous sixteen months. Within a few weeks all active
resistance was broken and the military regime in full control.

MARTIAL LAW: SOLUTION OR NEW DILEMMA?

Of the many questions surrounding the military takeover, perhaps the
most intriguing concerns possible Soviet involvement in its preparation
and execution. The sixteen months of Solidarity's legal existence was
clearly a very trying period for the Kremlin, which was surely tempted
more than once to use its military might to bring the Poles to heel. Among
Western observers there was substantial agreement that this latest Polish
crisis represented the most serious challenge not only to Soviet state interests, but to the whole body of Marxist-Leninist doctrine, since the
Titoist heresy of 1948—far more serious than either the Hungarian Revolution of 1956 or the Czechoslovak reform movement of 1968. It was in
effect a synthesis of the Hungarian and Czech challenges. As in the first,
the workers' rebellion soon acquired a mass character with overwhelming
popular support, while the process of democratization with the ruling
party strongly resembled the ideas put forward by the architects of the
Prague Spring.[35]

In view of the use of Soviet military force to put an end to these sins
when committed separately, there was every reason to expect that an
invasion of Poland in response to the combined challenge was only a
matter of time. In the end, the potential for large-scale resistance within
Poland and the certain damage that overt military action would have done
to the Kremlin's relations with the West dictated "invasion by proxy." But
there can be little doubt that Moscow was extensively involved both in
precipitating martial law and even in its execution. As early as the Warsaw
Pact maneuvers in late March and early April of 1981, Western intel-

35. See, e.g., Seweryn Bialer, "Poland and the Soviet Imperium," *Foreign Affairs*, 59, no.
3 (1980), 522–39, and Jiri Valenta, "Soviet Options in Poland," *Survival* (London), 23
(Mar./Apr. 1981), 50–59.

ligence sources reported a buildup of supplies at the main Soviet military base within Poland, as well as the construction of a wholly independent communications network in and around the country. In addition, Soviet Marshal V. G. Kulikov, commander of the Warsaw Pact, made numerous trips to Warsaw during the summer and fall, arriving in Poland again only a few days before martial law was declared. In light of numerous reports in the weeks after the coup that some "Polish" soldiers and border guards appeared not to know the Polish language, it is even possible that a small number of Soviet troops (disguised in Polish uniforms) were deployed in key noncombat positions.

In the year between the imposition of martial law and its partial suspension at the end of 1982, the Jaruzelski regime, no doubt with some prodding from Moscow, eliminated most of the gains won by Solidarity during the preceding sixteen months, most importantly the dissolution of the union itself, which was replaced by a new system of government-sanctioned (and -controlled) unions. Other "normalization" measures included a reversal of the democratization process within the PUWP (especially the removal of locally elected party officials); formation of a new "popular" organization, the so-called Patriotic Movement of National Rebirth (PRON), to replace the discredited Front of National Unity as a vehicle to mobilize broad nonpartisan support for the military regime; and the dissolution of a whole range of independent professional and student associations that had sprung up during the Solidarity period and were now replaced by a system of traditional "transition-belt" organizations.

Nonetheless, from the perspective of mid-1983 the imposition of martial law has merely altered Moscow's dilemma in Poland while leaving its essence unresolved. Having cajoled and intimidated the Poles into doing the job for them, thus escaping the onus for crushing Solidarity, the Soviets must now accept the fact that they have less direct control over the normalization process than was the case in Hungary or Czechoslovakia. Moreover, they must work through a regime which not only has an agenda of its own, but which has also been so totally compromised in the eyes of the population, and which remains so torn by factionalism, that it has so far been unable to make visible progress toward political reconciliation or economic reconstruction. Thus, even before the pope's dramatic return visit to his homeland in June 1983, Moscow had good reason to be less than satisfied with the situation, whether military, political, or economic.

The mere fact that the Polish Communist party proved incapable of restoring order and had to be replaced by the military as the supreme authority in the country had far-reaching security and political implications to which the USSR could not remain indifferent. There can be little doubt, for instance, that the crisis in Poland has seriously affected Soviet strategic-military planning in Europe. As long as the Polish Army continues to run the country, it cannot be available for possible deployment against NATO, a fact that has obviously weakened the military posture of the WTO and provided further incentive for Moscow to seek faster political and economic normalization.

Politically, too, the necessity of martial law reflected the total bankruptcy of the system. By mid-1983 it was clear that all attempts to regain a degree of legitimacy among the general population had failed. None of the new organizations—not the new unions, or PRON, or any of the student or professional associations—has managed to attract much support. Moreover, the party's efforts to reassert its authority or even to put its internal house in order have been wholly ineffective. In the three years after the 8th Congress in February 1980 the PUWP lost one-third of its members through resignations and expulsions; by early 1983 the numbers were still declining, although at a much reduced rate while the remaining rank and file membership was demoralized and apathetic.[36] Perhaps the greatest irony was that the two factions of the party that might have had a fighting chance of bridging the chasm between regime and society have been weakened or discredited in the eyes of the population far more effectively than they could have been by years of hostile Soviet propaganda: the genuine reformers by purges or voluntary resignations, the moderates (such as Deputy Prime Minister and former editor of the party weekly *Polityka,* Mieczysław Rakowski) by their complicity in martial law and the crushing of Solidarity.

Finally, although official explanations for martial law stressed the need to halt the tailspin of the Polish economy, 1982 witnessed a continuing slide in overall economic activity, down 8% from 1981 after a drop of 13% the previous year. Preliminary estimates for 1983 have projected a slight rise over 1982, but at best that will bring the economy back only to 1974 levels.[37] The failure of the Polish economy to recover more quickly has cost Moscow dearly. According to the most detailed data available, Soviet bloc assistance to Poland directly related to the crisis amounted in 1980 and 1981 to at least $3.1 billion, almost all coming from the USSR itself, while Poland's trade deficit with the Soviet Union in 1982 likely added another $1.5 billion. In addition, depressed production in Poland continues to have an adverse impact on economic performance throughout the region.[38]

36. *Trybuna Ludu,* Feb. 11, 1983; *RFER,* Polish Situation Report/3 (Feb. 21, 1983).

37. *Business Week,* May 30, 1983, p. 105

38. Elizabeth Ann Goldstein, "Soviet Economic Assistance to Poland, 1980–81," in John P. Hardt, ed., *Soviet Economy in the 1980s: Problems and Prospects,* pt. 2, selected papers submitted to the Joint Economic Committee, Congress of the United States (Washington, D.C.: GPO, 1983), p. 567. These figures are exclusive of the price subsidies on Soviet energy

Already in the late summer of 1982 there were indications that
Moscow was becoming impatient with the slow pace of normalization,
particularly with the unwillingness of the martial law regime to apply
strong measures against the persistent opposition. In contrast to the
warm reception given Jaruzelski during his first post-coup visit to Moscow
in March 1982, his subsequent meeting with Brezhnev in the Crimea in
August was marked by a coolness that suggested dissatisfaction.[39]

There is no evidence that Brezhnev's death and his replacement by
Yuri Andropov in November 1982 had any immediate effect on Moscow's
policy toward Warsaw. Nonetheless, the following May two stinging attacks in prominent Soviet journals on the Polish party, and at least indirectly on Jaruzelski himself, seemed to initiate a new and more open
phase in Soviet criticism. The first, in the weekly *New Times*, was ostensibly
aimed at *Polityka*, which was described as being "allergic to real socialism"
but was in fact a thinly veiled attack on its former editor, Rakowski. The
second, viewed by some as more ominous because it appeared in *Kommunist*, the main theoretical journal of the CPSU, was a partial translation of
an article published several months earlier in the PUWP's theoretical
monthly. It, too, was sharply critical of pragmatic elements in the Polish
party, accusing them of a purely "mechanical" approach to Marxism, and
warning that failure to draw "ideological dividing lines" clearly could
"lead to a return of opportunistic tendencies within the party, and outside—facilitate the penetration of rightist and counterrevolutionary
forces and groups."[40]

The timing of these two articles, which came at a delicate point in
internal Polish politics and barely a month before the Pope's visit—and
which also coincided with signs that the physical and political health of the
new Soviet party leader might be weakening—suggests several possible
motives on Moscow's part. The most obvious was to strengthen the hand
of hard-liners in the faction-ridden Polish party as it was preparing to put
its ideological house in order; in fact, the *New Times* attack was cited as a
major reason for the postponement of a long-awaited debate on ideologi-

---

and raw material exports, which result from the prevailing CMEA price formula irrespective of the Polish crisis. According to one estimate, these subsidies amounted to an additional
$7.5 billion in 1980–81 but would have been far less in 1982. For a critical review of the
subsidy issue, see chap. 6.

39. Bruce Porter, "Brezhnev and Jaruzelski Meet in the Crimea," *RLR*, no. 328/82, Aug.
18, 1982.

40. "When Bearings Are Lost: Scanning the Warsaw Weekly Polityka," *New Times*, no. 19
(May 1983), pp. 18–20; *Kommunist*, no. 7 (May 1983), pp. 85–87. The original Polish articles,
entitled "Social Consciousness and Political Struggle," appeared in the February 1983 issue
of *Nowe Drogi*. For reports on these two articles (and the Polish response to the first), see John
Kifner in the *New York Times*, May 10, 12, and 21, 1983.

cal questions by the Central Committee, which had been scheduled for mid-May. A second, closely related motive may have been to signal Soviet uneasiness over the attention being lavished on PRON, which had just held its first national conference. For, while some Polish Communists (including, it would seem, Jaruzelski) regard the organization as a "last chance" to bring about national reconciliation, others apparently see it as a potential threat to the party's dominant position.

It is also possible that the more critical tone out of Moscow was somehow related to political infighting in the Kremlin, either to a subtle shift in the balance of power as a result of Andropov's infirmities or perhaps to his own efforts to protect his political flanks in a stage of the succession process that typically sees a closing of ideological ranks. Alas, all this must remain in the realm of speculation. What is not speculation, however, and what was surely a fourth motive for Moscow's outbursts, was intense concern on the part of the Soviet leaders over the impact of Pope John Paul II's second visit to his homeland. Indeed, on the very day of the pope's arrival in Poland, Soviet Foreign Minister Andrei Gromyko warned the West against interfering in Polish affairs, declaring that "Poland . . . has been and remains an inalienable part of the socialist community."[41]

That concern was not misplaced. Since the imposition of martial law the role of the church had been ambivalent. On the one hand, the suspension of Solidarity had enhanced its status as the sole bastion of Poland's independence; on the other hand, to the surprise and chagrin of some of its supporters, church leaders frequently warned against antigovernment protests. Its most visible act came in November 1982, when Józef Cardinal Glemp, head of the Polish episcopate, sided openly with the regime in opposing the underground's call for a national strike following delegalization of the union. However, the church extracted a high price for its support by forcing the regime to agree to the June 1983 papal visit. In consenting to the pope's return, Jaruzelski in effect bought six months of relative social peace—the visit having been made contingent on continued calm in the country—and the hope that it would lend his regime a measure of vicarious legitimacy both at home and abroad and lead to a lifting of Western economic sanctions.

At this writing, less than a month after the visit, it is far too soon to tell whether Jaruzelski has won his gamble or what the long-term effects will be. What can be said is that the events of that dramatic week—not only the tumultuous crowds and outpouring of affection for the pope and church, but the week-long celebration of Solidarity—are certain to intensify the ongoing political tug-of-war in the Polish party. For some, the massive

41. *New York Times*, June 17, 1983.

demonstration of support for the now-banned union will be seen as decisive proof that only a more concerted effort to stamp out all remnants of Solidarity will remove the political threat to Communist rule. Others, no doubt Jaruzelski among them, will argue that the scale of repressive measures necessary to achieve that end would merely succeed in further alienating the population, thus setting the stage for another explosion, and that only consistent pursuit of national reconciliation can bring about lasting normalization.

Who eventually wins this tug-of-war will likely depend as much on decisions made elsewhere (in Moscow, the Vatican, and various Western capitals) as on those taken in Warsaw. In an effort to break the deadlock on sanctions and tip the balance toward moderation, the church has proposed to establish a foundation that would raise an estimated $2–5 billion from church, government, and private sources in the West and would channel those funds into Poland's private agricultural and small-business sectors. It is an offer that even the old men in the Kremlin, for whom both the Catholic church and Poland's 3 million private peasants are embarrassing anachronisms, will find it hard to turn down. Thus, as so many times before in history, Moscow's choices in Poland are "between the disagreeable and the intolerable."[42] Only the future will tell how far they are willing to compromise ideological principles for the promise of political stability and economic viability, or which they regard as more vital to their security in Eastern Europe.

42. See the last paragraph of chap. 12.

4

Soviet Policy toward Hungary and Czechoslovakia

JIRI VALENTA

Between the Soviet-Yugoslav break of 1948 and the Polish crisis of 1980–81, the two most traumatic events for the Soviets in Eastern Europe were the Hungarian Revolution of 1956 and the Prague Spring of 1968. As the only two occasions involving Soviet military invasions in the region since World War II, the Hungarian and Czechoslovak episodes provide a unique opportunity to examine the use of that ultimate sanction in Soviet-East European relations.[1] My purpose in this chapter is to compare the mundane dimensions of Soviet policy toward the two countries and, specifically, the circumstances surrounding the decisions to invade, as well as the postinvasion patterns of consolidation and normalization. Finally, I attempt to assess how these experiences have influenced Soviet policies toward the rest of Eastern Europe.

Current Soviet perceptions regarding Czechoslovakia and Hungary have been influenced, of course, by earlier relations with these two countries. Until 1968 the Soviets regarded the Czechs and Slovaks as traditionally friendly Slavic nations. Though tending to patronize the Russians as cultural inferiors, the Czechs and especially the Slovaks by and large shared this friendly sentiment; moreover, in the past both nations often looked to Russia for salvation from Austrian and German oppression. After World War I and establishment of the Czechoslovak state, relations were cordial, except for the Soviet government's brief conflict with the Czechoslovak legion in Siberia (1918–20).[2] During World War II Czecho-

I am indebted to the following scholars for their comments: Robert Legvold, Charles Gati, A. Ross Johnson, Béla K. Király (formerly a major general of the Hungarian Army), Vladimir V. Kusin, János Radványi (former Hungarian ambassador to the United Nations), Iván Völgyes, Sarah Terry, and Virginia Valenta, and to many former Hungarian, Czechoslovak, and Soviet officials for interviews. I am particularly grateful to Nagy's close associate during the Hungarian Revolution, the late Zoltán Vass.

1. The Soviets now recognize that the threats to their interests in Hungary and Czechoslovakia were primarily of an internal nature. Thus the former chief of staff of the Warsaw Treaty Organization, General S. Shtemenko, has stated that the USSR must defend Eastern Europe not only from threats from the West but also from "the encroachments of internal counterrevolution" such as occurred in 1956 and 1968 ("Fraternity Born in Combat," *Za rubezhom* [Moscow], no. 19 [May 6, 1976], p. 7).

2. It is interesting that the memory of this historical episode, which seems to have been almost forgotten at the time, was revived by both the Soviets and the Czechs during the crisis of 1968.

slovakia was an ally of the USSR. Czechoslovakia's mass-based Communist party, which the Soviets considered "outstanding among the European parties," further enhanced the natural affinity between the two countries.[3]

In contrast, the non-Slavic Hungarians reject Pan-Slavism and have harbored traditionally anti-Russian and anti-Soviet sentiments, exacerbated by memories of Russia's suppression of Lájos Kossuth's 1849 uprising, by the short-lived Soviet Hungarian republic of Béla Kun in 1919, and by Hungary's struggle against the Russians in both world wars. These traditional feelings of antipathy were reciprocated by the Russians and were heightened, as Nikita Khrushchev admitted, following World War II, especially among the Red Army.[4] Weakness in the Hungarian communist movement—the party's small, conspiratorial nature prior to World War II—contributed to negative Soviet perceptions.

Generally speaking, contemporary Soviet interests in Czechoslovakia and Hungary are consistent with the general strategy the Soviets have envisioned for all of Eastern Europe. Nonetheless, the differences of perception and historical experience continue to be reflected in the somewhat greater importance that Moscow appears to attach to its Czechoslovak ally. While together they form the central sector of the security *cordon sanitaire* (Warsaw Treaty Organization, WTO) along the USSR's western flank, it is Czechoslovakia, on the West German boundary, that provides a buffer between the USSR and NATO; Hungary borders only on neutral Austria and quasi-neutral Yugoslavia. Similarly, both countries form part of a less visible but no less vital political *cordon sanitaire* guarding the Soviet Union from hostile ideological incursions and generally enhancing its international respectability. However, while Moscow displayed an equal degree of sensitivity toward the emergence of pluralistic socialism in Budapest and Prague, the postinvasion periods in the two countries have witnessed marked differences, with greater importance attached to the preservation of political orthodoxy in Czechoslovakia than in Hungary. Finally, while both Czechoslovakia and Hungary are integral members of the Council for Mutual Economic Assistance (CMEA) and contribute to the realization of Soviet economic goals in the Third World, it is again Czechoslovakia, with its highly developed industrial base and advanced arms industry,[5] that has played the more important role. A question to be

3. *Khrushchev Remembers*, ed. Strobe Talbott, (Boston: Little, Brown, 1970), p. 362.
4. Veljko Mićunović, *Moscow Diary* (New York: Doubleday, 1980), pp. 134–35. Mićunović was the Yugoslav ambassador to the USSR from 1956 until 1958.
5. This was reported by many Czechoslovak leaders and their advisers, including the director of the Institute of International Politics and Economy, the late Josef Šnejdárek. See Jiri Valenta, *Soviet Intervention in Czechoslovakia, 1968: Anatomy of a Decision* (Baltimore: Johns Hopkins University Press, 1979), p. 134.

addressed in the course of this chapter is whether the lessons of the 1970s and the changing economic and political conditions of the 1980s may alter Soviet perceptions—and expectations—of these two East European allies.

THE HUNGARIAN REVOLUTION AND THE PRAGUE SPRING

Similarities exist between the Hungarian Revolution of 1956 and the Czechoslovak peaceful revolution of 1968, known as the Prague Spring. Both occurred because of the complex interaction of a number of common internal and external factors. In each case the population was generally dissatisfied with political and economic conditions, especially the suppression of individual liberties, the Sovietization of the way of life, and power struggles culminating in a polarization of the leadership between reformers and discredited politicians. These were the most significant internal factors that would lead to revolutionary change.

In both countries, broader Soviet domestic and foreign policies played a role. In the Hungarian case, the evolving Soviet strategy of peaceful coexistence with the West, including the peace treaty with Austria, rapprochement with Yugoslavia, and the program of de-Stalinization, shaped the course of events. Coupled with these issues was a succession struggle within the Soviet Presidium, centering on Khrushchev's controversial foreign and domestic policies, which was linked to a factional struggle within the Hungarian leadership.

During the Czech crisis, Soviet preoccupation with China and the internal problems accompanying Brezhnev's consolidation of power at home significantly affected the setting within which the Czechoslovak reforms unfolded. Soviet absorption with these problems allowed the Czechoslovak reform program of democratization and serious infighting between members of the Czechoslovak ruling elite to go almost unnoticed by the Soviet leadership until matters came to a head in 1968.

However, there were also many significant differences between Hungary in 1956 and Czechoslovakia in 1968. Hungary's revolution did not come about so gradually as the revolution in Czechoslovakia twelve years later. In 1953 Hungarian Premier Imre Nagy initiated, with Soviet approval, the New Course program, which, among other things, abolished police terrorism and political prison camps and promoted policies favoring economic consumerism. Even though there were reforms, the reforms did not lead directly to the revolution. On the contrary, optimism generated by Nagy's New Course gave way to frustration after his removal in early 1955, which in turn set the stage for the radicalization of Hungarian society. When revolution came, it was not the climactic phase of a gradual process of reformism, as in Czechoslovakia, but rather a sudden response to a series of events in Poland that reached a peak when the Soviets threatened to intervene against the new regime of Władysław Gomułka in October 1956. Popular sympathy for Poland, Hungary's traditional ally, approached a critical point during a peaceful student demonstration in Budapest on October 23, 1956. This event provoked the first outbreak of violence. Thus, like most violent revolutions, the one in Hungary did not come at a time of popular despair but rather during a period of increased expectations for rapid social change.

Soviet mismanagement of the situation in Hungary shortly before the actual revolution contributed to the conflagration. After some hesitation, Soviet leaders chose the discredited politician Mátyás Rákosi to implement de-Stalinization in Hungary. When this solution failed, they selected another equally disreputable politician, Ernö Gerö. Although the Soviets did not anticipate the revolution, shortly beforehand they did assess Hungary as "the weakest point in the socialist camp"[6] because conservative leaders there were already having to fight the emerging freedom of dissidents and intellectuals. Just a few days before the revolution, the Soviets placed their units in Hungary and Romania on a state of alert.[7]

Nagy was restored to the premiership shortly after the wave of street violence that occurred on October 23. A first Soviet intervention at this time, involving only a few battalions of tanks, was ill-planned and poorly executed. It only made the situation worse. In response, demonstrators joined by some Hungarian military units formed pockets of resistance and battled the Soviets. After four days the Soviets concluded a cease-fire with the Nagy government and agreed to withdraw their troops from Budapest, giving an illusion of victory to the rebels. Afterward, the Soviet leaders A. I. Mikoyan and M. I. Suslov were sent to Budapest to negotiate, if possible, a diplomatic solution to the crisis.

A somewhat romantic Communist with humanistic tendencies, much like Alexander Dubček, Nagy was the last individual in Hungary to want a revolution. He was completely unprepared for his new role.[8] His supporters convinced him that a new program of sweeping political reforms going far beyond the New Course program might be implemented successfully. However, the revolution soon went far beyond Nagy's and his advisers' ideas of reform. Nagy became prime minister in order to restore order, but by then the revolution had assumed its own dynamics. The party had almost entirely disintegrated. The revolution became a spon-

6. Mićunović, *Moscow Diary*, pp. 116–21.

7. See "The Report on Hungary," *United Nations Review*, vol. 4 (Aug. 1957), p. 7, and J. M. Mackintosh, *Strategy and Tactics of Soviet Foreign Policy* (London: Oxford University Press, 1962), pp. 165–78.

8. See the most comprehensive analysis of the Hungarian Revolution by Bill Lomax, *Hungary 1956* (New York: St. Martin's Press, 1976), p. 69.

taneous mass movement, often without leadership and marred by incidents of violence by street mobs. Nagy's name was frequently used for actions he did not know about and would have opposed.

The situation in 1968 in Czechoslovakia was very different. The enthusiasm of the Czechs did not match the revolutionary temper and élan of the Hungarians in 1956, and, perhaps for this reason, their Prague Spring was more gradual, legalistic, and tolerant. Unlike the Hungarian Revolution, the peaceful revolution in Czechoslovakia was a broad and very thorough program, initiated from above and implemented without violence over a period of several months.

Notwithstanding the differences, factional struggles within Czechoslovakia's leadership, like those in Hungary, served as catalysts for subsequent developments. The power conflict in the Czechoslovak Communist party resulted in the replacement of First Secretary Antonín Novotný by Dubček in January 1968.[9]

In contrast to their actions in Hungary on behalf of Rákosi, the Soviets did not attempt to back indefinitely the discredited Novotný, who had desperately sought their support to prevent his ouster. Recognizing that Novotný's position was untenable, the Soviet leadership did not try to prevent his fall. Nor did they dictate his successor.[10]

Novotný's fall was not the result merely of a power struggle but, as with Rákosi, it was conditioned by mounting internal discontent. The domestic sources of the crisis were a belated de-Stalinization program, the economic problems of 1962–63, the ensuing economic reforms, the unresolved Slovak question, the slow process of political rehabilitation, and the open expression of dissent from reform-minded party intellectuals.

Over the several months preceding invasion, the factional struggle evolved into a battle for the democratization of Czechoslovak society. The protracted nature of the political crisis, the continued resistance of Novotný and his supporters to Dubček—a resistance that paralleled that of Rákosi to Nagy in Hungary—and the relaxation of censorship further mobilized public support.

In April 1968, reformist leaders of the Czechoslovak Communist party incorporated their pluralistic concept of socialism "with a human face" into the Action Program, which became the Magna Charta of Dubček's new leadership. This was a comprehensive program that went much further than the initial program of Nagy in Hungary. The main domestic features were greater intraparty democracy; more autonomy for state

9. For the most comprehensive and well-balanced analysis of the origins of the Czechoslovak crisis, see H. Gordon Skilling, *Czechoslovakia's Interrupted Revolution* (Princeton: Princeton University Press, 1976).

10. See Valenta, *Soviet Intervention in Czechoslovakia*, and "Soviet Bureaucratic Politics and Czechoslovakia," *Political Science Quarterly*, 94 (Spring 1979), 55–76.

bureaucracies, other political parties, and the Parliament; restoration of civil rights (freedom of assembly and association); investigations of secret police excesses; greater national rights for Slovaks and other ethnic minorities within a new federal structure; and comprehensive economic reforms. In addition, Dubček permitted the establishment of new political clubs and subsequently abolished censorship. In foreign affairs the Action Program pledged to pursue increasingly autonomous policies but, mindful of the lessons of 1956, Dubček's leadership did not advocate policies that would threaten Soviet security interests. Thus Czechoslovakia's foreign policy orientation, especially its Warsaw Treaty Organization status, would remain unchanged.

Though fanned by an unrestrained news media and not always under control, Czechoslovakia's peaceful revolution was not a spontaneous mass movement, and it was not anticommunist. It was rather clearly socialist in nature. Whereas in Hungary the party had disintegrated, the Czechoslovak party was in the vanguard of the revolution and the primary vehicle for change. Limited pluralism did not cause the party to lose general control; although somewhat diffused, power remained in the hands of the party leadership.

Yet Dubček's Czechoslovakia, no less than Nagy's Hungary, directly challenged Soviet political and ideological interests. While it is true that in Czechoslovakia reforms were only gradually introduced and their outcome was far from certain, from the Soviet point of view the revival of freedom of the press created a dangerous political precedent. As in Hungary in 1956, the situation had the potential to affect the whole East European region and the Soviet Union itself.

Undoubtedly, the Soviet leaders were unanimous in their aversion to the reforms in Czechoslovakia. However, for a long time they were reluctant to invade, viewing force as a last alternative to be used only in an emergency, such as the establishment of a genuinely pluralistic system, Dubček's withdrawal from the WTO, or civil war. It was in May 1968 that the Politburo began to contemplate invasion as a viable option, although warranted only, as Brezhnev later explained, by "extreme circumstances."[11] As in Hungary, some Soviet leaders had sought a nonmilitary solution. This became evident in various negotiations with the Czechoslovak leaders during which Soviet officials began to exert political pressure on Dubček and his colleagues to curb reforms. Among the most crucial of these talks was an unparalleled Politburo-to-Politburo summit conference in the Slovak town of Čierná-nad-Tisou in late July 1968.[12] While

11. Zdeněk Mlynář, *Nightfrost in Prague: The End of Human Socialism* (New York: Karz Publishers, 1980), p. 162. Mlynář was a former secretary of the Czechoslovak Communist Party Control Committee.

12. For a comprehensive analysis, see Valenta, *Soviet Intervention in Czechoslovakia*, pp. 71–85.

political pressure was being applied, the Soviets also exerted psychological pressure on Czechoslovakia under the guise of WTO military maneuvers. WTO troops were deployed on Czechoslovakia's borders and several thousand remained there throughout June and July, despite the Czechoslovak leadership's insistence that they be withdrawn immediately.

THE SOVIET INVASIONS

As conventional wisdom goes, the invasions of Hungary and Czechoslovakia were inevitable in that both were determined by Soviet rules of the game in regard to East European politics. However, the evidence indicates more accurately that both invasions resulted from a complex policymaking process that in turn affected Soviet behavior prior to and during the crises, thereby creating uncertainties about the rules of the game. Ambiguous Soviet actions led the Hungarians and the Czechs and Slovaks to believe that they had a wider latitude for experimentation than was the case.

What were the crucial factors in the Soviet decision to intervene in Hungary? The Soviet ruling elite was undoubtedly united in its belief that developments in Hungary constituted a challenge to the immediate security, political and ideological interests, and long-term economic interests of the USSR in Hungary and potentially in all of Eastern Europe. Although Hungary probably figured lower on the list of security priorities than did other countries in the Northern Tier of the Warsaw Pact, the Soviets nevertheless felt that their security interests lay in preserving intact their East European alliance system. As Khrushchev explained to the Yugoslav ambassador to Moscow, Veljko Mićunović, on October 25, 1956, "Anti-Soviet elements have taken up arms against the 'camp' and the Soviet Union. . . . The West is seeking a revision of the results of World War II and has started in Hungary, and will then go on to crush each socialist state in Europe one by one."[13] Although in Hungary there was a cease-fire and some return to normalcy after the initial outbreak, Nagy did not succeed entirely in restoring order. Occasional acts of brutality against the secret police continued to create an impression of chaos. As Khrushchev is reported to have emphasized with emotion whenever he referred to Nagy's government, "They are slaughtering Communists in Hungary."[14]

The Hungarian Revolution, with its anti-Soviet undertones, had grave short-run political and ideological consequences not only for Hungary but for the entire region. Since there was considerable support for the Hungarian Revolution in Poland and substantial interest and curiosity in other East European countries, the Soviet leadership probably feared

13. Mićunović, *Moscow Diary*, p. 127.
14. Ibid., p. 140.

that the revolution would spill over into these and other countries and undermine Soviet political hegemony in Eastern Europe. According to Khrushchev, "If the counterrevolution did succeed and NATO took root in the midst of the Socialist countries, it would pose a serious threat to Czechoslovakia, Yugoslavia and Romania, not to mention the Soviet Union itself."[15] Indeed, the hard-line regimes in Romania, Czechoslovakia, and East Germany viewed Soviet inaction with alarm and pressed for a speedy solution. In Romania the large Hungarian minority followed the reports about Hungarian revolution sympathetically, while the Romanian regime offered to send troops to help suppress the revolution. Inaction could have produced immediate repercussions in unstable Poland, which might have been tempted to follow the example set by Hungary. Even the Yugoslavs were uneasy. The Soviet media published little actual information about the subject with the exception of a few articles in *Pravda* regarding "counterrevolutionary elements" in Hungary. Nevertheless, Soviet intellectuals and students in large cities such as Moscow followed developments in Hungary with interest through the Voice of America and other Western stations.[16]

Considering the perceived threats to Soviet interests in Hungary and the surrounding region, the second military intervention on November 4 should not have come as a surprise. What is surprising, and revealing, was the hesitation and vacillation of the Soviet leadership, which met almost nonstop between the first and second interventions. Evidence points to substantial indecision and debate during the 10-day cease-fire. Some pushed for an invasion while others such as Khrushchev preferred to "seek a political solution, if such a solution was still possible." During this period Soviet leaders conducted extensive talks with their Warsaw Pact allies, Yugoslavia, and China. As a result, Soviet behavior was an ambiguous mix of compromise and hostility. The ambiguity seemed to be reflected in a Soviet government declaration of October 30 that was published in *Pravda* on October 31.

Although the Soviet leadership was united in its belief that something had to be done in Hungary, they differed, for specific domestic, bureaucratic, and personal reasons, about the means to be used. Furthermore, they could not agree, at least for some time, about the likely response of the West. Moreover, as Khrushchev explained after the crisis, "one or two of our comrades" questioned whether the Hungarians would "take it in the right spirit if we hastened to come their aid."[17] It is probable that

15. *Khrushchev Remembers,* ed. Talbott, p. 417.

16. Julian Gorkin, "Young People Look to the Future (Hungary, Poland and Spain)," *The Review* (Brussels) (Imre Nagy Institute for Political Research), 3 (Oct. 1961); Mićunović, *Moscow Diary,* p. 153.

17. *Népszabadság* (Budapest), Dec. 3, 1958. The author benefited from Professor Paul Milch's assistance with Hungarian sources.

Khrushchev was referring to Mikoyan, who, according to the Hungarian negotiators, had expressed a certain predisposition toward a political solution during the October talks. According to subsequent admissions by Khrushchev, there were "internal" factors leading to the invasion. He believed that his rivals would blame him personally for the Soviet "defeat and the loss of Hungary."[18] Later Khrushchev was more specific, admitting that "Molotov thought that it was my policies that had led to the trouble in Hungary . . . [and] that my tolerance of Tito had encouraged the Hungarians."[19] Indeed, although the invasion did take place, nine months afterward V. M. Molotov and his supporters were almost at the point of ousting Khrushchev, blaming him for the mismanagement of the Hungarian crisis, among other things. According to Khrushchev, the Soviet armed forces also figured prominently in the final decision to intervene.[20]

October 30 was a turning point in the crisis. Under popular pressure, Nagy proclaimed the establishment of a multiparty political system organized around a coalition of several parties as in 1945, thereby violating the first commandment of Soviet rule in the region dictating political control by the local Communist party. Almost immediately the Soviet leadership coalesced around a now commonly perceived set of political, ideological, and security stakes. At the same time, the costs of an invasion were lowered by new international developments. The United States, preoccupied with the coming presidential elections, gave clear signals that it would do nothing in the event of an invasion. Moreover, there occurred a major split in the Western camp when the United States firmly opposed military intervention by England, France, and Israel in Suez, Egypt, on October 30, 1956. This factor, according to Khrushchev, created a "favorable moment" for the second Soviet military intervention in Hungary.[21] Shortly afterward, the Soviet leaders decided in favor of invasion.

On the night of October 31, the Soviet armed forces stationed in Hungary were reinforced with many additional units from the USSR and Romania, a move that contravened an earlier Soviet-Hungarian agreement about the partial withdrawal of Soviet troops from Budapest and signaled active preparation for the actual invasion. The following day, November 1, Nagy, probably suspecting Soviet deception and desperate, announced that Hungary would withdraw from the Warsaw Treaty Organization and assume full neutrality. On the same day, János Kádár, the new first secretary of the Hungarian Socialist Workers' Party and a member of Nagy's government, left Budapest and apparently separated him-

18. Mićunović, *Moscow Diary*, p. 133–34.
19. Khrushchev, in conversation with Egyptian president Anwar Sadat (Mohamed Heikal, *The Sphinx and the Commissar* [New York: Harper & Row, 1978], p. 92).
20. Mićunović, *Moscow Diary*, pp. 153–54.
21. Ibid., p. 134.

self from Nagy's government. He would later serve as head of the new "revolutionary government of workers and peasants" established after the invasion.

The invasion came after three days of tactical deception during which the Soviets, while pursuing further negotiations with a Hungarian governmental delegation, were in fact putting the final touches on the invasion plan. The invasion was a bold, surprise move preceded by the arrest of the Hungarian delegation. Whereas the first intervention involved only 6,000 troops, the second was undertaken by 120,000—those already deployed in Hungary and new troops from the Ukraine and Romania. Hungarian resistance was wiped out, except at two or three points, in only 24 hours. The Soviet commander-in-chief of the operation, General M. S. Malatin, could have almost duplicated the message sent to the Czar in 1849 by Russian Field Marshal Paskiewicz: "Hungary lies at the feet of your Majesty."[22]

Soviet behavior during the Czechoslovak crisis also combined hostility with a spirit of compromise. Because of the peaceful nature of the Czech revolution, however, it took the Soviets longer to agree about the best way to deal with the threat in Czechoslovakia than in Hungary. The Bratislava Declaration of August 3, 1968, drafted at the end of the protracted negotiations between Czechoslovakia and its Warsaw Pact allies, seemed a confirmation of the last-ditch effort made at the earlier Čierna negotiations by those Soviet leaders responsible for foreign affairs who feared the international costs of an invasion and hoped to find a political solution.[23] Although in this respect it resembles the Soviet declaration of October 30, 1956, the Bratislava Declaration contains escape clauses to justify, if necessary, an invasion.[24]

Czechoslovakia was in a better position than Hungary on the eve of invasion. In Hungary the Soviet leadership had committed itself to only a limited retreat from the capital city of Budapest, whereas the Soviets had withdrawn all their forces from Czechoslovakia before the invasion. The last Soviet units left Czechoslovak territory on August 3, 1968, the day the Bratislava Declaration was signed.

22. C. A. Macartney, *Hungary: A Short History* (Chicago: Aldine, 1962), p. 163.

23. During the conference, First Secretary of the Ukrainian Central Committee P. E. Shelest reportedly attempted to break up the negotiations by insulting some Czechoslovak leaders and accusing them of actively supporting separatist tendencies in the Transcarpathian Ukraine. In contrast, Politburo member M. A. Suslov reportedly tried to find a political solution to the crisis. See a posthumously published interview with former member of the Czechoslovak Presidium, J. Smrkovský, in *Listy* (Rome) 5 (Mar. 1975), 4–25, and Valenta, *Soviet Intervention in Czechoslovakia*, pp. 71–92.

24. Compare the Declaration of the Soviet Government in *Pravda*, Oct. 31, 1956, with the Bratislava Declaration, *Pravda*, Aug. 4, 1968.

However, the WTO units halted their homeward trek just outside the Czechoslovak borders, where they remained in encampments poised to invade if necessary. Their disposition highlights the ambiguous nature of the compromises reached at Čierna and Bratislava. The Soviet leaders, still divided and uncertain about future developments, regarded the verbal agreement made at Čierna and Bratislava in the same light in which their predecessors had viewed the understanding reached in Budapest in 1956: provisional accords allowing the option to invade should the situation deteriorate further or the Czechoslovak reformers fail to implement the agreements. From August 3 until August 20, Czechoslovakia, like Hungary, lived out the last moments of a fragile independence, whose precarious nature Dubček, like Nagy, failed to comprehend.

Dubček and his supporters did not have a firm grasp on the domestic situation. The Czechoslovak leadership was divided between those who supported the reforms and those who opposed them, with a sizable number of centrists. Fearing their defeat at the forthcoming party congress on September 9, the Czechoslovak antireformists intensified their efforts during the summer to discredit Dubček and his supporters. They tried to secure Soviet "fraternal assistance" by providing "proof" of "counter-revolution" in Czechoslovakia. Such "proof," supplied to the Politburo by Soviet Ambassador S. V. Chervonenko and KGB operatives in Czechoslovakia, was essential in convincing those in the Soviet leadership who had questioned the wisdom of an invasion.[25] It seems that Chervonenko played a more important role in the resolution of the Czechoslovak conflict than did his counterpart Yuri V. Andropov, who was Soviet ambassador to Hungary in 1956. Unlike Andropov, Chervonenko had a reputation for supporting the most conservative elements in the Czechoslovak leadership opposing Dubček. In Czechoslovakia, where the main threat to the USSR lay in possible future trends of the peaceful revolution, Chervonenko's reports were of crucial importance.

Dubček, like Nagy, was a romantic Communist and a man of integrity incapable of pursuing Machiavellian policies. Although both Nagy and Dubček showed considerable expertise in domestic politics, they were inexperienced in foreign affairs, Dubček particularly so. During the Čierná negotiations, for example, Dubček apparently gave Brezhnev foolish assurances that the radical opponents of reform would remain in the Presidium, a promise he could not hope to keep. Subsequently, Brezhnev felt betrayed by Dubček's interpretation and implementation of this and other agreements.[26]

Dubček's continued implementation of reforms tipped the balance

25. Valenta, *Soviet Intervention in Czechoslovakia*, pp. 123–28, 136.
26. Ibid., pp. 83–84.

toward a more radical Soviet solution. The Soviets did not fear a dramatic change in Czechoslovak foreign policy; it was obvious, particularly after Čierná and Bratislava, that the Dubček government would not deviate from the basic Soviet foreign policy line. Moreover, they knew that Czechoslovakia was not really threatened by NATO or West Germany, in spite of Soviet propaganda to the contrary. What Kremlin leaders did fear was that the security of the Soviet Union would be jeopardized by the "creeping counterrevolution" in Prague. In varying degrees, the Soviet leaders' shared image of Soviet stakes in Eastern Europe—primarily the cohesion of the Warsaw Pact countries and thereby the preservation of the security, political, and, most importantly, ideological status quo—contributed to the tipping of the scales in the Politburo during the debate in August 1968.[27] Soviet fears were not that Czechoslovakia would withdraw from the Warsaw Pact or CMEA but that it would continue to belong to these organizations and influence other members. If Czechoslovak reformism were validated at the forthcoming party congress, it would infect other Warsaw Pact members and perhaps ultimately the Soviet Union itself.

The Soviets were not alone in their apprehension about the Prague Spring contagion. Both Walter Ulbricht of East Germany and Gomułka complained that Dubček was not complying with the agreement[28] and warned Soviet leaders that no guarantee of political stability in their respective countries could be secured unless the Soviet Union used military force to restore order in Czechoslovakia.[29]

As in the case of the Hungarian Revolution, Soviet leaders were also influenced by internal considerations. Foreign radio broadcasts kept Soviet intellectuals, would-be reformers, and especially dissidents in the Ukraine apprised of the crisis in Czechoslovakia. Events in that country were closely followed and there was some support and even sympathy for the Czechs and the Slovaks. Here, particularly, the Soviet leaders responsible for domestic affairs, such as First Secretary of the Ukrainian Central Committee P. E. Shelest, feared the spillover of "Dubčekism" and pushed for a radical solution. Brezhnev, cognizant of Khrushchev's position in 1956, could ill afford to tolerate the image of Czechoslovakia as a "second Hungary." As he told one reformist Czechoslovak leader, "If I had not voted in the Politburo for military intervention, what do you think would have happened? You almost certainly would not be sitting here now. And I probably wouldn't be sitting here either."[30]

27. Ibid., p. 136.

28. For Ulbricht's and Gomułka's roles in the crisis, see the memoirs of the Polish translator for Gomułka, Erwin Weit, who now lives in the West: *At the Red Summit: Interpreter Behind the Iron Curtain* (New York: Macmillan, 1973).

29. Valenta, *Soviet Intervention in Czechoslovakia*, pp. 114–18.

30. Mlynář, *Nightfrost in Prague*, p. 163.

As in Hungary, the decision to intervene was the result of a complex cost-benefit analysis. In the end, the Soviet Politburo concluded that invasion, from a military standpoint, would be a low-risk operation. Dubček's unwillingness to fight and clear signs of U.S. noninvolvement noticeably increased the chance of success. The United States—caught up in Vietnam, racial disturbances, and presidential politics—was, as during the earlier crisis in Hungary, unwilling to do anything on behalf of Czechoslovakia. This position was implied by the public statements of Secretary of State Dean Rusk in July 1968, by President Johnson's strong interest in the early start of SALT negotiations, and by the behavior of the U.S. armed forces in West Germany.[31]

During the night of August 20–21, 1968, 23 Soviet divisions, together with 2 divisions from the Polish and East German armies, 1 from Hungary, and a token brigade from Bulgaria, boldly took Prague and other vital centers. The Soviet generals had obviously learned from their experience in Hungary in 1956, where the first small-scale military intervention was ineffective. The military invasion of Czechoslovakia, on the contrary, was a surprise action, rapid and overwhelming. The Czechoslovak armed forces were unprepared for the invasion. Furthermore, they were given orders not to resist by Dubček, who was anxious not to take any action that might be construed as unfriendly to the Soviets. In 24 hours Czechoslovakia was an occupied country. As in 1956, the Soviets immediately set about establishing a new "revolutionary government," led by Dubček's foes, Alois Indra and Vasil Bil'ak.

SOVIET CONSOLIDATION IN HUNGARY AND CZECHOSLOVAKIA

The following sections compare the processes of consolidation and normalization in postinvasion Hungary and Czechoslovakia. Consolidation refers to the immediate measures initiated by the Soviets to reestablish control not only in Hungary (1956–59) and Czechoslovakia (1968–71) but also in Eastern Europe as a whole. Normalization, on the other hand, describes long-term policies encouraged by the Soviets and developed under specific national conditions over a period spanning a decade or more.

The consolidation-normalization cycles in Hungary and Czechoslo-

---

31. At this point it was not important whether Brezhnev, as he told the Czechoslovak leaders in Moscow, had actually received President Johnson's assurance on August 18 that the United States still honored the Yalta and Potsdam agreements and, by implication, would not try to resist an invasion. (This was reported by the eyewitness Mlynář, *Nightfrost in Prague*, p. 241, but it was denied by Secretary of State Dean Rusk and by Dr. Walt W. Rostow, National Security Adviser to President Johnson, in interviews with this author.) By this date the Soviet Politburo already had enough signals from the U.S. government to know that it would not take action on behalf of Dubček's regime.

vakia occurred under two different Soviet regimes and in two very different periods of Soviet history. Consolidation in Hungary occurred during Khrushchev's own consolidation of power after his victory over the so-called antiparty group, some of whose members opposed his program of de-Stalinization and decentralization of the Soviet economy. The era that followed was characterized by continuous de-Stalinization at home and a premature globalism abroad sparked by the launching of Sputnik in 1957. In contrast, consolidation in Czechoslovakia was colored by more restrictive antireformist policies in the Soviet Union and the selective, yet vigorous and mature globalism of Brezhnev's leadership.

Normalization in Hungary during the 1960s coincided with the emergence of the Czechoslovak reform movement and, for some years, with the period of Khrushchev's reforms in the Soviet Union, in a climate quite different from that which has prevailed since 1968. The invasion of Czechoslovakia and the subsequent consolidation in that country obviously impacted on Soviet policy in Hungary. The Soviets' Hungarian policy was also affected by Brezhnev's recognition of Kádár's substantial achievements. Ironically, these achievements were largely the result of the more permissive atmosphere that characterized Khrushchev's later years.

Yet Soviet consolidation policies in Hungary and Czechoslovakia had some similar features. In both instances, the Soviets renewed their efforts to assure stability, not only in the invaded countries but elsewhere in Eastern Europe. In so doing both Khrushchev and Brezhnev encouraged closer coordination and integration among East European nations in order to better monitor any "deviations." Hence, in November 1957, a year after the Hungarian invasion, the Soviets organized a conference of 12 ruling Communist parties, mostly from Eastern Europe, to formulate a joint declaration specifying the limits of "specific roads toward socialism."[32] After this conference similar attempts were made to develop closer economic coordination within the CMEA.

As in Hungary earlier, the lessons learned in Czechoslovakia strongly influenced the Soviet Union's relations with its Warsaw Pact allies. Soviet policymakers were determined to prevent the occurrence of a "future Czechoslovakia" by curbing the far-reaching reforms that had begun during Khrushchev's era and culminated in the Prague Spring.[33] Shortly after the invasion, Brezhnev followed Khrushchev's example and tried to strengthen the alliance system in Eastern Europe. His policy of integration was multidimensional and included all aspects of Soviet-East Euro-

---

32. "The Declaration of the Twelve Communist Parties," *Pravda* (Moscow), Nov. 1, 1957.

33. See Brezhnev's speech, *Pravda*, Mar. 31, 1971.

pean relations. The insistence that multilateral meetings at all levels be held at "regular intervals, and not from time to time" reflected the Soviets' quest for more effective coordination and control.[34]

In both countries there was initial confusion over who should be in charge of consolidation on the local level. During the invasions the Soviets referred to Nagy and Dubček as "right wingers" who paid lip service to "counterrevolution,"[35] although several days later they tried to involve both Nagy and Dubček in the consolidation process. Nagy refused. In Czechoslovakia, the more compliant Dubček was released from prison and reinstated to commence the consolidation process. The Soviets soon realized, however, that they could not hope to consolidate postinvasion developments in either Hungary or Czechoslovakia without first replacing Nagy and Dubček and the reformers around them whom they considered weak and unreliable. At the same time, the Soviets also recognized that compromised politicians such as Rákosi and Novotný were unsuited to the task of consolidation. This was particularly true of Rákosi, whom Khrushchev described as an "idiot" who "does not understand the most elementary things."[36]

Soviet influence upon the selection of the new leaders was decisive though not exclusive. On November 3, after the decision to invade Hungary had been made, the Soviet leaders still were not disposed to accept Kádár as head of the new government. Although Khrushchev thought that Kádár was a "good guy," the Soviets' original choice was the old Comintern official, Ferenc Münnich. Had Münnich been chosen, the process of normalization in Hungary might have been much harsher. Khrushchev displayed flexibility when he apparently heeded the Yugoslav leadership's objections to Münnich on political grounds.[37] Kádár was a more attractive candidate in part because he had spent much of the Stalinist era in prison while Münnich served as ambassador to Moscow.

In Czechoslovakia the Soviets also displayed flexibility in selecting a new figure to help consolidate their control. The original plan had been to replace Dubček and his supporters with a new pro-Soviet government led by Dubček's opponents, Indra and Bil'ak. For two days, Chervonenko tried unsuccessfully to create a pro-Soviet government under their leadership. Subsequently the Soviet Politburo decided to compromise, at least temporarily (until April 1969), with Dubček and other "right-wing opportunists" who had been arrested as traitors during the invasion. Gustáv Husák became a possible Soviet choice as Dubček's successor during

34. Brezhnev, *New Times* (Moscow), no. 9 (Feb. 1976), p. 32.
35. For a similar indictment of Nagy and Dubček, see *Pravda*, Nov. 4, 1956, and Aug. 22, 1968.
36. Mićunović, *Moscow Diary,* p. 136.
37. Ibid., pp. 136–37.

postinvasion negotiations in Moscow in August 1968, when Soviet Premier A. N. Kosygin praised him as "a competent comrade and a wonderful Communist." Kosygin admitted that "we didn't know him personally before, but he quite impressed us *here*."[38] Husák, like Kádár, had been imprisoned during Stalin's time and this undoubtedly strengthened his candidacy.

During the years of consolidation, the policies of the Hungarian and Czechoslovak regimes were greatly influenced, if not almost wholly determined, by the Soviets. In both countries the Soviets were committed to the policy of eliminating all political opposition, even if this necessitated using coercion and terror. In Hungary, as a consequence of Soviet pressure, Nagy and some of his associates were tried and executed while others were jailed. In Czechoslovakia, the Soviets did not impose exemplary punishment on Dubček and his supporters. Nevertheless, repression in Czechoslovakia was more insidious than in Hungary. In Hungary repression lasted only a few years, but in Czechoslovakia it persisted into the late 1970s.

Hungary and Czechoslovakia were viewed by the Soviets as highly unreliable allies after their respective revolutions, particularly in terms of security and politico-ideological matters. Although the revolution in Hungary came as a shock to the Soviets, the anti-Russian and anti-Soviet sentiments that accompanied it were perhaps less of a surprise. Czechoslovak "deviation" was probably more shocking, since it altered the image of Czechoslovakia as one of the Soviet Union's more loyal allies.

Not surprisingly, the military and party establishments were the most heavily influenced by the consolidation processes. Soviet leaders encouraged a purge of officers in the armed forces of both countries. In Hungary, approximately 20% of the officer corps were purged. The Czechoslovak armed forces were not involved in actual fighting against the Soviets as some of the Hungarian units had been in 1956. Still, the invasion was detrimental to their morale. Subsequently, 9,000 officers, including 20 generals, were dismissed. Moreover, 57.8% of the officers under 30 later left the army of their own accord. Many of those who remained continued to feel bitter about the invasion.[39] There was also a KGB-instigated purge of the secret police in both countries.

The Hungarian party disintegrated during the revolution and had to be rebuilt (there were only 17,818 members in December 1956). Although the purges affected several thousand "revisionist" elements in

38. Mlynář, *Nightfrost in Prague*, p. 221 (emphasis added).

39. Iván Völgyes, "The Political and Professional Perspectives of the Hungarian Armed Forces," *Journal of Political and Military Sociology*, 5 (Fall 1977), 279–94; Rudolf Woller, *Warsaw Pact Reserve System: A White Paper* (Munich: Bernard & Graefe Verlag, 1978); private interviews.

Hungary, they never reached the proportions of the Czechoslovak purges. In Czechoslovakia the party itself had led the Prague Spring and therefore tens of thousands of so-called unhealthy elements had to be eliminated. Membership in the Czechoslovak party subsequently dropped from 1,700,000 to 1,200,000. Many were purged, but others left of their own accord.[40]

NORMALIZATION IN HUNGARY AND CZECHOSLOVAKIA

Although the consolidation processes in Hungary and Czechoslovakia in the aftermath of the Soviet invasions had similar features, the long-term processes of normalization encouraged by the Soviets have differed considerably. In Hungary the pattern of normalization led to the evolution of a flexible regime tolerated not only by the Soviets but also to a great extent by the Hungarians. In Czechoslovakia the pattern of normalization adhered to up to the early 1980s has helped to fortify a regime acceptable to the Soviets but a good deal less acceptable to the Czechs and Slovaks. Indeed, it can be argued that in Czechoslovakia consolidation has not given way to genuine normalization due to the vestiges of 1968.

The same is not true of Hungary. Kádár's famous slogan of 1961—"Whosoever is not against us is with us"—reflects his strategy for building national alliances and achieving domestic liberalization.[41] The fact that Kádár's pattern of normalization was encouraged by Khrushchev and tolerated by Brezhnev attests that normalization in Hungary has not changed the basic features of the system. Hungary remains a Communist state in which strategic policymaking is still concentrated at the top of the ruling elite. At the same time, Kádár's normalization brought an end to terror and ushered in political relaxation. Normalization in Hungary has included a general amnesty for political prisoners, the relaxation of censorship, and the uninterrupted transmission of Western radio broadcasts (which had been jammed prior to this). It also resulted in such political innovations as increased duties for Parliament, limited multiple-candidate competition in national elections, and greater responsibilities for social organizations such as trade unions. The gradual liberalization of the Hungarian political scene has been accompanied by increasing economic and cultural relaxation as well as contacts with the West, including active reconciliation with the Hungarian diaspora. Thus both Khrushchev and Brezhnev tolerated the implementation, in subdued form, of some of Nagy's original ideas and certain aspects of the Prague Spring.

This was especially true in the economy, where the introduction of the

40. Vladimir Kusin, *From Dubček to Charter 77: A Study of "Normalization" in Czechoslovakia, 1968–1978* (New York: St. Martin's Press, 1978).

41. Kádár's interview with *L'Unità* (Rome), Dec. 1, 1969.

New Economic Mechanism (NEM) in January 1968 took Kádárization beyond what Khrushchev used to call "goulash socialism"—contemporary consumer satisfaction often bought at the cost of future productivity and economic growth. The new policy, tolerated by Brezhnev's leadership even after the invasion of Czechoslovakia, advocated not only a shift in economic priorities favoring consumer and agricultural sectors but also substantial decentralization of the command economy. This was achieved by granting autonomy to individual enterprises and introducing new forms of the market-type economy, including a new system of pricing. As a result of the cautious liberalization under Kádár's leadership, Hungary in the 1970s became one of the most prosperous East European countries, with a more or less satisfied population. These achievements, though perhaps not the means by which they were achieved, are viewed positively by the Soviet leadership.

Kádár's slogan can almost be reversed in describing the process of normalization in Czechoslovakia in the 1970s: "Whosoever is not with us is against us." Husák's normalization was a great deal more oppressive than normalization in Hungary. Even now, in the early 1980s, thousands of Dubček's supporters who were expelled from the party are forbidden to pursue their professions while their children are denied access to higher education.

Czechoslovak citizens enjoy fewer civil liberties than their Hungarian neighbors. Since the invasion the Czechoslovak regime has repeatedly used coercion and persecution to maintain stability. Unlike in Hungary, there is a limited but nonetheless significant dissident movement of at least several hundred centered on the Charter 77 platform, which calls for a strong defense of civil liberties and political rights. In contrast to Hungary, the Czechoslovak regime sometimes uses detention, forced exile, and even political trials, that is, Soviet methods, to deal with dissidents.

In the 1970s, while Hungary continued on the path of market-oriented reform, Czechoslovakia, at Soviet insistence, gradually returned to more centralized economic planning. Although the Czechoslovak regime has never returned to Dubček's experimentation with market-oriented changes and enterprise autonomy, some limited economic measures, needed to improve efficiency, were introduced in the late 1970s. The current regime places primary emphasis on social security and stability through the constant improvement of the standard of living—devoid of "heretical reforms."

The complex of factors that has conditioned the evolution toward domestic liberalization in Hungary and the retardation of the same process in Czechoslovakia includes, in particular, the changing political climates in the USSR and Eastern Europe, Soviet perceptions of the overall domestic situations in the two countries, actual Soviet policies, Kádár's and Husák's personalities, and factional struggles within their leaderships.

The political environment in the USSR and Eastern Europe changed a great deal between 1956 and 1968. Whereas Khrushchev's reformism helped to advance Kádár's normalization process in Hungary, normalization in Czechoslovakia was conditioned by the more restrictive Soviet and East European environment that began to materialize in 1968–69. The more conservative nature of Brezhnev's politics and perhaps such foreign policy considerations as the perceived need to forestall the erosive influence of détente in the 1970s contributed to the new milieu.

Another factor that favored Kádár's policies was the Soviets' perception of the domestic situation in Hungary, which was conditioned by the memory of 1956. In Hungary, unlike Czechoslovakia, the Soviets suffered several thousand casualties. This commanded Soviet respect for the Hungarian temper and willingness to fight and softened Soviet policies toward Hungary. After the revolution the Soviets had basically two policy choices regarding Hungary: They could reign with terror or tolerate gradual liberalization. Kádár, for whom 1956 was not merely a "counterrevolution" but a national "tragedy,"[42] sensed then that Khrushchev would eventually opt for the latter choice. It seems that the costs incurred by the Soviets in 1956 were a bargaining chip played skillfully by Kádár in subsequent negotiations with the Soviet leaders on the nature of normalization. The Soviets did not want a recurrence of the bloodshed.

A third reason—perhaps the most important one—for Soviet tolerance was Kádár's personality, which, Charles Gati has argued, makes him unique among East European leaders.[43] He is an extraordinarily skillful and flexible politician with a gift for survival, but Kádár is also a simple man of modest upbringing and education, qualities that have made him a popular figure in Hungary. This is a remarkable achievement for any East European politician, but it is especially so in this case since Kádár was considered a traitor by most Hungarians during the period of consolidation. At the same time, he has convinced the Soviets of his loyalty and ability to maintain stability in Hungary. In contrast to their view of Nagy and Dubček, the Soviet leaders have confidence in Kádár and in his skill in managing the reforms instituted in Hungary.[44]

Though not Khrushchev's first choice in 1956, Kádár was able to gain

42. Kádár's speech in Denis Sinor, ed., *Modern Hungary: Readings from the New Hungarian Quarterly* (Bloomington: Indiana University Press, 1977), p. 42.

43. Charles Gati, "The Kádár Mystique," *Problems of Communism*, 23 (May–June 1974), 23–27; William Shawcross, *Crime and Compromise: János Kádár and the Politics of Hungary since Revolution* (New York: Dutton, 1974).

44. See Soviet praise of Kádár's able struggle on two fronts (*Pravda*, Nov. 25, 1970).

the latter's confidence by virtue of being a "centrist" politician, determined to resist all extremism, yet reform-minded, with an impeccable anti-Stalinist background. Under Khrushchev's patronage, Kádár became the sole acceptable choice for Hungary. His position was strengthened in 1957 after Khrushchev's victory over the "antiparty group" and again during the second wave of de-Stalinization initiated at the 22d Congress of the Communist Party of the Soviet Union (CPSU) in 1961.[45] Only after this congress was Kádár able to remove from the leadership those who opposed his policies of national reconciliation. Kádár's successes would have been impossible without Khrushchev's support. In contrast, the more restricted political climate in which Czechoslovak leaders had to work in the 1970s ruled out the possibility of introducing reforms.

The fall of Khrushchev in 1964 shocked Kádár. Still, he was able to develop a special relationship with Brezhnev, although not so close as the one he had enjoyed with Khrushchev. The crucial test of the Brezhnev–Kádár understanding occurred in 1968 during the Czechoslovak crisis. Kádár was aware of the ongoing Soviet debate about the events in Czechoslovakia and he had serious reservations about a military invasion. Czechoslovak reforms were a boon to Kádárization in Hungary—particularly the NEM experiment begun in January 1968. As Kádár stated in a private conversation with Czechoslovak leaders, "Successful reforms in Czechoslovakia would spell hope for similar developments in Hungary."

On August 17, three days before the invasion, Kádár initiated a meeting between himself and Dubček in what appeared to be a last attempt to warn Dubček about the limits of Soviet patience. Although he revealed neither the plans nor the timing of the invasion (perhaps because he was unaware of them), Kádár's words indicated that his understanding of the Soviet leaders was very perceptive: "Do you *really* not know what kind of people you are dealing with?"[46] Given his own experience, Kádár could only accept the invasion as an unhappy necessity.[47]

After the invasion, some Soviet and East European writers began to criticize the Hungarian New Economic Mechanism. Subsequently, in the early 1970s, the Soviets encouraged a curtailment of its more controversial policies. However, because of Soviet preoccupation with the crisis and consolidation in Czechoslovakia and because of Kádár's skillful bargaining, the NEM reforms survived. The Soviets' reserved tolerance of the NEM after 1968 contrasts sharply with their rejection of comparable economic measures in Czechoslovakia and with their immediate stifling

45. For a detailed discussion see the study by William F. Robinson, *The Pattern of Reform in Hungary: A Political, Economic and Cultural Analysis* (New York: Praeger, 1973).
46. Mlynář, *Nightfrost in Prague,* pp. 156–57.
47. Valenta, *Soviet Intervention in Czechoslovakia,* p. 143.

of similar attempts at reform in the USSR. To date, Kádár's regime has managed to maintain domestic flexibility despite Soviet insistence on a return to orthodoxy in Czechoslovakia and its continued preservation in the USSR. Notwithstanding setbacks and slowdowns, the core of the Hungarian reform program has survived. Stubborn and skillful, Kádár has been able to win many concessions from the Soviet leaders.

To what extent was normalization in Czechoslovakia a result of changing Soviet political conditions and preferences and to what extent was it influenced by other factors, such as the personality of Czechoslovak First Secretary Husák, factional struggles in the Czechoslovak leadership, and linkages between Czechoslovak and Soviet politics? The most important factor appears to have been the changing political environment in the USSR and Eastern Europe during the last two decades. In the 1970s, under Brezhnev, there was a marked retreat from Khrushchev's reformism. This change, moreover, favored Soviet *Westpolitik*, which necessitated close coordination of ideological orthodoxy among the countries of Eastern Europe.

Second, in contrast to Hungary, the Soviet military victory in Czechoslovakia was "easy." The Czechs and the Slovaks confirmed an almost unbroken tradition of unarmed resistance against foreign invaders. Only a few dozen Soviet soldiers were killed and most of these mortalities were accidental. Thus Soviet memories of Czechoslovakia in 1968 are less traumatic than their memories of the brutal confrontation in Hungary.

Third, the different patterns of normalization were shaped by the contrasting political positions of Husák and Kádár. When he came to power in April 1969, Husák was viewed by many observers as a possible Czechoslovak Kádár. Like Kádár, Husák had not compromised himself as a politician. Both possessed anti-Stalinist credentials. As Kádár had supported Nagy, so Husák had championed Dubček during the Prague Spring. Despite these similarities, Husák's and Kádár's positions upon assuming power were very different. Husák did not possess the sort of capital Kádár was able to wield in negotiations with Soviet leaders. In other words, Husák's bargaining position was weakened by the Soviets' foreknowledge that the Czechs and Slovaks, who did not resist the invasion, also would not resist the imposition of harsh normalization policies, as the Hungarians probably would have. Furthermore, though Husák was the best candidate from the Soviet point of view, Czechoslovakia had other politicians with centrist beliefs who could have replaced him. Kádár, on the other hand, was indispensable.

Other important differences between Husák and Kádár pertain to their personalities and styles. Although both are good politicians with an instinct for survival, Husák is more conservative. Unlike the proletarian Kádár, who is humble and jovial, Husák, a trained lawyer, is an ambitious individualist and, some would say, an arrogant intellectual with a messianic sense of mission. He is not a member of the dominant Czech nationality and in the past vigorously resisted Prague's traditional centralism, more so than most other Slovak Communist leaders. He is more committed to protecting Slovak national interests than to instituting genuine reforms.

Unlike Kádár, Husák has been challenged at times and even overruled by leaders more conservative than he, such as Bil'ak, Indra, and Antonín Kapek. Nevertheless, there are signs that Husák would like to emulate some of Kádár's normalization policies or at least display greater flexibility. For example, during the early stages of normalization he is credited with having resisted the attempts of his more conservative colleagues to put Dubček and his supporters on trial.[48]

Finally, Husák's failure to model Czechoslovak normalization on the Hungarian pattern is also related to internal Soviet politics, Brezhnev's particular leadership style and attempts by Soviet officials to manipulate Czechoslovak politics. Soviet Ambassador Chervonenko, who played a critical role in preparations for the invasion, was in charge of supervising normalization in Czechoslovakia until 1973. Throughout his service in Czechoslovakia, Chervonenko continued to support the most conservative line and objected to Husák's efforts to remove more conservative rivals such as Bil'ak and Indra.[49] Husák may have inspired Brezhnev's personal confidence but Brezhnev's attitude probably was not shared by all Soviet leaders, at least for some time. Brezhnev's leadership style, certainly during the first half of the 1970s, was more collective than Khrushchev's after 1957, and this probably contributed to factional struggle in the Czechoslovak leadership. The fact that some of Husák's rivals reportedly speculated about Brezhnev's downfall before or during the 24th Congress of the CPSU in 1971 seems to substantiate this.[50]

Brezhnev's victory over Shelest the following year probably strengthened Husák's position. After Shelest was purged, there were reports about the Soviet leadership's review of the situation in Czechoslovakia which indicated Shelest was to blame for providing inaccurate information to the Soviet leadership about developments in Czechoslovakia prior to the invasion.[51] Although this created uncertainties in the Prague leadership, Husák did not succeed in eliminating his more conservative rivals, as Kádár had done in the early 1960s.

48. Kusin, *From Dubček to Charter 77*, p. 161.
49. Private interviews. For the disagreement of Bil'ak with Husák's "blue sky theory," according to which the party would forgive Dubček's supporters their sins of 1968, see *Rudé právo* (Prague), Nov. 13, 1972.
50. Kusin, *From Dubček to Charter 77*, p. 139.
51. *Le Monde* (Paris), June 17–18, 1973.

Khrushchev's overwhelming dominance after the purge of his rivals in 1957 and his direct support of Kádár's leadership enhanced Kádár's ability to consolidate power and dismiss his rivals. Likewise, Brezhnev's consensus style, which was unaffected by Shelest's purge, has helped to sustain factional politics within the Czechoslovak leadership. Also weighing on Czechoslovak internal politics is the probability that the Soviet leaders, including Brezhnev himself, had no desire for Husák to become another Kádár. In the absence of a strong figure at the top it became easier for Brezhnev and his colleagues to play off one faction against another.

SOVIET POLICIES TOWARD CZECHOSLOVAKIA AND HUNGARY, 1970 TO THE PRESENT

To what extent are Soviet relations with Hungary and Czechoslovakia burdened by the legacies of 1956 and 1968? How do the Soviets view Hungary's and Czechoslovakia's military, security, political, ideological, and economic contributions to the Warsaw Pact alliance?

In both Hungary and Czechoslovakia there is great dependence on the USSR, whose presence is strongly felt. There are some significant differences, however, in Soviet attitudes toward Hungary and Czechoslovakia. The circumstantial evidence suggests that at the beginning of the 1970s the Soviets considered Hungary to be more stable than Czechoslovakia. In real terms this is attributable to the success of Kádár's program of normalization, although subjectively it is also partly a result of the fading memories of the 1956 revolution. In contrast, the legacy of the 1968 invasion of Czechoslovakia is still strong in the early 1980s, not only because the invasion and consolidation were recent events but also because they led to a different course of normalization.

Czechoslovakia's diminishing role as a reliable and active Soviet ally is nowhere more evident than in Czechoslovak relations with the Third World. Until 1968, Czechoslovakia was a major proxy for Soviet policies in the developing countries, supplying substantial quantities of arms as well as military, security, and economic advisers and technicians. Czechoslovakia's key position declined after the Soviet invasion. Although still an arms supplier to Soviet allies in the Third World, Czechoslovakia has been surpassed in the second function by the German Democratic Republic, whose military and security advisers were active in the 1970s and early 1980s in Africa (Angola, Ethiopia, and Mozambique), the Middle East (South Yemen), and Central America (Nicaragua).

Because it lacks the large industrial base and the indigenous arms industry of Czechoslovakia, Hungary has never played an important role in assisting the Soviets in the Third World. In Moscow's division of labor among its East European clients the more reliable Hungary is best suited as a liaison with the Western countries, Yugoslavia, and the West European Communist parties. The more effectively Kádár demonstrated his firm grip on Hungary in the 1960s and 1970s, the more Hungary's value and usefulness as a Soviet ally improved.

Neither Hungary's nor Czechoslovakia's armed forces are viewed as a great asset to Warsaw Pact security.[52] Reconstruction of the armed forces of both countries began only after the purges of the consolidation period. There are numerous Soviet advisers in both armed forces, though they seem to have assumed a more active role in Czechoslovakia than in Hungary.[53]

As far as contributions to the political viability of the alliance are concerned, Kádár's regime rates higher than Husák's. In Soviet eyes, the reliability of the Hungarian regime has risen in proportion to the ability of Kádár to demonstrate his control and to improve his rapport with the Hungarian people. Although ostensibly at variance with some tenets of orthodox Soviet ideology, the Hungarian regime under Kádár functions within the limits set by the "general laws of socialist construction." As one Soviet commentator stated in 1978:

Does a "Hungarian model" exist? It does. But not in the way Western papers write about it. In Hungary the general laws of socialist construction are in every respect clearly and tangibly asserted. It is not forgotten in Hungary what the country owes the socialist community.[54]

The conduct of internal affairs is almost exclusively in the hands of the Hungarian government, provided that its policies do not pass significantly beyond the outer limits set by the Soviets.

Nevertheless, some short-lived ideological differences between the USSR and Hungary developed during the early 1970s. Soviet commentators at the time revealed a degree of anxiety over ideological reliability in Hungary and for a short while criticized "various manifestations of nationalist ideology," "pro-Western sentiment," and "philistine attitudes" in connection with the NEM program.[55] There was some speculation that the Soviets were very reluctant to commit themselves to the delivery of

52. Dale R. Herspring and Iván Völgyes, "Political Reliability in the Eastern European Warsaw Pact Armies," *Armed Forces and Society*, 6 (Winter 1980), 270–96.

53. In addition to Soviet military advisers, there are also a number of Soviet secret service advisers in both countries. However, the activities of the Czechoslovak secret service seem to be more integrated with those of the KGB than do the operations of the Hungarian secret service. (This information is from private interviews.)

54. V. Kuznetsov, *New Times* (Moscow), no. 14 (Apr. 1978), p. 24.

55. See V. Gerasimov and M. Odinets, "Measures of Responsibility," *Pravda*, Dec. 1971, and "Coordination of Solidarity," *Pravda*, Feb. 3, 1972. For Kádár's defense of his reforms, see hints in his speech published shortly afterward in *Népszabadság* (Budapest), Feb. 13, 1972.

raw materials on a long-term basis and that they might have been contemplating using economic instruments to curb Hungarian reforms. This Soviet policy of pressuring Hungary occurred during Soviet-sponsored consolidation in Czechoslovakia, which was bound to affect Hungarian policy. Being Hungary's most important trading partner and its almost exclusive supplier of raw materials, including oil, has put the USSR in a position of significant economic power.

The "mini" ideological dispute of 1972 was soon overcome because, unlike Dubček, Kádár demonstrated his ability to limit the reforms. Under pressure and attacks from Soviet as well as East German and Czechoslovak ideologists, Kádár was forced to curb some liberal features of his domestic policies. In 1974–75 he came under internal pressure, most likely prompted by Soviet criticism, and had to agree to demote some of his more liberal associates in the leadership: Rezső Nyers, Lajos Fehér, and Jenö Fock. At the same time, despite rumors of his impending retirement, Kádár was able to skillfully circumvent conservative opposition to his reforms at the 1975 Party Congress. Kádár seemed to be even more successful at this during the Party Congress of 1980, when he brought about a surprise reshuffle in the leadership aimed at strengthening his position and facilitating continuation of his cautious reform policy. This happened, as on a few earlier occasions, with Soviet consent. Kádár is too valuable an asset for the Soviets to forsake on the grounds of ideological misdemeanors.

By contrast, although the Soviets probably see maintenance of the status quo as their only option under the circumstances, they appear to be somewhat dissatisfied with the precarious stability that exists in Czechoslovakia. Not all Soviet leaders, in the first half of the 1970s, were pleased with the unnecessary excesses of normalization. This is suggested by the still unexplained contacts of Soviet officials with former Czechoslovak Presidium member and Dubček supporter Josef Smrkovský in the years 1972 through 1974. It is said that Smrkovský was asked by his Soviet contacts to critically evaluate Husák's program of normalization.[56] Furthermore, the Soviets never permitted the trial of Dubček and his supporters, and only in 1979 did they back the Czechoslovak decision to conduct political trials of some Charter 77 members, but without enthusiasm. It is quite possible that there were some earlier Soviet attempts to moderate extreme hard-line policies in Czechoslovakia. Czechoslovak Minister of the Interior Jaromír Obzina, who had close relations with his Soviet counterpart, then-KGB chief Yuri Andropov, was reported on several occasions to have expressed more moderate attitudes toward Charter 77 than some other officials, who pressured for a "tough" re-

56. "About Soviet Connections and a Letter from Brezhnev," *Listy*, 5 (Feb. 1975), 10–12.

sponse.[57] In Hungary, in marked contrast to the situation in Czechoslovakia, several leading intellectuals expressed their support of the Chartists without any significant repercussions. Because of Kádár's flexible policies and the Soviet toleration thereof very little dissidence exists in Hungary.

Because the Soviets fear the residues of Dubčekism in Czechoslovakia, they have perhaps encouraged the development of competing factions within Husák's leadership and have advocated more orthodox policies for the purpose of maintaining stability. The excesses of the Czechoslovak hard-liners is the price that the Soviet leadership has to pay for this kind of stability.

How do the Soviets view Hungarian and Czechoslovak economic performance, especially in the plan period that ended in 1980? The economic performance of both countries was affected by the skyrocketing price of world energy sources beginning with the OPEC price increases of 1973–74. Furthermore, new policy concerns and economic pressures on the Soviet leaders, resulting from the Polish crisis of the early 1980s, seem to have altered their usual expectations concerning their allies' economic behavior. The Soviet leaders probably still look upon Czechoslovakia's highly developed industry as more significant than that of Hungary. However, Hungary's economic recovery since the revolution and its growing contributions to CMEA prosperity and integration processes have caused the Hungarian economy to become increasingly important to the USSR. Because of this and the emergence of new economic pressures in the last half of the 1970s, particularly the critical energy situation referred to, the Soviets seem to be well disposed toward Kádár's unorthodox, though flexible, economic policies and less approving of Husák's management of the problematical Czechoslovak economy.

The Soviets closely monitor events in Hungary and Czechoslovakia and try to influence policies through their local representatives in the Warsaw Treaty Organization, the KGB, the Department of Liaison with Communist and Workers' Parties (DLCWP), the Ministry of Foreign Affairs, and the Ministry of Foreign Trade. The presence of Soviet advisers is especially apparent in defense and security matters. In addition Soviet leaders try to control events in both countries by involving them in varying degrees in the multilateral integration of the Warsaw Pact alliance. Strong Soviet influence and, at times, firm direction were present in almost every facet of the foreign affairs of Czechoslovakia and Hungary during the 1970s. Although neither country deviates significantly from Soviet policy guidelines, a close look at how the East European states correlate their foreign policy with that of the USSR suggests that Hunga-

---

57. Private interviews.

ry occupies a middle ground among Soviet allies while Czechoslovakia, since 1969, is among the most conformist. Though Hungary does not exercise autonomy in foreign affairs, occasionally its treatment of such issues as the Czechoslovak crisis in 1968, détente and Eurocommunism during the 1970s, and the Polish crisis in 1980–81 displayed nuances not found in the formal Soviet line concerning these issues.

In the 1970s Kádár was supportive of all aspects of Soviet *Westpolitik.* Given his regime's performance, Kádár naturally did not fear détente with the United States or rapprochement with West Germany, as did some of his Czechoslovak colleagues. In fact, he seemed to be more enthusiastic about some aspects of détente than even Brezhnev because of the economic needs and European orientation of Hungary and his own desire to demonstrate more flexibility in foreign affairs. Hungary generally gives vigorous support to the USSR on most important security and foreign policy issues. Kádár's reputation as a liberal and a skillful mediator is an asset that the Soviets value for its usefulness in dealing with the countries of the West, the West European Communist parties, and Yugoslavia.

The less secure Czechoslovak regime has been more fearful of détente and rapprochement with the West. During the 1970s some elements of the Czechoslovak leadership displayed remarkably paranoid attitudes toward détente, fearing (with some reason) that opening the East to Western influences, including Eurocommunism, could lead to a new Prague Spring. As the Soviet leaders value Kádár's mediating skills, they also value the orthodox and generally subservient orientation of the Czechoslovak leadership. Whenever they need to criticize various deviations in other ruling and nonruling parties, but do not want to do the "dirty work" themselves, Czechoslovak hard-liners such as Bil'ak are more than happy to serve as instruments of Soviet foreign policy. Bil'ak was even said to have offered Czechoslovak "fraternal aid" to Poland, if it was thought necessary, during the crisis in 1970 and again during the crisis in 1980–81.[58]

However, some of the foreign policy excesses of the Czechoslovak leaders are probably viewed unfavorably in the Kremlin. Such was the case with Czechoslovak rapprochement with West Germany, when the Czechs dragged their feet and on one occasion were publicly critical of Soviet policy. Intransigence on the issue of rapprochement with West Germany originated in Prague and not in Moscow, though it was tolerated for a short time by Brezhnev—until 1973, when the Soviet leader

58. *Listy,* Apr. 13, 1977; Jiri Valenta, "Eurocommunism and Czechoslovakia," in V. V. Aspaturian, J. Valenta, and D. Burke, eds., *Eurocommunism Between East and West* (Bloomington: Indiana University Press, 1980), pp. 157–80.

personally pressured the Czechoslovaks to pursue further negotiations with West Germany. Czechoslovak-West German rapprochement succeeded only after the Soviets overcame Czechoslovak objections.[59]

It is doubtful that the Soviets were behind the offending statements of the Czechoslovak Embassy in Vienna, Austria, in 1979 which declared that it is not in the Austrian interest to support dissidents from Czechoslovakia because "Austria needs the Czechoslovaks now and in the future, more than vice versa." It is also doubtful that the Soviets masterminded the political provocations by the Czechoslovak press against Yugoslavia over the touchy Macedonian issue.[60]

CONCLUSIONS

What conclusions can be drawn from the foregoing discussion regarding future Soviet policies toward Hungary and Czechoslovakia and about Soviet rules of the game in Eastern Europe in general? Are Soviet policy choices in Eastern Europe clearly defined and predetermined or are they only vaguely defined and reactive? As they have demonstrated in Hungary and Czechoslovakia and more recently in Poland, Soviet leaders have clear-cut political, ideological, and economic stakes in Eastern Europe that are conditioned by their Leninist orientation: Eastern Europe is vital to the security and political, ideological, and economic well-being of the Soviet Union. To maintain maximal influence in that region, the Soviet Union must prevent the spread of what it views as anti-Soviet tendencies, which may be "bourgeois," "revisionist," or Eurocommunist in nature. Accordingly, (a) the withdrawal of an East European country from the Warsaw Pact (Hungarian scenario of 1956) is not permissible;[61] (b) the restoration of a genuinely multiparty system in any of the Warsaw Pact countries (Hungarian scenario of 1956) or the institution of genuinely pluralistic forces such as independent trade unions (Polish scenario of 1980–81) would jeopardize the control of the Communist party and therefore cannot be allowed; (c) the weakening of a regime's loyalty, such as in Czechoslovakia in 1968, or the inability of a regime to contain pressures for change within acceptable limits (Czechoslovak scenario of 1968 and Polish scenario of 1980–81) cannot be tolerated.

When confronted in Eastern Europe with developments such as these,

59. Igor Prástka, "Po Dohodĕs NSR (After an Agreement with the FRG)," *Listy*, 4 (Feb. 1974), 9–12; George Klein, "Détente and Czechoslovakia," in Peter J. Potichnyj and Jane P. Shapiro, eds., *From the Cold War to Détente* (New York: Praeger, 1976), pp. 181–98.

60. *Arbeiter Zeitung* (Vienna), Oct. 9, 1979. For an attack against Yugoslovia, see an article in *Rudé právo*, Mar. 31, 1973.

61. It should be noted, however, that small Albania withdrew from the Warsaw Pact in 1968. This was a special case, its uniqueness having to do with Albania's small size, its geographical location, and its willingness to fight the Soviets.

Soviet leaders argue that they have a right to use military force, if necessary, to protect their interests. Another drastic solution is to pressure the guilty country's military and security leaders to intervene on their own as we saw happen in Poland on December 13, 1981. The view that the Soviets have the right to intervene under these conditions has been called the Brezhnev doctrine by Western and Chinese observers. This may be inaccurate since Brezhnev never inaugurated any doctrine. Rather, he seemed to follow the Khrushchev doctrine (if not the Lenin and Stalin doctrine) inasmuch as his justification for the invasion of Czechoslovakia was similar to Khrushchev's justification for the invasion of Hungary.[62]

One can only speculate as to what Andropov has learned from the resolutions of the Hungarian and Czechoslovak crises and how he will respond to similar challenges. Soviet management of the ongoing Polish crisis (which is, at the time of writing, far from being resolved) will undoubtedly provide more definitive answers. One thing that can be ascertained from the events in Hungary, Czechoslovakia, and Poland is that the Soviets are determined not to permit pluralistic socialism. Another is that Soviet responses to such developments are not automatic.

The outcomes of the invasions of 1956 and 1968 suggest that the results of Soviet intervention can be both beneficial and costly to the USSR. In both cases substantial benefits accrued to the USSR in terms of East European stability. The invasions demonstrated the limits of autonomy set by the Soviet leadership and served as warnings to other ruling Communist parties. At the same time, both invasions were costly. The most serious repercussions of the invasion of Czechoslovakia are still being felt. That country, with its dissident movement centered on Charter 77, is, at the outset of the 1980s, far from being normalized. Moreover, the stability in Eastern Europe achieved by the invasions has not endured and liberalist trends have persisted. Thus Kádár's regime has managed to introduce and sustain some important structural reforms, and in Poland the liberal trend of the 1970s produced the Polish summer of 1980.

In the long run, however, neither invasion indicated a significant alteration in Soviet perceptions of the general pattern of East-West relations. As Khrushchev asserted, the invasion of Hungary showed the West that the USSR was "strong and resolute."[63] The same can be said of the

---

62. The ideological justification for the invasion, formulated as the Soviet right to "defend the achievements of socialism" in Eastern Europe, can be found in the Warsaw Pact letter to the Czechoslovak leadership of July 1980 and as an "escape clause" in the Bratislava Declaration. It is also clearly stated in an article by S. Kovalev in *Pravda*, Sept. 26, 1968 (published after the invasion). Brezhnev implicitly endorsed it later in a manner similar to the manner in which Khrushchev had justified the Soviet invasion of Hungary 10 years earlier. Compare Brezhnev's speech (*Pravda*, Nov. 4, 1968) with Khrushchev's speech (*Pravda*, Apr. 1, 1958).

63. Mićunović, *Moscow Diary*, p. 156.

Soviet invasion of Czechoslovakia, for it strengthened the Soviet posture of deterrence and made the Soviet policy of *Westpolitik* more credible in the 1970s.

As the events in Hungary and Czechoslovakia demonstrated, the limits of Soviet tolerance are often not well defined. Soviet leaders sometimes have poor and inaccurate information and they are often taken unawares by events in Eastern Europe. Also, they are sometimes distracted by their own power struggles. Before 1968 the laying of ground rules for permissible behavior in Eastern Europe was often erratic. Hence, it was difficult for the Hungarians and the Czechs to know when they had misbehaved. If confronted by a situation in Eastern Europe similar to the Hungarian situation in 1956 or the Czechoslovak situation in 1968, the Soviet leaders might again respond with a military invasion, particularly if faced with something similar to the Hungarian scenario. However, they might be more patient, putting considerable pressure to intervene on the country's own leadership, as they did in Poland in 1980–81.

So far the Soviets have successfully imposed their most basic political preference—the maintenance of the status quo and the containment of what they regard as anti-Sovietism—in Hungary and Czechoslovakia. A new-found (late 1950s) and renewed (1960s–1970s) emphasis on integration in the CMEA and WTO organizations constituted important consolidation policies in both cases and reflected the Soviet search for durable and acceptable control mechanisms. Following the invasion of Czechoslovakia, the main goals of this policy appear to be the prevention of another Prague Spring and the protection of Eastern Europe from increasing "ideological diversion" during détente. To achieve their objectives the Soviets have been willing to allow a certain degree of "particularism," be it a liberal one as in Hungary or an orthodox one as in Czechoslovakia. However, there was a lessening of Soviet emphasis on the WTO integration process in the late 1970s. This trend coincided with the Soviets' vigorous global pursuits during the second half of the 1970s in strategic areas of the Third World. During this period the Soviets acted out of a desire to exploit perceived opportunities (Angola in 1975–76 and Ethiopia in 1977–78) and out of what they perceived to be necessity (Afghanistan in 1979–80).

Again, the Soviets' principal concerns during the 1980s with regard to Hungary and Czechoslovakia may be the threats to their stakes in these countries springing from internal attempts at liberalization. In the 1980s the task of safeguarding stability in Hungary and Czechoslovakia may become more difficult. In addition to old problems the Soviet leaders will confront new problems in both countries. With the deterioration of the worldwide economic situation, the high cost of energy, the huge indebtedness to the West (in this respect Hungary is in a weaker position), and other socioeconomic dislocations, like the shortage of food (which in the early 1980s was a more serious problem for Czechoslovakia than for Hungary), there has been a decline in economic growth in Czechoslovakia and Hungary. Both countries are approaching a period of increasing economic difficulty. A reduction in the standard of living may be unavoidable and may be a catalyst for worker dissatisfaction, as it was in Poland in 1980–81. Czechoslovakia and especially Hungary have been particularly vulnerable to the USSR's inability since 1974–75 to satisfy their energy needs. Will a serious deterioration of the overall economic situation and the inevitable economic and social sacrifices it entails, coupled with ideological stagnation, overtake the Hungarian and Czechoslovak regimes? Will the Soviets be able and willing to pay the enormous economic price they paid for stability in Poland in 1976 and have continued to pay ever since? The Polish situation of 1980–81 may not be unique. Czechoslovakia's unpopular regime is highly vulnerable to future challenge.

As long as the Soviets are able to afford it they will continue to pay an economic price for political and ideological conformity in Hungary and Czechoslovakia. Yet their ability to do so may decline significantly as they discover that their cardinal success of the 1970s—maintenance of the restrictive status quo—is a major stumbling block and a source of economic stagnation in the 1980s. This is suggested by Andropov's 1983 approval of Kádár's efforts to refurbish the NEM and the advocation by some Czechoslovak leaders of limited economic reforms.

The post-Brezhnev succession will probably introduce another major element of ambiguity into Soviet behavior during the 1980s. As in the past, the transference of power in the USSR may produce an absence of clear direction with resulting irresolution and contradictions in policies. Brezhnev's succession by Andropov and his consolidation of power may be accompanied by Hungarian and Czechoslovak successions. This could introduce additional elements of instability into Hungarian and Czechoslovak politics. In turn, this could lead to an augmentation of the infighting within both leaderships. Kádár's death or retirement in Hungary, where the liberal Hungarian particularism owes much to his personality and skill, might bring hidden antagonisms resulting from Kádárization into the open. Furthermore, corruption and a decline in morale of the Hungarian people (prices paid for limited liberalization in Hungary) might become more evident. A new generation of Hungarians who have little memory of 1956 may not share their predecessors' sense of realism. The Czechoslovak succession of Husák can also bring about some unforeseen changes in the Czechoslovak leadership and internal politics.

If there is an extended continuation of martial law in Poland, it may have some effects on Soviet policies toward Czechoslovakia and Hungary as well. Should the repression succeed, thus stabilizing the Polish situation, the Soviets may decide that more repressive policies will have a greater chance of success in the unpredictable decade ahead, not only in Poland but also in Czechoslovakia, and perhaps even in Hungary. Should the repression in Poland fail, and should the regime turn gradually toward a Polish version of Kádárism as the means of normalization, the Soviets might conclude that cautious reforms could provide the solution elsewhere in Eastern Europe, even in Czechoslovakia.

Finally, Soviet policies toward Hungary and Czechoslovakia in the 1980s will be influenced, as in the past, by the general nature of Soviet relations with the West. A cold war environment will be less conducive to Soviet tolerance of experiments such as reform in Hungary and might even produce a Soviet endorsement of Czechoslovak orthodoxy. Although prudent U.S. policies toward the USSR and Eastern Europe might have an impact, they could hardly pry the regimes of Eastern Europe from the Soviet sphere of influence.

5

Soviet Relations with Yugoslavia and Romania

WILLIAM ZIMMERMAN

What is the international solidarity of revolutionaries. . . . Does it consist, under justified, extraordinary conditions, in rendering material aid including military aid, all the more so when it is a case of blatant, massive outside intervention?

The history of the revolutionary movement confirms the moral and political rightness of this form of aid and support.

Novoye Vremya
No. 3, 1980

It has recently become fashionable to slander our good relations with [Yugoslavia] and to spread the most absurd fabrications about them. The authors of these fairy tales try to depict Yugoslavia as some kind of poor, defenseless Little Red Riding Hood whom the terrible, rapacious wolf—the Soviet Union—threatens to tear to pieces and devour.

Leonid Brezhnev
November 16, 1976

Few generalizations about Soviet foreign policy hold for the entire period 1945–80. One that does is that successive Soviet leaderships have sharply distinguished between the USSR's relations with Eastern Europe and its relations with all other states, communist and noncommunist. Soviet policy toward Romania and Yugoslavia is a dimension of Soviet foreign policy in which the boundary—that is, exactly where Eastern Europe ends and the rest of the world begins—has long been difficult to ascertain. Indeed, a central part of the story of Soviet-Yugoslav and Soviet-Romanian relations pertains precisely to bargaining over whether the smaller states are, in a politically relevant sense, part of Eastern Europe.

In the years since Stalin's break with Yugoslavia in 1948, Yugoslavs have steadfastly maintained that Yugoslavia is not part of Eastern Europe. For Yugoslavs, belonging to Eastern Europe signifies having full membership in the Warsaw Treaty Organization (WTO) and in the Council for Mutual Economic Assistance (CMEA) and obligatory consultative ties with the Communist Party of the Soviet Union (CPSU). Moreover, it is a place where socialist states are aligned rather than non-aligned and where the other major world states, the United States most notably, have recognized Soviet hegemony.

For Romania, the issue is more complicated. In 1958 the Romanians succeeded in persuading the USSR to withdraw its troops from their country. Since then Romania has pursued a policy of reducing the salience of the boundaries that separate the Soviet-East European regional system from the dominant international system.[1] This in turn has been part of a carefully conceived and executed effort to create an environment in which Romania can conduct a foreign policy that differs in substantial ways from that of the Soviet Union. It is illustrated most thematically in the Romanian leaders' claim that Romania is both a socialist and a developing country, with the result that along with its membership in CMEA and the WTO Romania has achieved guest status at the Conference of Nonaligned States and become one of the Group of 77 developing nations (a group now exceeding one hundred members). It has also joined that notorious capitalist front, the International Monetary Fund. Its actual autonomy from the Soviet Union and the delicate ambivalence of its position were vividly demonstrated most recently by its decision to absent itself from the United Nations General Assembly votes condemning the December 1979 Soviet intervention in Afghanistan.

Likewise, for Soviet leaders, Yugoslavia and Romania have posed the issue of the nature of Soviet stakes vis-à-vis the European communist states. Is the Soviet stake in Yugoslavia akin to its stake in East European socialist states located more centrally in Europe? Is Romania as central to Soviet interests as the Northern Tier states of Eastern Europe? Soviet relations with Yugoslavia and Romania provide insight into the question of whether Soviet priorities have changed as the USSR has emerged as a world power. Should the USSR's stakes in Romania and Yugoslavia grow in the 1980s, in comparison with its stakes in other European socialist states, this will be most plausibly interpreted as evidence that prior Soviet preoccupation with Eastern Europe reflected only the limits of Soviet power and will strongly suggest that in Soviet eyes the boundaries between Eastern Europe and the rest of the world will become increasingly obscured as the 1980s progress.

In this chapter, I will summarize the challenges that Yugoslavia and Romania pose for the USSR and describe the divergent circumstances that led to their autonomous positions vis-à-vis Moscow. Then I will depict Soviet policy toward Yugoslavia and Romania after the Soviet invasion of

1. "Hierarchical Regional Systems and the Politics of Systems Boundaries," *International Organization*, 26 (Winter 1972), 18–36.

Czechoslovakia and describe the military, economic, and political challenges that these two states have represented for the USSR in the 1970s. Finally, I will speculate on whether the Soviet Union has the requisite resources to deal with the Yugoslav and Romanian challenges in the 1980s.

In comparing Soviet relations with Yugoslavia and Romania, I do not intend to suggest that the two situations are identical. Rather they are paired because in the 1970s and 1980s they have adopted strikingly similar stances versus the Soviet Union, despite many significant differences in their relations with the Soviet Union and in the circumstances that led to their autonomy. Certainly the degree of animus they have toward the Soviet Union and the extent to which each represents a challenge to Soviet interests are appreciably different. Romania's strategic position is not central from either a defensive or an offensive perspective, although it does serve as an important buffer between Yugoslavia and the Soviet Union. Romania's clashes with the Soviet Union have not been as voluble as Yugoslavia's or as extensive. Romania's differences with the Soviet Union over CMEA integration, over the cohesiveness and domain of the WTO, and in international forums pertain almost exclusively to international relations. Even though the Romanian leadership has played the Soviet card in order to stimulate nationalist sentiments, Romanian-Soviet differences, with one major exception, have shown no indications of spilling over into the domestic political domain. (The one exception pertains to Romanian interests in Bessarabia, now the Moldavian SSR.) Furthermore, Romania has not cast itself, or found itself cast, in the role of exemplar. The Romanian model is not a commodity for export—even though there are substantial tactical lessons about great power–small power interactions to be derived from Romania's efforts to extricate itself from Soviet dominance.

Yugoslavia constitutes a considerable challenge to a broad range of Soviet interests even though strategically Yugoslavia in no way threatens the Soviet Union. From the perspective of Soviet global force projection, however, Yugoslavia matters a great deal. The Slovenian Alps represent an obvious natural obstacle to any Soviet incursion into Italy. Yugoslav airspace facilitates direct Soviet aid to states in the Middle East. Yugoslav ports could greatly enhance Soviet naval power projection in the Mediterranean. Yugoslavia in Tito's last years was a major impediment to Soviet efforts to dominate the nonaligned movement. Overt, explicit, and sometimes vituperative polemics have taken place between the Soviet Union and Yugoslavia on several occasions. Interestingly, however, international relations and specifically interstate relations have been the most manageable areas of dispute between the Soviet Union and Yugoslavia. In up periods of Soviet-Yugoslav relations the pattern has usually been to negotiate matters pertaining to international relations first—to start, as Veljko Mićunović (the former Yugoslav ambassador to Moscow) put it, "at the shallow end" of the pool[2] and then progress, the two sides hope, to deeper, more profound matters. Rather it is internal Yugoslav developments that have constituted the "deeper" dimension of Soviet-Yugoslav relations. An important reason for this is that the Yugoslav example has been very much available for export: many of the attributes of Yugoslav communism—a private sector in agriculture, workers' self-management—that have been the basis of Yugoslav claims of distinctiveness have found an echo at some junctures among change-oriented elites in Eastern Europe.[3]

Romania is a fractious, albeit subordinate, member of the Soviet-East European system seeking, inter alia, to circumscribe the Soviet Union's freedom of action by insisting that peaceful coexistence ought to characterize not merely global adversary relations (e.g., Soviet-American relations) but also relations between the socialist countries, a view the USSR has always counterposed to its position that Soviet-East European relations ought to be governed by the (higher) principles of proletarian internationalism. By contrast Yugoslavia, like other states in the general international system, can point to authoritative bilateral statements affirming principles associated with Soviet notions of peaceful coexistence. One recent example occurred at the time of the Brezhnev visit in November 1976, which repeated the commitment to the "strict observance of the principles of sovereignty, independence, equality and noninterference in internal affairs."[4]

THE ORIGINS OF YUGOSLAV INDEPENDENCE

The origins of the Yugoslav and Romanian deviations from the USSR prior to 1968 also differed substantially. The origins of the Yugoslav deviation must be seen in large part in the way Yugoslav communism came to power. By and large the Yugoslavs emulated the Soviet pattern. Like the Bolsheviks, the Yugoslavs came to power more or less on their own; they created a monolithic party organization headed by a charismatic leader, and they set out immediately to transform Yugoslav society through such characteristically Soviet means as nationalization and ex-

2. Veljko Mićunović, *Moscow Diary* (Garden City, N.Y.: Doubleday, 1980), p. 63.

3. The direct role of Yugoslavia as an exemplar diminished in the 1970s as the Yugoslav economic situation deteriorated, but the Hungarian New Economic Mechanism has clear roots in Yugoslav practice, and moderate Polish reformers have been influenced by Yugoslav ideas of self-management. See, for instance, the chapter by Stanislaw Gebethner in Morris Bornstein, Zvi Gitelman, William Zimmerman, et al., *East-West Relations and the Future of Eastern Europe* (London: Allen & Unwin, 1981).

4. *Pravda*, Nov. 18, 1976.

propriation. Not only did they emulate the Soviet political model in seizing power and organizing the state and party apparatus, the Yugoslavs in the 1940s also patterned their economy after the Soviet Union's: a command economy, forced savings, deferred gratification, five-year plans, full employment, state foreign trade monopoly, bilateral trade flows, and autarky.

The hubris that accompanied successful power seizure, however, produced a kind of naiveté about Yugoslav foreign policy leading Yugoslavs to believe that close alignment to the Soviet Union and the pursuit of specifically Yugoslav foreign policy concerns were compatible. Although Stalin likely was troubled by evidence that in domestic politics Yugoslavia was *more* Stalinist than Stalin, in that socialism was being built much faster there than in Eastern Europe, the Yugoslav domestic system was not the source of the dispute with the Soviet Union. Stalin was evidently concerned that Yugoslavia had parochial interests pertaining to Albania, Trieste, the nature of the Danube River regime, and a possible Balkan federation. Simultaneously, the Yugoslavs were increasingly aware that Stalin was attempting to impose satellite status on Yugoslavia through such traditional control mechanisms as joint stock companies, the appointment of Soviet advisers at strategic points in the governmental apparatus and economy, the penetration of and recruitment of spies and agents in the Yugoslav army, and insistence on a special, satrap-like status for the Soviet ambassador. Yugoslav resentment of such treatment and the evidence of Yugoslav autonomous behavior were important backdrops to Stalin's break with Yugoslavia in 1948.

And break with Yugoslavia he did. In June 1948 the Cominform attacked the Yugoslav leaders "for their anti-Party and anti-Soviet views incompatible with Marxism-Leninism."[5] Mass nationalist discontent was encouraged, notably among the non-Slav Albanian and Hungarian minorities. The USSR employed an economic blockade that had severe consequences. The Soviet Union and its allies engaged in troop concentrations and mobilizations near the Yugoslav borders with Hungary, Romania, and Bulgaria and provoked numerous border incidents, almost 1,500 by Yugoslav reckoning during 1948–50.

For several reasons Yugoslavia weathered the storm. First, and perhaps most important, the Leninist model served Tito in good stead. Having paralleled the Soviet Union by building socialism in one country, a little Soviet Union would not easily become a satellite of *the* Soviet Union. Second, for the Yugoslavs, the conflict was a struggle in which core values were at stake; for the USSR the dispute was far less significant. In such

5. For the Cominform attacks on Yugoslavia, see Robert Bass and Elizabeth Marbury, eds., *The Soviet-Yugoslav Controversy, 1949–58* (New York: Prospect Books, 1958), pp. 44–46.

instances it is not just power asymmetries that matter. Equally, and perhaps more, important is the asymmetry in value intensity. Khrushchev notwithstanding, Stalin did not merely wave his little finger at Tito: rather he shook his fist. In what has proved an enduring theme in Soviet-Yugoslav relations, Yugoslav cohesion and its concomitant implication of an augmented capacity to withstand Soviet pressure were furthered unintentionally by the Soviet threat. Likewise, the Soviet blockade of Yugoslavia was like most blockades: as an instrument of coercion by great powers against lesser states, a blockade is not highly efficacious in the absence of great-power consensus. Failing such consensus, a state may easily substitute trade with one state for trade with another. The Soviet blockade allowed Yugoslavia to export to the West the minerals, notably copper and iron, it had previously committed to the USSR.

It need not have worked that way. Western decision-makers had to decide explicitly that Western interests were well served by a Communist-led Yugoslavia independent of the Soviet Union. This they did in one of the brightest pages in post-World War II Western policymaking. Moreover, they made the decision even though after the Cominform attack the Yugoslavs initially *intensified* collectivization, and even though the Yugoslavs persisted for more than a year after the break in inveighing against Anglo-American imperialism.

Finally, credit should be given to the Yugoslav leadership. Having successfully fought the Germans, Italians, Chetniks (Serbian monarchists), and the Ustaše (Croatian fascists), they had had considerable experience under stress. Tito and his colleagues manifested the self-confidence born of successful power seizure. There were no barricades that they, as good Bolsheviks, could not hurdle, not even ones set up by Stalin himself. Also, they were not lacking in political skill. While much of the continued Yugoslav praise of Stalin after the Cominform attack stemmed from ideological dogmatism and revolutionary élan, the persisting eulogies of Stalin were also intended to diminish mass and elite support for Stalin and the Soviet Union: Stalin, by his vitriol, thus convinced all but the most ardently pro-Soviet Yugoslavs that it was not a contradiction to be a good Communist and loyal to Tito's Yugoslavia.

Having protected themselves on that front, the Yugoslavs then turned to policies that strengthened their support domestically and rendered them more acceptable to the West as well. After it became clear that Soviet-Yugoslav relations had become fundamentally altered, the Yugoslavs embraced the rightist, conciliatory policies that most associate with Titoism and that have led over the years to charges of revisionism. Forced collectivization was abandoned, the Communist Party of Yugoslavia was renamed the League of Yugoslav Communists, and workers' self-management was stressed. In foreign policy, relations with the West improved substantially, with the Yugoslavs restricting their ambitions significantly—as the settlement with Italy over Trieste exemplified. Similarly, Yugoslavia early on discovered the advantages of cultivating, especially at the United Nations, what came to be known as the Third World and moving toward what subsequently became a full-fledged policy of nonalignment.

These changes occurred against the backdrop of a persistent aspiration for some form of association with the European socialist states. For seven years after 1948, Soviet policy toward Yugoslavia remained hostile and, indeed, vituperative. As part of a radical overall reorientation in Soviet foreign policy, however, Khrushchev—over Molotov's strenuous objections—proceeded to ameliorate Soviet-Yugoslav relations, going to Belgrade, where on June 2, 1955, the two states declared that "for the purpose of strengthening confidence and cooperation between the peoples" of the Soviet Union and Yugoslavia, each state affirms its "respect for the sovereignty, independence, integrity, and equality of states in their relations with each other" and pledges the observance of the principle of mutual respect and of noninterference in internal affairs for any reason "because questions of the internal structure, of different social systems, and of different ways of advancing to socialism are exclusively a matter for the peoples of the individual countries."[6] Khrushchev's move was not only part of a strategic reorientation in foreign policy; it was intimately linked to internal Soviet changes and in particular to Khrushchev's effort to de-Stalinize.

His efforts found a ready response in Belgrade. Tito welcomed the opportunity to have a major voice in matters pertaining to Eastern Europe. Events developed rapidly in the aftermath of the Khrushchev visit and the 20th Congress of the CPSU in 1956. Yugoslavia acquired a special favored status in Soviet eyes, and in Eastern Europe the Soviet reconciliation with Yugoslavia seemed to portend Soviet tolerance for separate, national paths to communism. In Poland and Hungary, the discrediting of Stalin was taken to imply a rejection of all things Soviet, and in Hungary of Communist rule.

In Eastern Europe matters came quickly to a head. The Hungarian Workers' Party collapsed, multiparty rule was restored, and Hungary declared its neutrality. The Yugoslavs, while providing asylum for Imre Nagy in their embassy in Budapest, acquiesced in the Soviet intervention in Hungary, characterizing it as a "lesser evil . . . if it leads to the preservation of socialism in Hungary." That degree of Yugoslav support, coupled with the granting of asylum to Nagy, was not sufficient. An almost instantaneous reversal in Soviet-Yugoslav relations occurred. By Novem-

6. *Review of International Affairs*, 6 (June 1, 1955).

ber 7, Moscow was signaling that "there is no longer any special relationship [with Yugoslavia], as there was only three days ago."[7]

After the Hungarian Revolution, the Yugoslav leadership came increasingly to articulate an explicit posture of nonalignment. While never
abandoning the notion that Yugoslavia had a role to play in Eastern
Europe, the Yugoslav leadership, and Tito in particular, turned consciously toward the global "South." Yugoslav-Soviet relations waxed and
waned in the late 1950s and early 1960s, but largely for reasons that had
little to do with Yugoslavia. Rather, the crucial elements seem to have
been Soviet domestic politics and the intensifying Sino-Soviet split in
which Chinese attacks on Yugoslavia were a surrogate for attacks on the
Soviet Union. (Just as Khrushchev and Molotov had clashed in 1955 over
Soviet relations with Yugoslavia, so too Khrushchev and Frol Kozlov
seemed to be at loggerheads about Yugoslavia in the early 1960s.)

Likewise, as Chinese-Soviet relations deteriorated, although Yugoslavia was clearly pursuing an independent policy, Soviet-Yugoslav policies often seemed to follow parallel paths. In the early 1960s there was
some basis for the case that Yugoslavia was acting in collusion with the
Soviet Union against both the United States and (in response to exceedingly sharp attacks from the Chinese) the People's Republic of China.

Two major events in the late 1960s fundamentally altered, once again,
Soviet-Yugoslav relations. The first was the Yugoslav economic reforms
instituted in 1965 and fully implemented in 1966 after the defeat of
Aleksandar Ranković. The reforms, advocated primarily by the Croatian
leader Vladimir Bakarić and endorsed by Tito, envisaged an economic
strategy of consciously linking Yugoslavia to the international system.
International market performance would constitute the primary criterion by which enterprise performance would be evaluated and the country's borders would be opened to the in-migration of Western capital and
the out-migration of Yugoslav workers.

The second event was linked to the first. The Prague Spring found
much of its inspiration in Yugoslav market socialism and was demonstrably supported by Tito. The subsequent intervention in Czechoslovakia
constituted a fundamental challenge to Yugoslavia. Nothing, with the
possible exception of the 1948 Stalin attack, had a greater impact on
Yugoslav perceptions of the Soviet Union. Unlike Hungary in 1956, when
Yugoslavia could rationalize Soviet behavior by averring that socialism
really had been in danger, the 1968 Soviet action in Czechoslovakia was,
in Yugoslav eyes, intended to thwart the prospering of alternative modes
of socialist construction and was viewed as representing a direct threat to
Yugoslavia. After Czechoslovakia and throughout the 1970s, most

7. Mićunović, *Moscow Diary*, p. 151.

Yugoslavs (though arguably not Tito) operated on the assumption that the Soviet Union was the major source of external military threat. That premise was reconfirmed on the eve of the 1980s by the Vietnamese invasion of Kampuchea (Cambodia) and the Soviet invasion of Afghanistan.

THE ORIGINS OF ROMANIAN AUTONOMY

In contrast to Yugoslavia, the origins of Romanian Communist rule must be seen in the advance of the Soviet army at the end of World War II. The destruction and social transformations of the war produced what could be considered a revolutionary situation in several East European countries at the end of the war. Not in Romania: there the skillful coup d'état on August 23, 1944, and the switching of sides by King Michael resulted in Romania's suffering relatively little in the war and ending the war on the Soviet side. In the absence of anything approaching a revolutionary situation, the Communist seizure of power was the very model of revolution at rifle-point. The coalition government of late 1944 gave way in early March 1945, after a Soviet ultimatum, to a bogus coalition headed by Petru Groza, with the Communists in a preeminent position. Over the next two years the Communists systematically whittled away at the power of the non-Communist forces. Finally, King Michael went into exile on December 31, 1947, the Romanian Socialist Republic was proclaimed on January 1, 1948, and a period of unambiguous aping of the Soviet experience began.

Little happened in the ensuing seven years to suggest that Romania was anything but a compliant satellite. Khrushchev's secret speech and the developments in Poland and Hungary, however, found considerable reverberation in Romania. Student demonstrations and workers' meetings, in particular by railroad workers, were called—suggesting that had the revolution not been suppressed in Hungary, dramatic changes might have taken place in Romania too. Nevertheless, the Soviet intervention in Hungary had a chilling effect on the Romanian citizenry.

Ironically though, the Romanian leadership, headed by Gheorghe Gheorghiu-Dej, began to show some signs of pursuing an independent policy. A glimmer of such a policy was evident in the Romanian leadership's stance toward Yugoslavia after Hungary. Its party-level criticism in 1957 was muted when compared with that of, say, Bulgaria and Albania. Most importantly, it persuaded the Soviet leadership that the presence of Soviet troops was an affront which intimated that the Romanian Workers' Party could not stay in power without the presence of Soviet troops.[8]

8. Nikita S. Khrushchev, *Khrushchev Remembers: The Last Testament*, ed. Strobe Talbott (Boston: Little, Brown, 1976), pp. 227–29.

There are several possible reasons why Khrushchev acquiesced in the request. Ghita Ionescu suggests the move was designed "to show that Khrushchev's promise to withdraw troops from European countries would be carried out were it not for the alleged danger of the NATO forces in Europe."[9] Khrushchev by his own account was mollified by the argument that Romania was strategically insignificant.

Whatever the reason, the consequences of the decision were profound for Soviet-Romanian relations, for it greatly enhanced the room for maneuver by the Romanian leadership. With that wedge and after implementing intensive repressive measures domestically, the Romanian leadership became the first derivative Communist regime—one brought to power by the Red Army—successfully to challenge Soviet interests. Over the span of a decade, Romania managed to stake out an impressively autonomous position. Thus in the course of the 1960s the Romanian leadership insisted that Romania be included among the less developed countries at the first session of the United Nations Conference on Trade and Development (UNCTAD 1), and increased Romania's activity at the United Nations (as Yugoslavia had done in the late 1940s). In like fashion, Bucharest skillfully diversified its trading patterns, thus reducing its dependence on intra-CMEA trade or on the Soviet Union specifically.

Then it became bolder. Citing Lenin, needless to say, in 1964 it openly opposed Soviet CMEA integration efforts, which would have relegated Romania to the role of a grain supplier, on the ground that supranational planning bodies were "not in keeping with the principles that underlie the relations among the Socialist countries,"[10] and by the mid-1960s it was posing as a mediator in the Sino-Soviet split.

By the late 1960s the evidence of Romanian independence was dramatically manifest in numerous domains. In 1967 it refused to sever diplomatic ties with Israel following the Six-Day War, it broke ranks with the other East European states by establishing diplomatic relations with West Germany, and it refused to attend the Karlovy Vary conference of European Communist parties. Moreover, Bucharest apparently resisted the effort by Moscow to select a new commander-in-chief for the Warsaw Treaty Organization because it objected to Soviet domination of the alliance. Indeed, during the course of the 1960s, it had taken various measures to disengage itself somewhat from WTO control, such as ceasing to send its officers to study at Soviet military academies, prohibiting joint WTO maneuvers in Romania, and sending only token forces to WTO

9. Ghita Ionescu, *Communism in Rumania* (London: Oxford University Press, 1964), p. 289.

10. For an English version see William E. Griffith, *Sino-Soviet Relations* (Cambridge: MIT Press, 1967), p. 282.

exercises in other countries. Also in 1967 the new Romanian leader Nicolae Ceaușescu (Dej had died in 1965) indicated that Soviet ideas of "perfecting" the WTO were as unacceptable as was the Soviet conception of an integrated division of labor within CMEA.

Contrary to the views of many, it is not difficult to figure out how Romania managed to pursue an independent foreign policy. Once Moscow had withdrawn its troops, it had few resources to employ *between* the sticks and stones of military intervention and the words (polemics) that would not substantially hurt the Romanians. As Yugoslavia had been at the onset of the Stalin–Tito clash, Romania was a little Soviet Union quite capable of resisting pressures from the motherland of socialism. Unlike other East European states, Romania was fortunate in that in the 1960s and throughout the 1970s it was not dependent on the Soviet Union for energy sources. Consequently, economic pressures were likely to be ineffective, and the Romanian leadership further reduced Soviet leverage by redirecting Romanian trade to the global West, the global South, and China. Romania's domestic security organs were every bit as effective as Tito's had been in 1948, with the result that, while it appears that Moscow encouraged pro-Soviet forces within Romania during the mid-1960s,[11] such efforts were neither likely to succeed, nor did they. Being relatively immune to economic pressure and largely invulnerable to subversion, the Romanians avoided steps that would constitute a pretext for Soviet intervention and instead undertook a series of small moves, relatively modest in themselves, but the total effect of which was substantial. A specially striking aspect of Romanian independence was the skill with which the leadership acted to increase Romania's capacity to operate independently.

All these efforts, however, presumed that the Soviet Union would not intervene militarily. Romania was, consequently, almost as shaken by the Soviet invasion of Czechoslovakia as was Yugoslavia. Romania was the only Warsaw Treaty Organization state not to invade Czechoslovakia and, instead, characterized the attack as a "flagrant violation of sovereignty."[12] For the Romanians, as for the Yugoslavs, the invasion of Czechoslovakia was a signal event that was to define the context of Soviet-Romanian relations throughout the 1970s, an event that for the Romanians found an ominous echo in the Vietnamese invasion of Kampuchea and the Soviet invasion of Afghanistan on the eve of the 1980s. Unlike with Yugoslavia, however, there was no ambiguity as to whether Romania was one of the states where abstract notions of sovereignty would be dis-

11. At least if we take Ceaușescu's statement of May 7, 1967, at face value.

12. As quoted in Robin Remington, *The Warsaw Pact* (Cambridge: MIT Press, 1971), p. 92.

regarded if they clashed with the class principle. Whatever might be the operative Soviet definition of the area in which the Soviet Union felt free to intervene—and even the Chinese betrayed some anxieties on this score[13]—it was indisputable that Romania, its efforts to muddy the waters notwithstanding, was a member of the socialist camp. Romania had to live with the reality that in the Soviet view "the Warsaw Pact was concluded not only to defend the signatory states' national borders and territory" but "was concluded in order to defend socialism," which "is not only the internal affair of that country's people, but also a problem of defending the positions of world socialism."[14]

THE MILITARY DIMENSION

The strategic "challenge" that Yugoslavia represented in the 1970s may be described briefly. For the Soviet Union, Yugoslavia is more an attraction than it is a challenge: but it does constitute a challenge, against which some kinds of defensive measures must be taken. Indeed, there is a sense in which Yugoslavia became more attractive strategically in the 1970s than it had been in 1948 at the time of Stalin's break. In 1948 a Soviet-linked Yugoslavia threatened Italy and Greece. (It should not be forgotten that the termination of the Greek Civil War was linked directly to the Stalin–Tito split.) In the 1970s and 1980s a substantial Soviet military presence in Yugoslavia, one well beyond the privilege that the Soviet navy, like other navies, enjoys to use Yugoslav ports for repairs and rest stops, would threaten the states bordering Yugoslavia—Italy, Greece, Austria, Albania, and Turkey—and then some. The USSR's military force projection capabilities in 1948 were almost entirely continental. The opportunities such a presence would afford now were suggested during the 1973 Arab-Israeli War, when Yugoslavia allowed Moscow the use of Yugoslav facilities and air space to fly supplies to Egypt. There was nothing in the 1970s to suggest, however, that short of a cominformist coup or actual Soviet attack, Yugoslavia would be willing to allow Moscow such a procedure as a general practice. (The 1973 decision must be seen against Yugoslav enthusiasm for the Arab cause.) Rather, the cool Yugoslav response to Brezhnev's request, during his 1976 visit, that Yugoslavia permit Moscow to increase significantly the servicing of warships in Yugoslavia's ports was more characteristic.

Yugoslavia is a challenge to the Soviet Union in several ways. Yugoslavia has the potential to be a formidable military power. One cost of nonalignment, in fact, has been the relatively high percentage of its GNP

13. See "Theories of 'Limited Sovereignty' and 'International Dictatorship' are Soviet Revisionist Social-Imperialist Gangster Theories," *Peking Review* (Mar. 28, 1969), p. 24.
14. *Izvestiya*, Aug. 25, 1969, as cited in Remington, *Warsaw Pact*, p. 107.

that Yugoslavia devotes to defense. With its doctrine of All-People's Defense, it could put an enormous army in the field. The usual calculation is that it would require 30 divisions for a Soviet army to subjugate Yugoslavia unless the latter were on the verge of civil war. This is not a price that the Soviet Union, by its past behavior, has suggested it is willing to pay (except perhaps under very specific and unlikely circumstances). Were a civil war or major upheaval on the horizon, the situation might be quite different. Tito reported that in 1971 the Soviet Union offered to help Yugoslavia maintain domestic order; it was such an offer that led him, in justifying the actions he took against the Croatian Party leadership, to say that the nationalist outburst in Zagreb in 1971 had brought the country to the verge of civil war—and "you know what that would have meant."[15] Much of the 1970s was given over to domestic moves designed to reduce the likelihood of a repetition of 1971 or its equivalent, to signal externally that Yugoslavia would fight if attacked, and to cultivate military ties with Soviet rivals.

Thus in the 1970s the Soviet Union found itself confronted by the challenge that the Yugoslavs might resume major weapons purchases from the United States. In general Moscow would doubtless like to discourage such a development, although the 1970s brought home the prospect that there were circumstances in which this might seem the lesser of two evils to Moscow. (In 1977 Yugoslav General Ivan Kukoć observed: "Whether Yugoslavia will ever be forced to think about an atomic bomb of its own . . . depends least of all on Yugoslavia."[16]) Yugoslavia had made no major arms purchases from the United States since 1961. In the 1970s it found itself in the awkward position of receiving many of the weapons it imports (it has a rather substantial armaments industry) from the Soviet Union, the country it is most likely to fight. The Soviet Union is in a position, especially by denying spare parts, to make it a costly process for the Yugoslavs to reduce their dependence on the Soviet Union for military hardware.

This is not to assert that the Soviet Union has the capacity to induce Yugoslavia to forgo major weapons purchases from the United States. In 1976 it was actually announced that major U.S. arms sales to Yugoslavia were to be resumed, a decision that was relegated to the back burner at Yugoslavia's request later during that same year. In October 1977 U.S. Secretary of Defense Harold Brown visited Yugoslavia, the Yugoslav Defense Minister General Nikola Ljubičić came to the United States in September 1978, and in May 1979 General Bernard Rogers, at that time

15. *Borba*, Dec. 19, 1971.
16. *Nedeljne Informativne Novine (NIN)* (Mar. 13, 1977) and reproduced in Slobodan Stanković, "General Denies Yugoslavia Has Atomic Bomb," *Radio Free Europe (RFE) Research Report*, Mar. 16, 1977.

U.S. Army Chief of Staff, visited with Yugoslav army commanders in Belgrade.

A related problem is the near military alliance that came to exist, after Czechoslovakia, between Romania and Yugoslavia.[17] Romania by contrast is more a modest military challenge to the Soviet Union than an attraction; but it is an attraction. Romania currently attracts the USSR militarily in two ways. Romania's radar contributes to WTO defense. The reentry of Soviet troops—even the reestablishment of the practice of sending Soviet troops into Romania for field exercises—would greatly facilitate Soviet capacity to exert pressure on Yugoslavia.

Romania represents a military challenge in several ways. For almost two decades Romania has declined to cooperate with Moscow when the latter has called for the "strengthening" of the Warsaw Treaty Organization. Throughout the 1960s and 1970s the Romanians had a common theme: control over troops in Romania should be exercised by Romanian authorities, and actual orders to fight should be administered by Romanian authorities: "The Romanian army will only take orders from the supreme party and state bodies and at the call of the people, and . . . it will never receive orders from outside."[18] The result has been that Romania has intermittently participated in exercises and has even allowed map exercises in Romania, for instance in 1973 and 1974. However, "after the 1963 exercises, Romania never again permitted maneuvers on Romanian soil, although it has sent to the WTO exercises personnel whom the Romanians have described as observers, and the Soviets have described as participants."[19]

The Romanians' insistence on a narrow construction of the Warsaw Pact also served to thwart Soviet ambitions to mobilize the WTO for use outside Europe—against the Chinese most notably. Throughout the decade after the Soviet intervention in Czechoslovakia, the Romanian theme was that the WTO was designed to cope with the threat to peace in Europe and that in the event of such a threat Romania will fulfill its commitments. Thus, for instance, Ceaușescu stressed in 1978 that Romania will "fulfill its obligations under the Warsaw Pact in the event of imperialist aggressions *in Europe* directed against the socialist member-countries of this pact."[20] Such a statement was carefully phrased. For what it succeeded in doing—probably with the private support of other East European states, notably Poland—was to limit the domain of the WTO commitment precisely to Europe.

17. Christopher Jones, "Soviet Military Doctrine and Warsaw Pact Exercises," unpublished paper, pp. 2–3.

18. *Scînteia*, Nov. 26–Dec. 2, 1978, as reported in *Yearbook on International Communist Affairs, 1979* (hereafter cited as *Yearbook 1979*) (Stanford: Hoover Institution, 1979), p. 69.

19. Jones, "Soviet Military Doctrine," p. 20.

20. *Scînteia*, Nov. 26–Dec. 2, 1978, in *Yearbook 1979*, p. 69. [Emphasis added]

Finally in the military realm, throughout the 1970s Romania showed that small states contribute less proportionately for defense than do larger states, even in an alliance whose protective function, as Robert Keohane once noted, smacks of protection as provided in Chicago in the 1920s: "You've got a nice place here. You wouldn't want something to happen to it. What you need is some protection." Romania's expenditures on defense as a percentage of GNP were only 2.1% in 1970 and declined to 1.7% by the mid- and late 1970s. Indeed, as recently as 1978 Romania rejected Moscow's advice, broadly phrased but targeted at least partially at Romania, that it increase its military expenditures. To Moscow's stern "Can one economize on security? Overestimating a threat would mean shouldering a heavy additional burden, of course, but underestimating a threat would mean risking everything,"[21] Bucharest responded that "there is no imminent danger of war" and "Romania has good relations with all NATO member countries."[22]

THE ECONOMIC DIMENSION

As other studies in this volume and elsewhere amply testify, when one thinks of Soviet interest in and influence over Eastern Europe, one thinks as immediately of economics, most notably energy, as one does of things military.[23] With regard to economics (as in the military realm) Yugoslavia and, to a lesser extent, Romania have long been linked to, but only peripherally part of, Eastern Europe. A Polish economist, Wiesław Iskra, was correct in 1969 when he declared that "as a matter of fact Yugoslavia is part, not of the socialist, but of the capitalist [read: global] international division of labor," and when in 1968 he inveighed against Yugoslavia as a country that "for a long time," and Romania as one that "for some time now," have been carriers of "tendencies" that "strive to . . . maintain separatist positions, to expand continuously economic relations with capitalist countries."[24]

After the 1948 Stalin–Tito clash and over the course of many years, Yugoslavia opted for an open economy for economic and political reasons. Such an economy had close links with the global economic system, particularly with Western Europe, and involved nominally parallel ties

21. *Pravda*, Dec. 16, 1978, and cited in *Current Digest of the Soviet Press*, 30, no. 50 (1978), 8.

22. *Scînteia* (Nov. 26–Dec. 2, 1978), in *Yearbook 1979*, p. 69.

23. See my "Western 'Stagflation' and The Evolution of Soviet-East European Relations," in Egon Neuberger and Laura Tyson, eds., *The Impact of International Economic Disturbances on the Soviet Union and Eastern Europe* (New York: Pergamon, 1980), pp. 409–37.

24. "Economic Integration of the Socialist Countries," *Zagadnienia i Materiały*, Jan. 15–28, 1969, reprinted in *RFE Research Report*, Apr. 16, 1969, and as reported by PAP (Sept. 9, 1968), cited in "The Problems of Comecon," *Radio Liberty*, Dec. 27, 1968. Only a few years later Poland joined the ranks of those seeking to increase economic ties with the West.

with the European Common Market and CMEA, but in practice entailed greater economic links to Western Europe and the United States than to Eastern Europe. It resulted in considerable economic penetration of the economy by foreign capital and an immense outflow of Yugoslav workers to Western Europe, especially to West Germany.[25]

The late 1960s and the 1970s brought renewed attention to the vulnerabilities of interdependence. The Soviet invasion of Czechoslovakia in 1968 and the Croatian nationalist outbursts in 1971 indicated that there might be an imminent danger to Yugoslav independence stemming from an external threat and/or intense internal divisiveness. Military security concerns prompted Tito in 1972 to decry the fact that "three big armies" were working abroad in Western Europe.[26] Tito's effort to harness the republic party organizations (in large part to prevent the recurrence of an episode like the 1971 Croatian events) became linked to the seemingly intractable problem of Yugoslavia's trade imbalance with Western Europe. Moreover, that imbalance worsened throughout the 1970s as the OPEC-induced global rise in oil prices and the subsequent Western stagflation made it increasingly difficult for Yugoslavia to sell its exports to Europe and increasingly important that Yugoslavia export substantially to the Soviet Union in order to pay for Soviet oil, which by 1978 constituted half of Yugoslavia's oil imports. (The shift in Yugoslavia's trade patterns in the 1970s is summarized in table 5.1.) Even with the immense oil bill from the Soviet Union (and a correspondingly large one from Iraq and other Third World oil producers), however, Yugoslavia's trade deficit throughout the 1970s remained largely with the West. In response to its substantial economic dependence on the West and fearful that the country was becoming too greatly dominated by the forces of "technocratism and anarcho-liberalism," the Yugoslav leadership turned in the early 1970s to Moscow for credits.

The promise of credits was forthcoming, to the tune of U.S. $1.3 billion over several years, mostly for the purchase of Soviet equipment and raw materials. (In practice the amounts actually delivered were much smaller and slower in coming than the Yugoslavs thought they had been given to understand, in large part because Yugoslav firms were often disinterested in acquiring Soviet equipment.) Yugoslavia's search for Soviet credits, however, is probably not to be interpreted primarily as a turn eastward per se but rather as part of what became a new Yugoslav strategy of independence for the 1970s.

The issue of course is the stake Moscow has in being "used" in this

25. See my "National-International Linkages in Yugoslavia," in Jan C. Triska and Paul M. Cocks, eds., *Political Development in Eastern Europe* (New York: Praeger, 1977).

26. *Borba,* Dec. 9, 1972.

TABLE 5.1   Geographical Distribution of Yugoslav Trade, 1971–78 (In percentage shares)

	1971	1972	1973	1974	1975	1976	1977	1978
Developed West								
Exports	52.9%	56.9%	55.7%	46.6%	35.7%	41.8%	40.0%	38.8%
Imports	65.8	65.3	62.5	60.5	60.8	54.8	56.9	56.6
Deficit	81.9	84.6	74.3	74.6	89.0	80.3	77.2	—
Planned economies								
Exports	36.7	36.1	34.0	41.6	47.2	42.4	40.1	43.1
Imports	23.9	24.8	24.8	23.3	24.8	30.7	28.9	30.1
Deficit	7.8	−0.5	8.9	4.7	−0.5	7.6	15.4	—
Developing economies								
Exports	10.4	7.0	10.3	11.8	17.1	15.8	19.9	18.1
Imports	10.3	9.9	12.7	16.2	14.4	14.5	14.2	13.3
Deficit	10.3	15.9	16.8	20.7	11.5	12.1	7.4	—

SOURCE: Laura Tyson, *The Yugoslav Economic System and Its Performance in the 1970s* (Berkeley: Institute of International Studies, 1980), p. 89.

fashion. During the 1970s part of the answer was political. The Soviet Union provided aid to Yugoslavia to restrict the latter's proclivities for affiliating even more with Western Europe than it does—exemplified by the trade agreement with the EEC signed just prior to Tito's death. In the early 1970s, moreover, the Yugoslav quest for credits from Moscow led to what seemed a major political concession by Belgrade. On that occasion, an apparent price of the loan was the ouster of the popular liberal Slovenian political figure Stane Kavčič. Whether the Soviets insisted on the ouster as a quid pro quo is unknown. We do have Mićunović's testimony that on several other occasions Moscow had made it known that it was distressed because certain Yugoslav leaders had anti-Soviet tendencies. We do know that in 1972 the Yugoslav leadership gave the impression that such concerns existed and were in some sense legitimate. Thus Edvard Kardelj attacked those who advocated a "one-sided linkup with Western Europe or Bavaria" and, addressing himself pointedly to those like Kavčič who maintained that Yugoslavia's place was in Western Europe, asked, "How would the East European countries react to such a separatist and antisocialist orientation?"[27]

Moscow's trade and aid to Yugoslavia in the 1970s makes sense, eco-

27. Ibid., Sept. 22, 1972.

nomically, even if no political calculation is involved. The Yugoslav-Soviet bauxite-aluminum trade is a good example. Soviet consumers, moreover, are highly attracted by the products, largely consumer goods, that Yugoslavia sells on the Soviet market but that it would have difficulty selling to the West. However much Moscow's ideologists may polemicize with market socialism, Made in Yugoslavia stands for quality in Moscow's central department store, GUM.

Romania has nothing like the open economy of Yugoslavia. The regime's attitude to foreign travel and work parallels that of the Soviet Union. Although joint investments with foreign companies are substantial in comparison to those of other East European states, the amount and scope are relatively modest by Yugoslav standards. Romania is of course a full member of CMEA, but in numerous respects it does not behave like a model East European state. One central element of the Romanian disengagement from Soviet preeminence has been the calculated reorientation in its trade patterns. At the beginning of the 1960s two-thirds of its trade was within CMEA; in 1970, less than half was. By the late 1970s only two-fifths of Romania's trade was within CMEA. A second element was its much more modest participation in CMEA joint projects. The third feature that differentiated Romania from the rest of Eastern Europe during the 1970s is that (until 1979) it imported no oil from the Soviet Union.

Views have been expressed that in the 1970s, after the Soviet invasion of Czechoslovakia, Romanian foreign policy lost its distinctive cast. From the vantage point of the early 1980s, however, such views may be safely disregarded in the realm of economics. What has happened is that Moscow and Bucharest have achieved a kind of modus vivendi within CMEA. Through the "interested party" principle, participation in collaborative schemes in particular areas has been restricted to those who wish to join. Moscow thus gets the participation in joint ventures it seeks from the industrialized CMEA states and Romania can opt out if it chooses. Neither the intimidation as a by-product of the Soviet intervention in Czechoslovakia nor the global jump in oil prices (which greatly aggravated Romania's trade problems with the West) has deterred the Romanian leadership from its previous course. During the 1970s Romania joined the International Monetary Fund and became the first East European country to achieve most favored nation status from the United States under the Jackson amendment.[28] As Romanian trade problems with the West became aggravated by West European stagflation, moreover, it reoriented its trade away from the West to the global South, *not* to the East.

28. See, for instance, Ronald Linden, "Romanian Foreign Policy in the 1980s," unpublished paper prepared for a conference at George Washington University, Apr. 4–5, 1980.

At the end of the 1970s, however, one notable change in Romania's economic situation occurred that did have ramifications for Soviet-Romanian relations. The ouster of the Shah of Iran deprived Romania of an important source of its oil. Reports exist that in 1979 Romania made a deal with the Soviet Union to import oil from the latter for the first time.[29] (It participates in the Orenburg gas scheme with the Soviet Union.) Such a development might have repercussions for other aspects of Soviet-Romanian relations, at least in the economic realm. It should be known, however, that Soviet interest in Romanian products (for instance, meat and other food products) is probably as intense as Romania's need for oil.

THE POLITICAL-IDEOLOGICAL DIMENSION

For Moscow, Yugoslavia constituted a political-ideological challenge in three closely related respects by the end of the 1970s. For years, Yugoslavia has stood for an entirely different pattern of relations among communist states and nonruling parties than Moscow has traditionally preferred. Its internal political structure has served as a possible alternative to be emulated in Eastern Europe and even in the Soviet Union, or at least as a reminder that communist alternatives exist. Finally, while Soviet and Yugoslav global interests have often coincided, by the end of the 1970s Yugoslavia represented a major impediment to the optimal fulfillment of Soviet aspirations in the global system. Each of these elements of the Yugoslav challenge is well known and has been widely discussed. What warrants attention here are some relevant developments in the 1970s.

In relations among communist parties and states, Yugoslavia has long stood for an autonomous and all-inclusive framework. During the 1970s, for instance, it lent considerable support to Eurocommunism, at least as it applied to Western Europe, and was conspicuously supportive of both the Social Democrats and the Communists (for whom the Social Democrats were anathema in Portugal). How Yugoslavia's conception of relations among Communists confronted the Soviet Union was vividly illustrated by the 1976 meeting of East European and West European Communist parties in East Berlin, which finally convened on the condition, in considerable measure due to Tito's efforts, that no document binding on the participants would result.

Similarly, the Yugoslavs cultivated relations with China, the USSR's communist archrival, during the 1970s. Whereas in the 1950s China had been at the forefront in excoriating Yugoslav revisionism, mutual fear of Soviet designs and internal changes in China drew the two states together after 1968. Surely no one would ever have expected that Tito would be

29. Linden, "Romanian Foreign Policy," p. 49, cites *RFE Research Report*, Nov. 23, 1979, as having said that both Reuters and UPI reported an unpublished deal according to which 350,000 tons of oil were imported from the USSR in 1979.

the first non-Chinese Communist leader to visit Mao's grave. More important for Soviet notions about communist international relations, Yugoslavia has sought ties to those, left and right, who aspire to a loosely structured world of communist states and parties, behavior that not only suits Yugoslavia but adds to Soviet difficulties with other Communist parties, such as the Italian, and states, for example, Romania.

For Romania, the Yugoslav challenge to Soviet interests stems from its advocacy of party and state autonomy and the vaguest and most benign possible construction of proletarian internationalism. For other East European states, Yugoslavia still constitutes a challenge to Soviet interests ideologically because its internal organization, or aspects thereof, may be deemed worthy of imitation. For this reason, the Soviet Union was quick to remark favorably upon recentralizing tendencies in Yugoslavia such as occurred in the early 1970s. Because such steps discredit the Yugoslav experiment in East European and Soviet eyes, Moscow acted as if it preferred a strong Soviet-type Yugoslavia to a weakened Yugoslavia.[30] In addition, Moscow seemed to believe that a Yugoslavia that is more like the Soviet Union domestically would pursue a foreign policy more in line with Soviet interests than one bent on market socialism.

In the early 1970s there were grounds for believing that Yugoslavia was once again drawing closer to the Soviet Union. (The context, it will be recalled, included the U.S. war in Vietnam, the re-Leninization of the Yugoslav League of Communists in the aftermath of the 1971 Croatian events, and the partial reorientation of Yugoslav trade away from Western Europe.) Tito himself gave cause for such speculation when in 1973 he declared that the Soviet invasion of Czechoslovakia—which Yugoslavia had vigorously condemned—"had been transcended" and that, contrary to the views of "some of our people in foreign affairs, I do not think it is logical to equate the USSR and the U.S. . . . [just] because both . . . are big powers. . . . That is incorrect."[31] Similarly, by participating with other communist states in showing solidarity with the Arab cause, Yugoslavia prompted some observers, including the then U.S. ambassador to Yugoslavia, Laurence Silberman, to wonder if, as had been the fashion for a brief while in the early 1960s, Yugoslav nonalignment meant nonalignment on the side of the Soviet Union.[32]

Neither the Soviet leadership nor Silberman was correct. After the reconsolidation of the early 1970s, with its renewed emphasis on Leninist themes, Yugoslavia moved in the latter half of the decade to reassert

30. *Izvestiya*, Apr. 21, 1974, represents an especially good example of a Soviet article praising the Yugoslavs for tightening up domestically.

31. *Vjesnik*, Feb. 23, 1973.

32. "Yugoslavia's 'Old' Communism: Europe's Fiddler on the Roof," *Foreign Policy*, no. 26 (Spring 1977), pp. 3–27.

distinctively Titoist socialist elements.[33] A parallel occurrence transpired in Yugoslavia's foreign policy, although the two phenomena were not necessarily causally connected. The Yugoslavs more and more stressed the aspects of their foreign policy that differentiated it from Soviet foreign policy.

Specifically, by the end of the decade Yugoslavia found itself defending the nonaligned against the claims of the "radicals" within the movement, headed by Fidel Castro, that the socialist camp and the nonaligned movement were natural allies against imperialism. The year 1979, for instance, provided several dramatic occasions for Yugoslav actions that challenged Soviet interests. It is striking testimony to the increasingly global ambit of Soviet power that each incident—which the Yugoslavs depicted as threats to nonalignment—involved communist states. Throughout 1979, for example, Yugoslavia and Cuba (the latter with strong Soviet encouragement) struggled over the themes to be stressed at the 6th Conference of Nonaligned Nations that met in Havana in September 1979. There were numerous indications that the Yugoslavs were bent on making certain that the nonaligned movement be directed against both Western and Eastern [read: Soviet] interests in the Third World. One utterance that nicely captures the flavor of Yugoslavia's challenge to Soviet interests faulted Iraqi leaders for emphasizing "exclusively the anti-imperialist and anti-Zionist aims of the nonalignment movement" (the United States and Israel) instead of taking a "like stand in the equally important direction of our struggle against hegemony and all forms of political and economic domination which are not classic imperialism" (the Soviet Union).[34]

Much sharper and more explicitly anti-Soviet remarks were prompted by the Vietnamese invasion of Kampuchea. The Yugoslavs were forthright in expressing their alarm and disapproval of such actions. They obviously feared that the Vietnam proxy invasion could serve as a "precedent which might endanger the security of other countries" and warned that "armed confrontations between nonaligned and socialist countries reflect negatively on both the strength and the prestige of the nonaligned movement."[35]

The Soviet response in turn was equally sharp. In Yugoslav eyes perhaps the most ominous element in that response came in November 1979,

33. See my "The Tito Legacy and Yugoslavia's Future," *Problems of Communism,* 26 (May–June 1977), 33–49.

34. Radio Belgrade (Feb. 6, 1979), as cited in *Yearbook 1980* (Stanford: Hoover Institution, 1980), p. 103.

35. *Yearbook 1980,* p. 102, citing *Večernji List* (Jan. 6 and 7, 1979), and *Borba* (Feb. 21, 1979). Like American official statements, Yugoslav commentary about the PRC's subsequent attack on Vietnam was more restrained.

when the Soviet news agency TASS observed that the Vietnamese action was analogous to the assistance rendered Yugoslavia in 1944 by the Soviet Red Army. Besides being a gratuitous affront, such statements undercut Soviet efforts to characterize as "absurd" the possibility of Soviet intervention in Yugoslavia after Tito's death, to deny that the Soviet Union was a "terrible and rapacious wolf" lusting after a "defenseless Little Red Riding Hood."[36]

That the Yugoslavs had reason to wonder which nonaligned socialist state would be next was made even more manifest when in December 1979 the wolf itself intervened in Afghanistan. The Yugoslav leaders' reaction was predictable; they took the lead in condemning the Soviet invasion in their own press and in international forums such as the United Nations General Assembly. Once again the Soviet response made it clear that the Yugoslavs had reason to feel threatened should Moscow conclude that socialism was endangered in Yugoslavia. The Soviet *New Times* inveighed against the "tendentious comments of some communist press organs" who ignore "totally . . . the main point . . . the fundamental difference between the nature and goals of the foreign policy of socialism and imperialism." *New Times* noted:

The Soviet Union acts in full accordance with the norms of peaceful coexistence enshrined in international enactments. . . . To fail to come to Afghanistan's aid would have meant handing over the Afghan revolution and people to be torn to pieces by the class enemies, imperialism, and feudal reaction and at the same time objectively aiding imperialism.[37]

Romania represents much less of a challenge to Soviet political and ideological interests than Yugoslavia. Domestically, Romania has remained highly orthodox. The Soviet Union and Romania retain close party ties, although the exact degree of proximity has been the subject of bargaining. Globally it does not have the stature that Yugoslavia has, as one of the leading nonaligned states. Rather, it must in several respects be regarded by Moscow as a nuisance more than a challenge. What Romania did, however, over the decade of the 1970s was to shape its foreign policy in a way that brought it into a stance almost parallel with that of Yugoslavia. There were a few notable exceptions, the major one being Romania's relations with Israel and its position on such items as the Camp David accords, which Romania supported. Table 5.2 compares Romania's voting in the UN General Assembly with that of Yugoslavia and Poland. Poland here symbolizes the kind of solidarity in the international realm that the Soviet Union has normally secured from its East European allies.

36. *Pravda*, Nov. 16, 1976.
37. *Novoye Vremya*, no. 3 (1980), and translated in *Foreign Broadcast Information Service (FBIS)*, Jan. 23, 1980.

TABLE 5.2. Voting Affinity of Selected Communist States with the USSR,
1970–80, in the United Nations General Assembly Plenary Sessions
(In percent)

	Country		
	Poland	*Romania*	*Yugoslavia*
1970	94	84	70
1971	99	83	70
1972	97	74	62
1973	98	72	70
1974	100	76	71
1975	99	69	74
1976	94	80	75
1977	98	74	72
1978	92	65	63
1979	95	67	67
1980	96	71	69

Because, moreover, Romania's foreign policy rests firmly on a strategy of cultivating good relations with all communist states and parties and on insisting that principles such as nonintervention are universally binding, it found itself ranged against the Soviet position in many instances in the 1970s. An advocate of autonomy, it has fostered close relations with the Spanish Communist party and has persisted in having close ties with China. The most striking illustration of the latter tie was Hua Guofeng's visit to Romania in August 1978, exactly a decade after the Soviet invasion of Czechoslovakia. As an advance of nonintervention, analogously, Romania maintained ties with Kampuchea's Pol Pot regime and criticized the Vietnam invasion. Rather than seem to support the Soviet Union or intervention, it took politically motivated walks when the General Assembly votes criticizing the Soviet intervention in Afghanistan took place.

There is even a sense in which Romania does pose a slight political challenge to the Soviet Union. For one thing, its statements at Soviet Party Congresses (the same can be said for those of several other Communist leaders) contribute very modestly to the pluralization of the Soviet internal dialogue. Soviet citizens encounter a less homogeneous press merely because Ceauşescu's speeches to Soviet Party Congresses, which repeat Romanian positions articulated elsewhere, appear in the Soviet media. More significantly, Romania has a territorial claim, Bessarabia, that it could invoke against the Soviet Union (and has in an oblique fashion). Ceauşescu's 1976 visit to Moldavia (erstwhile Bessarabia) has, however, generally been construed as a Romanian signal that it would desist from any claims against the Soviet Union.

The real political challenge Romania posed for the Soviet Union in the 1970s related to Eastern Europe. East European elites, in Poland and Hungary especially, probably had more than one occasion to muse that if Romania did not exist it would have to be invented: surely such an idea crossed the minds of East European elites when Moscow suggested in 1969 that WTO forces be sent to the Far East; in the mid-1970s, when various Soviet economic integration schemes were thwarted; and in 1979, when Moscow apparently again sought to create a role for the WTO outside Europe in response to the Chinese attack on Vietnam. In addition, Moscow's reputation probably suffers from its inability to muster complete foreign policy solidarity from its East European allies; there is little doubt that Soviet elites, with their doctrinal penchant for unanimity, perceive this to be the case. Pulling the superpower's tail can be infectious.

SOVIET OPTIONS IN THE 1980S

I have now assayed the Yugoslav and Romanian challenges to the Soviet Union in the military, economic, and political-ideological domains in the decade after the Soviet invasion of Czechoslovakia. That invasion set the tone for Soviet-Romanian and Soviet-Yugoslav relations for the 1970s. In particular, it contributed substantially to the evolution of a military quasi-alliance between Yugoslavia and Romania. Indeed, by the end of the 1970s Yugoslavia's and Romania's foreign policy positions with respect to the USSR were strikingly similar and generally incongruent with Moscow's preferences.

The Soviet invasion of Afghanistan in December 1979 has been thus far, and is likely to be throughout the 1980s, as salient an event for setting the tone of Soviet-Yugoslav and Soviet-Romanian relations in the 1980s as the Soviet invasion of Czechoslovakia was for the 1970s. Thus far, moreover, the evidence suggests that the proclivity of Yugoslavia and Romania to challenge, or at a minimum be perceived as representing a challenge by, Moscow will persist throughout the 1980s. It also suggests that there have been some changes in the stakes the Soviet Union attaches to Yugoslavia and Romania and some alterations in the resources available to the Soviet Union with which to influence the two smaller states.

As the Soviet Union's global force projection capability has continued to grow, the attractiveness it attaches to Yugoslavia has very likely also increased. Evidence for this was already available in the 1970s; almost certainly such items as greater access to Yugoslav ports for servicing Soviet ships will continue as part of the Soviet agenda in the 1980s. In the early 1980s the post-Tito leadership has shown no more enthusiasm for such a request than did Tito, for instance, in 1976.

Similarly, one can confidently assert that the issues that have divided

the Soviet Union and Romania militarily will persist and, more tentatively, that Romania's strategic significance to a more globally focused
Soviet Union will increase. Romania will continue to assert a narrow
construction of its obligations to the WTO and insist that the WTO's
domain be limited to Europe. Likewise, Romania will continue to be a
beneficiary of the free-rider principle in the WTO and, despite pressures
from Moscow, to contribute a disproportionately small share to the alliance. In this it may find more overt support than it has in the past from
states like Poland and Hungary.

Economically, the Soviet Union and Yugoslavia are likely to continue
to regard each other as valuable trading partners in the 1980s. The stakes
for the USSR will remain as they were in the 1970s. Whatever other
motivations prompt Soviet economic ties with Yugoslavia, the USSR will
seek, through trade and aid, to offset tendencies to orient the Yugoslav
economy increasingly to the West, tendencies greatly enhanced by
Yugoslav hard-currency debts. In addition the Soviet leadership will continue to find Yugoslavia a valuable source for consumer goods of a quality
far better than that produced in the USSR. Yugoslavia's need for Soviet
oil will continue; by the mid-1980s the USSR will probably not be able to
provide Yugoslavia with as much oil as the latter would like to purchase.

Romania, too, will persist in resisting Soviet pressures for economic
integration within CMEA. It will continue to be more differentiated in its
trade patterns, less involved in CMEA joint projects, and much less dependent on the Soviet Union for energy than are other East European
states. Here, however, one may witness some subtle changes in Soviet-
Romanian relations: a Romania that imports some oil from the Soviet
Union is much likelier to participate in CMEA joint projects than one that
imports no oil at all. It is probably also likely to be more attentive to Soviet
concerns in all other domains as well—especially if its major Middle Eastern suppliers are as unpredictable in their ability to deliver commitments
as were Iran and Iraq in the early 1980s.

In the political-ideological realm too, Yugoslavia will continue to represent a challenge to the Soviet Union. It is difficult, for instance, to
envisage Yugoslavia abandoning its ties to West European Communist
parties, and it will probably seek to improve relations with China as long as
the latter does not engage in vigorous antirevisionist polemics. The direct
relevance of Yugoslavia to reforms in Eastern Europe probably diminished in the 1970s and is not likely to cause Moscow great concern in the
1980s. The economic problems that have plagued Yugoslavia—inflation,
unemployment, and maldistribution of income—are precisely the most
grievous economic fears for those raised under "real" socialism. Less
directly, however, Yugoslavia will continue to be a source of Soviet concern with regard to Eastern Europe. While the particular Yugoslav path

may seem less attractive than it did in the 1960s, Yugoslavia will remain as testimony to the plurality of paths, and testimony to the possibility of reconciling with socialism particular symbols (most notably pluralism) and practices (open boundaries, strikes) that in the Soviet mind are anathema to socialism. Moreover, the Yugoslavs will continue to engage Soviet and East European critics in direct polemics; Soviet and East European ideologists have been reminded on several occasions in the early 1980s that there exist Communists in power who as a matter of course place quotations around the *real* in Soviet-style real socialism and who are publicly contemptuous of mandatory planning and other attributes of *state socialism*.[38]

In foreign policy Yugoslavia will remain a distinct hindrance to Soviet interests. The range of options in Yugoslav-Soviet relations is fairly broad and contingent on acts by decision-makers in Washington, Beijing, and Third World capitals as well as in Moscow and Belgrade. Nevertheless, Moscow will surely be confronted in the early 1980s by a Yugoslavia bent on directing the nonaligned in paths that are incompatible with Soviet (and Cuban) interests.

Romania, too, represents a challenge to Soviet interests in the 1980s. As in the 1970s, it is unlikely, despite some Romanian popular discontent, that there will be a major domestic upheaval in Romania that will produce a Soviet intervention. It is conceivable, though, that an intense Romanian reaction to Soviet intervention elsewhere, for example in Poland, might produce an upheaval that would result in Soviet military intervention in Romania as well.

In short, Yugoslavia and Romania are likely to constitute challenges to Soviet foreign policy throughout the 1980s. If we exclude for the moment the direct use of force, severe constraints will restrict the Soviet capability to alter Yugoslav and Romanian behavior. The Soviet Union has real difficulty dominating the foreign policies or internal development of a state like Yugoslavia that came to power on its own, has effective control over its society, is prepared to fight for its independence, and is able to muster considerable political support internationally. The Soviet Union even finds it difficult to dominate the foreign policy of a "derivative" regime like Romania, which exercises the control over its society one associates with Soviet and even Stalinist patterns of rule, given that there is no actual Soviet military presence in the country. (The Romanian example suggests that it might be appropriate for the United States government to attach greater value to a negotiated troop withdrawal in Central Europe than it has done heretofore.) It helps, moreover, from the van-

---

38. For a recent example see *Politika,* Sept. 27, 1980, as cited in Slobodan Stanković, "International Marxist Conference in Yugoslvaia," *RFE Research Report,* Oct. 16, 1980, p. 2.

tage point of a small socialist state seeking to defy the USSR, if one is not virtually dependent on the Soviet Union for something like oil.[39] While the USSR can certainly influence Romania and Yugoslavia much more than either Yugoslavia or Romania can influence the USSR, power asymmetries do not point to domination in circumstances where the larger power does not resort militarily to force. In the absence of force, the room for maneuver on the part of the small state is often substantial.

This is not, however, to portray the Soviet Union as a helpless giant. Rather it has impressive resources short of actual force that it can use (and has used) to influence Yugoslav and Romanian behavior. Although it is difficult for someone lacking access to classified information to sort out rumored and real troop movements, Moscow has doubtless used such posturing to communicate to Belgrade and Bucharest. Moscow has succeeded in convincing both that there are limits, and each has been constrained by such knowledge.[40] Exactly what those limits are is subject to context and bargaining. What passes for the rules of the game depends on the manner in which things are accomplished. Bucharest, as we have seen, has been especially adroit in encroaching systematically and incrementally on the putative limits. The limits for Romania, nevertheless, are demonstrably greater than for Yugoslavia. The full-fledged opening of the borders and the adoption of market socialism in Romania might, for instance, prompt Moscow to intervene.

There also are limits for Yugoslavia. There has been considerable sentiment over the years for pluralism in Yugoslavia,[41] and even Yugoslav establishment representatives have been at pains to make the case that pluralism is not inextricably linked with (bad) bourgeois rule. Part of the reason, however, that Yugoslav elites have persistently rejected proposals that would result in placing a multiparty system on the agenda is that they have perceived such an option as being unacceptable to Moscow. (There are obviously more instrumental and self-serving reasons as well.) Instead, the Yugoslav internal dialogue has centered on the merits of a one-party versus a "no-party" system.[42]

In addition the Soviet Union has exerted and will continue to exert

39. But, it should be stressed, only *helps*. Elites seeking to reduce their dependence on the Soviet Union have other resources—the threat to collapse, for instance—as well.

40. Even granting the instrumental use of such statements, see in particular Kardelj's remark, as cited in text and n. 27.

41. In a survey conducted in the early 1970s, an absolute majority of Croatian rural youth indicated they "agreed strongly" or "tended to agree" that "a multiparty system is the only possibility for creating democracy in society" (Ivan Šiber, "The Political Socialization of Rural Youth," *Sociologija Sela*, nos. 3–4, 1975, p. 129).

42. Edvard Kardelj in particular emphasized the notion that Yugoslavia was evolving into a "no-party" system.

political leverage over both Yugoslavia and Romania through its use of economic resources. If the Soviets linked Yugoslav republic-level political changes to the offer of economic assistance, it would represent a striking illustration of the use of the economic instrument for political purposes. Moscow will doubtless try such ploys in the 1980s as well. It may have greater leverage over both Yugoslavia and Romania in the 1980s than it did in the 1960s and 1970s. Here, the key element is oil. Yugoslavia now derives nearly half its foreign oil from the USSR. Romania will import Soviet oil in the 1980s. In a world where power grows out of a barrel this could give Moscow leverage it did not have in the 1970s. Should that happen, Yugoslavia and Romania would be more in the position of typical East European states than either was in the 1960s and 1970s. In 1983, however, it appears that the Soviet Union will not have such an abundance of oil, and oil will not be so difficult to obtain elsewhere as to render this an important change. Viewing Soviet-Yugoslav relations generally, moreover, I remain impressed by how little political mileage Moscow has derived from its economic credits and aid, except to the extent that it has reinforced Yugoslav notions that too great economic ties to the West would not serve Yugoslavia's interests.

Additionally, Moscow still has some lingering capacity to provide symbolic rewards. This matters less for the Yugoslavs than for the Romanians. (In retrospect, though, one is impressed by how often Tito seems to have responded to flattery rather than pressure from the Soviet side.) Leaders of communist states generally turn out to like Orders of Lenin, and the Soviet Union can withhold such kudos—as it did to Ceauşescu[43]—until Moscow deems the circumstances appropriate.

Finally, there are many ways the Soviet Union has intervened, and doubtless will continue to intervene, in Romania and Yugoslavia short of military force. It is difficult to imagine Moscow stifling the urge to encourage "healthy forces" by indicating that certain persons have known anti-Soviet tendencies—with the implication that relations would be better if they were ousted—thus establishing the principle that domestic cadre questions are a legitimate concern of the Soviet Union. It will continue to introduce its agents into the country, or recruit them from among the Yugoslav citizenry who are manifestly pro-Soviet: Mićunović reports that in 1956, "The Russian priest from Belgrade, Tarasiev, . . . behaves so that you might think he represents not only the Russian Orthodox community in Belgrade but also some other, much more powerful 'secular' Soviet organizations in our country."[44] There are Soviet "sleepers" in deep

43. He received the medal on August 1, 1979, a year-and-a-half after it had been awarded him on his 60th birthday.
44. Mićunović, *Moscow Diary*, p. 120.

cover in both countries. In the Yugoslav case the Soviet Union can give aid and comfort to Cominformist forces in exile (many of whom are in Kiev) seeking to restore an order untarnished by the Titoist infection. Already there are rumors of KGB ties to Croatian separatists in the post-Tito era just as there were during the 1971 Croatian national upsurge.

In both Yugoslavia and Romania, Moscow can and has played the minority card. For Yugoslavia the central concern is, with respect to Moscow, Bulgarian attitudes to Macedonia and Macedonians. (Croatia and Kosovo are other obvious danger spots; Albania's incipient succession crisis may well impinge on Soviet-Yugoslav relations.) Although Moscow has played the nationality card cautiously in the past, there is no doubt that in Yugoslav minds, Bulgarian-Yugoslav relations and the Macedonian question are linked intimately to Soviet-Yugoslav relations. Significantly, in the first three years after Tito's death, Yugoslav-Bulgarian relations were as cordial as they had been for years. The Romanians are likewise convinced that Hungarian-Romanian relations and the problem of the Hungarian minority in Transylvania are linked to Soviet policy. (For good reason: Ceauşescu probably traded a cease-fire in the battle of words between Soviet and Romanian historians over Bessarabia for a muting of polemics over Transylvania.)

The question of course is which of these resources Moscow will use. Some crystal-ball-gazing about Yugoslavia may provide illumination on this score. In the first three years of the post-Tito period, Soviet behavior toward Yugoslavia has been very restrained. Yugoslavia in those years did not provide a setting that would encourage an active Soviet foreign policy. Great risk taking has never characterized Soviet behavior, and in the environment Yugoslavia has offered Moscow has been content to pursue a relatively subtle game. Despite major economic difficulties, the Tito succession has been largely uneventful, even though there have been major upheavals in heavily Albanian Kosovo. Part of the reason for Moscow's quiescence doubtless has been that Moscow's attentions have been elsewhere: at home with the end of the Brezhnev era, in Afghanistan, and in Poland. Paradoxically, by its actions in Afghanistan and its support of Vietnam in Kampuchea, the Soviet Union has thoroughly offset whatever purchase its economic aid and credits may have achieved and has convinced the Yugoslavs that Moscow really is a "big ferocious wolf." In any event, Kosovo aside, Yugoslavia has not presented the kind of setting in which an opportunistic but exceedingly cautious Moscow would move overtly against Yugoslavia.

By such action, as Moscow doubtless realizes, it would stand to lose a lot. There would be some risk, however modest, of a general war. The Soviet Union would suffer great political losses in the Third World, and it would have a real fight on its hands were it to attack a unified Yugoslavia.

(It is a sobering commentary that none of the above would be attributes of a Soviet intervention were a domestic upheaval to occur in Romania. The Soviet Union may draw the line less finely between Eastern Europe and other socialist states now that it is a world power, but noncommunist elites still make the distinction sharply.)

Unfortunately there may yet be a time for Soviet military intervention in Yugoslavia during the 1980s. The Partisan generation is rapidly passing from the scene and is being replaced by elites raised under Tito. Although the current leadership's talents have been the subject of sharp and open criticism in the Yugoslav press, it is not at all evident that the generation of political leaders raised under Tito has either the political skills or the commitment to Yugoslavia of those who fought with Tito in World War II. It is easy to imagine the current economic crisis coupled with nationalist agitation able to produce a mass uprising in the near future at a time when elite consensus was absent. Such circumstances might produce the kind of worst-case scenario many feared in regard to Soviet-Yugoslav relations in the aftermath of Tito's death. Once again the Soviet leadership might phone the Yugoslav leadership or some part thereof and offer, as Brezhnev did Tito in April 1971, to render comradely mutual assistance. Thus far, it should be stressed, Moscow has not acted as though this is a scenario it looks forward to; on the contrary, Moscow has consistently acted as though it preferred a strong, centralized Yugoslavia, one governed by a strong hand, which neither represented an alternative to Moscow nor, because of Yugoslavia's inherent fissiparous qualities, would come to represent a military opportunity for Moscow. If the scenario we have outlined should occur at some juncture in the 1980s, however, it may be that Soviet-Yugoslav relations will also take a highly ominous turn.

A generation after Stalin effectively expelled Yugoslavia from Eastern Europe, a post-Brezhnev Soviet leadership, in the name of "the international solidarity of revolutionaries," may attempt forcibly to reintegrate Yugoslavia with Eastern Europe. Should such a scenario come to pass, it will pose a challenge to American policymakers that will make the decisions the United States took in supporting Yugoslavia in 1948 pale in comparison.

6

The Political Economy of Soviet Relations with Eastern Europe

PAUL MARER

The most significant general factor in the relations between the Soviet Union and the countries of Eastern Europe,[1] whether individually or collectively, is the large disparity between their populations, territories, resource endowments, and military power. Given these differences, and given the objectives of Soviet policy, intrabloc relations are inevitably asymmetrical, marked by the dominance of a superpower and the dependence of six relatively small client states, and like any relationship of asymmetrical interdependence offering opportunities for the strong to take advantage of the weak.

My focus in this chapter is the evolution of the Soviet Union's economic relations with Eastern Europe since 1945 and the prospects for those relations in the 1980s. The basic question it will attempt to answer is how Soviet-East European relations should be characterized: Has the USSR used its power to dominate the East European countries economically, or has it subsidized them heavily, as some claim? Or is the relationship one of mutual costs and benefits?

First I trace the Soviet Union's postwar economic objectives and policies under Stalin, relevant because Eastern Europe's economic institutions and structures were established then; their legacies continue to be important even in the 1980s. Next I describe post-Stalin changes in Soviet economic policies and the main institutions and mechanisms of the Council for Mutual Economic Assistance (CMEA), as essential background for understanding the nature of Soviet economic relations with Eastern Europe. Then I discuss a most controversial issue: Can it be established statistically and unambiguously that the Soviet Union provides large subsidies to Eastern Europe and, if so, how can that be reconciled with Soviet

I would like to thank Morris Bornstein, Robert W. Campbell, Ed. A. Hewett, Marie Lavigne, Sarah Terry, and Thomas Wolf for their helpful comments and Michael Marrese and Jan Vanous for making available a prepublication copy of their book and for clarifying discussions. This acknowledgment should not imply their agreement with any statements or interpretations.

1. For the purposes of this chapter, Bulgaria, Czechoslovakia, the GDR, Hungary, Poland, and Romania. Yugoslavia is included in this chapter only if specifically mentioned.

power and domination of the region? Finally, I describe how Soviet and East European economic performance and prospects are expected to influence Soviet economic policy during the rest of the 1980s, and conclude with a discussion of the USSR's political goals and economic policy options.

HISTORICAL BACKGROUND (1945–55)

During World War II, much of the industry of what subsequently became the German Democratic Republic (GDR) was destroyed or severely damaged, and a good part of what remained was dismantled and taken by the Soviets. The economies of Poland and Yugoslavia were also largely destroyed, while Hungary's suffered very serious damage.

Postwar economic recovery was slowed by Soviet exploitation, mainly via conventional types of economic extraction: carting away machinery from the former enemy countries; so-called joint stock companies, through which the Soviet Union took a significant share of Eastern Europe's current output; and by paying less than world market prices for Eastern Europe's commercial exports (particularly well documented in the case of Poland). Reparations represented further unrequited transfers (principally from East Germany but also from Hungary and Romania). The GDR carried the largest combined burden by far, but substantial resources were extracted from the other countries as well. I have estimated the value of the unrequited flow of resources from Eastern Europe to the Soviet Union during the first postwar decade to be roughly $14 billion, or of the same order of magnitude as the aid the United States gave to Western Europe under the Marshall Plan.[2]

With the completion of basic postwar reconstruction by 1948–49 (later in East Germany), the development strategies of all East European countries followed the Soviet model: increasing the share of investment in national income to very high levels at the expense of consumption and concentrating investment in mining, metallurgy, and machine building. The policies pursued during 1948–53 and the reorientation of trade from Western Europe to the USSR laid the foundations of an industrial structure that largely determined the course of postwar economic development in Eastern Europe as well as the subsequent pattern of Eastern Europe's commercial relations with the USSR and with the rest of the world. Therefore, it is of interest whether the adoption of the Soviet

2. Paul Marer, "Soviet Economic Policy in Eastern Europe," in John P. Hardt, ed., *Reorientation and Commercial Relations of the Economies of Eastern Europe*, compendium of papers submitted to the Joint Economic Committee, Congress of the United States (Washington, D.C.: U.S. Government Printing Office [hereafter GPO], 1974).

model by national Communist leaders during the 1948–53 period was voluntary or imposed.

Long aware of their relative economic backwardness, the East European countries had periodically attempted to overcome it by spurts of import-substitution industrialization, although with little success. In light of past frustrations, it is not surprising that there was significant support after the war for a strategy of rapid industrialization, not only in the newly separate Eastern Zone of Germany and in the already highly industrialized parts of Czechoslovakia but in all the other East European countries as well. However, the breakneck speed of industrialization and its extremely skewed pattern were externally imposed. Countless eyewitness accounts testify to the decisive role played by Soviet advisers and shopping lists in the industrialization and trade patterns of Eastern Europe during this early period; many argue that Soviet shopping lists have remained important in determining the composition of the region's industrial output.

Czechoslovakia after the war was already a relatively highly developed country whose industrial base had not been destroyed. The double coup d'état of 1948–49—of the Communist party over parliamentary democracy and of the Muscovite faction over the rest of the party—was immediately followed by two successive, very large, revisions in the original draft of the First Five-Year Plan (1950–55). According to an economics text published in Prague in 1969, the first revision arose out of long-term trade contracts with CMEA, especially the 1950–55 agreement with the USSR, which "raised demands upon Czechoslovak heavy industry, in particular upon the production of heavy machinery and equipment. . . . These articles were highly material-intensive and required the construction of new capacities, or the reconstruction of existing ones." Concerning the second revision in 1951, the same text contended that demands from the military sector were "considerable, and [that] the entire economy was subordinated to them"—indeed, that "these tasks were no longer integrated into a modified plan but represented a plan of their own." As a result, planned growth of industrial output was increased from 10 to 20–25% per annum, while armaments production increased sevenfold from 1948 to 1953.[3]

The situation was quite similar in East Germany. War destruction and dismantling by the Soviets in metallurgy and in the chemical and engineering industries had left the GDR's manufacturing capacity predomi-

3. R. Olšovský and V. Průcha, eds., *Stručný hospodářský vývoj Československa do roku 1955* (Prague: Svoboda, 1969), p. 397; cited in V. Holešovský, "The Czechoslovak Economy in Transition" (unpublished manuscript, 1972).

nantly in light and food industries and light machine building. Yet, while these latter industries often operated below capacity because of supply shortages, and in 1958 were still producing far below 1939 levels, branches founded or expanded to produce for Soviet export (shipyards, railroad equipment plant, precision machinery, electrical machinery, and heavy industrial equipment) were operating above 1939 levels.[4]

The situation appears to have been similar also in Poland and Hungary. As postwar reconstruction was nearing completion, both governments opted for an industrialization drive spearheaded by heavy industry. But it was the subsequent Soviet-inspired upward revisions that became decisive and created extreme hardships. As Poland's one-time economic czar, Hilary Minc, later admitted, the buildup of defense industries at Soviet behest "skimmed the cream of output . . . [and] led to the creation of a half-war economy in 1951–53."[5]

Romania, Bulgaria, and for a short time Yugoslavia also copied the Soviet model, although trade data do not show that their priorities for heavy industry were imposed on them by Soviet import demands, since much of their exports to the USSR during the 1950s (Yugoslavia until the Stalin–Tito break in 1948) consisted of raw materials, semifabricates, and foodstuffs. But even in Romania there were efforts in its newly created machine-building sector to produce goods such as drilling equipment and ships for export to the USSR.[6]

The primary mechanism through which the USSR imposed its preferences on Eastern Europe during this period has been called the "Soviet embassy system" of plan coordination. The Soviets decided which countries should produce which articles, were involved in the drawing up of long-range plans, and operated certain enterprises in every country except Poland. In the GDR, "all high economic functionaries had their 'partner' in the Soviet embassy whom they consulted for every important move."[7]

A second important instrument of control was the Council for Mutual Economic Assistance, which was formed in 1949 ostensibly to promote

4. E. M. Snell and M. Harper, "Postwar Economic Growth in East Germany," in John P. Hardt, ed., *Economic Developments in Countries of Eastern Europe*, compendium of papers submitted to the Joint Economic Committee, Congress of the United States (Washington, D.C.: GPO, 1970).

5. See, for instance, Minc's speech at the 8th Plenum of the Polish Central Committee in 1956, cited in J. M. Montias, *Central Planning in Poland* (New Haven: Yale University Press, 1962), p. 123, and S. Ausch, *Theory and Practice of CMEA Cooperation* (Budapest: Akadémia Kiadó, 1972), p. 43.

6. J. M. Montias, *Economic Development in Communist Rumania* (Cambridge, Mass.: MIT Press, 1967).

7. F. L. Pryor, *The Communist Foreign Trade System* (Cambridge, Mass.: MIT Press, 1963), pp. 200–01.

multilateral economic integration among its members. CMEA's real purposes were political: as Stalin's reply to the Marshall Plan and to the economic integration of the West European countries that the plan was intended to promote; as an instrument of the Soviet bloc's stand, including initially a trade embargo, against Yugoslavia; and as a means of pre-empting and aborting the several proposals for subregional integration that were being promoted by nearly all the East European regimes in the late 1940s.[8] Far from fostering multilateral links, CMEA served in its first years to enhance Soviet control over each of its individual members; indeed, up to 1955, its activities were confined to the registration of bilateral commercial agreements.

The foregoing evidence leads to the conclusion that during the first postwar decade the USSR was chiefly responsible for turning the East European countries' industrialization strategies, which were probably voluntary and largely balanced to begin with, into an imposed, un-economical, and excessively paced parallel development of high-cost industrial branches throughout the region. There were probably several interrelated reasons. First, the Soviets apparently did believe that their own pattern of industrialization was ideologically correct and had universal applicability for the new socialist states. This belief was not challenged by the Communist leaders in Eastern Europe, many of whom were trained in the USSR and had witnessed the example of impressive Soviet economic progress during the 1930s and military success during the 1940s. Second, this model also had the beneficial political ramification of placing limits on the East European states' interaction with one another, at least more so than regional specialization would have, and thereby prevented the building up of a politically stronger Eastern Europe. Third, the Soviet policy of encouraging Eastern Europe to specialize in heavy industrial products regardless of their raw material base may have been designed to reorient trade to the USSR and to heighten each state's dependence on Soviet raw materials (which at the time could not readily be sold on world markets) and the Soviet market (at a time when the Western embargo limited Soviet access to Western goods).

The outcome was a grossly inefficient allocation of resources. Its chief manifestations were the building up of parallel industrial capacities in the East European countries and a rapid movement toward all-East European deficits in raw materials. The forced pace of industrialization led to

8. Proposals for various kinds of subregional integration schemes, all well documented, included those made by Czechoslovakia with Poland, Hungary with Yugoslavia and Czechoslovakia, Yugoslavia with Bulgaria, and Bulgaria with Romania. See I. Berend, "The Problem of Eastern European Economic Integration in a Historical Perspective," in I. Vajda and M. Simai, eds., *Foreign Trade in a Planned Economy* (Cambridge, England: Cambridge University Press, 1971).

declining living standards after 1950 and to terrorized and resentful populations, thereby contributing to the political upheavals in the region in the 1950s.

SOVIET POLICIES AND THE MECHANISMS OF CMEA INTEGRATION (1956–83)

Policy Changes after Stalin

There was a sharp break in Soviet economic policy toward Eastern Europe after 1956 as the high political cost of economic extraction and pervasive direct interference was brought home to Moscow by the turmoil of the first post-Stalin years. The essence of the post-1956 policy was to place trade with Eastern Europe on a reasonably equitable commercial basis—a process that began earlier with the dismantling of the joint stock companies—and to activate the CMEA.

After 1956 CMEA became useful as a mechanism through which to maintain and expand Eastern Europe's economic ties with the USSR, while allowing for the formal economic and political independence of the region. Formal, and to some extent real, independence for the East European countries is useful to the Kremlin both for its global foreign policy (because it can be charged less evidently with outright domination and because its allies can support the USSR's global objectives more effectively as nominally independent than as captive states) and for its regional policy (because giving up direct control should help to allay the resentment of the East European populations, which in turn should contribute to the domestic political stability and thus also to the economic viability of these regimes). To be sure, the Soviet Union continued to view its trade with the region as yielding important economic and security, as well as political, benefits.

Although CMEA has not proved to be a strong integrative mechanism, it has played and continues to play a significant role in Soviet-East European economic relations. It is through CMEA that many of the rules of intrabloc commerce are codified. CMEA also serves as the main forum for debating proposals to improve the intrabloc divisions of labor, debates that yield insight into the economic objectives and policies of member countries.

Economic integration among a group of centrally planned economies (CPEs) is fundamentally different from integration among market-type economies. In Western economies much of international commerce is conducted by private enterprise seeking profit opportunities wherever it can find them. Hence, a reduction in or elimination of barriers to the movement of goods, factors of production, and money across national borders goes a long way toward integration. By contrast, under central planning all movement of goods and factors across national borders requires an explicit action by the governments involved. For CPEs, with no mechanism for determining comparative advantage in manufactures, it is difficult to reach agreement about specialization or to implement agreed policies effectively in each country.

Proposals for Integration

During the first postwar decade the Soviet concept of integration was for each country to carry out Soviet instructions. During the second half of the 1950s the USSR probably had no clear-cut policy on integration. To be sure, large and useful blocwide projects had been completed, such as an electricity grid and other infrastructure projects, which in the CMEA literature of this period were equated with movement toward regional integration. There was much discussion of the need for improved blocwide specialization and integration, but without specifying clearly the economic content of these broad objectives. It is conceivable that during this period the USSR had no definite idea or policy on what type of specialization would provide the Kremlin maximum long-run benefits from intrabloc trade.

By the early 1960s the wastefulness of the parallel industrial development strategies of the 1940s and 1950s became apparent. To remedy the problem, Khrushchev proposed to transform CMEA into a supranational organ: that is, CMEA rather than the national planning authorities would make key new investment decisions ex ante rather than try to coordinate ex post the decisions independently made. This proposal brought to the surface the fear of the East European countries that bloc integration under a supranational authority would mean even more domination by the USSR. The most uncompromising stand against supranationalism was taken by Romania, whose famous 1964 statement brought the conflict to world attention.[9] In the face of Romania's firm stand—and perhaps recalling that earlier pressures on Yugoslavia and Albania had contributed to those countries' defections from the bloc—the USSR decided not to press its proposals.

The 1964–70 period was one of much debate and experimentation about economic reforms. Domestic reform proposals usually contained suggestions for CMEA reforms also. One proposal, most clearly articulated by the Hungarians, favored greater reliance on market mechanisms for socialist integration. Its advocates predicted better prospects for gains from regional specialization and for the maintenance of greater national

9. Montias, *Economic Development*, chap. 4.

autonomy. Other proposals favored planned integration, relying on the traditional concepts and institutions of central planning.

The outcome of the debate was the 1971 Comprehensive Program for socialist integration. Although the document appears to be a compromise between those advocating market mechanisms and those favoring joint planning, the emphasis since 1971 has definitely been on the second approach and on the initiation of joint investment projects in priority sectors. Aspects of the Comprehensive Program stressing the market approach to socialist integration, such as eventual currency convertibility or the establishment of direct and autonomous trade links among enterprises in the different countries, appear in retrospect to have been more a recognition of need rather than a statement of intent.[10] To reduce the fears of the East European countries about supranationalism, an important compromise recognized by the Comprehensive Program that appears to have become a permanent feature of CMEA is the "interested party principle." This permits member countries to confine their participation to those CMEA projects or programs in which they have an interest.

The Comprehensive Program stresses improved plan coordination, joint CMEA investment projects, and cooperation in "long-term target programs." Under the old system, plan coordination meant little more than exchanging background information preparatory to bilateral trade negotiations, after national plans had been completed and the pattern of investment (formally not subject to coordination) had been decided. Improved plan coordination today means that the procedure begins earlier (three years before the end of the current quinquennium), so that there is at least the possibility that as a result of discussions, a member country's investment plans could be altered.[11] Each country must include a special section in its national plan document elaborating the specific details of its integration measures. In practice, plan coordination appears to involve a standardization of economic information concerning projects that involve a long-term linking of two or more CMEA economies. This should facilitate a better assessment of what is really going on in CMEA and checking of the bilateral and multilateral consistency of national plans, but it does not appear to have brought about fundamentally new modes of CMEA integration.[12]

10. C. H. McMillan, "Some Thoughts on the Relationship Between Regional Integration in Eastern Europe and East-West Economic Relations," in F. Levcik, ed., *International Economics: Comparisons and Interdependencies* (Vienna: Springer Verlag, 1978).

11. W. Brus, "Economic Reform and Comecon Integration," in *Wirtschaft und Gesellschaft* (Berlin: Duncker und Humblatt, 1979).

12. For a more detailed discussion of the theory and practice of integration among CPEs, see Paul Marer and J. M. Montias, eds., *East European Integration and East-West Trade* (Bloomington: Indiana University Press, 1980).

CMEA Joint Projects

The joint investment program represented the major new form of CMEA activity during the 1970s. For some time, the Soviet Union had been pressing the East European countries to participate in joint investments in the USSR, pointing out that it alone had the exploitable natural resources and that such investments would represent partial compensation for supplying its CMEA partners with energy and raw materials.

The total value of joint investment projects agreed upon for the 1976–80 period was approximately $12 billion (at the 1975 official ruble–dollar exchange rate of $1.30). The largest undertaking involving all six East European countries was the Orenburg project, consisting of a natural gas complex at Orenburg in Western Siberia and a 2,677-kilometer natural gas pipeline connecting Orenburg with the Soviet Union's western border. The total estimated cost of the project was between $5 and $6 billion, accounting for about 50% of the value of all CMEA joint investment projects in the 1976–80 plan period.[13] The second largest joint undertaking was a giant pulp mill at Ust Ilim in Central Siberia.

The two features that distinguished the Orenburg and Ust Ilim projects from all other joint CMEA investment projects were the joint participation of the investing countries in construction on the territory of the host country (other projects were jointly planned but not jointly built, each country being responsible for construction on its own territory) and the extensive degree of Western participation with technology, machinery and equipment, and financing. The ownership benefits accrue to the USSR, which is repaying the East European countries' investment with a 2% simple interest rate, by delivering to them agreed quantities of gas and pulp, respectively.

In the absence of accurate information about future prices for the commodities used to repay the investment and accurate information about the opportunity cost of investment participation, it is difficult to undertake a meaningful cost/benefit calculation. Some of the East European literature suggests that investing in CMEA joint projects—which take the form of delivery of labor, capital, consumer goods, technical know-how, and hard currency—is not economical. Among the factors cited are: the high manpower costs of these projects (employing East European workers in the USSR costs about three times more than employing them at home, while their contribution is valued by the USSR at Soviet wage rates and overhead schedules); the low interest rate received; the burden of large hard-currency contributions; and the disadvantageous terms of repayment (since the prices of the goods received in

13. See also chap. 7.

payment are tied to world market prices). In short, the East European countries do not obtain ownership benefits for their contribution; however, they do gain assured supplies and will enjoy price concessions as long as CMEA prices are set on the basis of historical world market prices *and* world market prices of energy and raw materials continue to rise steeply.

The joint investment formula à la Orenburg does not appear to have been continued into the 1980s, certainly not on the scale implemented during 1976–80. No new major multilateral projects have been announced for the 1981–85 period. East European contributions to Soviet resource development are primarily through deliveries of specialized machinery and equipment as agreed on bilaterally. The reason for this, in addition to those already mentioned, is that such large-scale projects as the pipeline, which lend themselves more readily to joint construction and financing than projects in the manufacturing sector, have been exhausted.

Instead, there appears to be a new emphasis on bilaterally determined investment specialization, with the East European economies providing machinery and other inputs for multilateral resource development projects in the USSR, and on implementing the so-called long-term target programs. The latter involve selected sectors and projects of major importance, where coordination is supposed to take a more binding and all-embracing form: joint forecasting for 15 to 20 years of production, consumption, and trade trends to identify prospective shortages and surpluses; coordination of medium- and long-term plans for the sector's main branches of production and key commodities; and joint research and development programs. Such long-term target programs have been mentioned for five sectors: fuels, energy, and raw materials; machine building; industrial consumer goods; agriculture, especially foodstuffs; and transportation.

It is unclear whether much progress has been or can be made in increasing CMEA specialization under these programs. One problem is that too many priorities means no real priority for any sector. The more general problem, however, is that which hinders CMEA specialization in all sectors: how to determine an economically sound pattern of specialization in production and trade. Calculations of static or dynamic comparative advantage involve comparisons of relative costs in the member countries; but the internal price systems of the CMEA countries cannot provide the necessary information on domestic costs because administratively set prices and exchange rates neither incorporate all relevant costs nor measure relative scarcities of inputs and outputs. This is the reason why intra-CMEA trade is valued at world market prices, an approach that gives rise to a new set of complex problems.

Prompted by unresolved problems relating to the fundamentally unsatisfactory mechanism of economic integration in the CMEA and the immediate economic and trading difficulties experienced by the East European countries in recent years, there have been repeated calls since 1980 for a summit meeting of the first party secretaries and heads of governments of the CMEA countries to deal with the problems. The first publicized summit proposal was made by Romania in June 1980, another by Leonid Brezhnev in February 1981; the latter's formulation of the purpose of the summit was endorsed by Gustáv Husák of Czechoslovakia in April 1981. Yet the disagreements about which problems are the most important and how to solve them are so fundamental that at the time of writing (November 1983) no summit had been convened even though plans have been announced repeatedly to hold one. While Moscow, complaining that ordinary plan coordination as hitherto practiced no longer suffices to support production integration, wants to harmonize the economic systems and policies of the countries and to set up joint production units,[14] the East European countries wish to discuss how the CMEA in general and the USSR in particular can assist them in alleviating the economic crisis they face as a result of their rapidly deteriorating terms of trade with the USSR, hard-currency balance-of-payments problems, and deteriorating East-West political, economic, and financial relations. Romania seeks especially increased supplies of Soviet energy at CMEA prices. Waiting for a clarification of Yuri Andropov's economic policies and prospective reform proposals has been another reason for repeatedly postponing the summit.

CMEA Price System and Commodity Composition

CMEA countries employ different pricing mechanisms in East-West and intra-CMEA trade. With partners outside the bloc, they try to trade at current world market prices (generally succeeding when they import but obtaining lower prices when they export), while prices in intrabloc trade are linked to world market prices of an earlier period according to successive formulas agreed upon since 1958. Because each CMEA country sets its domestic prices differently and essentially arbitrarily, no country is willing to accept the prices of the others for valuing exports and imports. Therefore, as a practical matter, they formally rely upon an agreed variant of the world market price even though cost ratios and scarcities are different in CMEA from those in the West.

Under the Bucharest formula of 1958, average 1957–58 world market prices remained in effect until about 1965. For 1965–70, average

---

14. *Pravda*, Oct. 15, 1982. This article and the material contained in this paragraph of my text were called to my attention by Jozef van Brabant.

world prices of 1960–64 were used; for the 1971–75 period, intra-CMEA prices were based on average world prices of 1965–69. However, in early 1975, prices were revised at Soviet insistence one year ahead of schedule, and today are changed annually on the basis of world prices of the preceding five years. This procedure will remain in effect at least through the 1981–85 plan period.[15]

This price-setting mechanism has several problems and consequences. For one, the mechanism prompts bargaining because it is difficult to establish "the" world market price.[16] Bargaining power may be exerted through prices (obtaining high prices for exports and paying low prices for imports) and through quantities (supplying certain goods in specified amounts). Thus, if we find the price of a commodity high or low relative to current world prices, this may be due to (1) the price that is "out of line" being compensated by offsetting deviations in the prices or quantities of other export and import items; (2) one country purposefully exploiting or subsidizing another; or (3) current world market prices having moved much higher or lower than the historical Western prices on which the CMEA price is based.

For energy, raw materials, and other primary products, CMEA prices can be determined relatively easily because these are mostly standardized commodities traded on the world markets at published prices. Since 1973–74, world prices of energy and many raw materials have risen sharply; CMEA prices, because of the price rule, more slowly. Thus, if the CMEA price rule is observed, the USSR as a net exporter of energy and raw materials will obtain for those goods prices lower than current world prices. One may call this difference an implicit Soviet subsidy to Eastern Europe, though it is important to stress that, to the extent the price rule is followed, the subsidy results automatically from the mechanisms of intra-CMEA price determination, which, for institutional and political as well as economic reasons, it would be difficult for the Soviet Union to change.

For most manufactured goods, there is a range of world market prices for similar but in most cases not identical products. In bilateral bargaining between countries with nonconvertible currencies, prices typically tend to gravitate toward the upper end of the world market price range. One reason for this is that the shortage of convertible currencies causes each

15. Kálmán Pécsi, *The Future of Socialist Economic Integration* (Armonk, N.Y.: M. E. Sharpe, 1981), p. 101.

16. That there is considerable price bargaining is readily acknowledged even by Soviet experts: "In [intra-CMEA trade] negotiations, both sides cite prices that satisfy their notions of effectiveness of exchange and subsequently arrive at some variant as a result of 'bargaining.'" See N. M. Mitrofanova, "The Economic Nature of Contract Prices in the Mutual Collaboration of CMEA Countries," *Izvestiya Akademii Nauk SSSR (Seriya ekonomicheskaya)*, no. 5, 1977, translated in *Soviet and East European Foreign Trade*, 15 (Spring 1979), 9.

side to prefer to import the commodities needed from other soft-currency countries, which places the seller in a position to charge the highest possible price. Indeed, during 1958–64, when world market prices were comparatively stable, East European computations showed that the intra-CMEA price levels of manufactures were slightly above world market prices, though after 1965 the price level gap apparently narrowed.[17] What has happened to CMEA/world market price ratios for manufactures since then is difficult to say because world market prices of industrial products have also risen rapidly during the 1970s, and there is insufficient reliable information on whether CMEA prices of machinery and industrial consumer goods have kept pace or lagged behind changes in world market prices.

Be that as it may, it is our impression that in the battle of documentation to set prices for manufactured goods in intra-CMEA trade, the USSR has not leaned heavily on its economic and political leverage to obtain favorable prices. In fact, during the 1960s and early 1970s East European negotiators may well have been better equipped with price documentation and thus more skillful price bargainers than those of the USSR, perhaps because of greater initial experience in these matters and because each East European country has relatively more at stake in its trade with the USSR than vice versa. If so, the Soviet Union, as a net importer of manufactures from Eastern Europe, may have granted implicit net price subsidies on this segment of trade also. It must be stressed, however, that the evidence on this point is "soft" and that other considerations must also be taken into account in assessing who is subsidizing whom and by how much in intrabloc trade.

A further important point is that the real value of a commodity is judged by each country's planners not only by its price but also by how strongly it is in demand, either because (1) the exporter is able to meet the technical and marketing specifications of the importer, (2) the import alleviates shortages and bottlenecks in the domestic economy, or (3) the commodity can be sold in the West for convertible currency. Goods in greatest demand are called "hard goods," commodities in surplus "soft goods." Commodities have different degrees of hardness or softness that can change as production patterns and priorities change. Energy, raw materials, and basic food items such as grain that can be sold readily on the world market are the hardest; standard machinery, for which there is not a great deal of demand by the importing country, softest.[18]

17. Paul Marer, *Postwar Pricing and Price Patterns in Socialist Foreign Trade (1946–1971)* (Bloomington: International Development Research Center of Indiana University, report 1, 1972).

18. Pécsi, *Future of Socialist Economic Integration, p. 131.*

CMEA countries try to balance with each trading partner not only total exports and imports but also trade within each category of hardness and softness. This partly compensates for the fact that prices and money balances in CMEA do not play the allocative role they do on the world market. Approximate bilateral balancing of hard goods and soft goods is the practice in all CMEA links except between the USSR and Eastern Europe. This is evident from the commodity composition of Soviet trade with the East European Six combined (table 6.1) and the corresponding trade balance by main commodity categories (table 6.2). A brief discussion of the CMEA currency system and exchange rate practices is a useful background for interpreting the data in tables 6.1 and 6.2. One reason why it is difficult to obtain a firm handle on price subsidization is CMEA's elusive exchange rate system; another is that actual price adjustments do not always follow the formal price rule.

Currency and Exchange Rates

Intra-CMEA trade transactions valued according to the agreed set of historical world market prices (usually expressed in dollars) are translated into and settled in "transferable rubles" (TRs), an artificial currency whose only function is to serve as an accounting unit. The exchange rate of the TR vis-à-vis the dollar is for all practical purposes the same as that of the Soviet domestic ruble, which remained unchanged at 1.00 Rb = 1.00 TR = \$1.11 until 1972, when both the ruble and the TR began to fluctuate, initially with an appreciating trend, to reflect the depreciation of the dollar in terms of other currencies. Thus, by 1980, 1 TR = \$1.50, which the subsequent appreciation of the dollar changed to 1 TR = \$1.30 by mid-1983.

The significance of a changed valuation of the TR is that, ceteris paribus, it changes the prices of *some* of the commodities traded in CMEA. If the prices of *all* goods traded were determined each year from a dollar base, a change in the dollar/TR rate would not matter because all prices would change proportionately. But it appears that only the prices of crude oil, of other important primary products, and of newly traded items are derived each year from dollar prices, probably by averaging the dollar prices of the years to be included in the formula and then applying the current dollar/TR rate. The prices of most manufactured goods tend to remain unchanged in CMEA over a longer period and, when changed, the usual method is to adjust the TR price by an agreed percent. The net result is the existence of de facto multiple exchange rates and the continued separation of domestic, East-West, and intra-CMEA price levels and ratios. These represent significant obstacles to intra-CMEA specialization, especially in the manufactures sectors.

Owing to these difficulties, a significant development during the 1970s was that a growing share of intrabloc trade began to be priced at current world market prices and paid for in convertible currency. These transactions involve mainly hard goods exported to a CMEA partner over and above the quantities agreed upon in the five-year trade agreements. Thus, a certain portion of Soviet oil and raw materials is sold to the East European countries at current world prices and paid for in dollars, and a portion of Soviet imports from Eastern Europe is also priced and settled in the same way. No systematic information is available on the size and balance of this trade except for Hungary, for which it represents between 8 and 15% of its total "socialist" trade (i.e., with CPEs).

In addition to "direct" there is also "indirect" convertible-currency trade. This refers to the Western import content of East European exports to the USSR that have been paid for in convertible currencies. These have increased very rapidly in recent years, as a growing proportion of imported inputs have had to be obtained from world market rather than CMEA sources. Of course, the Soviet Union can be said to compensate, in part, its East European trade partners for such "embodied" Western imports by providing a certain "ruble content" for Eastern Europe's hard-currency exports to the West. Although calculations of this type are fraught with statistical difficulties, it is interesting to note that during the mid-1970s, the dollar content of Hungary's ruble exports was roughly 20% and rising rapidly, whereas the ruble content of its dollar exports was only about 7%.[19] The point, of course, is that East European "transshipping" of Western goods to the Soviet Union is a benefit the USSR obtains from its CMEA partners, just as Eastern Europe obviously benefits from "transshipping" imported Soviet energy and raw materials in the other direction. The benefits to each side will be determined by the use value as well as by the price (relative to opportunity cost) of the items involved.

Invisible Transactions and Credits

Even less is known in the West about so-called invisible transactions in CMEA. Prices of invisibles reportedly are not covered by the CMEA price rules noted above and therefore change infrequently. Poland, for example, is known to be a large exporter of transit services, primarily to the USSR, mostly on rails. Uniform CMEA freight rates remained unchanged from 1973 through 1980—a fact that Poland protested strongly—at a time when freight costs rose steeply due to rising energy prices.

Intrabloc tourism is another significant item. Apart from the question of how realistic tourist exchange rates are, net exporters of tourist ser-

19. Ibid.

vices—especially Hungary and Bulgaria but also Poland and Romania—provide a high-value service to the net importers because tourists have open access to most of the consumer goods available in the host countries and can thus take advantage of large differences in the availability and relative prices of consumer goods in the CMEA countries.

Another aspect is the settlement of invisible transactions in the balance of payments. Net balances are converted into TRs by an agreed coefficient and settled by shipping goods from the deficit to the surplus country. Depending on the coefficients and the kinds of goods that the deficit country is willing to export to the surplus country, substantial hidden gains or losses may derive from such transactions. It is my strong impression that the USSR and the GDR obtain substantial net benefits on invisibles from the rest of Eastern Europe, but further research would be required to validate and to try to quantify this. That the issue is important was suggested by the headline news when, on August 1, 1979, Romania decreed that all foreign tourists must immediately pay in convertible currency for gasoline and oil purchases. This order, at the height of the summer tourist season, stranded thousands of Soviet and East European tourists in Romania, a country that in effect repudiated the CMEA clearing system for invisible transactions. The decree provided that tourists from the other CMEA countries would be able to pay in their own currencies only after an interstate agreement had been negotiated providing reimbursement to Romania in specified commodities—presumably goods more acceptable than the deficit countries had been willing to ship to Romania up to then.

Credits are among the most important and complex issues in Soviet-East European economic relations. The size of credits, the type of goods or currency in which the loans are supplied, settlement provisions, and the "grant equivalent" of credits jointly determine the distribution of costs and benefits in a loan transaction. In recent years credit transactions between the USSR and the East European countries have been significant, but no comprehensive balance-of-payments-type accounting is available on them. However, since most credit transactions involve the delivery of goods, bilateral trade balances do offer clues.

During 1971–73 the East European countries combined had a positive trade balance with the USSR of TR 1.7 billion. During 1974–80, however, Eastern Europe had an import surplus every year, the cumulative total reaching TR 6 billion (table 6.2). A portion of this surplus represents 10-year Soviet terms of trade credits.

A great deal of uncertainty, however, surrounds the interpretation of observed trade balances because they typically reflect some combination of: delays in planned deliveries by one partner, settlement of balances on invisible transactions, extensions of new credits, and repayment of earlier loans. Matters are further complicated by the involvement of CMEA's International Bank for Economic Cooperation (IBEC) and the International Investment Bank (IIB) in convertible-currency credit transactions because one side of such a transaction will not be reported in intra-CMEA trade statistics. To be specific, in recent years IBEC and IIB have borrowed, jointly on behalf of the USSR and the East European countries, billions of dollars on the Eurocurrency markets, primarily to finance imports from the West for CMEA projects located in the USSR, such as the Orenburg gas pipeline. The East European countries are responsible for servicing their share of these loans, which in the case of IIB amounted to 95% of the total between 1971 and 1978.[20] The USSR repays the East European countries with additional gas shipments that may show up as a Soviet trade surplus with Eastern Europe, while the hard-currency portion of the credits the East European countries grant to the USSR remains invisible. A further important aspect of such credits is that, while the East European countries pay the Euromarket rate of interest on their hard-currency loans (which in recent years has fluctuated between 8 and 20% per annum), they receive interest from the USSR that ranges between 2 and 5% per annum.

IS EASTERN EUROPE AN ECONOMIC ASSET OR A LIABILITY FOR THE USSR?

The aggregate growth and structure of Soviet trade with the six East European CMEA countries between 1960 and 1980 are presented in table 6.1; the trade balance by main commodity categories is shown in table 6.2. The data presented reveal that the USSR has had a large export surplus in two of the "hardest" commodity groups—fuels as well as nonfood raw materials and semimanufactures—and a large deficit in machinery and industrial consumer goods, which on balance are "softer" commodities.

This pattern of trade is in part a consequence of the energy- and raw-material-intensive development strategy of the East Europeans during the late 1940s and early 1950s, which has in many ways constrained their subsequent pattern of industrial development and trade. It is a consequence also of the relatively poor energy and mineral resource endowment of most of these countries, of the wasteful consumption of inputs that characterizes all CPEs, and of the fact that the East Europeans have redirected some of their domestic output of hard goods to the West to pay for needed imports. As a result, the region's import requirements for energy, raw materials, and semimanufactures, a large part of which were met by the USSR, have grown rapidly over the last three decades. By 1980 the Soviet Union's export surplus in these commodity categories exceed-

20. M. Lavigne, "The Soviet Union Inside Comecon," *Soviet Studies*, 35 (Apr. 1983), 146.

TABLE 6.1. Soviet Trade with the Six East European Countries Combined, by Main Commodity Categories, 1960–80 (In millions of transferable rubles)

	Fuels	Nonfood raw materials and semimanufactures	Agricultural and food products	Machinery	Industrial consumer goods	Total
Exports						
1960	372	1,205	476	637	77	2,767
1961	438	1,335	424	784	80	3,060
1962	527	1,438	544	976	89	3,574
1963	598	1,482	504	1,081	83	3,747
1964	668	1,717	322	1,274	68	4,049
1965	679	1,758	340	1,241	79	4,097
1966	660	1,777	380	1,327	79	4,223
1967	682	1,836	485	1,442	91	4,535
1968	742	2,048	493	1,671	118	5,073
1969	846	2,228	559	1,826	119	5,578
1970	914	2,600	487	1,944	138	6,083
1971	1,051	2,653	576	2,090	147	6,517
1972	1,174	2,740	351	2,301	161	6,727
1973	1,324	2,849	347	2,682	179	7,381
1974	1,577	3,185	496	3,185	263	8,705
1975	3,138	4,344	455	3,581	347	11,866
1976	3,717	4,610	177	4,216	387	13,107
1977	4,692	4,878	326	4,982	388	15,266
1978	5,670	5,115	109	5,605	448	16,946
1979	6,977	4,968	260	5,908	436	18,549
1980	8,582	5,478	152	6,219	488	20,919
Imports						
1960	187	535	171	1,153	470	2,516
1961	173	586	247	1,198	536	2,740
1962	164	627	229	1,551	660	3,231
1963	164	680	267	1,806	816	3,732
1964	158	757	289	2,001	801	4,005
1965	171	741	366	2,113	815	4,205
1966	158	662	349	1,926	922	4,016
1967	159	733	400	2,175	1,117	4,583
1968	145	802	417	2,471	1,245	5,079
1969	148	865	475	2,645	1,278	5,410
1970	144	962	555	2,899	1,411	5,970
1971	174	1,001	639	3,048	1,671	6,533
1972	205	1,202	759	3,720	1,801	7,687
1973	211	1,152	728	4,214	1,788	8,093
1974	196	1,208	889	4,450	1,857	8,600

TABLE 6.1   (*continued*)

	Fuels	Nonfood raw materials and semimanufactures	Agricultural and food products	Machinery	Industrial consumer goods	Total
1975	418	1,630	1,317	5,616	2,330	11,312
1976	407	1,798	1,226	6,321	2,474	12,226
1977	411	1,981	1,358	7,331	2,771	13,852
1978	497	1,941	1,220	10,065	3,049	16,776
1979	471	2,155	1,506	10,196	3,163	17,491
1980	401	2,777	1,864	10,585	3,468	19,095

SOURCE: Official Soviet foreign trade statistics as compiled, reconstructed, or estimated in *Wharton Centrally Planned Economies Foreign Trade Data Bank*, Vol. 1 (Washington, D.C.: Wharton Econometrics, Jan. 1982).

TABLE 6.2.   Soviet Trade with the Six East European Countries Combined, Total and by Main Commodity Categories, 1960–80 (In millions of transferable rubles)

	Fuels	Nonfood raw materials and semimanufactures	Agricultural and food products	Machinery	Industrial consumer goods	Total
1960	185	670	305	−516	−393	252
1961	265	749	177	−414	−456	320
1962	363	811	315	−575	−571	343
1963	434	802	237	−725	−733	15
1964	510	960	33	−727	−733	44
1965	508	1,017	−26	−872	−736	−108
1966	502	1,115	31	−599	−843	207
1967	523	1,103	85	−733	−1,026	−48
1968	597	1,246	76	−800	−1,127	−6
1969	698	1,363	84	−819	−1,159	168
1970	770	1,638	−68	−955	−1,273	113
1971	877	1,652	−63	−958	−1,524	−16
1972	969	1,539	−408	−1,419	−1,640	−960
1973	1,114	1,697	−381	−1,532	−1,609	−712
1974	1,382	1,977	−393	−1,265	−1,594	105
1975	2,720	2,714	−862	−2,035	−1,982	554
1976	3,310	2,812	−1,049	−2,105	−2,087	881
1977	4,281	2,897	−1,032	−2,349	−2,383	1,414
1978	5,173	3,170	−1,112	−4,460	−2,601	170
1979	6,506	2,813	−1,247	−4,288	−2,727	1,058
1980	8,181	2,700	−1,712	−4,365	−2,980	1,824

SOURCE: Calculated from table 6.1.

ed $16 billion at intra-CMEA prices (TR 10.9 billion at the official exchange rate of approximately $1.5); at prevailing world market prices the surplus would have been significantly higher.

This surplus in Soviet exports of primary products to its CMEA partners, together with the sharp differences between world market and intra-CMEA prices for these products, is an important component of what has been called the USSR's "implicit subsidies" to Eastern Europe. According to the subsidy argument, as presented in its most dramatic form by economists Michael Marrese and Jan Vanous, "the Soviet Union has transferred resources equivalent to almost $80 billion in 1980 dollars during the decade 1971–80."[21] Their calculations are based on two assumptions: the first concerning the disadvantageous commodity structure of Soviet-East European trade for the USSR; the second concerning the disadvantageous pricing of Soviet trade with Eastern Europe, compared with the hypothetical situation of the same goods being traded by the Soviets with Western countries. An examination of these two assumptions will show that the subsidy argument is open to serious qualification in principle and that the Marrese–Vanous estimate of the burden that Eastern Europe imposes on the USSR is greatly overstated. Let us look first at the commodity structure of trade and then at the question of valuation.

In the 1950s the exchange of Soviet primary products for East European manufactured goods was advantageous for the USSR because its partners were able to supply machinery and other manufactures denied by the Western embargo, and because there was no world shortage of energy and raw materials and therefore no strong demand for Soviet supplies. By the 1960s this pattern had become to some extent ossified: Soviet planners had become used to the routinized supply relationship with East European producers, just as East European planners had come to count on routine acquisition of Soviet primary products and semi-manufactures. Moreover, there was no great economic pressure on the USSR to alter the pattern; on the contrary, it was able to expand energy and raw material production quickly and at reasonable cost.

During the 1970s circumstances began to change. The rapid expansion of Soviet trade with the West increased the opportunity cost of being a large net supplier of hard goods to Eastern Europe, as did the rising cost of extracting and transporting these goods from increasingly remote Siberian regions. Moscow began to complain more persistently that its

---

21. M. Marrese and J. Vanous, *Implicit Subsidies and Non-Market Benefits in Soviet Trade with Eastern Europe* (Berkeley: University of California Press, 1983). These estimates have been prominently reported in influential publications such as the *Wall Street Journal* (Jan. 15, 1982), *Time* (Jan. 18, 1982), and *Fortune* (July 13, 1981).

pattern of trade with Eastern Europe was disadvantageous, but mitigating circumstances still limited the trade pattern's disadvantage. Most important were the substantial windfall gains the USSR enjoyed in the form of improved terms of trade with the West, and to a lesser extent with Eastern Europe, as it benefited from OPEC price increases, the rising price of gold, and its ability to tap into the OPEC surplus by selling military hardware for dollars to several newly rich oil-exporting countries.[22]

These windfall gains—which may have yielded as much as $50 billion between 1973 and 1980—enabled Moscow to increase its hard-currency export revenues almost as rapidly as it expanded its hard-currency imports, that is, without incurring excessively large foreign debts. Moreover, in view of systemic limitations on the capacity of the Soviet economy to absorb a greater volume of Western technology than it purchased during the 1970s (indeed it could not utilize fully even what it did import), in view also of supply and transport limitations on the import of larger amounts of grain, the opportunity cost of supplying increased amounts of energy and raw materials to Eastern Europe probably did not appear to be a crushing burden. In addition it should be remembered that Moscow's improved terms of trade with Eastern Europe meant that the growth rate of the volume of Soviet hard-goods exports to its CMEA partners declined steeply during the 1970s, while the volume of Soviet purchases from them accelerated, thus delivering a double-barreled blow to the region's hard-currency balances. On the one hand, the East Europeans were forced to turn to the world market for a growing share of their hard-goods imports; on the other, they had fewer exports to pay for them.

Let us now turn to the question of prices in Soviet-East European trade. This is an important issue on which firm, empirically based conclusions are exceedingly difficult to reach. The first problem is the selection of the appropriate standard against which to assess intra-CMEA prices. Although relative scarcities in CMEA are different from those on the world market, in the absence both of meaningful prices within CMEA and of an effectively functioning regional market, most specialists (Western and Eastern) have concluded that current world market prices are the appropriate standard. Next, one must select the appropriate world market price concept: Is it to be the set of prices at which Western countries trade with one another or prices in East-West trade? This is a vital distinction because, although as a rule CPEs are able to import from the West at West-West prices, they are often able to export to the West only at substantially lower prices, especially on finished manufactures.

22. Ed. A. Hewett, "Foreign Economic Relations," in Abram Bergson and Herbert S. Levine, eds., *The Soviet Economy: Toward the Year 2000* (London: Allen & Unwin, 1983).

A further difficulty is how one should interpret the fact that a commodity is traded in CMEA at a higher or lower price than the current world market level. As noted earlier, this may be due to: (1) offsetting deviations in the prices or quantities of other export or import items, (2) changes in world market prices that have not yet been factored into the CMEA formula, or (3) outright exploitation or subsidization. In short, proper interpretation of price anomalies in intra-CMEA trade depends on an evaluation of all aspects of economic (and political) relations among the countries concerned—an evaluation that is made difficult, if not impossible, by the fragmentary nature of available data. It is here, in the interpretation of intra-CMEA prices, that the subsidy argument is most vulnerable to statistical inaccuracies.

Assuming that the USSR could have substituted trade with the industrial West (settled in dollars) for the transactions it entered into with the East European Six countries (settled mainly in TRs), Marrese and Vanous argue that the prices paid to or received from the West represent the Soviets' opportunity cost; hence, trade with Eastern Europe should be revalued in those hypothetical dollar prices. That is, if trade reported by the Soviet Union as balanced in TRs yields a Soviet export surplus in dollars, the surplus is the amount of Soviet subsidy to Eastern Europe; if a deficit, an East European subsidy to the USSR. If trade in TRs is not in balance, an adjustment is made in dollar values. For purposes of their calculations, Marrese and Vanous further divide Soviet-East European trade into two categories: (1) energy, raw materials, semimanufactured products, and agricultural and food products (primary products); and (2) machinery, equipment, and industrial consumer goods (manufactures).

In the case of primary products, Marrese and Vanous first compute TR "unit values" for a sample of commodities and then try to find matching unit values in dollars. For Soviet exports to Eastern Europe, the dollar values are Soviet-to-West prices for the same commodity; for Soviet imports from Eastern Europe, they use West-to-Soviet prices. The ratio of dollar-to-TR unit values are called derived dollar/ruble exchange rates. The authors compute as many sample derived $/TR ratios as published trade statistics allow and estimate the hypothetical dollar value of each commodity category by multiplying the published or reconstructed TR value by the weighted-average-derived $/TR exchange rate obtained from unit value samples in that commodity category. Although gaps in the data force them to make a series of assumptions that create potentially large margins of error, the dollar values and corresponding subsidies they compute for trade in primary products may be accepted as reasonable approximations.

Far more difficult is the establishment of "true" dollar values for intrabloc trade in manufactures. On the basis of a study done nearly 20 years ago by CMEA experts, Marrese and Vanous estimate that in 1960 intra-CMEA prices of manufactures were 25% higher than West-West prices for comparable goods. Next, they note that the Soviet Union and the East European countries could sell to the West the manufactures they trade with each other only at large discounts from world market prices—discounts ranging up to 50% and assigned arbitrarily by country—due to the poor quality and service features of these products. Each of these assumptions gives a major upward bias to their estimates of the amount of the Soviet subsidy to each East European country.

Three sets of factors account for the large discounts on East-bloc exports of manufactures to the West. One is the poor quality of the East's products. A second is the systemic shortcomings of Eastern export pricing: exporting on the basis of plan directives, which reduces the flexibility required to obtain the best price; preference for barter and compensation deals inconvenient for the Western partner, who therefore pays a low price for such products; and hard-currency balance-of-payments pressures, which often force Eastern countries to make drastic price concessions. The third set of reasons for Eastern export price discounts is Western discrimination—whether in the form of high-tariff or nontariff barriers to CMEA goods.

Since Marrese and Vanous argue that a portion of Soviet subsidy arises because the Soviet Union pays more for imports from Eastern Europe than it would have to pay if the same goods were purchased from the West, the correct dollar opportunity cost is not East-to-West export but East-from-West import prices. If the Soviet Union imported the same manufactured goods from the West, it would not be able to obtain as large discounts as when the East exports to the West because the second and third sets of discount factors would be absent. In missing this point and assuming that they can substitute East European export prices for Soviet import prices to value Soviet purchases from Eastern Europe, Marrese and Vanous introduce a significant upward bias into their calculations.

There is an even more fundamental criticism of their subsidy computations. Just because an East European machine or consumer product is not of the latest Western design—that it is not equipped with the ultimate series of gadgets, does not have all the assortment, packaging, and other convenience features that characterize the most modern Western products—does not mean that the Soviet importer of these goods provides a subsidy to Eastern Europe equivalent to the Western quality discount. There must be many instances where the East European products are as, or even more, suitable to Soviet conditions than the most modern Western counterparts. Thus, while Marrese and Vanous are probably correct that as a net importer of manufactures the USSR provides some subsidy to the exporters, there is simply not enough statistically meaning-

TABLE 6.3. Net Soviet Subsidies (+) and Taxes (−) on Trade with the Six East European Countries Combined, by Major Commodity Categories, 1960–80 (Millions of current dollars)

	Total (1)	Fuel (2)	Nonfood raw materials and semimanufactures (3)	Agricultural and food products (4)	Primary products (2) + (3) + (4) (5)	Machinery (6)	Industrial consumer goods (7)	Manufactures (6) + (7) (8)
1960–70	3,862	−2,099	−3,502	−594	−6,195 (−160%)	4,953	5,104	10,057 (260%)
1971	900	−31	−311	−38	−380 (−42%)	472	808	1,280 (142%)
1972	1,134	−114	−411	22	−503 (−44%)	736	901	1,637 (144%)
1973	2,001	293	−132	2	163 (8%)	934	904	1,838 (92%)
1974	6,227	3,525	1,450	215	5,190 (83%)	449	588	1,037 (17%)
1975	5,030	2,028	31	496	2,555 (51%)	1,304	1,171	2,475 (49%)
1976	5,144	2,547	43	298	2,888 (56%)	1,155	1,101	2,256 (44%)
1977	5,209	2,333	106	288	2,727 (52%)	1,165	1,317	2,482 (48%)
1978	5,637	959	−145	345	1,159 (21%)	2,856	1,622	4,478 (79%)
1979	9,653	4,041	−376	481	4,146 (43%)	3,527	1,981	5,508 (47%)
1980	20,482	14,294	−341	477	14,430 (70%)	3,933	2,120	6,053 (30%)
1960–80	65,280	27,776	−3,588	1,992	26,180 (40%)	21,484	17,617	39,101 (60%)
As percentage of total								
1960–80	100%	43%	−5%	3%	(40%)	33%	27%	(60%)
1960–79	100%	30%	−7%	3%	(26%)	39%	35%	(74%)

SOURCE: M. Marrese and J. Vanous, *Implicit Subsidies and Non-Market Benefits in Soviet Trade with Eastern Europe* (Berkeley: University of California Press, 1983).

ful information to attach a dollar price tag to the amounts that might be involved.[23]

By breaking the Marrese–Vanous subsidy estimates down into two basic categories—first, those that arise from net Soviet exports of primary products to Eastern Europe (which are acceptable estimates); and second, those that arise from net Soviet imports of East European manufactures (which are unacceptable due to the statistical uncertainties, upward biases, and omitted compensatory gains to Moscow noted above)—we can readily see that 60% of the cumulative subsidy is accounted for by the second, less reliable category (table 6.3). In addition, more than half the cumulative 1960–80 total fuel subsidy arose in 1980 due to the explosion of the world market price for crude oil in 1979–80, which the CMEA price formula and other considerations did not allow the Soviet Union to pass on to Eastern Europe immediately.

Detailed computations covering the period 1971 to 1978, the latest year for which these calculations could be made, show that on trade in fuels, nonfood raw materials, semimanufactured goods, and agricultural products combined, the USSR implicitly provided a net cumulative subsidy of about $14 billion to the six East European CMEA countries. This amount was somewhat greater than 10% of cumulative total Soviet exports to these countries during the period. The distribution of this subsidy total by country was as follows:

	Total (billion $)	Per capita ($)
Bulgaria	3.5	390
Czechoslovakia	2.6	170
GDR	4.8	290
Hungary	1.0	100
Poland	2.1	60
Romania	−0.1	−0.5

The amount of the implicit subsidy is determined largely by the bilateral commodity structure of trade, which has evolved gradually during

23. Marrese and Vanous have responded to some of the criticisms here and those made by others at the various debates we have had on these issues by including in the appendix to their book (n. 21) a sensitivity analysis, varying the assumed quality discount on intra-CMEA trade in manufactures. However, in their text, summary statements, and press releases they continue to cite only the original high numbers, without qualifications. They also claim that these statistical issues make little difference in any event because much of the subsidy arises on Soviet primary exports to, rather than manufactures imports from, Eastern Europe. I do not agree with their claim; our disagreement on this issue arises from differences concerning the correct statistical formula to use to decompose the total subsidy.

the postwar period, and by the extent to which an East European country depends on trade with the USSR; but it may also be influenced by the politically determined preferences of Moscow. It seems that for all these reasons Bulgaria has been favored because the amount of the subsidy received by that country, especially in per capita terms, is substantial. Particularly notable is the contrast with Romania, which has been much more oriented toward the West and was self-sufficient in energy until the late 1970s, although political considerations by the Kremlin may also have played a role.

In 1982 crude oil and other fuel prices began to decline sharply whereas intra-CMEA prices continued to rise. If fuel prices were to stabilize at their early 1983 levels or decline further, intra-CMEA prices will equal and then exceed world market prices sometime in 1984 or 1985, so that subsidies in this important commodity category would begin to flow from Eastern Europe to the USSR.

Making similar calculations for manufactured goods is much more difficult for the reasons indicated. Trade in manufactures leads to the question of dynamic gains from trade. Significant trade benefits are forgone by the exporter if the preferential, sheltered CMEA market absorbs over a long time poor-quality goods and obsolete equipment, thereby reducing the incentive to innovate and produce "for the market," causing the exporter to fall more and more behind its competitors on the world market. This cost appears to fall disproportionately heavily on the smaller and relatively advanced CMEA countries like the GDR, Czechoslovakia, Hungary, and Poland; the bill is presented when they must expand their manufactures exports outside the sheltered CMEA market. The importer of shoddy goods loses potential productivity gains, too; yet it may not be able to resist buying such goods if its own producers have become dependent on the same CMEA suppliers for exports and imports.

ECONOMIC PERFORMANCE OF THE CMEA COUNTRIES AND SOVIET POLICY OPTIONS

During the second half of the 1970s two factors that became increasingly important in Soviet calculations were the USSR's own deteriorating economic performance and prospects and the growing economic weakness of the East European countries, with obvious implications for political instability, actual or potential. Since economic performance in the USSR and Eastern Europe represents constraints on Soviet foreign policy during the 1980s, this section will highlight the main trends.

Economic Performance of the USSR and Eastern Europe

The rate of growth of the Soviet economy declined considerably during the 1970s. The consensus of Western experts is that the slowdown will continue so that, during the 1980s, growth rates are unlikely to exceed the 1 to 2.5% range per annum. Given the Soviet Union's low labor-force growth, growing global commitments, the heating up of the arms race, and the great need for additional investment to respond to bottlenecks in infrastructure, energy, and other sectors, this projected slowing of the growth rate suggests the possibility of stagnation in the level of per capita consumption, with attendant political difficulties for the Soviet leadership. Thus, from the perspective both of prospects for the Soviet energy sector (see chap. 7) and of overall economic performance since the late 1970s, the opportunity cost of supplying subsidized energy and other raw materials to Eastern Europe has risen significantly, as have pressures to obtain additional resources from the region.

At the same time, the rapidly deteriorating economic performance of the East European countries caused the Soviet leaders to proceed cautiously about raising export prices too sharply or curtailing energy and raw material shipments too precipitously. Since the late 1970s Eastern Europe, too, has been in a fundamentally new situation that in many ways is more precarious than that of the USSR, and that can best be explained by providing a brief historical perspective.

From the late 1940s until the late 1970s, the East European countries appear to have performed well, some exceptionally well, by international comparisons. One reason for using the word *appear* is that Western experts consider the exceptionally high growth rates reported by some East European countries—Romania, Bulgaria, and the GDR especially—to be exaggerated because of unconventional statistical methods of index number construction, although even after a downward adjustment the rates remain impressive. More important is the fact that the growth rate of output should not be the only performance indicator. The performance of an economy should be judged by multiple indicators, such as efficiency, consumer satisfaction, and its external trade and financial balance. An economy may be able to achieve spectacular growth rates by borrowing large sums abroad. But if the borrowed resources are not put to good use, the high growth rates of one period may be achieved at the expense of stagnation or decline in a subsequent period, as is best shown by the case of Poland.

One reason the East European countries were able to achieve impressive growth rates over the past 30 years was that, until the 1980s, these countries were able to rely on three consecutive sets of temporary support mechanisms. During the early 1950s the regimes used extreme methods to mobilize underemployed resources and to squeeze agriculture and the consumer to finance a rapid growth in investments. These strong-arm methods, however, proved to be economically and politically counterproductive. Political excesses and the absence of material incentives undermined political stability and the economic efficiency of resource use.

During the 1960s the East European economies were boosted by increased trade with the USSR (in the case of Yugoslavia increased trade with, and some assistance from, the West were more important), involving a rapidly growing exchange of inexpensive Soviet energy and raw materials for East European machinery and other manufactured products. However, during the 1970s the annual increments in the volume of Soviet exports to Eastern Europe slowed and became more expensive; by the early 1980s their absolute level began to stagnate and, in the case of some key commodities like oil, actually declined, wherein energy conservation and the recession in Eastern Europe played some role also.

During the 1970s growth rates were helped by official Western credits and private bank loans that became newly available to CPEs. The banks had large surpluses of loanable funds, and lending to Eastern Europe was considered safe because central planning was viewed as synonymous with effective control over the balance of payments (since planners, supposedly, could always cut imports and push exports) and because a Soviet umbrella was believed to exist. Yet in 1981 Poland was forced to reschedule; in 1982 Romania joined Poland, and net lending to Eastern Europe stopped. Most of the other East European countries also experienced debt-servicing difficulties, owing partly to economic and political factors outside their control—such as the Western recession, high interest rates, and the increased level of East-West tensions in the wake of Afghanistan and Poland, which also had an adverse impact on Western trade and the extension of credits.

By the late 1970s all the East European countries were experiencing increased economic pressures: from their own consumers who expected that living standards would continue to improve or at least not deteriorate; from their trade situation with the USSR, whose energy and raw materials had become less readily available and much more expensive; and from Western creditors, who were no longer willing to make large *new* loans to Eastern Europe but expected the countries to service their large debts, which meant a new outflow of resources from Eastern Europe to the West. Depressed economic conditions in the West since the mid-1970s contributed further to Eastern Europe's problems as demand for their products declined, competition (especially from the less developed countries) increased, and protectionist forces in the West grew. The most immediate observable outcome of this new situation has been drastic reductions in growth rates or levels of production, and even more drastic cuts in domestic utilization, as shown in table 6.4.

Net foreign borrowing makes it possible for domestic utilization—private and public consumption plus investment—to increase more

TABLE 6.4.   Average Annual Growth Rates of National Income Produced and Utilized by the East European Countries, 1971–82 (In percent)

National income produced	1971–75	1976–80	1981	1982ᵃ
Bulgaria	7.8	6.1	5.0	4.0
Czechoslovakia	5.7	3.7	−0.4	0.5
GDR	5.4	4.1	4.8	3.0
Hungary	6.2	3.2	2.0	1.5
Poland	9.8	1.2	−12.1	−8.0
Romania	11.2	7.3	2.2	2.6
Yugoslaviaᵇ	6.6	5.6	2.0	n.a.ᶜ

National income utilized	1971–75	1976–80	1981	1982ᵃ
Bulgaria	8.6	2.8	7.7	4.0
Czechoslovakia	6.1	2.2	−4.5	−3.0
GDR	4.7	3.6	1.7	0.5
Hungary	5.6	1.9	0.1	−2.0
Poland	11.6	−0.2	−12.3	−12.0
Romania	n.a.	6.9	−4.9	−1.5
Yugoslaviaᵇ	n.a.	4.5	−4.9	n.a.

SOURCE: Compiled from official East European reports.
ᵃPreliminary.
ᵇSocial product.
ᶜNot available.

rapidly than production, which it did during the first half of the 1970s in most East European countries. A net outflow of resources—which occurs if the sum of debt service payments and the deterioration in the terms of trade exceeds the sum of new loans obtained from abroad—means that domestic utilization must remain below production, as it has in all these countries except Bulgaria since the late 1970s. This in fact is the adjustment—the price—the borrowing countries have had to pay as debt levels rose too high and as new credits became unavailable.

Although similar pressures are felt by all the East European countries, there are very important differences among them in terms of policies, performance, and prospects, as suggested by the data presented in table 6.4. Most striking is the case of Poland, where economic mismanagement and overly ambitious expansion plans led to costly mistakes, with outcomes that are detailed elsewhere in this volume. What economic role is played by the USSR and other members of CMEA in Poland? Although we do not have the full picture, evidence suggests that in 1980 and 1981 the USSR provided economic assistance in the form of additional deliveries to and reduced imports from Poland, as well as substantial hard-currency loans, but that since 1982 only relatively small trade credits have been granted. The East European countries, on the other hand, while clearly being hurt economically by disruptions in Poland's export delivery obligations and the deteriorating creditworthiness of the entire region induced by the Polish and Romanian debt rescheduling, do not appear to have provided large-scale assistance. After the imposition of martial law, the Soviet Union seems to have reduced sharply its economic aid to Poland. This may well be a move motivated not only by economic but also by political considerations: to place the blame for that country's economic hardships on Western sanctions and lack of credits, which Poland's leaders have been doing publically since introducing martial law.

Highly significant also is the dramatic slowdown in Romania's growth. Though due in part to special circumstances, there are similarities with Poland: overly ambitious growth targets in earlier years, serious shortages of consumer goods, economic mismanagement, and a balance-of-payments crisis compounded by external circumstances, such as a disruption of oil imports due to the Iranian revolution and the war between Iran and Iraq.

The growth of the absolute level of the net hard-currency debt of Eastern Europe and the USSR between 1970 and 1982 is shown in table 6.5. Although since 1981 the debt levels have stabilized, in most cases because of the absolute unavailability of new credits, the debt service ratios (percent of exports that must be devoted to service the debt) are still very high and will remain high for several years, except in Bulgaria and Czechoslovakia (and the USSR), whose debt burdens are relatively modest.[24] The unavailability of substantial new credits to the East European countries since about 1979 has forced them to adjust quickly, which has meant not only the slowing, leveling, or decline of production growth rates (depending on country) but also the reduction of consumption and especially investment rates or levels.

The basic conclusion concerning Eastern Europe's economic performance is that these countries will continue to face serious difficulties. Although by 1983 the worst of the economic crisis may be over (with the likely exception of Poland), these countries can no longer count on the temporary support mechanisms mentioned earlier. Moreover, their continued high debt service obligations, the trade difficulties faced within CMEA, and the related stagnation in consumption but especially the decline in investment levels, indicate that East European growth rates will

24. Bulgaria, which had a very high debt burden during the early 1970s, carried out a successful adjustment policy between 1977 and 1982.

TABLE 6.5. Net Hard-Currency Debt of Eastern Europe and the USSR to the West, 1970–82 (In current billion U.S. dollars)

	1970	1975	1980	1981	1982[a]
Bulgaria	0.7	2.1	2.5	2.1	1.8
Czechoslovakia	0.6	1.2	3.4	3.4	3.2
GDR	1.4	4.8	11.2	11.0	9.2
Hungary	0.6	2.3	5.8	6.2	6.2
Poland	1.1	7.7	22.0	23.2	24.1
Romania	1.6	3.1	9.3	9.7	8.8
CMEA-Six	6.0	21.2	54.2	55.6	53.3
USSR	1.0	7.8	8.7	10.8	8.0
CMEA banks	0.3	2.2	4.1	3.9	3.6
CMEA-Seven[b]	7.3	31.2	67.0	70.3	64.9
Yugoslavia	1.9	5.7	16.8	18.0	18.3
Eastern Europe and USSR total	9.2	36.9	83.6	88.3	83.2

SOURCE: Wharton Econometrics, *Centrally Planned Economies Outlook* (Washington, D.C.: Wharton Econometrics Forecasting Association, Mar. 1983).

NOTES: Net hard-currency debt to the West is defined as gross hard-currency debt to Western banks, Western governments, and international financial organizations (IMF and the World Bank, in the case of Romania and Yugoslavia), minus deposits in Western banks. Categories of debt included are long-, medium-, and most short-term debts, evaluated at year-end foreign currency/dollar exchange rates.

[a]Estimated.

[b]CMEA-Six plus the USSR.

not soon return to levels achieved to the mid-1970s. The greatest difficulties, of course, will be faced in Poland.[25]

Soviet Economic Options in Eastern Europe

J. F. Brown has identified succinctly the Soviet Union's policy dilemma in Eastern Europe: conflict between its desire for alliance cohesion and for political viability in the region. Cohesion requires conformity of ideology, of domestic and foreign policies, and of implementing institutions. Viability demands credible and efficient economic performance in East-

25. A more detailed assessment by country can be found in Paul Marer, "East European Economies: Achievements, Problems, Prospects," in Teresa Rakowska-Harmstone, ed., *Communism in Eastern Europe*, 2d rev. ed. (Bloomington: Indiana University Press, 1984).

ern Europe that will increasingly legitimize Communist rule. The two objectives are difficult to reconcile because a uniform set of institutions and policies is at odds with the need for flexible responses to country-specific problems.[26] Stalin opted for cohesion; the post-Stalin leaderships have more and more emphasized viability, as long as East European policies remained within "limits" that were uncertain and constantly changing.

Moscow does not appear to have a great deal of room for maneuver in Eastern Europe. Since it is quite certain that no Soviet leadership will want to give up the ideological, military, political, and economic alliance system it dominates in the region, it cannot contemplate telling the East Europeans that it will change quickly, drastically, or unilaterally the existing institutional arrangements, such as the CMEA pricing mechanism or basic trade patterns. Therefore, the realistic question in assessing Soviet options is this: To what extent and through what mechanisms can the Soviet Union reduce, gradually, the economic cost of its East European empire while increasing the economic and political viability of the regimes in the region?

For the USSR the economic cost of trade with Eastern Europe declines rapidly as the gap between intra-CMEA and world market prices of raw materials and energy products narrows or disappears. A substantial movement in this direction has been taking place since 1980 for most raw materials and since 1982 for energy, owing to the continuing rise in intra-CMEA prices of these products under the CMEA pricing formula, while world market prices have declined. The Soviet Union has also been insisting that the East European countries improve the quality of their manufactured exports.

For the future, one may also envision a gradual change in the pattern of the Soviet-East European division of labor. Given relative factor endowments, including historical traditions and skills, and the Soviet Union's great excess demand for agricultural and food products and industrial manufactures, it would make economic sense to encourage the East European countries to move toward increased specialization in those products for the Soviet market.

Over the next few years much will depend on how the situation evolves. One can envision a scenario in which Poland's economic contacts with the West will continue to decline, and the regime will remain afloat only through substantial Soviet and some East European economic assistance. Such an option would be costly for the USSR. The previously

26. J. F. Brown, *Relations Between the Soviet Union and Its East European Allies: A Survey*, Report R-1742-PR (Santa Monica: The Rand Corporation, 1975).

cited evidence for 1981 and 1982 does not suggest that Moscow is prepared to carry a continuous and large economic burden in Poland. For
this reason, eventually the Soviet Union will probably support—or at least
permit— moves toward political accommodation and economic liberalization, provided that its fundamental security, ideological, and political
interests will not thereby be threatened.

Eastern Europe's long-run economic viability can be improved significantly only by undertaking fundamental economic reforms. Economic
logic and the evidence cited suggest that reform pressures are gaining
strength throughout the region because of the need both for greater
efficiency in the use of limited inputs and for expanded production of
hard goods, especially manufactures salable for hard currency. Further
pressures for reforms come from consumers, neglect of whom has an
adverse impact on productivity and political stability.

Given its own economic performance and constraints, the Soviet
Union may well become more tolerant of basic economic reforms in Eastern Europe. Yet domestic opposition will remain a major obstacle. Problems in the domestic and international economic environments paradoxically contribute to pressures both for and against reforms. Balance-of-
payment pressures add to the tautness of the economy, whereas reforms
require some slack—that is, reserves of materials, machinery, labor, consumer goods, and foreign exchange—to cushion predictable and unforeseen difficulties during the transition period. Tautness also means operating under conditions of repressed inflation; thus reforms that give a
greater role to market forces are especially feared because of the increased likelihood of rapid, open inflation and possibly significant unemployment. The crisis in Poland warns other East European countries to
undertake reforms in time to prevent a crisis, yet the current tense economic and political situation is not conducive to reform initiatives in every
country.

What about Soviet attitudes toward economic reforms in Eastern Europe, a topic explored by Sarah Terry (chap. 8)? My view is that, since
Khrushchev, the Soviet leadership has become first more ambivalent,
then more tolerant, toward a system evolution along the lines of the
Hungarian New Economic Mechanism (NEM). There is no question that
past and present Soviet leaders have felt and feel more comfortable dealing with Soviet-type centrally planned economies in Eastern Europe than
with decentralized ones; the former are easier for them to understand
and to manipulate. At the same time, they are aware of the shortcomings
of traditional central planning and probably realize also that for historical, cultural, geopolitical, and economic reasons carbon copies of the
Soviet model would not be appropriate for all of Eastern Europe. Some

surely must also consider that an East European country's reforms may serve as a laboratory to find out what works and what does not and with what consequences.

The East European countries' room for maneuver regarding economic reforms is likely to increase regardless of what happens in Poland. One reason for this is the example of Poland. From the point of view of the Soviet leadership, the contrast between Hungary's reasonably successful economic decentralization[27] versus Poland's economic crisis, which has contributed greatly to an almost complete loss of political control, must be so clear-cut that the Soviets must now realize even more strongly that their own long-term political interests require a much greater stress on economic viability than on political conformity and control over economic decisions. But the manner in which the strong pressures for and against basic economic reforms are to be resolved will be determined by factors that are country specific.[28]

27. A comprehensive discussion of Hungary's economic reforms can be found in Paul Marer, "Hungary's New Economic System: Evaluation, Assessment, Prospects," paper presented at the conference Hungary in the 1980s, Columbia University, New York City, Oct. 28, 1983.

28. The basic features of a traditional centrally planned economic system, the pressures for and against reforms, and the type of reforms that so far have been introduced in Eastern Europe are discussed in Paul Marer, "Management and Reform in Centrally Planned Economies," in Richard N. Farmer and John V. Lombardi, eds., Readings in International Business, 3d ed. (Bloomington: Cedarwood Press, 1984).

7

Soviet Energy Policy in Eastern Europe

JOHN P. HARDT

Energy policy has always loomed large in Soviet-East European economic relations. Under the impact of recent global energy trends, however, it has become a key lever of Soviet political control in the region. While there is little doubt that Moscow can exercise sufficient military power to back up its policies, resort to that ultimate weapon in intra-CMEA (Council for Mutual Economic Assistance) affairs has been expensive, crude, and often counterproductive. By contrast, energy policy provides the USSR with a more effective and flexible mechanism of control—one that can be calibrated to particular Soviet needs and discreetly applied and that, in theory at least, is less likely to have political and economic side effects inimical to Soviet interests. Yet energy is a double-edged sword. The same global trends that have enhanced the leverage exerted by energy policy now threaten to combine with an increasingly taut domestic and regional economic environment to impose sharp constraints on Soviet use of that tool in Eastern Europe in the 1980s.

Besides its vital goal of maintaining control over Eastern Europe, the Soviet Union is also interested in fostering the overall economic health and political stability of the region. Although supplies of Soviet energy are critical to attaining both these goals, the economic and political criteria for energy policy may conflict. On the one hand, flexible energy rationing by the Soviet Union in a tight supply market greatly increases its leverage and expands its policy options for dealing with a variety of problems in Eastern Europe. On the other hand, a reduction of energy deliveries, necessitated both by the declining growth of Soviet energy supplies and by expanding demand at home and abroad, may lead to slower growth in national and personal incomes in Eastern Europe and perhaps to political instability.

Moreover, Soviet energy rationing poses systemic dilemmas within CMEA. Preferential supply and pricing policies favoring Eastern Europe tend to tie the CMEA economies closer to the USSR, fostering integration

For purposes of this chapter, *Eastern Europe* consists of the six full members of CMEA (the GDR, Poland, Czechoslovakia, Hungary, Bulgaria, and Romania). The term *CMEA-Five* refers to the above less Romania, while Yugoslavia is treated only marginally.

and system conformity while bolstering the political stability of the current regimes in the region. At the same time, in an effort to reduce the burden on the USSR, CMEA plans now call for a sharp change in the pattern of East European energy consumption—via conservation through economic slowdown and cutbacks in energy-intensive industries—that are likely to increase pressures for systemic reform. Thus, although energy policy appears to have the potential of being the most discreet and effective tool of Soviet influence in Eastern Europe, the implementation of policy reveals serious future dilemmas, constraints, and double-edged consequences. At best, Soviet leaders may orchestrate East European policy and economic performance by effectively using energy policy. At worst, they may find their energy policy to be a costly burden foreclosing opportunities for needed domestic supply, exports to the West, or "energy diplomacy" in the Third World, while being blamed for East European economic slowdowns, falling living standards, and political instability.

While Soviet leaders from Stalin through Brezhnev apparently perceived the critical role Soviet energy policy could play in Eastern Europe and fostered its development, the ends and means of policy have differed markedly over the course of the post-World War II period. From 1945 to the OPEC price increases of 1973–74, the USSR shifted from a policy that encouraged autarky, use of indigenous fossil fuels, and deliveries of energy supplies to the USSR to one of regional integration, hydrocarbons imports from the Soviet Union, and selective interdependence with world energy markets. I discuss these shifts in the immediate pages that follow. The dawning of the OPEC era was succeeded by a reexamination in CMEA planning of the assumption that Soviet oil and gas would be cheap and abundant and by a new phase in CMEA energy integration as the East Europeans found themselves priced out of OPEC markets—a shift I then examine. Finally, I address the increasingly difficult allocation and systemic choices that will confront Moscow in this decade.

FROM AUTARKY TO INTEGRATION, 1945–74

Under three successive leaders—Stalin, Khrushchev, and Brezhnev—the Soviet Union's energy policy in Eastern Europe passed through several stages, from autarky toward integration, between the end of World War II and the OPEC price increases of the early 1970s.

Autarky and Soviet Economic Recovery: The Stalinist Policy

In the Stalinist period, energy relations paralleled the overall pattern of Soviet-East European economic relations. All the East European countries were encouraged to strive for maximum self-sufficiency, relying on their own raw material base with the USSR as a residual supplier. Thus, the Stalinist policy toward Eastern Europe may be thought of as a modified form of autarky, in which the socialist camp was to be independent of the West and linked to the Soviet Union through bilateral rather than multilateral ties among members. In 1950, 92.7% of all energy consumed in Eastern Europe was solid fuel, primarily indigenous coal. Romania, with its extensive petroleum and natural gas deposits, was the exception with less than half its energy provided by solid fuels.

From 1945 to 1955–56, several of the East European countries had special relationships with the Soviet Union: Poland supplied coal to the USSR in substantial quantities at less than world market prices, even below the cost of production. Romania—a World War II enemy—had its petroleum industry controlled by a Soviet-Romanian joint stock company, with the bulk of exports going to the USSR. Czechoslovakia and the Soviet Zone of Germany (after 1949, the German Democratic Republic [GDR]) provided uranium, again at less than world market prices. These were all key energy sources for the economic recovery and expansion of the European regions of the USSR and were provided as direct or indirect war reparations, or at highly preferential terms of trade.[1]

On the other hand, even in the Stalinist period, the USSR also exported energy to Eastern Europe. In particular, the industrially advanced economies of the Northern Tier—the GDR and Czechoslovakia—developed an increasing reliance on Soviet coal and oil. These countries became significant trading partners: the Soviet Union as the primary supplier of industrial materials—crude oil, coal, iron ore, cotton—the two East European countries as exporters of machinery and industrial equipment. East Germany was further encouraged to develop its coal-based chemical industry to meet Soviet needs. Bulgaria and Poland were also modest importers of Soviet oil, while Romania and Hungary were net importers of coal.

Despite these considerable Soviet energy exports, however, Eastern Europe as a whole remained a net exporter of fuel through 1960 (see table 7.1), mostly to the USSR on the preferential terms noted above.

1. John P. Hardt, "East European Economic Development: Two Decades of Interrelationships and Interactions with the Soviet Union," in John P. Hardt, ed., *Economic Developments in Countries of Eastern Europe*, compendium of papers submitted to the Subcommittee on Economic Policy of the Joint Economic Committee, Congress of the United States, Joint Committee Print, 91st Cong., 2d sess. (Washington, D.C.: U.S. Government Printing Office [hereafter GPO], 1970) (hereafter cited as *Economic Developments*), pp. 5–24. My $15–20 billion estimate of Soviet impositions covering dismantling, reparations, and occupation costs is similar to Paul Marer's estimate of $14–20 billion. For the latter, see chapter 6.

TABLE 7.1.   Eastern Europe: Energy Balance Sheet, 1950–67

		Total energy (thousand metric tons of standard fuel)[a] (1)	Solid fuels (thousand metric tons of standard fuel) (2)	Hydrocarbons (oil and gas) (thousand metric tons of standard fuel) (3)
1950				
	Production	200,930	185,762	14,168
	Net trade	−22,645	−20,569	−2,076
	Consumption	178,285	165,193	13,092
1955				
	Production	268,792	237,937	30,855
	Net trade	−21,006	−15,960	−6,036
	Consumption	247,786	221,977	25,809
1960				
	Production	319,273	278,880	40,393
	Net trade	−5,375	−8,756	+3,381
	Consumption	313,898	270,124	43,774
1967				
	Production	384,694	322,694	62,000
	Net trade	+24,159	−7,018	+31,177
	Consumption	408,853	315,921	92,932

SOURCE: Calculated from Polach, "The Development of Energy in East Europe," in *Economic Developments* (see n. 1), p. 356.

[a]One metric ton of standard fuel equals 7,000 kilocalories.

Energy Modernization under Khrushchev and Brezhnev

The beginnings of a policy of economic modernization in the late 1950s brought about a corresponding modernization of the energy balance, first in the USSR and later in Eastern Europe, which accelerated during the 1960s. Although in 1967 solid fuels accounted for nearly four-fifths (as late as 1970 still 70%) of the energy consumed in Eastern Europe (see table 7.1), substantial increases occurred in the absolute use and relative shares of oil and natural gas. On a region-wide basis, the 1960s saw a 217% rise in the consumption of hydrocarbons (against a 57% increase in total energy use), while the share of hydrocarbons rose from 14% in 1960 to 29% in 1970. Especially marked was the rising share of oil and gas in the energy balances of the GDR, Czechoslovakia, Bulgaria, and Hungary.[2]

2. Central Intelligence Agency (National Foreign Assessment Center), *Energy Supplies in Eastern Europe: A Statistical Compilation*, ER-79-10624 (Washington, D.C.: Dec. 1979), pp. 4–7.

The two partial exceptions were Poland and Romania. The former, relying on abundant and high-quality coal, was slowest to modernize its energy balance, although even here hydrocarbon consumption rose from 6 to 17% of energy use in the same period. Romania, already an exception in the early period, again moved in a somewhat different direction: while indigenous hydrocarbons, especially natural gas, continued to be the mainstay of the energy balance, the more rapid expansion of coal use, presumably dictated by a desire to stretch its oil reserves and to remain independent of Soviet energy deliveries, freed Romania of Soviet energy leverage once the dismantling of the joint stock companies removed Moscow's control of their oil fields. Surplus oil supplies also permitted an increase in Romania's exports, now largely to the West, and became an important basis of its economic and foreign policy independence.

Despite these two special cases, energy modernization was reflected in a fivefold increase in East European imports of Soviet crude, from 7 million metric tons (MMT) in 1960 to 35 MMT in 1970, accounting in the latter year for nearly 90% of their total crude imports. The increases in Soviet oil deliveries in turn necessitated the building of an energy infrastructure and provided the context of energy-led integration within CMEA. Before 1960, oil was transported exclusively by rail and sea. By 1963, with construction of the Friendship (*Druzhba*) Line, all the East European members of CMEA except Bulgaria and Romania, the lone nonimporter, could be supplied by pipeline. The pipeline, a large-scale jointly financed venture in which each country undertook the construction of an assigned section of the line within its own boundaries, represented a major step in the development of regional energy planning in CMEA. Although integration was still primarily bilateral, tying the individual East European countries closer to the USSR, the pipeline initiated a period of very modest multilateralism, still closely controlled by Moscow. In addition Czechoslovakia and the GDR each entered into separate agreements in 1966 and 1967, respectively, whereby they would supply the Soviet Union with industrial machinery and equipment on credit, to be repaid with Soviet oil at a fixed price between 1971 and 1984. (In the Czech case, the amounts were reportedly $550 million in machinery for 60 MMT of oil; details of the agreement with the GDR were not released.)[3]

By contrast, deliveries of natural gas to Eastern Europe remained low throughout the 1960s, as increments in consumption were largely based on increased domestic production. Only Poland and Czechoslovakia were

3. John B. Haberstroh, "Eastern Europe: Growing Energy Problems," in John P. Hardt, ed., *East European Economies Post-Helsinki*, compendium of papers submitted to the Joint Economic Committee, Congress of the United States, Joint Committee Print, 95th Cong., 1st sess. (Washington, D.C.: GPO, 1977), pp. 390–91.

significant importers at this stage. By the second half of the decade, however, Soviet policymakers were clearly interested not only in expanding oil deliveries (as indicated by the doubling of the capacity of the Friendship Line) but in developing a comparable pipeline network for natural gas.[4] But as long as Moscow offered its hydrocarbons at prices roughly equivalent to the then low world market prices and as long as world supplies remained plentiful, the East Europeans showed little interest in expanding energy integration.

Policy Uncertainty, 1967–73: Stringency or Abundance

The period from the late 1960s to the Arab oil embargo of 1973 was one of uncertainty, even vacillation, in Soviet energy policy over how to manage, or possibly take advantage of, soaring East European demand for hydrocarbons. It was also a period in which the allocation and systemic dilemmas converged in a way foreshadowing the situation Soviet decision-makers face in the 1980s. On the one hand, by 1966–67, the USSR was unsure whether its energy supplies would be adequate to meet both East European demand and its own needs, which were expected to increase sharply in the late 1960s and early 1970s, as well as other export requirements. This uncertainty during the early years of the Brezhnev regime led to a pause, a reassessment of the policy of energy modernization in CMEA based on "abundant" Soviet oil and gas at reasonable prices. On the other hand, energy deliveries were quickly coming to be seen as an important source of leverage over the smaller members of the bloc and continued to be used by Moscow to promote its political goals even after supply prospects brightened in the early 1970s.

Future energy supplies for Eastern Europe were the dominant issue at the annual CMEA meeting in 1967. By this time, the USSR's "second Baku," the Romashchino field in the Ural–Volga region, had begun to peak, perhaps a decade earlier than anticipated by Soviet planners. Therefore, production forecasts were not optimistic, even though the large West Siberian fields—in particular, the monster field of Samotlor from which more than three-quarters of the increment in Soviet petroleum production in the 1970s was to come—had already been explored.

Despite these uncertainties, the decision was to continue to meet Eastern Europe's needs. As J. G. Polach noted in 1969: "In the short run and

4. O. Bogomolov, "Integration by Market Forces and Through Planning," in Fritz Machlup, ed., *Economic Integration Worldwide, Regional, Sectoral*, Proceedings of the Fourth Congress of the International Economic Association, held in Budapest, Hungary, 1974 (London: Macmillan, 1976), especially pp. 313–15. (See also comments by Gottfried Haberler and John P. Hardt, pp. 318–24.)

in spite of objections often heard in 1966, the Soviet Union is ready to rearrange her priorities to meet the energy demands of East Europe" rather than risk the "danger that East European initiative to get the needed fuels from outside the bloc may threaten the bloc's political cohesion."[5] Thus, while there were occasional reports in this period of Soviet threats to interrupt or curtail oil deliveries for political reasons—to Czechoslovakia in 1968 and to Hungary in 1971[6]—Soviet "energy leverage" was exercised primarily by meeting the region's rising demand, although at a diminishing rate of increase compared with the 1960s. Under plans drawn up at the end of the 1960s, Soviet deliveries of crude and petroleum products during the first half of the 1970s grew 10.6% a year from 40.3 MMT in 1970 to 63.4 MMT in 1975, or by 58% over the five-year period.[7] It was these increases in readily available supplies of crude, together with the entry of West Siberian natural gas as a major factor in the CMEA energy balance, that facilitated the rapid growth of the East European economies in the early 1970s.

Nonetheless, the critical question for the longer term remained, in Polach's words, "How large will the East European energy deficit be . . . , say by 1980? And will the USSR be capable of filling the gap and willing to do so?" One alternative, Polach noted, would be "to permit liberalization of trade and let East Europe obtain her energy supplies, or at least a major part of them, on the world market." Such a course, however, would entail "grave risks":

The simple necessity of paying for the huge energy imports [involved] would force the East European countries to open their borders freely to the influx of foreign businessmen and align their export industries in accordance with the demand on the world markets rather than with their politically motivated targets. Monetary repercussions of such a policy (the question of convertibility) also would not be negligible. All this . . . would ultimately lead to a shift in political and social attitudes in East Europe.

Thus the potential impact of external energy imports on the socialist system was a constraint in the late 1960s.

As if anticipating the "energy heartland" option discussed by Western analysts at the end of the 1970s, Polach predicted that, rather than accept the risks of such a realignment, the Soviet Union would choose to increase its imports of oil and gas from Middle Eastern countries, such as Iran and Iraq, to supplement CMEA hydrocarbon production, at the same time ensuring Soviet control over the allocation of both their own and Middle

5. J. G. Polach, "The Development of Energy in East Europe," in *Economic Developments,* p. 410 (emphasis added).

6. See Peter A. Toma and Iván Völgyes, *Politics in Hungary* (San Francisco: Freeman, 1977), p. 155.

7. Haberstroh, "Eastern Europe," pp. 383–87.

Eastern supplies. His suggestion that an expanded nuclear electric power program might be necessary to the Soviet Union again seemed to fore-shadow the significant upgrading of nuclear power development called for at the June 1980 meeting.[8]

In the interim, none of these alternative strategies, except nuclear power, played a major role in Soviet energy policy. With the opening of the new Siberian fields in the early 1970s, Soviet planners could again be optimistic about their own long-term energy prospects.[9] As early as 1970, energy forecasters envisaged increased production of all forms of ener-gy—oil, natural gas, coal, hydroelectric and nuclear power—through 1990. Although no detailed breakdown of energy production goals was released by Gosplan (the State Planning Committee), it has been deduced from piecemeal data released by Soviet energy experts at the Academy of Sciences and state ministries and departments (see table 7.2). Of particu-lar note were the modest but steady increases in oil output forecasts and the more rapid absolute and relative increases in gas and nuclear electric power. By 1974 the Soviet Minister of the Petroleum Industry, Valentin Shashin, estimated that the long-range crude oil output of West Siberia *alone* would be 400–500 MMT annually (8–10 million barrels per day [MBD]), or more than total Soviet output in that year.[10]

Ironically, this optimistic long-term outlook for Soviet energy supplies was only partially reflected in planned energy deliveries to Eastern Eu-rope. In contrast to the late 1960s, when uncertainty over future supplies was combined with an apparent, if somewhat reluctant, willingness to meet escalating regional demand, the early 1970s witnessed yet another reassessment of Moscow's energy priorities, as evidenced by initial projec-tions that East European imports of Soviet oil in the 1976–80 plan period would rise by only 3% per annum, compared to the 10.6% rate of increase in the previous plan period.[11] The rationale for the shift in Soviet policy is not immediately self-evident: Did East European demand increase more rapidly than the Soviets expected, or could cope with? Did the Soviets at this stage try to make increases in energy supplies contingent on East

8. Polach, "Development of Energy," p. 412; Jonathan Stern, "Soviet and East Euro-pean Relations with the Energy Heartland," in John P. Hardt, ed., *Energy in Soviet Policy*, Joint Economic Committee, Congress of the United States, Joint Committee Print, 97th Cong., 2d sess., June 11, 1981 (Washington, D.C.: GPO, 1981), pp. 55–79.

9. John P. Hardt, "West Siberia: The Quest for Energy," *Problems of Communism*, 22 (May–June 1973), 26–28.

10. John P. Hardt, George Holliday, and Young C. Kim, *Western Investment in Communist Countries: A Selected Survey on Economic Interdependence*, prepared for the Subcommittee on Multinational Corporations of the Committee on Foreign Relations, U.S. Senate, Commit-tee Print, 93d Cong., 2d sess., Aug. 5, 1974 (Washington, D.C.: GPO, 1974), esp. pp. 34, 40–44; *New Times*, no. 15 (Apr. 1974), p. 21.

11. Haberstroh, "Eastern Europe," p. 387.

TABLE 7.2.   Soviet Projections of the Supply of Energy by 1980 and 1990 during
the Early 1970s

	1980 MMT/SCE[a]	Share (percent)	1990 MMT/SCE	Share (percent)
Oil	915	40.5	1,100	31.8
Gas	522	24.3	1,100	31.8
Coal	564	26.3	870	24.7
Peat, shale, and fuel wood	60	2.8	70	2.0
Hydroelectric power	24	1.1	35	1.0
Nuclear electric power	26	1.2	175	5.1
Other	36	1.7	50	1.2
Imports	50	2.1	100	2.5
Total supply	2,197	100.00	3,500	100.00

SOURCE: N. Y. Melnikov published a percentage breakdown of the energy balance for 1990 in *Toplivnoenergeticheskiye Resursy SSSR* in 1971. L. A. Melentyev wrote about energy supplies "for the next 10 to 15 years" in *Izvestiya Akademii Nauk SSSR: Energetika i Transport,* May–June 1974. Using the percentage breakdown from the Melnikov article and the absolute values from the Melentyev article, the Central Intelligence Agency derived energy supply data for 1990 in *Soviet Long-Range Energy Forecast,* CIA Research Aid A (ER) 75-17, pp. 6–7.

[a]MMT/SCE is million metric tons of standard coal equivalent, 7,000 kilocalories per metric ton.

European help in resource development (a Soviet interest as early as 1966), which the East Europeans then resisted in the climate of cheap energy in the preembargo period?[12] To what extent was Soviet policy influenced in the early 1970s by the sudden availability of large-scale Western credits, which meshed not only with the emerging policy of détente but also with their need for Western technology both to develop difficult sites and to increase recovery rates? And, finally, to what extent were the Soviets more confident by the early 1970s that they had contained the Prague disease of 1968, and could allow the East Europeans some latitude in dealings on world markets without undue fear of political contamination—even that this was preferable to reforms that, while they would increase energy efficiency, carried unpredictable political risks?

12. A. Makarov and L. A. Melentev, "Issledovaniya perspektivnoi struktury toplivnoenergeticheskogo balansa SSSR i osnovnykh zon strany" (Research on the prospective structure of the fuel and energy balance of the USSR and the main zones of the country); M. A. Styrikovich and S. Ya. Chernyavskii, "Puti razvitiya i rol yadernoi energetiki v perspektivnom energobalanse mira i ego osnovnykh regionov" (Paths of development and the role of nuclear power in the prospective energy balance of the world and its main regions), two papers provided to a U.S.-USSR energy exchange scheduled for October 1979 but canceled. The author of this chapter was to have been a U.S. delegate.

Whatever the reasons, it is evident that on the eve of the OPEC embargo of 1973 the assumptions underlying Soviet energy priorities had changed in important, if subtle, ways:

1. Domestic growth could be maintained by expanding supplies, with natural gas, coal, hydro, and nuclear rising to fill the falling share of oil in energy supply.
2. The hard-currency bill for importing Western technology would be financed in large part by petroleum sales. Natural gas sales would be expanded via "gas-for-pipe" arrangements with the Federal Republic of Germany and compensation deals with the United States and Japan (Project North Star in Western Siberia and the Yakutia project in Eastern Siberia).
3. Non-East European client states, such as Cuba, would be provided with oil as aid or for soft currency; likewise, oil sales and energy projects for such countries as India, Ghana, Greece, and Morocco would be orchestrated with diplomacy.
4. Basic CMEA energy requirements would be met, although with increased emphasis on natural gas; however, the East European countries would have to meet more of the increment in their petroleum needs through direct imports from OPEC.[13]

In line with these expectations, several of the East European countries launched ambitious projects to accommodate the influx of OPEC oil: Poland projected an expansion of refinery capacity to 28 MMT by 1980 (although Soviet deliveries were not scheduled to increase above the 10 MMT of crude provided annually in 1971–75; Hungary and Czechoslovakia joined with Yugoslavia to construct the Adria pipeline, which was expected to provide Yugoslavia with 24 MMT of Middle Eastern oil annually by 1980 and Hungary and Czechoslovakia with 5 MMT each, with large purchases planned by the other countries as well. Indeed, initial plans in the CMEA-Five alone—that is, excluding Romania and Yugoslavia—called for crude imports from the Middle East to skyrocket from 6.5 MMT in 1975 to 41 MMT in 1980.[14]

FROM ENERGY AFFLUENCE TO IMPENDING SHORTAGES, 1974–80

The Arab oil embargo and the subsequent quadrupling of OPEC oil prices in 1973–74 sharply altered both Soviet and East European expectations and options. For the East Europeans, the increases dealt a serious blow to expanding import plans and brought about a reversal of their

13. Cf. the energy trade data in Central Intelligence Agency, National Foreign Assessment Center, *International Energy Situation: Outlook to 1985* (Washington, D.C.: 1981).
14. Haberstroh, "Eastern Europe," p. 387.

previously cool attitude toward energy integration within CMEA. For the Soviets, the immediate impact was to present them with an unqualified bonanza, on the one hand enhancing their leverage over Eastern Europe in a way they could hardly have anticipated, on the other hand providing them with windfall profits on oil exports to the West.

In the longer term, however, the Kremlin leadership could ill afford to maximize the benefits to itself without concern for the effects on Eastern Europe's economic and political stability. This concern, together with the deterioration of détente in the mid-1970s—in particular, the collapse of plans for U.S. participation in Siberian natural gas development—led to a number of shifts in CMEA energy strategy and in Soviet-East European energy relations in the second half of the decade: the restoration of the region's dependence on the USSR for the bulk of incremental energy imports; a revival of intra-CMEA energy integration, this time in the form of joint development of Soviet resources; a marked revision in the terms of trade between the USSR and its regional partners; renewed emphasis on indigenous energy resources; and, ultimately, renewed attention to energy conservation with its obvious implications for the economic system.

Although in some ways reminiscent of the earlier pursuit of energy self-sufficiency within the bloc, these shifts implied tensions—between economic and political requirements, and between the domestic and external economic environments—that could not long be concealed. Thus, by the end of the 1970s, the combination of another sharp run-up in world oil prices, new fears over long-term Soviet energy supplies, and faltering economic performance throughout the bloc would pose new dilemmas (or, more accurately, old dilemmas in new forms) for Soviet energy policy in Eastern Europe.

Price and Allocation Policies

The initial reaction of the Soviet Union to the 1973–74 OPEC increases was to maintain the supply and pricing policies with Eastern Europe agreed to for the 1971–75 plan period. That is, for 1974 the price of Soviet crude oil within CMEA remained at the pre-Yom Kippur War price of $2.50 per barrel, or about one-fourth the new OPEC price; at the same time, the price of Soviet oil exports to the West rose to the new OPEC level. Thus, the effect of the OPEC price rises on Soviet trade revenues was to accentuate the benefits of trade with the hard-currency West over the CMEA East: In 1974 alone, shipments of Soviet oil and petroleum products to the West provided a hard-currency windfall on the order of $3 billion, without significant increases in volume—a windfall that coincided with an acceleration of Soviet hard-currency imports, especially of equipment for constructing the Baikal-Amur Mainline Railroad (BAM). At the same time, continued deliveries to the East represented what appeared to be an economic subsidy, which could be measured by world market prices and opportunities for sale; not only were the prices charged far below the OPEC level, but the USSR continued to accept a mixture of hard and soft goods.

In the meantime, spiraling prices rendered totally unrealistic East European plans to satisfy growing energy needs by vastly increasing oil imports from world markets. In the year after the embargo, imports by the CMEA-Five from non-Soviet sources dropped 25 percent, from 7.7 to 5.8 MMT, and recouped barely half that decline in 1975. (The declines for Bulgaria and Czechoslovakia were especially sharp, while only Poland and Hungary imported more from non-Soviet sources in 1975 than they had in 1973.) Still greater, however was the impact on import plans for 1976–80. Against the original 1980 target of 41 MMT from non-Soviet sources, the CMEA-Five actually imported about 9 MMT in 1978 (the last year for which relatively firm data are available), and probably little more than 11 MMT in 1980, or more than two-thirds below initial plans; even so, the estimated $2.4 billion hard-currency energy bill in the latter year (assuming an average price of $30 a barrel) was viewed as an intolerable burden. (Romania, always the exception, imported an additional 13 MMT in 1978 and probably close to 15 MMT by 1980, chiefly to satisfy overexpanded refinery capacity and export needs; but these imports were based on Romania's special trade relations with Iran and Iraq and were not part of the 41 MMT projection.)[15]

Concurrent with the realization that they would have to make up at least some of the increment in Eastern Europe's oil needs that the latter could no longer import from OPEC, the Soviets decided to adjust intra-CMEA prices upward. At the beginning of 1975, the 1958 Bucharest formula, under which fixed prices had been established for a given five-year plan period on the basis of world market prices for the preceding five years, was modified. Instead, prices for 1975 were based on an average of the preceding three years (no doubt to maximize the immediate increase for Soviet energy deliveries), while starting in 1976 prices were to be adjusted annually on a five-year moving average. At the same time, actual Soviet shipments of crude oil and petroleum products to the CMEA-Five

15. CIA, *Energy Supplies in Eastern Europe,* table 19; Ronald G. Oechsler and John A. Martens, "Eastern European Trade with OPEC: A Solution to Emerging Energy Problems?" in *East European Economic Assessment, Part 2—Regional Assessment,* compendium of papers submitted to the Joint Economic Committee, Congress of the United States, Joint Committee Print, 97th Cong., 1st sess. (Washington, D.C.: GPO, 1981) (hereafter cited as *East European Economic Assessment*), pp. 530–33; and Jan Vanous, "Eastern European and Soviet Fuel Trade, 1970–85," in ibid., p. 557.

TABLE 7.3. Soviet Exports of Crude Oil and Oil Products to CMEA, 1970–80

	1970		1975		1976		1977[a]		1978[a]		1979[b]		1980[b]	
	C	T	C	T	C	T	C	T	C	T	C	T	C	T
Exports to														
Bulgaria	4.8	7.1	9.9	11.6	10.0	11.9	10.8	12.9	11.3	13.4	13.0	14.1	13.0	14.0
Czechoslovakia	9.4	10.5	15.5	16.0	16.3	17.2	17.0	17.0	17.7	17.7	18.3	18.3	19.2	19.2
East Germany	9.2	9.3	15.1	15.0	16.0	16.8	17.0	17.0	17.8	17.8	18.5	18.5	19.0	19.0
Hungary	4.0	4.8	6.9	7.5	7.7	8.4	7.7	9.1	8.5	10.2	8.6	11.0	9.5	12.0
Poland	7.0	8.6	10.9	13.3	11.7	14.1	12.8	14.7	13.4	15.5	12.9	14.0	13.1	15.9
Romania	—	—	—	—	—	—	—	—	—	—	0.4	0.4	1.0	1.0
CMEA-6	34.4	40.3	58.2	63.4	61.7	68.4	65.3	70.7	68.6	74.6	71.7	76.3	73.8	81.1
Cuba	4.3	6.0	5.8	8.1	6.0	8.8	6.2	9.2	6.4	9.6	6.7	9.6	7.0	10.0
Vietnam	—	0.4	—	0.4	—	0.4	—	0.5	—	0.5	—	0.6	—	0.6
Mongolia	—	0.3	—	0.4	—	0.4	—	0.5	—	0.5	—	0.6	—	0.6
CMEA-9[c]	38.7	47.0	64.0	72.3	67.7	78.0	71.5	80.9	75.0	85.2	78.4	87.1	80.8	92.3
Entire world	66.8	95.8	93.1	130.4	110.8	148.5	NA	152.5	NA	165.6	NA	158.1	NA	NA

SOURCES: Prepared by Ed. A. Hewett for *Technology and Soviet Energy Availability*, Office of Technology Assessment (Washington, D.C.: U.S. Government Printing Office, Nov. 1981), p. 288. The data through 1976 are from Soviet foreign trade yearbooks (*Vneshnyaya torgovlya SSSR*). Figures concerning the proportion of crude and products for Cuba, Vietnam, and Mongolia are estimated. Data beginning in 1977 are estimates based on CMEA, *Vneshnyaya torgovlya* (Statistical Yearbook of the Member-Countries of the Council for Mutual Economic Assistance) (Moscow: Statistika, 1979, 1980), and the *Journal of Commerce*.

NOTES: C = crude, T = crude plus products. NA = not available.

[a] These estimates are necessitated by the fact that the Soviet Union stopped reporting quantity data on its energy exports in 1977; but they are probably fairly reliable indicators of actual shipments.

[b] These are estimates but somewhat less reliable than the 1977–78 figures. They should be taken only as indicators of general magnitudes; in some cases the actual number could be easily 1 ton larger or smaller.

[c] The nine countries listed individually above.

in the 1976–80 plan period rose well in excess of the 3% annual rate originally projected—reaching approximately 80 MMT in 1980, or twice the 1970 level. (See table 7.3; Romania began importing small amounts of Soviet crude in 1979 but these added only marginally to the total.)

The Orenburg Gas Pipeline and CMEA Energy Integration

Natural gas began to play an increasingly important role in Eastern Europe's energy balance in the 1970s and provided the vehicle for a renewal of energy-led integration within CMEA. Although earlier expressions of interest by the Soviets in constructing a natural gas equivalent of the *Druzhba* oil pipeline had fallen on deaf ears in the smaller CMEA countries, a combination of factors now revived interest on both sides.

From Eastern Europe's viewpoint, what had previously seemed either an unnecessary or even undesirable increase in dependence on Soviet energy deliveries now must have appeared a relatively attractive alternative. The region's consumption of natural gas had grown substantially in the second half of the 1960s, both in absolute terms and as a share of total energy consumption. Although these increases had been based almost entirely on domestic reserves, in most of the countries those reserves were limited and future expansion of gas use would depend primarily on imports, almost exclusively from the USSR. For instance, between 1970 and 1977 (still prior to completion of the pipeline), Eastern Europe's production of gas rose by 47%, while consumption increased by 80% and the region's level of self-sufficiency dropped from 94 to 77%. (If gas-rich Romania is excluded, the comparisons are even more dramatic, with production up 66%, consumption 165%, and self-sufficiency in gas down from about 80 to barely 50%.)[16] In light of Moscow's intensions, made evident already early in the decade, to limit future growth of oil deliveries, and with world prices for all forms of energy soaring while intra-CMEA prices were still stable, the case for Orenburg must have seemed overwhelmingly favorable to the East European leaderships in 1974.

From the Soviet point of view as well, East European participation in construction of the pipeline offered several advantages. In addition to the enhanced leverage it would give them over the region, it would also ensure some degree of external participation (including access to Western technology) in development of their natural gas reserves at a time when direct Western participation was becoming less certain. In 1973 and early 1974, the prospects for cooperative energy ventures with the United States and Japan seemed highly promising—with the former providing long-term financing, underpinned by $10 billion in government loans,

---

16. CIA, *Energy Supplies in Eastern Europe*, tables 7, 13, and 14.

for developing the massive gas projects in Western Siberia (Project North Star) and Eastern Siberia (Yakutia). In 1973 Japan's Prime Minister Tanaka and Soviet leader Brezhnev also discussed an oil pipeline from Tyumen province in Western Siberia to the Pacific Ocean to carry up to 40 MMT of oil per year for export. By late 1974, passage by the U.S. Congress of the Jackson–Vanik amendment, severely restricting the amount of any U.S. loans and linking them to political concessions from Moscow, together with the reluctance of the Japanese to proceed on their own, effectively aborted these projects.

The decision to build a natural gas pipeline from the Urals to Eastern Europe, made at the CMEA meeting in Sofia, Bulgaria, in 1974, marked a new departure in joint CMEA energy projects in at least one important respect: unlike the *Druzhba* project, in which each participant undertook construction of the pipeline only across its own territory, the Orenburg (or *Soyuz*) project obliged each of the East European participants (this time including Romania) to provide labor and equipment (including significant amounts purchased in the West) for a section of the line within the USSR. In return the Soviets agreed to provide the East Europeans with 15.5 billion cubic meters (BCM) of natural gas annually for twenty years.[17] As table 7.4 shows, deliveries through the Orenburg line, begun in 1979, reached the projected maximum delivery level of 15.5 BCM in 1980, with the largest relative impact on the Southern Tier (Bulgaria, Hungary, and Romania). In the latter year, imports of Soviet natural gas accounted for 6% of Eastern Europe's total energy consumption, with Orenburg alone providing nearly half that amount, or 2.9%.

The significance of the Orenburg project, as originally conceived, went beyond its role in facilitating Soviet gas exports to its CMEA partners, or in increasing their energy dependence on the USSR. It was also the centerpiece of the package of multilateral development projects adopted under the 1971 Comprehensive Program and intended to usher in a new stage in CMEA integration. In all, seven major joint investments were planned for the 1976–80 plan period, primarily in resource development and raw-material-based industries in the USSR, with a total estimated cost of 9 billion transferable rubles ($12 billion at the 1975 rate of exchange). One obvious justification for this joint investment program was the need to rationalize energy use by concentrating energy-intensive industries near the sources of energy and raw material supply—in effect reversing the inefficient Stalinist pattern of parallel industrial development throughout CMEA.

17. John Hannigan and Carl McMillan, "Joint Investment in Resource Development: Sectoral Approach to Socialist Integration," in *East European Economic Assessment*, esp. pp. 261–64.

TABLE 7.4.   Significance of Orenburg Gas Deliveries for Individual Countries'
Fuel–Energy Balances

Importing country		Estimated volume of imports of Soviet natural gas (million cubic meters)	Imports of Soviet natural gas as percentage of total energy consumption	Imports of Orenburg natural gas as percentage of total energy consumption
Bulgaria	1978	3,000	8.1	
	1980	6,000	15.2	7.1
Czechoslovakia	1978	5,400	5.6	
	1980	8,200	8.1	2.8
German Democratic	1978	3,600	3.6	
Republic	1980	6,500	6.2	2.7
Hungary	1978	1,000	3.2	
	1980	3,800	11.3	8.3
Poland	1978	2,800	1.7	
	1980	5,600	3.3	1.6
Romania	1978	—	—	
	1980	1,500	2.0	2.0
Total Eastern	1978	15,800	3.1	
Europe	1980	31,600	6.0	2.9

SOURCE: John Hannigan, *The Orenburg Natural Gas Project and Fuel-Energy Balances in East Europe* (Ottawa: Carleton, July 1980).

Although the original expectations for output and delivery are being fulfilled, Orenburg has been less successful as a step forward in genuine integration. Owing to shortages of skilled labor, most of the East Europeans could not meet their obligations for direct participation in construction; also, it seems, they were not entirely satisfied with the terms of participation. After careful analysis of available data, John Hannigan and Carl McMillan concluded that the rate of return to the East European countries on their investment in Orenburg was not unfavorable. On the other hand, they point out that, although Orenburg assured long-term access to Soviet supplies on favorable terms, it also served to increase Eastern Europe's dependence on the USSR and diverted resources from investment projects oriented toward Western markets while increasing the region's hard-currency indebtedness. For these and other reasons (including the difficulty of determining net benefits under complex CMEA accounting arrangements), Orenburg and other joint resource-development projects have been widely perceived in Eastern Europe as disadvantageous. Thus the USSR has backed away from multilateral construction projects on Soviet territory, with no new region-wide projects along Orenburg lines announced for the 1981–85 plan period.[18] (A partial exception appears to be the more limited participation in construction of two nuclear power plants in the Ukraine, discussed in the next section.)

Renewed emphasis on CMEA integration did not mean that Moscow now discouraged imports of oil and gas from OPEC; indeed, it facilitated them through Soviet-led negotiations with Iran and other Middle East countries. The initial Trans-Iranian Gas Trunkline (IGAT I) agreement in the 1960s, which provided Iranian gas primarily to the Soviet Caucasus, kindled expectations of OPEC hydrocarbons at manageable levels of financing. The IGAT II agreement, signed in 1975, was intended to bring additional supplies to the Transcaucasus, as well as to Eastern Europe (especially Czechoslovakia) and the Federal Republic of Germany, with the European deliveries as an offset arrangement—that is, transshipped through Soviet pipelines—thereby diversifying the burden of East European energy demand while maintaining control over supply. At the same time, several East European countries were pursuing independent plans to gain preferred access to OPEC oil. Even after the first round of price increases, oil for the Adria pipeline to Yugoslavia, Hungary, and Czechoslovakia was to come from Iran, Libya, and other OPEC countries on favorable terms. All these arrangements were adversely affected by a series of political events in 1979–80: the Shah's fall, followed by renunciation of most of the agreements by his successors, the new round of OPEC price increases, and the interruptions of oil deliveries due to the Iran-Iraq war. As a result, IGAT II was terminated and other cooperation arrangements were scaled down.

Energy Modernization and Energy Leverage

Thus two decades of energy modernization in Eastern Europe witnessed an eightfold increase in hydrocarbon use, against a rise in total energy consumption of approximately 150%, while the share of hydrocarbons in the region's energy balance grew from 14 to more than 40%. In the same period, Eastern Europe as a whole was transformed from a minor net energy exporter into an importer of close to one-third of its energy needs—largely in the form of oil and natural gas, of which about 90% was supplied by the USSR. Between 1961 and 1979 the value of Soviet hydrocarbon exports to the region increased approximately 18-fold.

18. Ibid., esp. pp. 290–92. For an interesting Hungarian comment on the disadvantages of these joint investments for the East European partners, see László Csaba, "Some Problems of the International Socialist Monetary System," *Acta Oeconomica*, 23, nos. 1–2 (1979), 1–7; among other things, Csaba claims that "the direct dollar content of the investment credits granted [by Hungary] within the CMEA amounted to 54.4 percent in the [1970s]." See also chapter 6.

The degree of energy dependence varied widely throughout the region, with the smaller countries such as Hungary, and especially Bulgaria, the most dependent. Although the volume of liquid fuels consumed by Czechoslovakia, the GDR, and Poland was far greater, their share in total energy consumption was less. Poland continued to maintain the largest share of total energy from solid fuels (with domestic coal still accounting for 82.6% in 1978), while Romania, with its indigenous hydrocarbon base and separate import arrangements, remained the most independent of Soviet deliveries. The relative independence of both, however, was eroded by the events of 1979–80.

Precisely how these ascending levels of dependence were translated into increased Soviet leverage over its East European clients remains largely in the realm of speculation, since negotiations over deliveries have traditionally taken place at the highest political level and have been shrouded in secrecy. Nonetheless, it is clear that Moscow retained substantial control over both the price and quantity of energy deliveries, especially oil. Available data suggest that, the CMEA price formula notwithstanding, some East European countries paid substantially less for their Soviet oil than others. Throughout the 1976–80 plan period the GDR (the most favored in this regard) appears to have paid more than 25% less for its oil than Hungary (the least favored); the average price to Czechoslovakia was only slightly above the GDR's, Poland's somewhat below Hungary's, while Bulgaria fell approximately in the middle. Poland and Hungary also suffered relative to the other three by having to satisfy a larger percentage of their oil needs on world markets.[19]

One partial explanation for these differentials was that the GDR and Czechoslovakia were still benefiting from the oil-for-equipment deals negotiated in the late 1960s, which will bring them some oil at preembargo prices through 1984. However, numerous ambiguities remained. How, for instance, were (and are) energy accounts calculated or cleared—in rubles at intra-CMEA prices, in dollars at world prices, or in some combination of the two depending on the mix of hard and soft goods shipped to the Soviet Union in exchange for its oil and gas? Has the GDR received more favorable treatment with respect to both price and quantity because of the relatively high hard-currency content of its exports to the USSR? Where above-plan deliveries are concerned, have both sides honored world pricing? That is, if the Soviets received world market prices for above-plan deliveries of oil, did the Poles get similar treatment for their coal? If so, the policy on bilateral pricing for intra-CMEA energy trade would be clearer and more equitable, although even world market pricing involves some ranges and judgment. But when the packages of

19. Vanous, "Eastern European and Soviet Fuel Trade," pp. 552–57.

goods involve combinations of hard and soft goods priced in various (and publicly unknown) ways, direct monetary pricing and calculation of a real exchange rate becomes complex and probably subject to political negotiation.

Political negotiation of hydrocarbon supplies and prices appears likely as annual negotiations on trade, including energy deliveries, take place at the highest party levels. One may also note that periodic comments on energy pricing and deliveries are often made by top East European and Soviet leaders after these summits. In this political context a number of considerations may play a role in Moscow's cost-benefit analysis, for example:

1. sharing of support costs for Warsaw Pact forces, bases, programs, and procurement, particularly where Soviet troops are directly stationed in East European countries;
2. military and economic aid to Soviet client states, target countries, or surrogates;
3. support of Soviet foreign policy positions generally; and
4. conformance to internal political and economic policies approved by the Soviet Union.[20]

Examples of specific East European actions or policies that might have weighed favorably on Soviet energy policy in the 1970s were the sending of GDR advisers to Yemen and other Soviet Third World clients, shipments of Polish meat to Soviet troops in the GDR, Czechoslovak aid to Vietnam, or Bulgaria's yeoman service in the campaign against Eurocommunism. While it is difficult to document these noneconomic or quasi-economic factors in Soviet energy policy, such positive contributions to the USSR's political and strategic goals may help to explain why the GDR, with its special support for the Soviet military presence abroad, or Bulgaria and Czechoslovakia, with their special loyalty to Soviet systemic orthodoxy, have generally received favorable prices and allocations relative to other CMEA countries. Conversely, economic weakness or political instability may have provided CMEA members with at least temporary leverage vis-à-vis Moscow, as witnessed by the latter's concern to satisfy Prague's energy needs after 1968; Poland too appears to have fared better in its energy allotments, at least temporarily, once the "renewal" process began to challenge systemic conformity and cause a sharp fall in output.

Rising OPEC prices and the resulting opportunity costs of supplying Eastern Europe at below world market levels have given rise to recent

20. Jan Vanous and Michael Marrese, *Implicit Subsidies in Soviet Trade with Eastern Europe*, Discussion Paper no. 80-32, Department of Economics, University of British Columbia, Sept. 1980, p. 6. For circumstantial evidence that "oil leverage" was used against the Poles in the mid-1970s to encourage greater domestic conformity with bloc norms, see chap. 6.

years to considerable debate over Moscow's "implicit subsidy" to the region. As articulated by Jan Vanous and Michael Marrese, the exchange of oil and gas (hard goods) for machinery and equipment (soft goods) amounts to a preferential trade arrangement in which the Soviets have had to forgo Western markets for hydrocarbons, as well as the more advanced Western technology that earnings from such sales would have brought, for increased imports of East European manufactures, much of which are overpriced by world standards and/or not salable on world markets. Moreover, the authors argue, this pattern would become only more pronounced with continuing increases in OPEC prices.[21]

The pros and cons of this "subsidy" argument are explored elsewhere in the volume. For our purposes, the important point is that the balance in the broader net cost-benefit assessment of Soviet-CMEA trade may be far more even than a narrower accounting of energy trade suggests, and that the perception of discrimination and disadvantage may be mutual. Against the opportunity costs to Moscow, the East Europeans must weigh the cost to themselves of the various benefits to Moscow noted above, which appear to influence both the quantity and price of hydrocarbons received and, therefore, the size of the Soviet subsidy to each. In addition the East Europeans undoubtedly perceive the Stalinist policy of parallel energy-intensive investments imposed earlier as responsible for many of their current energy problems, for which they must now pay with a rising volume of exports at a time of growing stringency at home. As Vanous himself has observed elsewhere:

The expected rapid increase in prices of Soviet oil will greatly increase the Soviet export revenue earned in Eastern Europe, which will most probably be spent on imports of Eastern European machinery and industrial consumer goods. This is already apparent in the USSR trade results for the year 1978; in 1978 Soviet imports of Eastern European machinery and equipment increased by an unprecedented 40 percent relative to 1977 (about 35 percent in real terms).[22]

By the end of the decade the Soviets had ample reason to ponder the double-edged nature of their energy leverage. On the one hand, the OPEC-inspired energy crisis of the 1970s had handed them a subtle but powerful tool of influence over the smaller members of CMEA. On the other hand, resolute use of that tool clearly threatened the latters' political stability—in the end limiting its effectiveness to providing or withholding

21. Vanous and Marrese, *Implicit Subsidies*, pp. 1–2. For a fuller discussion of the subsidy issue, see chap. 6.

22. Vanous, "Eastern European and Soviet Fuel Trade," p. 558. A possible explanation for the sharp increase in machinery exports may be an accounting entry for deliveries intended for the Orenburg gas pipeline, but not carried as such after the terms of the deal changed. But this does not alter the general observation concerning the economic burden imposed on the East Europeans by deteriorating terms of trade with the USSR.

increases in energy deliveries, a most expensive policy given domestic needs and opportunity costs on world markets. Moreover, perpetuation even in modified form of the CMEA energy umbrella, protecting the East European countries from the full brunt of world price increases, fostered expectations of a continuation of cheap energy supplies, which in turn discouraged the kinds of efficiency-oriented reforms that Moscow itself had been trying to avoid for more than a decade. It was a vicious circle that would come to an end, unhappily for Eastern Europe, only with the renewed sense of Soviet supply constraints evident in the plans for 1981–85.

SOVIET ENERGY PROSPECTS AND DILEMMAS IN THE 1980s: THE IMPLICATIONS FOR EASTERN EUROPE

Soviet energy policy in Eastern Europe during the 1980s will hinge on three critical variables. First, supply—that is, how much oil and gas can and will the USSR export to the region? Second, energy pricing choices— what will the terms of trade be? And, third, control of East European energy demand and economic growth—that is, can Moscow permit, or through enforced conservation impose, economic slowdown due to energy shortages? The combination of these policy variables in turn confronts the Soviet leaders with two fundamental dilemmas: the allocative and the systemic.

While maintaining the preferential energy supply and pricing policies of the past might promote the economic growth and political stability of the East European regimes, continuation of this allocation policy would almost certainly create serious shortfalls in supplies available to other claimants. On the other hand, a policy of rationing Soviet energy deliveries to Eastern Europe in the 1980s may prove to be both too little and too much. That is, a stable level of oil deliveries at 1980 levels may still not be enough to avoid serious slowdowns in growth, reductions in real income, and resultant instability there; at the same time, it is likely to lead to reduced income from energy exports to hard-currency nations, a decline in energy aid to key Third World countries, and, depending on Soviet plan fulfillments, shortfalls in energy available for pressing domestic needs.

The way in which this allocation dilemma is resolved will have significant systemic ramifications. On the one hand, the preferential aspects of Soviet energy policy in CMEA, while increasing the burden on the USSR, have the desired centripetal effects of fostering integration and system conformity in member countries. On the other hand, a policy of energy rationing, while encouraging conservation, generates centrifugal forces by increasing pressures on the East Europeans to carry out economic reforms requiring significant changes in planning and management, and by pushing them onto world markets in search of alternative energy sources and efficient Western technologies. Before assessing the risks and options open to Moscow, let us look briefly at the prospects for both Soviet and East European energy supplies.

Soviet Energy Supplies in the 1980s

Soviet energy prospects have been the subject of extensive debate among Western observers since the late 1970s, when the Central Intelligence Agency first began predicting a precipitous decline in the USSR's oil output in the coming decade. In somewhat revised form, the CIA's current view is that output will rise from slightly more than 600 MMT, or 12 MBD in 1980, to 12.6 MBD by mid-decade and to 11–12 MBD by 1990—that is, a drop in production of one-third in the 1981–90 period—with a continued decline thereafter. This view is based on a combination of negative conditions: a fall in major West Siberian field output, including Samotlor; difficulties in bringing in new oil reserves; and a slow rate of substitution of other energy sources. The CIA further argues that, in the current five-year time frame, only equipment on order in 1980 or already in the West's export pipelines could materially influence the efficiency of extraction or exploration, and that limited options are open to the Soviet energy industry for improvement in performance from domestic sources.[23]

Although differing among themselves, others within the U.S. and West European intelligence communities tend to treat the CIA estimate as a worst case and point to a number of offsetting factors: uncertainties over the fall of West Siberian recovery rates, more optimistic expectations for proving out and bringing in new reserves, especially in West Siberia, and for maintaining output levels or avoiding sharp reductions in other regions. The most optimistic forecasts were those made by the United Nations Economic Commission for Europe (ECE), which in 1981 pro-

23. Central Intelligence Agency, *International Energy Statistical Review*, Mar. 31, 1981. In 1983 the CIA further modified its earlier, dire oil forecast for the Soviet Union:

> The Soviet Union has thus far averted the downturn in oil production that the CIA had earlier predicted by virtue of an enormous development effort that has tapped a petroleum reserve base larger in size than we previously believed. The cost of doing this has been high, but we think that the Soviets have already allocated enough investment resources to the oil industry to permit them to come close to their production target of 12.6 million b/d by 1985.

The above is CIA Deputy Director of Intelligence Testimony before the Subcommittee on International Trade, Finance, and Security Economics of the Joint Economic Committee, Congress of the United States, Sept. 20, 1983.

jected rising Soviet oil production through 1990, reaching approximately 645 MMT (or nearly 13 MBD). Clearly, if the worst-case scenario were to obtain, CMEA as a whole might be transformed into a modest net petroleum importer in the near future, with particularly catastrophic consequences for the East European economies, but also seriously limiting Soviet policy choices and escalating the cost of meeting domestic and foreign commitments. On the other hand, the best case implies that the USSR may have an increasingly significant economic lever for use in global as well as bloc diplomacy.[24]

In drawing up their own targets for the 1981–85 period, Soviet planners appear to have used assumptions falling somewhere between the West's best and worst cases but with a definite bias toward the former. Guidelines for the Eleventh Five-Year Plan provide the following goals for each of the primary energy sources to 1985:

	1980	1985
Oil (MMT)	603	620–645
Natural gas (BCM)	435	600–640
Coal (MMT)	716	770–800
Electrical generation (BkWh)[a]	1,295	1,550–1,600

[a]Billion kilowatt hours.

Thus, Soviet planners concurred with Western observers to the extent of predicting a leveling off in the growth rate of petroleum output (to a range of 12.4 to 12.9 MBD by 1985, or 3 to 7% over 1980 output); indeed, even this target should be put in perspective by noting that the original goal for 1980 was 12.6 MBD. At the same time, they also foresaw an increased rate of substitution by other sources, especially natural gas, production of which was to rise by 38 to 47%, with coal output up by 8 to 12% and electrical generation (based largely on expansion of nuclear capacity) by 20–24%.[25]

In fact, Soviet performance in the first two years of the Eleventh Five-Year Plan has fallen well short of these expectations and lends support to some, although certainly not all, of the worst-case projections. Oil output rose barely 1% in 1981 and by half that amount in 1982 and appears to be leveling off between 12.2 and 12.3 MBD (613 MMT). Coal production actually fell 2% in 1981 (about 3% off peak production of 724 MMT in 1978). Although it recovered to 718 MMT in 1982, the 1985 target of

24. "Medium-Term Oil Perspectives in the ECE Region," *Economic Bulletin for Europe*, 33 (June 1981), 229–33.

25. For Eleventh Five-Year Plan projections and subsequent revisions, see *Pravda*, Mar. 15, Nov. 17, 18, 1981, and Jan. 24, 1982.

770–800 MMT appears to be out of the question (800 MMT was also the original plan target for 1980). Nuclear power development, too, has experienced serious delays; while the plan calls for 26 additional plants to be put into operation by 1985, of which 8 were to be commissioned in 1981, only 3 actually came on line in that year and at least 6 of the remaining 23 were behind schedule. Only natural gas production has increased at or slightly above plan (to 501 BCM in 1982).[26]

Prospects for East European Energy Supply

The implications of these constraints in Soviet energy supplies for deliveries to Eastern Europe are sobering at best. According to Kosygin's statement at the June 1980 CMEA meeting in Prague, the first such public pronouncement of Moscow's energy policy toward the region for the 1981–85 period, Soviet petroleum exports to Eastern Europe would remain at "the high level attained for 1980" and would total "almost" 400 MMT over the five years.[27] This implied that Eastern Europe would continue to receive approximately the 73.8 MMT of crude, or 81.1 MMT of crude and petroleum products, that it had received in 1980 (see table 7.3), for a total of slightly more than 1.6 MBD. Since this would mean an increase in total deliveries for the five years of only 7 to 8% over the 1976–80 plan period, even this provisional commitment was none too reassuring for those CMEA countries that were planning annual growth rates in energy needs of 3 to 5% through 1985. Moreover, each country had to wonder how Soviet oil deliveries would be averaged out over the five years, and how they would be allocated among the countries. Would Romania, with its limited imports of Soviet oil, be allocated more? Would large importers, such as Czechoslovakia or the GDR, be held down below previous levels? The one thing they could all be certain of was that the cost of Soviet oil would rise sharply as the 1979–80 OPEC price increases were factored into intra-CMEA pricing.[28]

---

26. *Pravda*, Jan. 28, 1983; *New York Times*, Jan. 16, 1983.

27. "Vystuplenie glavy delegatsii Soyuza Sovetskikh Sotsialisticheskikh Respublik tovarishcha A. N. Kosygina" (Speech of the Head of the Delegation of the USSR Comrade A. N. Kosygin), *Ekonomicheskoe sotrudnichestvo stran-chlenov SEV* (June 1980), p. 30.

28. Specific commitments as to both quantities and prices are made in the long-term and annual bilateral trade agreements with each of the East European countries; see, e.g., reports of the Soviet-Czechoslovak trade agreement for 1981–85 in *Pravda*, May 18, 1981, and Oct. 23, 1982. Vanous ("Eastern European and Soviet Fuel Trade," p. 553, n. 9) notes that, as of 1977, the Soviets ceased publishing data on quantities of key commodities traded (in particular fuels), thus making it "more difficult for analysts in the individual East European countries to compare how well they fare relative to each other."

Several months after the Kosygin pronouncement, Oleg Bogomolov, director of the Institute of Economics of the World Socialist System of the USSR Academy of Sciences, elaborated on Moscow's position. Affirming that deliveries of Soviet oil to CMEA would remain close to the 1980 level of 80 MMT (or about 85% of current oil needs), he suggested that, if present trends in East European oil consumption continued, by 1990 these countries would have to import half their oil from non-Soviet suppliers. Moreover, although prices for Soviet oil to Eastern Europe were still 40% lower than world market levels in 1979, the gap would progressively narrow as the modified CMEA formula caught up with OPEC prices, with the long-run Soviet goal being current world pricing within CMEA. In the meantime the past practice of permitting CMEA countries to build up deficits in their energy accounts with the USSR—"free" credits which in the Soviet view amounted to an additional temporary subsidy—would be discouraged. On the other hand, Soviet energy exports other than oil—especially natural gas and electricity, the latter increasingly from nuclear power—would continue to increase. Nonetheless, Bogomolov enjoined the East Europeans to maximize both the utilization of indigenous fuels and the potential for conservation. Noting that CMEA on average used 40% more energy per unit of GNP than the Common Market economies, he hinted that conservation through structural changes in energy demand was imperative, even though this might lead to a slowing of economic growth. In particular, additional energy-intensive industries in Eastern Europe should be discouraged, with their development shifted instead to Western Siberia.[29]

The constraints on Soviet oil supply are reflected in other aspects of CMEA energy planning for the 1980s. As Bogomolov implied, natural gas and direct transmission of electricity will increasingly be substituted for oil to satisfy Eastern Europe's incremental energy needs; because these forms of energy are priced closer to world market levels, such substitutions have the additional attraction from the Soviet point of view of speeding up the phaseout of its subsidy on energy exports to the region. While firm figures are difficult to obtain, one Western source suggests that Soviet gas exports to the region could increase by as much as 40 BCM a year by 1990 (for a total of more than 70 BCM compared with 31.6 BCM in 1980), as additional pipeline capacity to both Western and Eastern Europe is completed. In addition, electric power transmissions,

29. Oleg Bogomolov, *Problems of Peace and Socialism* (Prague: Aug. 1980). Bogomolov's views may also be found in *Pravda,* June 23, 1980, and "Mezhdunarodnyi rynok stran SEV" (The International Market of the CMEA Countries), *Voprosi Ekonomiki,* no. 4 (Apr. 1980), pp. 113–21.

presumably based largely on increased Soviet nuclear generating capacity, are expected to more than double, from 0.19 to 0.45 million barrels per day of oil equivalent (MBDOE), between 1979 and 1990.[30]

This last aspect of CMEA energy planning has apparently led to a partial revival of joint investments. Poland, Czechoslovakia, and Hungary have agreed to participate in the construction of the 4000 MW Khmelnitskii nuclear plant in the Soviet Ukraine at a total cost of 1.5 billion transferable rubles, one half of which will be borne by the three East European countries, who will be repaid in electric power over a twenty-year period from 1984 to 2003. (A second nuclear plant in the Ukraine, this one possibly involving wider CMEA participation, is also in the planning stage.) Given the less than satisfactory outcome of the joint investment program of the 1970s, the fact that this project was undertaken at all is in itself testimony to the seriousness of Eastern Europe's energy problems. Equally interesting, however, is Moscow's apparent concern to avoid a renewal of earlier complaints over the terms of participation by agreeing to compensation at fixed prices, the first time it has done so since its oil deals with Czechoslovakia and the GDR in the late 1960s.

In addition to these joint projects, the East European countries themselves have drawn up extremely ambitious plans for nuclear power development, calling for an expansion in nuclear generating capacity from 3 to 37 million kilowatts between 1979 and 1990, or from 0.083 to 0.991 MBDOE. This expansion program will be based largely on a series of blocwide specialization and cooperation agreements for the manufacture of equipment for nuclear power stations, with the Czechs as the primary producer of reactors for the region. Five of the East European countries are relying solely on Soviet nuclear power technology and fuel processing, while the sixth—Romania—initially opted for an independent nuclear program based on Canadian reactors.

East European plans also call for an increase in total coal output from about 700 MMT (4.72 MBDOE) to 992 MMT (6.86 MBDOE) by the end of the decade. More than half the increase is projected for Poland, with another one-third from the GDR and Czechoslovakia, while Hungary and Romania plan only modest increases. The latter's strategy also includes further hydroelectric development, which, together with its coal

30. For these and the following projections, see Wharton Econometric Forecasting Associates (WEFA), *Centrally Planned Economies Outlook* (hereafter cited as WEFA, *CPE Outlook*) (Washington, D.C.: Apr. 1982), p. 31; Office of Technology Assessment, *Technology and Soviet Energy Availability* (Washington, D.C.: Mar. 1981), pp. 283–312; and Cam Hudson, "CMEA Joint Investments in Soviet Nuclear Power Stations," Radio Free Europe Research (hereafter cited as RFER), *RAD Background Report 11*, Jan. 20, 1981.

and separate nuclear programs and plans for revived OPEC trade, is intended to return it to independence of Soviet oil and gas by 1990.

Despite these ambitious plans to maximize development and utilization of CMEA's own energy base, the East European countries plan to continue as modest importers of OPEC oil, although clearly the amounts will depend less on need than on their ability to pay for these imports. According to one Western estimate for the CMEA-Five (excluding Romania), imports from OPEC in 1985 will range from 13 MMT (or only slightly above the 1980 level) to a high of 23 MMT, at a probable cost of $4.3 to $7.7 billion. Although some East European specialists claim that planned imports (for example, via the Adria pipeline) can be paid for through exports and industrial cooperation with OPEC countries, recent experience suggests that most CMEA countries will have difficulty expanding these sources of revenue and, therefore, that the high estimate of OPEC imports would impose an intolerable hard-currency drain, in particular on Poland with its heavy debt burden. As the largest importer of OPEC oil in the region, Romania remains a special case, with import costs partially offset by hard-currency exports of refined products as well as by industrial cooperation agreements; nonetheless, Bucharest's deficits with OPEC will likely remain the largest in CMEA.[31]

Preliminary Trends, 1981–82

Whether overall CMEA energy strategy proves realistic in the longer term will depend on the degree of success in substituting alternative energy sources, primarily natural gas and nuclear, for Soviet and OPEC oil to satisfy Eastern Europe's incremental needs. What is certain is that in the shorter term, until these alternative sources become available, the region's energy situation is likely to be precariously taut. Particularly serious has been the failure of both Soviet oil deliveries and indigenous coal production to meet original expectations in the first two years of the current plan period.

Deliveries of Soviet crude and petroleum products to Eastern Europe appear to have been close to the promised 80 MMT in 1981. However, in 1982 Moscow imposed a 10% cut across-the-board on deliveries at intra-CMEA prices, and comparable cuts are expected in 1983. Although some

31. Oechsler and Martens, "East European Trade with OPEC," pp. 530–32, 540. The view that Eastern Europe can pay for OPEC oil by expanding exports and industrial cooperation is presented by István Dobozi of the Hungarian Institute of World Economy, although he provides no specifics; see his "Long-Term Policy Responses to the Energy Crises: East and West," in Christopher Saunders, ed., *East and West in the Energy Squeeze: Prospects for Cooperation* (London: Macmillan, 1980), pp. 304–05.

Western analysts initially assumed that Poland had been spared any cuts—and, indeed, interpreted the move in part as a means of supplying that country with oil it could no longer afford to buy on world markets— preliminary data suggest that the Soviet Union's primary motive was to increase its hard-currency exports to Western markets, which rose by an estimated 40% in 1982, to between 1.4 and 1.5 MBD (70–75 MMT).[32]

The impact of these cutbacks has been compounded by shortfalls in Eastern Europe's coal production, which suggest that the current emphasis on indigenous fuel sources is at best a temporary stopgap measure. Most disruptive have been the declines in Polish output and exports; hard coal production in that country fell from a 1979 peak (in all probability overstated) of 201 to 163 MMT in 1981. In the same period, Polish coal exports dropped even more steeply, from more than 41 to about 15 MMT, with sales to CMEA (mainly to the USSR, Czechoslovakia, and the GDR) dropping from 15 to little more than 7 MMT. There was a revival of output and exports in 1982 to 189.3 and 28.5 MMT, respectively, but at the cost of a return to the exploitative and uneconomic mining practices (and very likely the overstatement of output) that characterized the pre-1980 period and that put in doubt Poland's long-term export expansion plans. Brown coal exports, mostly to the GDR, have also declined sharply, while Poland's general economic crisis forced suspension of the development of a major new hard coal deposit near Lublin. Of the other five countries, production of coal and lignite during the first two years of the new plan was down fractionally in three—Czechoslovakia (despite urgent efforts to maintain or increase output), Bulgaria, and Hungary (where output is expected to trend downward); fell short of plan in a fourth (Romania); and appears to have been close to target only in the GDR.[33]

For the longer term, all these countries, with the partial exception of Poland, are faced with depleted and less accessible deposits and worrisome declines in the average caloric content of the coal and lignite mined.[34] Moreover, nuclear substitution is not likely to occur as rapidly as is called for in current plans. The Czech reactor program has been troubled by high costs and production delays. With Czechoslovakia as a key supplier of reactors under the CMEA cooperation and specialization program, nuclear power plans throughout the region will be set back. Romania's independent nuclear program, too, has fallen behind schedule and may be in further jeopardy as a result of that country's debt problems; as a result, the Romanians have recently showed interest in cooper-

32. WEFA, *CPE Outlook,* p. 32; *Wall Street Journal,* Feb. 18, 1983.
33. WEFA, *CPE Outlook,* p. 32; various RFER *Situation Reports* on the individual countries.
34. CIA, *Energy Supplies in Eastern Europe,* p. 1, and tables 10, 11.

ating with the CMEA nuclear power program and possibly participating in the second joint plant in the Ukraine.[35] Delays in the USSR's own nuclear program in all probability will affect these joint projects, from which the East Europeans anticipate drawing large amounts of electric power in the second half of the decade; moreover, any shortfalls in nuclear-generated power for domestic Soviet use can be expected to affect the availability of hydrocarbons for export, whether to Eastern Europe or the West.

The cumulative impact of these difficulties in current and prospective energy supply was already reflected across the region in more modest growth targets for the 1981–85 plan period. As early as 1980 one Western analyst, projecting growth rates at "barely half" the level of the 1970s, wrote that "in most countries, energy shortages are likely to account for half or more of the decrease in economic growth."[36] In fact, economic performance in the first two years has fallen short even of this gloomy prediction in several of the countries, and at least two have been forced to amend their plans. In Czechoslovakia the original targets for industrial production were revised downward twice even before the plan period began, but output still fell short of the 1981 target; the 1982 goal was further reduced, to an increase of 0.8%, but output at mid-year stood at one-half that level. According to the Czechs themselves, the main culprit is the decline in energy inputs, as a result of which they have launched a prohibitively costly effort to raise domestic coal production—an effort that will inevitably cut into other investment priorities. In Romania as well, energy constraints have prompted the Ceauşescu regime to embark on a crash program to increase domestic oil production to 15 MMT (from 11.6 in 1981) by reopening old wells and investing in new drilling equipment to improve recovery rates; as in Czechoslovakia, the program will be extremely costly, in terms of both hard-currency outlays and opportunity costs, and the prospects for success are doubtful.[37]

Soviet Policy Options: A Resolution of the Dilemmas?

In the various statements emanating from Moscow on CMEA energy policy—whether the Kosygin and Bogomolov pronouncements in 1980,

35. RFER, *Czechoslovak Situation Report, 15* (Aug. 25, 1982), and *RAD Background Report, 165* (Aug. 18, 1982). The Czechs also report that the Soviets will soon raise, perhaps substantially, the price charged for their nuclear fuel.

36. Robin A. Watson, "The Linkages Between Energy and Growth Prospects in Eastern Europe," in *East European Economic Assessment*, p. 477.

37. RFER, *Czechoslovak Situation Reports, 2 and 16* (Feb. 3, Sept. 3, 1982), and *Romanian Situation Report, 16* (Sept. 22, 1982). In addition, of course, Poland (whose economic difficulties were also partially caused by energy stringencies) was only in the initial stages of implementing a recovery plan by the end of 1982.

or the statement of Soviet Council of Ministers Chairman N. A. Tikhonov at the July 1981 CMEA meeting in Sofia[38]—one senses an element of uncertainty and frustration. It is evident that the Soviets find themselves pursuing a policy they view as costly but of limited effectiveness in terms of their own goals and needs. While they may expect and require of the recipient CMEA countries a planned slowing of economic growth, they are also aware that the consequence will be an aggravation of political instability and, possibly, a distressing lack of adherence to Moscow's policy line. At the same time, while they may wish to see more efficient use of available energy supplies, so far they have been unwilling to countenance the kinds of reform that would promote increased efficiency. Indeed, none of the East European economies has come close to meeting its goal for energy conservation.[39]

This new mood in CMEA energy policy suggests a Soviet perception of itself as hostage to an expensive but potentially unsuccessful policy, as Soviet energy policy mirrors the overall frustrations of the Soviet Union in the Eastern Europe of the 1980s. The energy policy lever may still be powerful but it has lost much of its earlier flexibility. Whereas in the 1970s Moscow felt constrained to limit use of its energy leverage to granting or withholding increases in deliveries because cuts in the face of spiraling world prices would have imposed an intolerable strain on the region, in the 1980s it may have no choice but to impose such cuts regardless of the consequences for the East European economies.

Soviet options for resolving these dilemmas are several, none of them particularly appealing and all entailing substantial cost or risk: (1) they could reallocate energy exports, increasing Eastern Europe's share at the expense of West European or Third World clients; (2) they could continue to subsidize Eastern Europe's energy imports, either by maintaining the preferential pricing policies of the past or by extending other financial or trade concessions; or (3) they could make a more concerted effort to control the region's energy demand, in particular by promoting efficiency-oriented reforms as well as by continuing to shift energy-intensive industries to Siberia. The uncertainties of the post-Brezhnev succession period only add to the hazards of predicting Moscow's policy choices; nonetheless, some preliminary trends can be discerned.

The 1982 results suggest that option 1 is the least likely. Indeed, the softening of world oil prices in 1982–83, combined with the succession of poor harvests in the Soviet Union, has heightened the pressure to maintain or even increase the volume of hard-currency energy sales. As for

38. Communiqué of the 35th Members' Meeting of CMEA, *Pravda,* July 7, 1981, p. 4.
39. Concerning the disappointing results of Czechoslovakia's efforts to improve energy efficiency, see RFER, *Czechoslovak Situation Report, 16* (Sept. 3, 1982).

subsidized exports to the Third World, because of the relatively small amounts involved, meaningful reallocation in favor of Eastern Europe would seriously impinge on Moscow's relations with key clients in this group. Still a third category of countries competing with Eastern Europe for Soviet energy exports are the non-European members of CMEA, most importantly Cuba; in fact, that country alone has been promised a 26% increase in deliveries of crude oil and petroleum products (to a total of 61 MMT) in the 1981–85 period.[40]

Option 2 presents a more complex picture. The 10% cut in oil deliveries to Eastern Europe in 1982, together with what is known of Soviet oil export plans for 1983,[41] demonstrates Moscow's determination to eliminate the subsidies on its energy exports to the region as quickly as possible. On the other hand, the fact that most of these countries have continued to run substantial deficits in their trade with the Soviet Union, despite the latter's stated intention of balancing those accounts, suggests a continuing sensitivity to Eastern Europe's fragile economic state. One possibility is that the Soviets could attempt to revive an "energy-heartland" approach, similar to the defunct IGAT II agreement, whereby increased Soviet energy exports to Eastern Europe were to be offset by Soviet imports of Iranian gas. Or, in a variant of this approach, Moscow might assist its CMEA partners in arranging for direct imports of OPEC oil and gas.[42]

However, neither of the above options addresses the critical long-term problem of controlling East European energy demand. Reduction of demand may be encouraged by offsetting development of petroleum/gas-intensive industries in Western Siberia, where the USSR is creating its "largest petrochemical base" presumably to satisfy both Soviet and incremental CMEA needs.[43] In the final analysis, however, the chief factors in reducing Eastern Europe's energy consumption short of crippling reductions in the level of economic activity will be, first, the structure and technical specifications of the region's existing industrial plant

40. Lawrence H. Theriot, "Cuba Faces the Economic Realities of the 1980s," in John P. Hardt, ed., *East-West Trade: The Prospects to 1985,* studies prepared for the use of the Joint Economic Committee, Congress of the United States (Washington, D.C.: GPO, 1982), p. 115.

41. See, e.g., Czechoslovak data on prospective Soviet oil deliveries suggesting another 10% cut in 1983 (RFER, *Czechoslovak Situation Report, 2,* Jan. 31, 1983).

42. One interesting development since 1981 has been the sharp increase in Eastern Europe's hard-currency arms exports to such oil-exporting countries as Iran and Libya; although the issues involved are broader than Soviet-East European energy trade, the possibilities are intriguing. See *Soviet and East European Aid to the Third World* (Washington, D.C.: U.S. Department of State, Mar. 1983).

43. A. Aganbegyan, "Behind the Lines of the Basic Guidelines: The Siberia Program," *Sotsialisticheskaya Industriya,* May 8, 1981, translated in *Current Digest of the Soviet Press, 33* (June 17, 1981), 1.

and, second, improvement of the efficiency with which energy is used. On the first point, the prospects for the near to medium term are not hopeful. In each of the East European countries, although in varying degrees, the existing industrial structure still bears the marks of Stalinist priorities and energy-intensive technologies; altering those structures would require investment outlays and Western technology imports that are presently beyond the region's resources. The potential for near-term improvements in the second area is somewhat greater in that, even within the existing organizational and technological framework, reforms that provide incentives to use fuels (and all materials) more efficiently—for example, more realistic prices, emphasis on profitability as the key success indicator—could yield meaningful reductions in energy consumption.

There are, then, no easy solutions to Eastern Europe's energy problems or to the dilemmas they pose for Soviet policymakers. Under optimal circumstances, the new leadership in the Kremlin could minimize the pain of adjustment by a concerted effort to promote efficiency-oriented reforms in these economies while continuing to provide some form of assistance to ease them over the transition period. Yet past experience tells us that such a course would require an uncharacteristic degree of policy consistency and farsightedness, especially in a succession period. Thus, energy seems destined to remain a major source of economic weakness and political instability in the region and perhaps a growing source of Soviet-East European discord.

8

Theories of Socialist Development in Soviet-East European Relations

SARAH MEIKLEJOHN TERRY

In a subject area as replete with murky issues as Soviet-East European relations, none is more elusive than the question of how Moscow views problems of political, economic, or ideological change in its neighboring client states. This may seem a curious statement in light of past military interventions in Hungary and Czechoslovakia and, most recently, the "invasion by proxy" of Poland. Despite the apparently definitive character of these actions, however—despite also the extensive and presumably authoritative literature emanating from Moscow on the subject of "socialist development"—what are commonly called the rules of the game in Soviet-East European relations remain a matter of continuing debate and uncertainty, not only among Western observers but also among East Europeans themselves. For the Soviets' demonstrated willingness to use force against some transgressors must be weighed against their tolerance over the years of a considerable degree of diversity among, not to mention occasional insult from, their junior partners.

Since 1956 successive Kremlin leaderships have, however willingly or reluctantly, bowed to extensive concessions to national tradition and church in Poland, overseen and at times seemed to encourage a more flexible economic system in Hungary, and tolerated Romania's independent and at times even insolent foreign policy behavior. With the advent of détente in the early 1970s, the Soviets permitted (and with the fading of détente continue to permit) an unprecedented penetration of much of Eastern Europe by Western "bourgeois" influences with what might appear to be little more than verbal hand-wringing over the potential erosion of socialist élan. Finally, between August 1980 and December 1981, when Moscow at last managed to pressure the Warsaw regime to put an end to this latest "threat to socialism," the Poles repeatedly shattered taboos that observers in East and West alike had long regarded as inviolable. Thus it is hardly surprising that confusion persists not only over where the outer limits of Soviet tolerance lie, but whether indeed there

I wish to thank Robert Legvold for his comments on an earlier draft of this chapter and Donna L. Gold and Judith Scalesse Freedman for their research assistance.

221

are fixed boundaries that cannot be transgressed without evoking the ultimate sanction of armed repression.

It is not my purpose here to examine either Moscow's reactions to specific systemic challenges from Eastern Europe or the dynamics of Soviet interventionism in the region. Instead, I will focus on the ideological dimension of the relationship—on the evolution of the concept of socialist development as applied to Eastern Europe and on the role that it plays in Soviet policy toward the region. How, for instance, have Soviet interpretations of the stages of socialist development changed over time, and how have they compared with East European views? How rigidly has Moscow insisted on a single model of development, for all practical purposes indistinguishable from the Soviet one? Or are Soviet theorists sometimes responsive to, or influenced by, competing East European variants? Finally, what is the function of the concept of socialist development? Is it merely a rhetorical exercise, a smoke screen whose sole purpose is to obscure real power relationships, or does it play a more positive and central role in the Kremlin's attempts to guide and regulate its relations with the region? Or is Eastern Europe at times even a surrogate arena for theoretical debates over the future course of socialist development in the USSR itself?

In seeking answers to these questions, my analysis will focus on the developments of the last two decades and will be based on the following two hypotheses: first, that despite the"inexorable decay" of official Marxist-Leninist ideology,[1] the democratic and egalitarian value system together with the analytical perspective of Marxism retain their provocative, even subversive, potential in the context of contemporary Soviet-style socialism; and, second, that Moscow's attention to issues of socialist development in Eastern Europe, far from exhibiting the consistent concern for control and orthodoxy often attributed to it, has been highly erratic over the years, characterized by cycles of permissiveness and retrenchment reflecting both the conflicts inherent in the diversity of Soviet interests in the region and periodic debates within the USSR itself.

To understand the provocative nature of the ideology, we need to break it down into its component parts: (1) the Leninist underpinnings of the monopolistic political structure; (2) Marx's humanistic value system and image of the communist future; and (3) Marx's analytical perspective, with its emphasis on class conflict and the coercive nature of all states. The problem is that this linkage of the hierarchical and authoritarian imperatives of Leninism to Marxist analysis and utopianism can be sustained

---

1. George Schöpflin, "The Political Structure of Eastern Europe as a Factor in Intra-bloc Relations," in Karen Dawisha and Philip Hanson, eds., *Soviet-East European Dilemmas: Coercion, Competition, and Consent* (London: Heinemann, 1981), pp. 64–65.

without rending tensions only as long as a society is defined as being in a presocialist stage of development. Once a society has, in the obligatory jargon, "completed the building of the foundations of socialism," then the Marxist-Leninist synthesis (always more artificial in Eastern Europe than in the Russian heartland where it originated) begins to come unstuck, confronting the ruling Leninist party with an insoluble dilemma: the party is obliged to perpetuate a doctrine whose inner logic would destroy it. That is, it cannot jettison the original value system or vision of the future without undermining its own legitimacy; but neither can it be faithful to them without undercutting its power base. Moreover, the fact that Marxism-Leninism remains the only permissible language of political discourse means that the greater the tension between the promise and reality of socialism, the more likely that the critical, destabilizing elements of the ideology will be turned against its Leninist core.

With regard to the second hypothesis, if Moscow's sole or primary stake in Eastern Europe were to demonstrate the universal validity of the Soviet model of socialism, we could expect to find a consistent pattern of doctrinal guidance and enforcement. In fact, as the remaining chapters in this volume attest, Soviet interests in the region are complex and, as often as not, contradictory. That is, the requirements for economic vitality or political stability are not necessarily the same as those for ideological conformity. Nor are Soviet concerns in Eastern Europe always compatible with other policy goals, whether domestic or international. Against this background of Moscow's competing interests and commitments, Soviet-East European interactions on questions of socialist development tend to be cyclical in nature, each cycle consisting of the following phases: (1) a more or less permissive and flexible interpretation of a given stage of Eastern Europe's development, sometimes initiated by Moscow but with initiative quickly passing to the regional parties; followed by (2) miscalculations by one or more of the East European regimes as to how much diversity or autonomy Moscow will tolerate; provoking (3) rapid retrenchment, backed where necessary by a show of military force, and justified by a more restrictive definition of East European socialism in which the once permissive terminology is appropriated and reinterpreted in order to drain it of its innovative elements and restore the initiative to Moscow.

Thus, since 1945, Eastern Europe has passed through three such cycles: first, the stage of "people's democracy" in the initial postwar period; second, the brief revival of the notion of "separate roads to socialism" in the mid-1950s; and third, the stage of "developed socialism," extending from the early 1960s through the late 1970s, when hints of a return to greater flexibility suggested the beginnings of a fourth cycle. The first two cycles will not be reviewed here; instead, the chapter will focus on the third cycle, the hints of a reemergence of reformist tendencies, and the implications of the Polish crisis for systemic change in Eastern Europe.[2]

DEVELOPED SOCIALISM

Auspicious Beginnings

It is only within the last few years that Western scholarship on the Soviet bloc has begun to take cognizance of a newly delineated stage of socialist development: "developed socialism" (variously referred to also as "mature" or "advanced" socialism or, in some early statements, as a "second stage of socialist development" and the "period of the full construction of socialist society"). To date, the few analyses of developed socialism to appear in Western literature have focused largely on the Soviet conceptualization as elaborated since the 24th Congress of the CPSU in 1971. As such, this intermediate stage en route to the promised (if ever more distant) advent of communism is presented as a more or less consistent body of theory, still to be sure in the process of formulation, but not the subject of sharply opposing interpretations or fundamental differences of opinion among Soviet and East European theorists. Indeed, to the extent that Western sources on this topic deal with Eastern Europe at all, they tend to see the East Europeans not as articulating competing definitions of "developed socialism"—and certainly not as originators of the concept—but as following by and large in Moscow's footsteps.

In a sense, such neglect of the East European origins of developed socialism is not surprising. With the demise of the Prague Spring, early

---

2. One final comment by way of introduction concerns the nature of the source materials. Western observers tend to divide Soviet literature on political and theoretical questions into three categories: official or "authoritative," popular or propagandistic, and scholarly or professional—the last presumably "more revealing, more realistic in its assessment of the functioning of the system, more willing to discuss problems in a serious manner" (Ronald J. Hill, *Soviet Politics, Political Science and Reform* [New York: M. E. Sharpe, 1980], p. 18). While these distinctions may be useful at times, other factors complicate interpretation of the data. First, the fact that the early phase of each cycle has coincided with a period of uncertainty and debate in the USSR (sometimes but not necessarily related to a succession struggle) means that the significance to be attached to one or another category of literature varies markedly and that the dividing lines between categories become blurred, sometimes to the point where it is difficult to identify an "official" line at all. By the same token, in the final phase of a cycle (retrenchment and redefinition) even scholarly writings are only marginally distinguishable from the "official" view. Second, the special nature of the Soviet-East European relationship, in which the nominally independent East European states are viewed as central to the validation of the Soviet model, contributes to the pervasive opaqueness of discourse (both Soviet and East European) on questions of socialist development. And although major crises, such as the Prague Spring or the current crisis in Poland, produce welcome fallout in the form of more candid treatment of the real issues, the problems of interpretation remain substantial and require a hefty dose of informed speculation.

ruminations about the nature of this new stage were quickly and quietly discarded and have since been ignored by Soviet and East European authors alike. In reality, however, the term was introduced by the Czechoslovak party at its June 1960 Central Committee plenum, more than seven years before Brezhnev's first documented reference or attempts on the part of Soviet scholars to apply the term to the Soviet system itself; and the Czech example was shortly followed by the Hungarian, East German, and Bulgarian parties.[3] Subsequently, and despite both the variations in terminology and the sometimes rudimentary level of theoretical articulation, all the major East European reform movements of the 1960s were set in the context and justified by the requirements of this new stage of socioeconomic and political development. More important from the perspective of this chapter, the issues raised by these early conceptualizations of developed socialism have remained the subject of an ongoing if nuanced tug-of-war within the bloc—one that, after a period of retrenchment under Soviet tutelage through the better part of the 1970s, began toward the end of the decade to revert to ground marked out in particular by the Czech and Hungarian reformers of the 1960s.

Ironically, the earliest references to developed socialism in no way betrayed overtly reformist tendencies. The regimes in question were then securely in the hands of thoroughly conservative and reliable elements; only in Hungary were incipient signs of Kádár's relative populism evident to the astute observer. Rather, the inauguration of this new stage seems to have been occasioned by the completion (Poland excepted) of the final blocwide collectivization drive inspired by Khrushchev at the time of the 21st CPSU Congress in 1959. It was this achievement, marking for all intents and purposes the elimination of private ownership of the means of production and therefore also the end of the class struggle, that allowed the several client parties to proclaim that they had completed "the construction of the foundations of socialism" and were now embarking on the next stage, the building of a fully socialist or developed socialist society.

At the time, however, these early pronouncements had a perfunctory, almost ritualistic quality, suggesting at best only a minimal understanding of what this new stage might mean in systemic terms or of its latent ideological implications. Certainly there was no hint that it would entail a significant departure from the Soviet model, especially now that the latter had put the distortions of the cult of personality behind it. Indeed, the

3. *Foreign Broadcast Information Service [FBIS]*, Eastern Europe, July 8, 1960, pp. HH16, HH22; Gyula Kállay, "Hungary on the Eve of the Party Congress," *New Times*, no. 47 (1962), pp. 8–10; István Darvasi, "Hungarian Socialist Workers' Party Congress," *World Marxist Review*, 9 (Oct. 1966), 60–61; I. P. Ilinskii, *Po puti sotsialisticheskogo razvitiya* (Moscow: Mezhdunarodnye Otnosheniya, 1965), pp. 12–16; F. M. Burlatskii, *Lenin, Gosudarstvo, Politika* (Moscow: Nauka, 1970), pp. 426–27.

12th Congress of the Czechoslovak party in 1962 was marked by doctrinal confusion over the meaning of the "all-people's state" and by a retreat in the direction of stricter discipline and central control.[4] It was only later, toward mid-decade, as a result of internal pressures growing out of a realization of the connection between faltering economic performance and systemic rigidities, and only under the influence of the more permissive atmosphere of the last Khrushchev years, that these gropings toward a new stage of socialist development came to be associated with programs of far-reaching economic and political reform in Czechoslovakia and Hungary and more limited reforms elsewhere. As the Czech reformer Eduard Goldstücker later put it, the first "small chink [was] opened in the Stalinist armour by the combined effects of our economic bankruptcy and the 22nd Soviet Party Congress."[5]

My purpose here is not to review in any detail these several reform efforts, much less the range of dissident thinking, but simply to identify those issues, especially as articulated by Czech and Hungarian theorists in the 1960s, that were to become sources of contention in the reinterpretation of developed socialism following the Warsaw Pact invasion of Czechoslovakia and throughout the 1970s. These issues fall into four basic areas: (1) the system of economic planning and management; (2) the nature of class structure and social relations under full socialism; (3) the proper structure and functioning of political institutions; and (4) the continuing relevance of orthodox Marxism-Leninism and the Soviet model of socialist development, or what has come to be referred to with increasing frequency as "real socialism."

1. The common denominator of all East European reform efforts in the 1960s was a recognition of the need for fundamental change in the system of economic planning and management as a prerequisite for meeting the more demanding technological and productivity requirements of the new stage; likewise, this was the area in which East European thinking was most closely paralleled by developments in the USSR. The core of the problem, the obsolescence of the traditional centrally planned economy (CPE) whose structure had remained essentially unchanged since Stalin's time, was one that Marx would have understood well. As described by a prominent Polish economist at the time, "A basic contradiction [had arisen] between the old methods of planning and industrial management, evolved at another stage of economic development, and the current aims of economic policy, as determined by an objective need to substitute

4. H. Gordon Skilling, *Czechoslovakia's Interrupted Revolution* (Princeton: Princeton University Press, 1976), pp. 135–39.

5. Interview with Eduard Goldstücker, in G. R. Urban, ed., *Communist Reformation: Nationalism, Internationalism and Change in the World Communist Movement* (New York: St. Martin's Press, 1979), p. 21.

intensive methods of promoting economic growth for the extensive ones."[6]

Given the common nature of the ills generated by the traditional CPE, it was inevitable that there would be broad similarities among the remedies proposed throughout the bloc: a reduction in the number and rigidity of centrally determined plan indicators, with profit (or sales) to replace gross output as the key success indicator; increased emphasis at the center on long-term strategic planning, combined with some degree of decentralization of operational decision-making either to newly formed industrial associations or directly to the enterprise level; the introduction of a more realistic price mechanism and other financial tools (interest charges and variable interest rates, more highly differentiated wage and incentive scales, and so forth) to facilitate a more rational allocation of resources and to encourage increased productivity and technological innovation.

The broad similarities among reform blueprints in the several countries should not, however, obscure the equally important differences in approach and emphasis. Most important was the distinction between the limited "administrative decentralization" approach of most of the reform programs (including the Soviet) and the more comprehensive "economic decentralization" approach of the Czechoslovak and Hungarian blueprints, as well as briefly the Bulgarian. As described by Morris Bornstein, the intent of the former was

to "rationalize" the existing scheme of administering the economy, by transferring to lower levels some of the more detailed decisions regarding the composition of output, on the one hand, and production methods, on the other . . . [but] subject to constraints in the form of centrally set global output assignments and input authorizations. This shift would also reduce the burden of decision making at higher levels, freeing them to concentrate on their non-delegable responsibilities regarding investment, location, living standards, foreign economic policy, etc.[7]

By contrast, "economic decentralization" marked a major step in the direction of a "socialist regulated market economy" in that it

6. Quoted in Michael Gamarnikow, "Balance Sheet on Economic Reforms," in John P. Hardt, ed., *Reorientation and Commercial Relations of the Economies of Eastern Europe*, compendium of papers submitted to the Joint Economic Committee, Congress of the United States (Washington, D.C.: U.S. Government Printing Office [hereafter GPO], 1974), p. 165. See also Goldstücker's more forceful statement of this contradiction in Urban, ed., *Communist Reformation*, p. 29.

7. Morris Bornstein, "Economic Reform in Eastern Europe," in John P. Hardt, ed., *East European Economies Post-Helsinki*, compendium of papers submitted to the Joint Economic Committee, Congress of the United States (Washington, D.C.: GPO, 1977), p. 109.

envisioned a greater role for domestic and foreign market forces—and concomitantly a smaller voice for central planning and administrative control—in determining the composition of output, the allocation of resources, and even the distribution of income. . . . The state authorities would still control the "main directions and proportions" of the economy through macroeconomic policy decisions and instruments (taxes, subsidies, credit). . . . But within this regulatory framework, "the market," not "the plan," would guide the microeconomic decisions of the enterprises about what to produce and how to produce it.[8]

In addition, the East European reforms, in theory if not always in practice, tended to go beyond Soviet proposals in several respects: in the decontrol of agriculture through stimulation of local cooperative (or even private) initiative; in the importance attached to achieving a more acceptable balance between consumption and investment; and consequently, in a perceptibly more permissive attitude toward cooperative and limited private enterprise in small-scale industry, services, and housing—all despite the recently approximated goal of full nationalization of the means of production.

A final and crucial distinction concerned the urgency attached to meeting the challenge of the so-called scientific-technological revolution. While this phrase was to become a favorite buzzword in Soviet and East European literature in the 1970s—so ubiquitous, in fact, that it was quickly reduced to the abbreviation STR—it was the Czechs who first recognized the qualitative nature of the challenge and its systemic implications. In 1966 a special study team of the Czechoslovak Academy of Sciences depicted this revolution as a watershed in the development of human civilization with profound implications for the economic system of socialism. Starting from the impeccable Marxist position that science was "a direct productive force" and therefore part of the "base," the study team argued that technological innovation was becoming the "decisive factor" in a country's competitiveness. Since the existing "directive system of management," as part of the superstructure, was incapable of fostering the spirit of free inquiry and conflict of views essential to the optimal development of science, it had to be fundamentally restructured.[9]

2. A second area that was subjected to renewed scrutiny in the context of the transition to "developed" or "mature" socialism was the nature of the class structure and social relations. Viewed through orthodox Marxist-Leninist eyes, class structure is a function of property relations. Thus completion of the stage of "constructing the foundations of socialism"

8. Ibid., pp. 109–10.

9. Paul M. Cocks, "Retooling the Directed Society: Administrative Modernization and Developed Socialism," in Jan F. Triska and Paul M. Cocks, eds., *Political Development in Eastern Europe* (New York: Praeger, 1977), pp. 54–55; Skilling, *Interrupted Revolution*, pp. 125–27.

presumably signifies the elimination of hostile classes ("antagonistic contradictions") and the inauguration of a period of increasingly harmonious
relations among the remaining classes of "working people"—a catchall
phrase that includes manual workers, collective farm peasants, and the
intelligentsia, the last invariably referred to as a "stratum" rather than a
class—until such time as class distinctions disappear altogether. In the
meantime, the dictatorship of the proletariat (formed in a period of intense class struggle) would, in Khrushchev's phrase, be gradually transformed into a "state of the whole people."

Without explicitly rejecting the Marxian concept of class, the Czechs,
and more cautiously the Hungarians, chose to focus less on the growing
homogeneity of society than on the persistence within the framework of a
broad socialist consensus of specific group and individual interests ("in-
tra-class divisions" or "non-antagonistic contradictions"), which were no
longer based on property relations but on different positions in the socialist division of labor, and which had "come to the forefront" now that the
basic "capitalism-or-socialism alternative" had been resolved. Moreover,
given the complexity of the challenge posed by the scientific-technological revolution, and the concomitant need to stimulate productivity and
innovation, neither the division of labor nor the resulting social diversity
and conflicts of interest were likely to diminish in the foreseeable future.
In brief, after a period of social leveling and mobility, advanced socialist
societies no less than their capitalist counterparts were in danger of experiencing a restratification and a reemergence of such "bourgeois" phenomena as alienation.[10]

3. Recognition of the permanency and legitimacy of diverse and competing interests under socialism had profound implications for the reform of political institutions and processes in the stage of developed
socialism—implications most forcefully and consistently articulated by
the Czech theoretician, Zdeněk Mlynář. According to Mlynář, the "method of planning and management by directives from above" carried with it
a double-edged threat of distortion of the general interests of society: on
the one hand, the tendency to equate some "individual, specific interests
(which the central bodies could not anticipate and hence did not recognize) with anti-social behavior"; on the other hand, the comparable danger that official policy "advanced by the state in the name of the interests
of society as a whole" merely represented the equally specific and partial
interests of other groups or individuals (in this case, the central planners

10. See, e.g., Zdeněk Mlynář, "Problems of Political Leadership and the New Economic
System," *World Marxist Review*, 8 (Dec. 1965), 75–77, and Peter Toma and Iván Völgyes,
Politics in Hungary (San Francisco: Freeman, 1977), p. 47. See also Goldstücker's comments
on alienation under socialism, in Urban, ed., *Communist Reformation*, pp. 24–27.

or the *apparat*). Rather than ignoring or suppressing the inherent conflicts, the proper "function of leadership" therefore was "to coordinate
these interests" and to so construct "the machinery of economic management [and state administration] . . . as to allow such contradictions to
manifest themselves . . . [and] to help the socialist community of working
people to find its objective common interests in the process of solving the
non-antagonistic contradictions that may arise."

Thus, while he paid tribute to Khrushchev's new Soviet Party program
and occasionally borrowed some of its terminology (e.g., the "all-people's
state"), Mlynář's solutions to the problems of socialist democracy took the
form of institutionalized channels of interest articulation and control over
arbitrary bureaucratic rule. "The deepening of democracy," he noted in
an oblique criticism of Khrushchev's approach, "cannot be regarded
merely as a quantitative development of the forms of popular participation." Moreover, "it would be a mistake to associate the development of
[social] organizations merely with the mechanical transfer to them of
more and more functions now performed by state bodies" on the assumption that they could or should represent some abstract general social
interest. Instead, in phases reminiscent of the adversarial relationship
implicit in such bourgeois concepts as the "separation of powers" and
"checks and balances," Mlynář argued for a system in which all elements
of society—party, state, social organizations, and other interest groups—
would participate "as independent political subjects" on the basis of "mutual control and a certain equilibrium." The "leading role" of the Communist party was not rejected, but it was redefined to stress the importance of political processes and bargaining as opposed to the imposition of
a predetermined policy.[11]

4. Finally, Czech and, to a lesser extent, Hungarian and GDR reforms
rekindled the sensitive issue of Soviet ideological primacy. In particular,
thinly disguised pretensions on the part of the Czechs that "socialism with
a human face" would provide a more appealing model for West European societies than Soviet-style socialism implied, at least from Moscow's
point of view, an unacceptable disregard for "the general laws of socialist
development." Similarly, growing awareness of the inadequacies of

11. Based on the following of Mlynář's writings: "Problems of Political Leadership," pp.
75–82; "Our Political System and the Division of Power," *Rudé Právo* (Feb. 13, 1968),
translated in Robin Alison Remington, ed., *Winter in Prague: Documents on Czechoslovak
Communism in Crisis* (Cambridge: MIT Press, 1969), pp. 43–47; and *Nightfrost in Prague: The
End of Humane Socialism* (New York: Karz, 1980), esp. pp. 61–63. See also Skilling, *Interrupted
Revolution*, pp. 112–13, 333–35. Similar ideas were implicit in the New Economic Mechanism (NEM), although here they were far more cautiously articulated and not given clear
institutional expression; see, e.g., Resző Nyers, "Reform of the Economic Mechanism in
Hungary," *World Marxist Review*, 9 (Oct. 1966), 3–12.

orthodox Marxism-Leninism as a guide to contemporary social realities was reflected in a marked disinterest in still hypothetical questions concerning the future communist society and in a new perception of Marxism as, in Mlynář's words, "a rational, open-ended theory of social development with inner contradictions, . . . not identical with the political ideology of the communist movement." Recognizing that there was no "perfect" system—indeed, that the quest for such had led to a perversion of the movement's original ideals—he wrote in 1968 that the "fundamental problem facing [us] . . . does not lie in how we can 'perfect' the existing political system, but in how we can ensure its qualitative reform." In place of the old goal-oriented orthodoxy, the new preoccupation with political processes brought with it a revival of interest among Czech scholars in the discipline of political science—that is, a renewed appreciation of the value of a systematic study of politics, including such hitherto taboo subjects as the workings of bourgeois political systems as well as the role of the party in communist systems.[12]

The Soviet Role and Response

While these reform efforts were primarily the work of the East Europeans themselves, Soviet politics, both domestic and external, played a multifaceted and by hindsight curiously positive role in their development. In contrast to our retrospective view, filtered as it is through the prism of 1968 and Moscow's ultimate "No!" to the Prague Spring (an event that contributed to the reversal of all but the Hungarian reform), the most striking feature of Soviet behavior up to 1968 was the way in which it *fostered* the growth of reformism in the region. At times that influence was exercised more or less consciously; at other times, it was apparently inadvertent, the result of mixed signals or incoherent policy guidance from Moscow, due largely to the uncertainty and confusion attending the post-Khrushchev power struggle. But the weight of evidence strongly suggests that the East Europeans believed, and had fair reason to believe, not only that the CPSU was "well disposed toward reform" but even that it was itself the "spearhead of liberalisation."[13]

Moscow's pro-reform influence was most direct and unambiguous in the early part of the decade, when the impetuous Khrushchev seemed eager for the East Europeans to follow his lead toward renewed de-Stalinization and the still vaguely defined "all-people's state" proclaimed

12. Goldstücker, in Urban, ed., *Communist Reformation*, p. 74; Mlynář, *Nightfrost*, pp. 44–45, 75, and "Our Political System," p. 45; and Skilling, *Interrupted Revolution*, pp. 111–12.

13. Mlynář interview in Urban, ed., *Communist Reformation*, pp. 116–17.

in the 1961 CPSU program. It was, for example, Khrushchev's unequivo-
cal support of Kádár's "alliance policy" and "goulash communism" that
allowed the Hungarian leader to consolidate his domestic political position and embark on the course that led to the New Economic Mechanism
(NEM). Similarly, it was Khrushchev who encouraged and supported the
beginnings of reform in the GDR and Bulgaria and who in September
1964, just a month before his ouster, reportedly pressed a reluctant
Czechoslovak Central Committee to adopt its first economic reform
program.

   Although it is never an easy matter to pinpoint Khrushchev's motives,
in this case they were likely a mixture of the pragmatic and the ideological.
On the one hand, in view of declining growth rates throughout the bloc,
he was undoubtedly receptive to reforms that promised improved economic performance and an easing of the drain that Eastern Europe was
beginning to impose on the Soviet economy. On the other hand, the
prospect of Moscow's East European clients pursuing an orderly and
gradual transition toward the communist future, more or less in Moscow's
train, must have seemed welcome relief from Mao's "great leaps" and
vituperative accusations of "bourgeois revisionism" against Soviet policies. Apart from Khrushchev's own still ambiguous notion of the "all-
people's state," there is no evidence that he had a hand in delineating the
new intermediate stage of "developed socialism" (a term he himself seems
not to have used), but it is unlikely that he would have seen it as a threat to
Soviet ideological primacy. After all, he had already proclaimed the USSR
to be in the more advanced state of the "final construction" of communism. Moreover, the regimes in the forefront of this movement were
among the most loyal and stable in Eastern Europe; with some, Khrushchev's problem was more one of pushing them into de-Stalinization
than preventing them from overstepping the bounds of acceptable
change.

   None of this is to suggest that Khrushchev fully understood the forces
he was unleashing, or that he would have tolerated the Prague Spring any
more than his successors did. Although his own notions of increased mass
participation went well beyond the traditional Leninist concept of *pri-
vlechenie* ("drawing in") and implied a kind of adversarial relationship
between officialdom and populace,[14] they were still crude and restrictive
by comparison with Czech (and to a lesser extent Hungarian) concepts of
socialist pluralism and the latter's recognition of the legitimacy of competing social interests. Nonetheless, the "populist" thrust of Khrushchev's
policies, and his apparent concern to restore some of the original demo-

   14. See George W. Breslauer, "Khrushchev Reconsidered," *Problems of Communism*, 25
(Sept.–Oct. 1976), 18–33.

cratic and egalitarian ethos to the ideology, offered leverage to those in Eastern Europe who were attempting to open that "chink in the Stalinist armour." In other words, the Soviet contribution to the cause of East European reform in the first half of the 1960s came not in the form of a specific blueprint for the future but in its absence—in a release from some of the strictures of the past and an apparent green light to experiment on their own.

Looking back on the implications of Khrushchev's fall for the cause of reform in Czechoslovakia, both Goldstücker and Mlynář have recently stated that the Czechs' cardinal error lay (in the former's words) in:

> not subjecting our impressions of the political situation in the Soviet Union to more rigorous analysis. We assumed that the process of de-Stalinisation was continuing—whereas, in fact, it was not. . . . Khrushchev's fall meant re-Stalinisation, and the evidence was there for everyone to read, for example in the trial of Sinyavsky and Daniel. Why were we being misled? Because in Czechoslovakia the process of de-Stalinisation had been delayed until 1963, so that in 1968 we were out of phase with what was happening in Moscow. We were caught in the trough of the wave while imagining not only that we were acting in the interest of socialism, but that the men in the Kremlin would *recognise* our merit for doing so.[15]

Most contemporary evidence suggests, however, that the Czech (and other) reformers were not nearly so naive as this comment implies and that the telltale signs of the post-Khrushchev "restoration" became evident only with the benefits of hindsight. Indeed, what is most striking about the Soviet reaction to incipient reform in Eastern Europe in the years between Khrushchev's fall in 1964 and the invasion of Czechoslovakia in 1968 is not a perceptible reversal in attitude, but the lack of clear warning signs of a pending change in the direction of Soviet policy.

Mlynář himself recounts one of the most revealing episodes in his memoir *Nightfrost in Prague*. Having spent a number of years in the Soviet Union and keenly aware that reform in Czechoslovakia "would have to pass muster with the Kremlin," Mlynář writes that he went to Moscow in the spring of 1967 precisely "to determine what kind of reaction could be actually expected on the part of Soviet ideologists." Although "some highly placed academic ideologists" attacked his ideas—"In what way," one asked with obvious distaste, "do your opinions differ from bourgeois conceptions of pluralism?"—he reports that "most of the official reactions were very reserved: they found my ideas 'interesting,' without specifying whether this was meant in the positive or the negative sense." At the unofficial level, however, the reactions were "essentially different":

---

15. Goldstücker, in Urban, ed., *Communist Reformation*, pp. 73–74; for a similar comment by Mlynář, see ibid., pp. 116–17.

My Soviet counterparts . . . were of the opinion that although many of our reform conceptions could scarcely be considered practicable in the foreseeable future in the USSR, it would nevertheless be exceptionally important for them if something like them were in fact to take place in Czechoslovakia. They felt that reforms and democratization would become necessary in the Soviet Union as well. . . . Only in very isolated instances did I encounter pessimism about democratization in the Soviet Union.

Moreover, Mlynář reports, "the general opinion (particularly in the party apparatus) seemed to be that [Brezhnev] represented an 'interim government.'" Thus, although he recognized that there could be "no immediate hope of support from the Soviet theoretical and ideological institutes"—indeed, that despite a sympathetic majority among Soviet academics, the Czechs "had to expect a certain degree of ill will from the official . . . circles of such places"—he returned to Prague "convinced that the situation was not unpromising and that we could expect positive developments toward democratization in the Soviet Union as well."[16]

Mlynář readily admits that this was "one of the worst appraisals of any situation" he has ever made. Perhaps so, but he seems to have been in respectable company at the time, as evidenced by the most detailed study of Soviet politics in this period, Michel Tatu's *Power in the Kremlin*. Although Tatu did not directly address the issue of Soviet policy toward Eastern Europe, he did document in extenso the prevailing confusion over the post-Khrushchev direction of Soviet policy. In particular, his account of the tug-of-war between reformers and "re-Stalinizers"—the apparent neutralization of the latter, as well as Brezhnev's relative quiescence and difficulties in consolidating his hold over the secretariat—tends to confirm Mlynář's impressions and suggests how he (and no doubt others) could have so badly misinterpreted their reform prospects.

As Tatu described the domestic political scene at the time of the 23d CPSU Congress in March 1966, there was "a political vacuum without precedent for many years": that is, a situation in which the hard-liners (led, in Tatu's view, by Brezhnev) were strong enough to stop de-Stalinization but not strong enough to impose re-Stalinization. Instead, the conservatives' ploy for reversing Khrushchev's innovations was one of "revision through silence": for example, the principle of "systematic renewal" of party cadres was retained in the new party statutes even as it was being ignored in practice; mention of the 1961 party program and the "all-people's state" gradually disappeared from speeches and party slogans; and by the 23d Congress, both the 20th Congress and de-Stalinization were also taboo subjects. At the same time, the studied reticence of the antireform faction—throughout the critical period Brezhnev re-

16. Mlynář, *Nightfrost*, pp. 85–87, 173–74.

mained silent on the whole question of industrial reform, and such leading lights as Mikhail Suslov did not speak at all at the 23d Congress—created confusion among propagandists and tended to give far greater visibility to proreform elements than their relative numbers or support in high places would have warranted. Hence the illusion, especially after mid-1965 and likely well into 1967, that the reformers had emerged (or were about to emerge) victorious. Even as astute an observer as Tatu saw the evolution of the Soviet system toward "parliamentarianism" as inevitable, although he recognized the possibility of temporary reversals along the way.[17]

It is in light of this power vacuum and the temporary, albeit illustory, ascendency of proreform elements on the domestic political scene that one has to interpret Soviet commentary on East European developments of the period. At least until 1968, and to a limited extent for several years thereafter, such commentary should be read less as a reflection of official approval or disapproval of East European policy (much less as an attempt to guide it) than as an offshoot of internal Soviet policy debates in which reform—whether economic reform of the Liberman type or Khrushchevian populism—still seemed to be the order of the day, and in which East European innovations provided welcome evidence of the legitimacy of the desired changes as respectably "socialist."

From this point of view, two aspects of the literature are of interest. The first is the dearth of meaningful commentary at the official level. In retrospect, this is not particularly surprising. After all, if the likes of Secretaries Brezhnev and Suslov were reluctant to express themselves on critical issues at home, should one be surprised that they showed a similar circumspection about comparable developments in Eastern Europe? At the same time, given the controversial nature of some of the proposed reforms, the East European elites were, like Mlynář, looking for unambiguous signals as to the acceptability of their ideas and may have interpreted silence as an absence of objections. The second and more interesting phenomenon was the essentially positive tone of the commentary on East European developments in the professional and popular press. Not only was this in sharp contrast to the pattern of official reticence but, by comparison with Soviet writings on Eastern Europe in the 1970s, the literature of the 1965–68 period was notable for its candor, relative accuracy, and even enthusiasm about regional developments. (We can probably assume that some of this commentary reflected the policy preferences of higher authorities, but even that supposition must in most cases remain in the realm of conjecture.)[18]

17. Michel Tatu, *Power in the Kremlin: From Khrushchev to Kosygin* (New York: Viking, 1970), esp. pp. 429–93, 538–39.

18. East European developments were apparently drawn into Soviet policy debates on

It was questions of economic reform that drew the lion's share of attention from Soviet authors—and understandably so in view of the general belief that the Soviet Union was also on the road to genuine economic reform and, therefore, that this was a relatively safe topic. One can detect some differences in tone and emphasis between the professional journals (e.g., *Voprosy Ekonomiki* and *Ekonomicheskaya Gazeta*) on the one hand and the popular press (e.g., *New Times*) on the other—for instance, the latter's tone of unalloyed enthusiasm and tendency to highlight some of the more unorthodox aspects of East European reform proposals. With few exceptions, however, the overall tone of Soviet commentary in this period was highly positive.

Although some authors stressed the common features of reform programs throughout the bloc (including the Soviet), others pointed with apparent approval (or at least not disapproval) to the more comprehensive nature of the Czechoslovak and Hungarian blueprints and picked up on Czech themes concerning the qualitative challenge of the scientific-technological revolution.[19] Still others waxed lyrical over the anticipated benefits of such erstwhile heresies as the easing of restrictions on private and cooperative initiative in housing, services, and agriculture, not merely to improve the supply situation in these traditionally neglected sectors but as a way of tapping private savings for needed investments.[20] Finally, there was a general consensus that many of the measures proposed to improve domestic economic performance—in particular, price reform and the introduction of other economic regulators—would have the additional benefit of measurably improving the level of cooperation and specialization within the Council for Mutual Economic Assistance (CMEA) by

---

occasion, at least indirectly; see, e.g., Tatu's account of an exchange between Suslov and Podgornyi in 1965, in which the former praised developments in Bulgaria while the latter invoked the more radical changes proposed in Czechoslovakia (*Power in the Kremlin*, pp. 456–58). See also Zvi Y. Gitelman, *The Diffusion of Political Innovation: From Eastern Europe to the Soviet Union* (Beverly Hills: Sage Publications, 1972), and N. Osipov, "Hungary's Economic Reform," *New Times*, no. 27 (1966), pp. 9–12.

19. O. Bogomolov, "Khozyaistvennye reformy i ekonomicheskoe sotrudnichestvo sotsialisticheskikh stran," *Voprosy Ekonomiki*, no. 2 (Feb. 1966), pp. 76–86; N. Stolpov, "Sovremennyi etap stroitelstva sotsializma v evropeiskikh stranakh narodnoi demokratii," ibid., no. 3 (Mar. 1966), pp. 75–83; L. Dobysheva and K. Kedrova, "Aktualnye voprosy razvitiya tekhnicheskogo progressa v stranakh sotsializma," ibid., no. 9 (Sept. 1966), pp. 138–41; Fyodor Burlatskii, "On the Construction of a Developed Socialist Society," *Pravda*, Dec. 21, 1966 (condensed in the *Current Digest of the Soviet Press* [*CDSP*], vol. 18, no. 51, pp. 16–17).

20. See especially the articles by Valery Rutgaizer in *New Times*, nos. 12 (1967), 12 (1968), 19/20 (1969), and 39 (1969); also by Zinovy Mirsky, in nos. 48 (1966) and 14 (1967). On the importance of the consumer sector to productivity in the Soviet economy, see L. Kantorovich, "The Sphere of Services and Science," *Pravda*, Mar. 20, 1967 (*CDSP*, vol. 19, no. 12, pp. 9–10).

facilitating calculation of comparative advantage and increasing member interest.[21] Only occasionally in this period does one find hints of what was to become a major Kremlin concern, namely, that excessive concern for efficiency, profits, and technological innovation, especially when stimulated by even modest use of market forces, could have a disintegrative effect on CMEA, in particular by diverting key East European products or industries away from Soviet or CMEA markets.[22]

Compared with this modestly frank treatment of economic matters, Soviet coverage of East European thinking on the more sensitive issues of social and political change during the 1960s was both less extensive and more cautious. It was also lamentably unanalytical, for the most part devoid of any discussion of actual behavior as opposed to nominal or rhetorical change; moreover, the closer an issue cut to the underpinnings of political power, the more opaque and uninformative the commentary tended to become, falling back on old clichés and vague formulations about "improvements in socialist democracy" at the expense of accurately reflecting the attempts of some East Europeans to define institutionalized mechanisms of interest articulation and political control. These quantitative and qualitative deficiencies aside, the literature that appeared is interesting from several points of view: it is generally straightforward and uncritical, occasionally enthusiastic; and most of the concerns that motivated East European reformers in this period did find some resonance, albeit inconsistent, among Soviet writers.

Among the actual or proposed reforms receiving favorable comment were: electoral reform (broadening of the nomination process, introduction of multicandidate races); revitalization of representative institutions at all levels; broadening of trade union rights to participate in management and to defend workers' interests (including uncritical mention of Yugoslavia's self-management system); easing of censorship restrictions ("frank and full information is an essential element of democracy," including "unfavorable facts . . . and views we don't agree with"). Soviet writers were understandably coy when referring to the persistence of social tensions, or to a redefinition of the "leading role" of the Communist party. But even here one finds some intriguing allusions: to the complex-

21. B. Ladygin and Yu. Shiryaev, *Voprosy Ekonomiki*, no. 5 (May 1966), pp. 81–89; A. Alekseev and Yu. Shiryaev, "Aktualnye problemy razvitiya spetsializatsii i kooperirovaniya proizvodstva mezhdu stranami-chlenami SEV," ibid., no. 9 (Sept. 1966), pp. 66–75; B. Miroshnichenko, "A Good Start," *Izvestiya*, Mar. 26, 1967 (*CDSP*, vol. 19, no. 12, pp. 11–12); Boris Ladygin, Zdenek Chalupsky, and Yuri Shiryaev, "Cost Accounting in Economic Relations Between Socialist Countries," *World Marxist Review*, vol. 9 (Oct. 1966), pp. 13–18.

22. Peter Marsh, "The Integration Process in Eastern Europe 1968 to 1975," *Journal of Common Market Studies*, 14 (June 1976), 311–35; Alekseev and Shiryaev ("Aktualnye problemy razvitiya," p. 72, n. 6) also allude to this potential problem.

ity of the final socialist transformation of classes and social groups, especially where "petty bourgeois elements" had been well developed in the presocialist period; and, therefore, to the positive role that secondary parties could play even in the period of "developed socialism" because Communist parties did not necessarily represent all strata of society. Overall the East European systems were seen as making a creative contribution to socialist experience (with little or no reference to the Soviet model, much less to its primacy), and as possibly providing a more relevant model for those capitalist countries "standing on the threshhold of the transition to socialism." At the same time, a preference for citing Hungarian, Bulgarian, or East German experience, even before the 1968 invasion of Czechoslovakia, suggests continuing caution on the part of Soviet authors.[23]

As with Soviet commentary on economic reform in Eastern Europe, the generally positive coverage of social and political trends in the region can in no way be viewed as an expression of official policy or leadership preferences, despite the high-level origins of some of the literature. Rather, it should be seen in the context of the halting and partial emergence of empirical social science in the USSR in the mid-to-late 1960s. Although generally less bold than their East European counterparts, many Soviet scholars were clearly moved by similar concerns—especially by the need for a more open-ended view of Marxism, as an analytical perspective on socioeconomic change and not merely as a set of "ready-made answers [concerning] . . . the future of communist society,"[24] and therefore by a growing interest in political processes in the Soviet Union. It was in this period, for instance, that Soviet sociologists began to break with the myth of the growing homogeneity of Soviet society and to confront the realities and political implications of a complex pattern of social stratification under socialism.[25] The connection between reforms in Eastern Europe and possible reform in the Soviet Union was rarely made explicit, but tacit acceptance of the diversity of socialist forms

23. See, e.g., Ilinskii, *Po puti*, pp. 3–4, 44; Burlatskii, *Lenin, Gosudarstvo, Politika*, pp. 413–40; Irena Trofimova, "Hungary: New Electoral Law in Operation," *New Times*, no. 14 (1967), pp. 16; and *Obshchee i spetsificheskoe v diktature proletariata*, ed. jointly by the Higher Party School and the Central Committee's Academy of Social Sciences (Moscow: Mysl, 1967), esp. pp. 3–7.

24. Review of a new text, *Principles of Scientific Communism*, published by the Central Committee's Academy of Social Sciences, in *Pravda*, Dec. 27, 1966 (*CDSP*, vol. 18, no. 52, pp. 29–30).

25. O. I. Shkaratan, "The Social Structure of the Soviet Working Class," *Voprosy Filosofii*, no. 1 (Jan. 1967), pp. 28–39 (*CDSP*, vol. 19, no. 12, pp. 3–8); also the selection of Soviet articles from the late 1960s in Murray Yanowitch and Wesley A. Fisher, eds., *Social Stratification and Mobility in the USSR*, (White Plains, N.Y.: International Arts and Sciences Press, 1973).

and the creative contribution being made by the East Europeans served to validate the distinction between a social system (socialism) and a political regime (a specific pattern of institutional relationships) and thus the legitimacy of a search for new and more effective forms of political organization and "socialist democracy" in the USSR itself.[26]

RETREAT FROM INCIPIENT PLURALISM

Developed Socialism Redefined

By the end of the 1960s, then, the concept of developed socialism presented the Soviet leadership, now coalescing around Brezhnev, with both a challenge (a dual challenge really) and an opportunity. It was a challenge, first, in that the reformist interpretation posed a threat, much as had the original interpretation of people's democracy in the late 1940s, to the primacy of the Soviet model of socialism, which in the wake of the invasion of Czechoslovakia was coming under increasing attack from key nonruling Communist parties as well. In addition, the articulation of a theoretical framework for reform along with a thoroughgoing critique of the CPE, all with sound Marxist underpinnings, threatened to provide a supportive climate for similar if less sophisticated reformist tendencies within the Soviet Union itself. On the other hand, developed socialism offered a welcome opportunity finally to exorcize Khrushchev's ghost, in that the identification of a new and prolonged stage of socialist development en route to the classless and stateless communist utopia postponed into the indefinite future such disagreeable aspects of that final transition as the "withering away of the state." What was needed, then, at least from Moscow's point of view, was a redefinition of developed socialism both to eliminate its potentially destabilizing features and to confirm the legitimacy of the existing power structure.

That process of redefinition emerged only haltingly and over a period of several years. The period between the invasion of Czechoslovakia in August 1968 and the 24th Congress of the CPSU in March 1971 appears to have been one of indecision and vacillation in Moscow over both how to meet the challenge and how to exploit the opportunity. In effect, there was a hiatus of sorts: a rhetorical retreat in which the term "developed socialism" (still in its reformist guise) gradually disappeared from articles dealing with Eastern Europe (and from much of the East European literature as well), while the Soviets were slow to invest it with more orthodox content. The first reference to developed socialism as applying to the Soviet Union—to the effect that the USSR had completed the building of

26. See, e.g., Burlatskii, *Lenin, Gosudarstvo, Politika*, pp. 136–39, and his "Lenin and the Art of Management," *New Times*, no. 51 (1968), pp. 6–9.

a developed socialist society, while the East European states were only embarking on its construction—appears to have come in Brezhnev's speech on the 50th anniversary of the October Revolution in November 1967. The following month a Soviet scholar, later to become one of the more prolific writers on the topic, suggested that it was time to establish criteria for this new stage and hinted at a more restrictive interpretation.[27] Brezhnev's cryptic reference was repeated on a few ceremonial occasions over the next three years but without further elaboration.

Serious attempts to appropriate the concept and give it a specifically Soviet stamp as a new form of orthodoxy began only in 1971, in the wake of the 24th CPSU Congress, an event generally viewed as marking Brezhnev's ascendancy within the Kremlin leadership. In the avalanche of articles, books, and conferences that followed, every dimension of developed socialism was redefined to eliminate or emasculate the offending elements. Moreover, that this new interpretation reflected the considered judgment of the Soviet leadership is indicated by the highly visible role that key officials from the Central Committee Secretariat played in this process. What follows is a synthesis of the official Soviet view of the main features of developed socialism, circa the mid-1970s.[28]

1. Concerning the system of economic planning and management, the critical role of the scientific-technological revolution was retained but now was to be combined with the advantages not of the socialist market (condemned as "bourgeois revisionism") but of socialist planning. Partial decentralization and price reform were to be replaced by a "rationalization" or "streamlining" of economic administration. Once again, the degree of socialization of the means of production—including not only the "socialist transformation of the countryside" (a clear admonition to the Poles) but also the gradual merger of collective into fully state property—was given priority over such criteria as labor productivity or per capita production, both of which had proved something of an embarrassment.[29] Especially striking in the Soviet literature, professional and popular as well as official, was the disappearance in the early 1970s of the word "reform," now replaced by the cumbersome and often empty phrase "perfection of the economic mechanism." Finally, economic cooperation through CMEA, rather than being the beneficiary of economic reform in member countries, was now to serve as a spur to economic efficiency and

27. A. Butenko, "Socialism and Its Laws of Development," *New Times*, no. 52 (1967), pp. 8–11.

28. Although only a few selected sources can be cited in the following summary, it is based on a broader survey of these journals: *Kommunist, Nauchnyi Kommunizm, Voprosy Ekonomiki, Ekonomicheskaya Gazeta,* and *Sovetskoe Gosudarstvo i Pravo.*

29. See A. P. Butenko, "Razvitoe sotsialisticheskoe obshchestvo: sushchnost i problemy," *Voprosy Filosofii,* no. 6 (June 1976), pp. 29, 38–39.

technological progress through the mechanism of plan coordination and guarantees of a stable and large market. Economic integration was to serve additionally as an impetus to political, social, and cultural rapprochement, leading to a "growing similarity of [the] economic and political structures [of the individual countries]." Economics in the service of political purpose, rather than vice versa.[30]

2. In the area of class structure and social relations, earlier progress toward recognizing the complexity of social relations under socialism gave way to a reassertion of the old "two class, one stratum" formula (working class and collective farm peasantry plus intelligentsia, all coexisting in ever increasing harmony and unity). To the extent that the persistence of conflicting interests was admitted, they were now seen exclusively as a receding legacy of an obsolete class structure and the immaturity of socialist forms, but in no sense as a permanent feature of socialist society. By contrast, developed socialism would be marked by a "substantial reduction of social differences"; indeed, such a reduction was now viewed as a prerequisite for this new stage of development. The following statements are typical: "The determining feature of a developed socialist society is the socio-political and ideological cohesion of all classes and social groups. . . . Until this cohesion is achieved, a socialist society cannot be regarded as developed, no matter what economic and cultural level it may have attained." "The victory of socialism radically alters the nature of society. . . . [With] complete socialist ownership of the means of production, . . . class antagonisms disappear too. A socialist society consists entirely of working people, among whom there can be no class conflicts or class struggle." Gone now was any explicit recognition of stratification or conflicts of interest as permanent and legitimate features of any modern industrial society with its complex division of labor, and therefore as necessitating institutional mechanisms for their regulation and mediation. To the extent that the problem of lingering social differences under socialism was addressed at all, it would be solved in good Marxist fashion through economic and technological progress.[31]

3. However, the new orthodoxy discarded the notion that Marxist dialectics might be applied to the political system of "developed socialism"—that is, that the political superstructure, valid for an earlier stage of

30. B. Ladygin and Yu. Pekshev, "Zakonomernost postepennogo sblizheniya sotsialisticheskikh stran," *Kommunist,* no. 5 (Mar. 1977), pp. 20–31; I. Dudinskii, "The Present State of the CMEA Countries' Cooperation," *International Affairs,* no. 9 (Sept. 1978), pp. 13–22.

31. V. S. Shevtsov, *KPSS i gosudarstvo v razvitom sotsialisticheskom obshchestve* (Moscow: Politizdat, 1974), pp. 14–15. See also D. A. Kerimov, ed., *Sovetskaya demokratiya v period razvitogo sotsializma* (Moscow: Mysl, 1976), and N. I. Azarov, "Sotsialisticheskaya demokratiya w sisteme sovetskogo obraza zhizni," *Nauchnyi Kommunism,* no. 2 (1975), pp. 92–101.

development, had become an impediment to the continuing development of the socioeconomic base in the new phase of "intensive economic growth." While retaining the concept of the "all-people's state" as the successor to the dictatorship of the proletariat, the Soviet view now held that the transition would require no changes in institutional forms or fundamental political relationships:

The development of the state of the proletarian dictatorship into the state of all the people does not indicate a change in the nature of the socialist state, which has always been popular, but points rather to the expansion of its social base [through the emergence of a socially homogeneous society].

One finds no dearth of statements concerning constantly expanding opportunities for the "active participation [of the working masses] in social management" or for "popular supervision of the functioning of state bodies." But these are invariably accompanied by familiar calls for increased discipline and a strengthening of the role of the party "exercised through the formulation of an overall perspective, the correct political line, directives and instructions," as well as "the indissoluble unity . . . between the public and personal interests of the working people." Any suggestion of a "division of power" was now rejected as a "bourgeois" concept, while earlier hints of the need for popular checks on the power of the professional administrative apparatus gave way to assertions that the scientific-technological revolution enhances its role and to claims that the apparatus has "certain inherent characteristics of a representative nature." Similarly, the party was described as having "no local, professional, national or departmental interests" but as faithfully expressing "the general interests of the whole people and therefore each collective and each individual."[32]

4. On the question of the general validity of the Soviet model, Soviet writers in the 1970s tried hard to appear balanced, always stressing that the "general laws" of socialist development manifest themselves in "specific national forms." Yet they invariably came down on the side of the proposition that "Marxist-Leninists proceed from the fact that there is only one scientific model of socialism, common to all countries."[33] In other words, the roads to socialism may differ according to local conditions, historical and cultural traditions, or the level of socioeconomic development; but we are all moving in the same direction toward a single

32. Kerimov, ed., *Sovetskaya demokratiya*, pp. 89–92, 139; Shevtsov, *KPSS i gosudarstvo*, pp. 28, 100–102, 109. For one of the clearest statements on the independent role of the superstructure in guiding the development of the economic base, see "Ob ekonomicheskoi deyatelnosti gosudarstva i roli nadstroiki pri sotsializme," *Kommunist*, no. 1 (Jan. 1976), pp. 38–47.

33. A. P. Butenko, *Sotsializm kak obshchestvennyi stroi* (Moscow: Politizdat, 1974), p. 277.

goal. And, since the Soviet Union is by self-definition at a higher stage of socialist development, it represents a more mature (although admittedly not perfect) manifestation of the general laws. Missing from the literature now were earlier references to the "creative contributions" of the East European parties, independent of Soviet experience. Moreover, Soviet claims to preeminence were propped up by lengthy and tedious discussions of a question of minimal concern to the East European reformers of the 1960s—namely, the proper periodization of socialist development, in particular the relationship between "developed socialism" and the eventual transition to communism. As Academician P. N. Fedoseev put it in 1972, the questions of the general laws and stages of development "are at the epicenter of the contemporary ideological struggle."[34]

It is undoubtedly true, as some Western observers suggest, that such excessive claims about the nature of Soviet-style socialism were meant largely as exhortations, as expressions of "what ought to be rather than what is."[35] On the other hand, their constant repetition also reflected an unwillingness to make concessions to a contrary reality or to allow its institutional expression. Moreover, they served to narrow perceptibly the limits of permissible (public) discussion, to exclude certain questions as legitimate topics of inquiry, and to reverse the all too modest progress toward an empirical approach to social and political behavior that had been made in the 1960s. This is not to say that dissonant voices now vanished from the literature but they were distinctly less frequent and more muted, often amounting to no more than vague allusions buried in the middle of an otherwise unexceptionable passage or article.[36] In addition, some of the more outspoken voices from the earlier period simply withdrew from the public arena or turned their attention to safer topics.

Between 1971 and 1975, after several years of silence and confusion, all Moscow's East European client parties fell into line with the redefined orthodoxy—although the literature reveals more or less predictable differences of emphasis among them, as well as a fairly clear pecking order from the Kremlin's point of view. The bulk of Soviet attention has been focused on three parties—the Bulgarian, East German, and Czechoslo-

34. "Nekotorye problemy stroitelstva i razvitiya sotsializma," *Nauchnyi Kommunizm*, no. 1 (1973), pp. 140–44.

35. See Hill, *Soviet Politics*, pp. 122, 169.

36. See, e.g., V. A. Kopyrin, "Razvitoe sotsialisticheskoe obshchestvo: problema kriteriev," *Nauchnyi Kommunizm*, no. 3 (1976), pp. 29–37; Ts. A. Stepanian, "XXV Syezd KPSS o meste razvitogo sotsializma v stanovlenii kommunisticheskoi obshchestvenno-ekonomicheskoi formatsii," *Nauchnyi Kommunizm*, no. 5 (1976), pp. 13–23. The latter is particularly interesting for its provocative, if guarded, references to the "primitive" application of Marxist dialectics to socialism. Hill also notes (*Soviet Politics*, p. 29) that some reform proposals that had been broached in print in the 1960s—e.g., multicandidate elections—had by the mid-1970s retreated to the seminar rooms.

vak: the first two, both of which formally adopted the laundered version
of developed socialism at their respective congresses in 1971, as apparent
showcases of socialist development (although the Socialist Unity Party
had to repent the sins of the just-deposed Ulbricht);[37] the third as an
object lesson in the perils of "bourgeois revisionism" and "pseudo-social-
ist" distortions of real socialism. The other three have received relatively
less attention; but whereas the Hungarians (who continued to emphasize
national peculiarities over the "general laws") and the Romanians (who
persisted in maintaining their distance from Moscow 'in international
relations) were quickly included among those countries in the process of
"building developed socialism," the Poles were pointedly excluded from
that category until 1974 (no doubt largely because of the dominance of
the private sector in agriculture). In addition this process of bringing the
individual parties into line was accompanied by the inauguration of a
series of blocwide conferences clearly designed to forge a united front on
key ideological issues—or at the very least to stem the erosion.[38]

The Politics of Developed Socialism

Of primary interest, however, is not so much Moscow's appropriation of
the concept of developed socialism, or even the ritualistic adherence of
the East European parties to the redefinition. The critical issue is the
significance of this process, if any, for Soviet-East European relations and
for systemic reform in Eastern Europe in the 1970s. Was this sudden rash
of ideological initiative, with its posturing and arcane hairsplitting, merely a rhetorical facade behind which the East Europeans retained considerable latitude to define their own political and economic systems? Or was
the new orthodoxy emanating from Moscow a tool of sorts, consciously
manipulated by the Brezhnev leadership to contain the challenges to its
interests in the region? And if the latter, how was it used and with what
degree of success? The evidence is mixed and largely circumstantial and,
by virtue of the secretive nature of the Soviet-East European relationship,
difficult to interpret.

On the one hand, even in its new guise the concept of developed
socialism remained sufficiently ill-defined that it did not preclude con-

37. See chap. 2.
38. "Nekotorye problemy stroitelstva"; G. E. Glezerman, ed., *Razvitoe sotsialisticheskoe
obshchestvo: sushchnost, kriterii zrelosti, kritika revizionistskikh kontseptsii* (Moscow: Mysl, 1973).
See also a review of the second edition of the latter (1975) concerning the August 1971
conference of Soviet, East German, Czech, and Bulgarian scholars out of which the volume
grew: *Nauchnyi Kommunizm*, no. 3 (1976), pp. 142–44. Beginning in 1973, *World Marxist
Review* carried frequent articles, symposia, and reports of blocwide conferences on the
subject of developed socialism.

tinued systemic diversity; on the other, there is not enough hard evidence of direct interference to demonstrate a consistent pattern of Kremlin pressure to enforce conformity on the East European parties. On the contrary, within a few months of the crushing of the Prague Spring, Kádár was allowed to proceed with the NEM, despite the fact that it was based on the very principles of market socialism the Czechs were now obliged to condemn; and while Soviet writers now avoided explicit discussion of the NEM's less orthodox features (often of the reform itself), they did not openly criticize it. In Poland, too, the first years under Gierek witnessed active discussion of economic and limited political reforms, as well as some initial steps toward their implementation. That the NEM in practice fell short of the original reform blueprint, or that the Polish reforms quietly collapsed almost before they got off the ground—as well as the earlier reversals of reforms in the GDR and Bulgaria—were developments that cannot readily be traced to meddling on Moscow's part. In each case the timing and circumstances were such as to suggest that domestic constraints were a significant factor, perhaps sufficient to explain the retreat. The Bulgarian reform, scuttled even before the invasion of Czechoslovakia, seems to have fallen victim to the local leadership's fears of Czech-type political repercussions, while the East German New Economic System, never a reform of the more radical market type, was undermined by a return to taut planning in the early 1970s. In Poland and Hungary also, there was ample evidence of bureaucratic resistance to genuine decentralization, reinforced by strong blue-collar opposition to any reform that accentuated income differentiation on the basis of productivity. In brief, then, the blocwide retreat on reforms in the 1970s is not necessarily proof of petty dictation by Moscow. Moreover, the fact that the first half of the decade in particular witnessed a rapid expansion of East-West trade and other contacts—contacts tolerated if not always encouraged by Moscow—hardly suggests a Kremlin leadership gripped by fear of political or economic erosion in its backyard.

On the other hand, recent statements by two well-placed East European officials—the Hungarian economist and "father" of the NEM, Reszö Nyers, and one-time economic adviser to Gierek, Zdzisław Rurarz—suggest the opposite conclusion: that Moscow was indeed actively engaged behind the scenes, if not in imposing total conformity with the Soviet model of "developed" or "real" socialism, then at least in placing off limits any deviations from the model that would seriously jeopardize basic Soviet political and economic interests. Nyers, who was removed from his leadership posts in 1974 (most likely at Soviet insistence) and has only recently made something of a comeback in conjunction with efforts to revive the NEM, stated in a 1980 interview that domestic opposition had little to do with Hungary's "backpedaling" in economic policy in

1972, which he ascribed "mainly to external causes and in particular to the failure of reform movements elsewhere in the region," specifically in Czechoslovakia and "even" in the Soviet Union. "To a certain extent this, too, bade us to be more cautious and not to get involved in conflicts through our pioneering efforts, which may have appeared overambitious at the time." Moreover, Nyers singled out CMEA trade as a "negative influence on Hungary's economic development," ostensibly because "global economic problems reduced the rate of growth in every socialist country"; but one need not read far between the lines to suppose that he was also referring to the difficulties of introducing market mechanisms in a small economy closely linked to a far larger bloc still dominated by a command structure. Rurarz, who defected from his post as Poland's ambassador to Japan in December 1981, could afford to be less circumspect. He claims to have proposed a comprehensive economic reform program to Gierek in 1971–72, based on market principles similar to those in the original NEM blueprint as well as on "complete freedom of action for individual agriculture and handicrafts and even for some small business." Gierek reportedly rejected his advice, telling him, "You should not forget that we could do certain things if we were only alone," while his Soviet contacts accused him of "proposing the restoration of capitalism."[39]

One cannot, of course, draw general conclusions from one or two such statements. But given the extraordinary secrecy that surrounds many aspects of Soviet-East European relations, it would be equally naive to wait for the proverbial "smoking gun" before inferring a policy of more or less enforced compliance. The Soviets have at their disposal ample means of leverage, of both the direct and indirect varieties, to elicit the desired behavior. The mere fact that there are powerful built-in biases against change in these systems means that a reassertion of orthodoxy in the USSR, such as occurred after 1968, will automatically tip the balance against would-be reformers in Eastern Europe. Especially in the wake of the Czechoslovak experiment, a lack of explicit approval from Moscow for some proposed change was now likely to be interpreted as disapproval. (As one Polish writer noted, in an unmistakable allusion to Soviet complicity in the defeat of economic reform in Poland, Moscow was the place "where questions go unanswered.")[40]

There can be little doubt that such self-imposed compliance was (and remains) the preferred form of guidance: it avoided the need to spell out systemic requirements in minute detail; frequent repetition of vague but orthodox formulas was sufficient to convey the intended signals—under-

39. *Radio Free Europe Research [RFER]*, RAD Background Report/307 (Hungary), Dec. 19, 1980; *New York Times*, Jan. 24, 1982.

40. Waldemar Kuczyński, *Po wielkim skoku* (Warsaw: Niezależna Oficyna Wydawnicza, 1979), p. 17.

stood by reformers and conservatives alike—and at the same time to preserve the appearance of noninterference. Where the self-enforcing mechanisms failed to elicit the desired degree of conformity, however, Moscow could apply more direct forms of pressure: for example, a stepped-up schedule of supervisory visits by Central Committee functionaries; a reassertion of the traditional Stalinist role of the Soviet ambassador in Eastern Europe; manipulations of divisions within the local leadership; or various forms of economic leverage (the carrot as well as the stick), the most effective of which in the wake of the 1973 Arab oil embargo became Soviet energy deliveries.

To document Soviet exploitation of any of these sources of potential pressure, especially energy sanctions, is difficult at best; to attempt to tie them specifically to questions of ideological or systemic conformity is well-nigh impossible. Nonetheless the evidence, while speculative, is intriguing. Is it merely a coincidence, for example, that the two least orthodox regimes in Eastern Europe—the Hungarian and the Polish—have consistently paid higher prices for Soviet oil than the others? Or that Moscow reportedly attempted to restrict oil deliveries to Hungary in 1971, just as it began pushing its newly redefined version of socialist orthodoxy and just prior to the Kádár regime's retreat from the original NEM blueprint? Even more suggestive is a series of episodes or developments in Polish-Soviet relations in the mid-1970s, in which Soviet oil again appears as a possible inducement, implying veiled but persistent pressure on the Gierek regime to bring its policies more into line with bloc norms.[41]

REFORMISM RESURGENT?

If it is fair to assume that the theoretical elaboration of developed socialism was not simply a rhetorical exercise but part of a revamped strategy of alliance management, then by mid-decade Brezhnev had reason to be generally satisfied with the results. The centrifugal forces that had threatened to erode Soviet ideological primacy in the 1960s had been contained. No major reform movements had been initiated in the 1970s and the one holdover, Hungary's NEM, had been successfully curbed, as had Poland's more tentative moves in that direction. The new orthodoxy, now referred to with increasing frequency as "real socialism," had weathered the attacks of the Eurocommunists, who, while they had scored some rhetorical points (as at the June 1976 Berlin conference), failed to make significant inroads in the East European parties. Even the rapid expansion of East-West contacts associated with the first blush of détente seemed to have minimal political effects. Here the Brezhnev leadership proved more prescient than proponents of détente in the West in recognizing, contrary

41. See chap. 3.

to the standard propaganda line, that the most potent threats to the stability of the East European societies were their internal contradictions rather than alleged subversive influences from outside. Indeed, in the short term at least, détente contributed to Eastern Europe's stability by supplying the capital and technology to maintain growth rates as well as otherwise scarce foods and consumer goods.

Yet the cornerstone of Brezhnev's strategy of alliance management turned out to be its Achilles' heel as well. The policy of firm, if subtle, ideological guidance, supplemented where necessary by the judicious application of economic and political pressures, militated against the kind of miscalculation that had contributed to the Czech crisis. At the same time, by containing debate and experimentation within the narrow limits acceptable to Moscow, this policy also succeeded in insulating the East European regimes from the need to squarely address their systemic short-comings and to adapt their institutional structures to the changed re-quirements of socioeconomic maturity. Thus, once the faltering eco-nomic performance of the late 1970s had revealed the inadequacy of infusions of Western credits and technology in the absence of meaningful reform, the stage was set for a new cycle of debate over the nature of "socialist development." By now, however, economic stringency com-bined with rising social tensions had left little room for maneuver—as was evident from the 1976 food-price riots in Poland and the 1977 Jiu Valley disturbances in Romania long before the dramatic events of August 1980.

Characteristic of the early stages of this new cycle of "debate" were, first, the caution with which questions of reform were broached—indeed, the word "reform" was still generally avoided in favor of more neutral terms, such as "steps" or "measures"—second, the restriction of most "official" discussions to changes in the economic system, and, third, the extent to which the East European parties took their cues from Moscow rather than risk finding themselves, yet again, out on the wrong limb. The first sign that the Soviet Union might be moving out of the pattern of partial administrative reorganizations that had characterized most of the 1970s came in early 1978 with the publication of the first of a series of authoritative articles by prominent Soviet economists on improving the system of planning and management in which, for the first time in nearly a decade, serious attention was given to the need for greater reliance on economic tools. At about the same time, an unusually laudatory article in *New Times* on the Hungarian economy, containing a brief if ambiguous reference to a "Hungarian model of socialism," seemed to signal the East Europeans that they, too, could begin (or resume) experimenting.[42]

42. N. Fedorenko et al., "Manage Efficiently: Parameters of Management," *Pravda*, Mar. 23, 1978 (translated in *CDSP*, vol. 30, no. 12, pp. 6–7); subsequent articles by Fedorenko were excerpted in *CDSP*, vol. 30, no. 24, pp. 12–13, and no. 35, pp. 10–12; concerning Hungary, see *New Times*, no. 14 (1978), pp. 21–24.

Among the first to take advantage of the new opening were, not surprisingly, the Hungarians, who set about revitalizing their NEM, and the Bulgarians, who began articulating a modified version of their abortive economic reform from the 1960s. Others were more cautious, waiting for the verdict from Moscow before committing themselves to changes at home. With the announcement of the Soviets' "mini-reform" of July 1979, involving no fundamental changes in the system of planning and control, Poland, Czechoslovakia, and Romania quickly fell into line. Only the Hungarians, with Brezhnev's apparent approval, and possibly the Bulgarians (although they were now exceedingly reluctant to spell out their proposed reforms) proceeded with more comprehensive change.

At the same time, the more permissive atmosphere generated by the discussion of changes in the economic system encouraged those concerned over growing social and political tensions to revive some of the more controversial ideas and analytical perspectives of the original reformist conception of developed socialism from the 1960s. Most persistent were the Poles, spurred by their 1976 crisis and the active dissident movement that sprang up in its wake. But the Hungarians, too, remained sensitive to the defects of the political system. Among the recurrent themes were warnings, in the official party press and sometimes phrased in what can only be described as alarmist terms, that the development of the political superstructure must not be allowed to lag behind the socioeconomic base (the implication being that it already had); that the gaps between social groups not only were not diminishing but were growing, raising the prospect of "social disintegration"; that, despite orthodox assertions to the contrary, the administrative bureaucracies should be seen as representing not the "general interests" of society but their own specific interests that could alienate the people from the state in the absence of effective external controls; therefore, that failure to accommodate the institutional political structure to the growing functional complexity of society and to differing points of view would lead only to an increase in social tensions; and, finally, that faltering economic performance made the proper functioning of "socialist democracy" more rather than less important to the political stability of the system. As in the Czech literature of the 1960s, one again finds a greater concern with political processes than with ultimate goals, together with an implicit assumption that the futile quest for the "perfect" society of the future is antithetical to attainment of a more humane society in the present.[43]

43. The Polish literature from this period is voluminous; of primary interest in this context are not so much the dissident publications, or even uncensored party or "establishment" writings (e.g., the DiP reports and other writings that circulated privately), as articles that appeared in the official party press and signaled concern at the highest levels. Among the more interesting of such articles to appear in the late 1970s are the following: Sylwester Zawadzki, "Z zagadnień demokracji socjalistycznej," *Nowe Drogi*, no. 9 (Sept. 1976), pp.

There is little in the available record to indicate how sensitive the Soviet leaders were to the reemergence of these issues or to the deepening tensions in Poland prior to the explosion of discontent in the summer of 1980. But the circumstantial evidence detailed elsewhere in this volume suggests that they saw Poland's economic weakness and internal political divisions less as a warning of the need for fundamental reforms than as useful leverage over a vulnerable Gierek leadership.[44]

While one might have expected that the Kremlin's immediate response to the Polish crisis would be to abort the latest round of reform discussions throughout the bloc, the reaction was far less definitive. On the one hand, the Soviets repeatedly and categorically rejected the notion of an independent trade union in a socialist state (or any other change that could be construed as weakening the party's leading role); used every tactic short of outright military intervention to influence the Polish situation; and issued uncharacteristically blunt public statements warning other bloc parties to toe the line of Leninist orthodoxy.[45] On the other hand, harsh warnings of the need to rebuff "antisocialist" elements were accompanied by pleas that more attention be paid to the "representative" functions of existing "popular" organizations; interest in economic reform remained high, with no less than Brezhnev himself admonishing the CPSU at its 26th Congress to study the experiences of the East European parties; and, in at least one instance, Lenin's New Economic Policy was cited positively as an example of flexible response to crisis.[46]

At the time of Brezhnev's death in November 1982, such intimations of reform had yielded no concrete results. But the selection of Yuri Andropov as the new Soviet party leader raised widespread expectations, in East and West alike, of a more vigorous push for substantive change. In particular, Andropov's presumed association with the reform movements

---

40–53; "Teoria demokracji socjalistycznej," *Państwo i Prawo,* 32 (Aug.–Sept. 1977), pp. 249–52; Jerzy Kowalski, "Społeczne-ekonomiczne podstawy socjalistycznego systemu politycznego," *Państwo i Prawo,* 32 (July 1977), pp. 3–10; idem, "Kilka uwag o rozwoju demokracji socjalistycznej" and "Efektywność mechanizmów demokratycznych," *Nowe Drogi* (Mar. and Aug. 1979), pp. 122–26, 157–61; and Wacław Bielicki and Stanisław Widerszpil, "Z problematyki przemian społecznych w Polsce Ludowej," *Nowe Drogi* (July 1979), pp. 74–85. From the Hungarian literature, the following reflect similar concerns: György Aczél, "On the Approaches to Developed Socialism," *World Marxist Review,* 19 (Mar. 1976), 14–23; and György Szoboszlai and Imre Verebelyi, "Aspects of Developing Socialist Democracy Analyzed," *Társadalomtudományi Közlemények,* no. 1, 1980 (excerpted in Joint Publications Research Service, *East Europe Report,* no. 1799 (July 11, 1980), pp. 55–79.

44. See chap. 3.
45. *Pravda,* Aug. 23, 1981; reported in the *New York Times,* Aug. 24, 1981.
46. A. P. Butenko, "Socialism: Forms and Deformations," *New Times,* no. 6 (1982), pp. 5–7.

of the 1960s (especially in Hungary), combined with his reputation as a tough but sophisticated pragmatist, were cited as reasons why Moscow might now take a more tolerant view of NEM-type reforms in Eastern Europe, and perhaps in the Soviet Union itself. By the middle of 1983, however, what had looked like a fast jump off the starting block only a few months before began to resemble the all-too-familiar immobilisme of the later Brezhnev years. Whatever Andropov's policy preferences, it was clear that he was unwilling or, in light of his own uncertain health, unable to override powerful vested interests in the status quo.[47]

This is not to say that the signals emanating from the Kremlin are wholly negative. Pronouncements at more or less official levels continue to admonish Soviet planners to study the experiences of the more innovative East European systems—although apart from agriculture, where Hungary is routinely trotted out as a model of productivity, the more orthodox and centralized GDR and Bulgarian systems are cited as the examples to emulate. At the June 1983 CPSU Central Committee plenum and again in August at a special meeting for senior party officials, Andropov himself sharply criticized the half-measures and foot-dragging that had characterized past reform attempts. Speaking of the long-heralded shift to a more "intensive" mode of development as inevitable, he implied that this would require "a corresponding perfection of production relations" (the political superstructure).[48] At the quasi-official level, prominently displayed articles have shown an even greater flexibility reminiscent of East European thinking in the 1960s—including hints, albeit very ambiguous, to the effect that under the impact of the scientific-technological revolution society has become increasingly complex, and therefore that "the very concept of socialism becomes increasingly multiform as each social group views the socialist ideal in the light of its own interests, its own cultural standards and its own world outlook."[49] No

47. See, e.g., R. W. Apple, Jr., "Some Insights Into Andropov Gleaned From Budapest Role," and John F. Burns, "Andropov's Changes: Early Pace Bogs Down," *New York Times*, Dec. 28, 1982, and May 5, 1983; also Allen Kroncher, "Waiting for the Economic Reform," *RLR*, RL 133/83 (Mar. 29, 1983).

48. For the texts of Andropov's speeches, see *Pravda*, June 16 and Aug. 16, 1983; see also O. Bogomolov, "Obshchee dostoyanie: obmen opytom sotsialisticheskogo stroitelstva," *Pravda*, Mar. 14, 1983. One of the more fascinating, if still muted, aspects of current political struggle in the Kremlin concerns the apparent renewal of debate over precisely what stage of developed socialism the USSR has attained and what implications this has for the political system; see, e.g., Elizabeth Teague, "Andropov Putting His Mark on the New Party Program," *RLR*, RL 238/83 (June 16, 1983).

49. Fyodor Burlatskii, "Karl Marx and Our Time," *New Times*, no. 23 (1983), pp. 18–20; see also A. Aganbegyan, "Incentives and Reserves: Implement the Decisions of the November Plenary Session of the CPSU Central Committee," *Trud*, Dec. 12, 1982 (*CDSP*, vol. 34, no. 52, pp. 1–4).

doubt such statements will be welcomed by proreform forces in Eastern Europe as ammunition against their own hard-liners.[50]

Nonetheless, the emphasis in Moscow's attitude toward systemic reform in Eastern Europe has been on caution and cohesion—"the dovetailing of economic and social decisions" and "joint appraisal of collective experience," which will help "to bring the structures of economic mechanisms closer together." In other words, while the new Kremlin leadership may have a keener grasp than its predecessor of the need to study the applicability of East European experiments to the USSR, it is still reluctant to permit the smaller CMEA countries to move significantly ahead of Moscow in solving their problems of economic planning and management.[51] Nor do the "reform" measures announced by Moscow in late July and early August promise meaningful change in the foreseeable future. Once again, the Soviets have come down resoundingly on the side of compromise—partial and incremental reforms, stressing both "enterprise autonomy" and a strengthening of "centralized economic management"—in the end signifying little. For Eastern Europe, the return of stalemate to the Kremlin can only mean that the domestic political balance will again be tipped against genuine reform, at least temporarily, and that the thrust of Soviet policy toward the region will focus on political orthodoxy and bloc cohesion.[52]

Thus, three years after the birth of Solidarity and nearly two years after its suspension, perhaps the only thing that can be said with any certainty is that the Polish crisis has intensified the debate over the nature of "socialist development," in both Eastern Europe and the USSR, and has irrevocably placed the central dilemma of the Soviet-East European relationship on the agenda of the post-Brezhnev leaderships in Moscow. The essence of this dilemma is that the Soviet Union is a profoundly conservative power bound willy-nilly to a dynamic, revolutionary belief system which it has tried to truncate and tailor to its state needs, but which remains inherently subversive of its perceived interests. Measured against the values they espouse, the Soviet-style regimes of Eastern Europe are increasingly viewed as illegitimate by their own populations and especially by the working class in whose name and interests they claim to rule. These values then become the program of competing groups: either inside the

50. See, e.g., a Polish report on the June CPSU plenum in *Życie Gospodarcze*, no. 27 (July 3, 1983), p. 3.

51. Bogomolov, "Obshchee dostoyanie;" Hungarian Research Department, "Soviet Signals on Economic Management Picked Up in Hungary," *RFER*, RAD Background Report/68 (Mar. 31, 1983).

52. For initial reports of the partial and experimental changes to be introduced in Soviet economic management beginning in January 1984, see John F. Burns, in the *New York Times*, July 27, 1983.

party, as in the Prague Spring, or, far more threatening as Solidarity proved, from within the working class itself. The willingness of the next generation of Soviet leaders to come to terms with this dilemma, to begin to close the gap between the promise and reality of socialism in Eastern Europe, will determine whether history bears out Czech reformer Mlynář's prophecy that "if [the Central and East European countries] have to mark time until Russia, too, is ready for change—well, that would be a national disaster."[53]

53. Urban, ed., *Communist Reformation*, p. 129.

9

The Warsaw Pact: Soviet Military Policy in Eastern Europe

A. ROSS JOHNSON

Eastern Europe is and will remain the principal Soviet sphere of influence. Soviet hegemony in Eastern Europe has many dimensions, including political, economic, and ideological factors discussed in other chapters of this volume. But most fundamentally, the Soviet stake in Eastern Europe involves security considerations and is based on military power. The external and internal aspects of that military power have been inextricably linked since Stalin extended Soviet influence to the region in 1944–45. World War II demonstrated to Stalin and his successors the crucial importance of sufficient military power and secure border areas to counter opponents of the Soviet state. Security also implied, for Stalin and his successors, Soviet-style regimes in Eastern Europe. Except for Yugoslavia, Albania, and in part Czechoslovakia, Soviet military power was responsible for the creation of the communist states of Eastern Europe; these states were born not of revolution but of Soviet military liberation and occupation, as Soviet and East European officials alike freely acknowledge. Polish Communist leader Władysław Gomułka granted in 1945, for example, that the "transformation of Polish society" could begin in the absence of revolution because of the presence of the Red Army.[1] The reality of Soviet military power in Eastern Europe as a principal instrument of Soviet policy vis-à-vis Western Europe and as the ultimate

This chapter is based in large part on materials contained in my Rand Corporation studies of East European military issues, particularly: A. Ross Johnson, Robert W. Dean, and Alexander Alexiev, *East European Military Establishments: The Warsaw Pact Northern Tier* (New York: Crane Russak, 1982), and A. Ross Johnson, *Soviet-East European Military Relations: An Overview* (Santa Monica: The Rand Corporation, P-5383-1, Aug. 1977). Material on the Romanian military deviation is based in part on Alexander Alexiev, *Romania and the Warsaw Pact: The Defense Policy of a Reluctant Ally* (Santa Monica: The Rand Corporation, P-6270, Jan. 1979). Thomas W. Wolfe, *Soviet Power and Europe, 1945–1969* (Baltimore: Johns Hopkins University Press, 1970), provides a comprehensive analysis from the Soviet perspective. Extensive documentation is contained in these studies. I am indebted to my Rand coauthors and colleagues. I am also grateful to Michael Chécinski, Michael Sadykiewicz, and other former East European military officers who wish to remain anonymous, for sharing their insights.

1. Speech of Dec. 7, 1945, as quoted in A. Ross Johnson, *The Transformation of Communist Ideology: The Yugoslav Case, 1945–1953* (Cambridge, Mass.: MIT Press, 1972), p. 14.

guarantor of East European policies and regimes acceptable to the USSR has not changed—either in fact or in the minds of Soviet leaders. As Leonid Brezhnev, objecting to the liberalization in Czechoslovakia in 1968, told the Czechoslovak leadership at that time:

Your country is in the region occupied by Soviet soldiers in World War II. We paid for this with great sacrifices and we will never leave. Your borders are our borders. You do not follow our suggestions, and we feel threatened . . . we are completely justified in sending our soldiers to your country in order to be secure within our borders. It is a secondary matter whether or not there is an immediate threat from anyone; this is an issue of principle, which will hold, [as it has] since World War II, "forever."[2]

The USSR has both deployed large-scale Soviet forces in Eastern Europe and overseen the development of substantial national military forces. These military capabilities have served a variety of Soviet military and foreign policy goals vis-à-vis the West. In the late 1940s and 1950s, air defense forces in the region contributed significantly to defense of the Soviet heartland against American and British nuclear-capable bombers. More generally, Eastern Europe constituted a military staging and buffer zone that could be used for either defensive or offensive purposes. While Stalin could not have had much confidence in the reliability or competence of the newly developed East European forces, their buildup, as a supplement to the buildup of the Soviet armed forces themselves, tilted the regional military balance in Europe in favor of the USSR. This made Western Europe a "hostage" for American nuclear restraint, while casting a long political shadow over the western half of the continent.[3]

At the end of the 1950s the USSR sought to improve its military posture, and presumably to expand its political influence, through the development of Soviet military forces in Eastern Europe capable of rapid, offensive, nuclear-supported operations against NATO. Corresponding changes took place in the East European military forces, which as a consequence became more important to Soviet military planning for European contingencies. Just how important is not easily determined. Calculating the weight of non-Soviet Warsaw Pact military forces in total Warsaw Pact military capabilities in Europe is difficult because information is sparse, common measures do not exist, and the share of total Soviet military forces applicable to various European contingencies is a matter of interpretation.[4] Yet all available calculations indicate that the East Euro-

2. Zdeněk Mlynář, *Nachtfrost* (Cologne: Europäische Verlagsanstalt, 1978), pp. 300–01.

3. See Wolfe, *Soviet Power and Europe*, p. 43.

4. By the mid-1970s, Western officials and analysts commonly assumed that more than half the initial Warsaw Pact forces that would be utilized for an offensive against Western

pean armed forces have acquired a major role in Soviet military planning for European warfare, just as Eastern Europe has become a key staging ground for Soviet forces. Soviet military policy in Eastern Europe must be viewed primarily through this prism of East-West, Warsaw Pact-NATO relations.

Soviet policy has been influenced by other factors as well. Soviet military forces in Eastern Europe serve a very real internal policing function, even though this role does not explain the numbers or (in most cases) the specific deployment of forces in the region. Soviet military power is the ultimate—indeed, the only real—guarantor of the stability and the very existence of the East European Communist regimes. The USSR threatened or used military force or military ties in Eastern Europe for intrabloc policing functions nine times between 1945 and 1982.[5] In all these cases, it had to be concerned with the behavior of the national military establishments that it was responsible for creating in the pursuit of security objectives vis-à-vis the West but that were subsequently integrated into the East European political systems.

In the 1980s, greater competing demands on Soviet military resources at home and abroad give the Soviet leadership a strong incentive for developing an enhanced East European contribution to total Soviet-con-

---

Europe might be East European. Of the 58 Warsaw Pact in-place divisions commonly mentioned in Warsaw Pact attack scenarios, 31 are non-Soviet (e.g., *Annual Defense Department Report for Fiscal Year 1979*, Department of Defense press release, p. 6).

According to data from the International Institute of Strategic Studies, 43% of the in-place (fully mobilized) divisions in northern and central Europe are non-Soviet; in southern Europe, 81% are non-Soviet. (Data for southern Europe include Romanian forces, which would be of questionable utility to the USSR in many circumstances.) None of the ten category 1 (up to three-quarters strength) reinforcing divisions are East European, but 40% of the category 2 (up to half-strength) and 15% of the category 3 (cadre) divisions are non-Soviet. East European armies provide 36% of the total Warsaw Pact main battle tanks in northern and central Europe and 63% of those in southern Europe. Forty-four percent of Warsaw Pact tactical aircraft in northern and central Europe are East European; in Southern Europe, 61%. See The International Institute for Strategic Studies (IISS), *The Military Balance, 1980–1981* (London, IISS, 1980), pp. 110–15.

These figures may overstate the East European contribution. According to the calculation of a former Polish officer utilizing Soviet categories, in the European theater of war, non-Soviet forces account for 39% of First Strategic Echelon divisions, 30% of Northern Tier First Strategic Echelon divisions, and 32% of total Warsaw Pact European divisions (Michael Sadykiewicz, personal communication, Feb. 23, 1981).

5. Soviet forces guaranteed the Communist takeover of Eastern Europe in 1945–47; indirectly supported the coup of the Czechoslovak Communist party in 1948; exerted pressure on Yugoslavia in 1949–52; suppressed worker demonstrations in East Germany in 1953; attempted to influence the choice of Poland's leadership in 1956; suppressed the Hungarian Revolution in 1956; sought to influence Albania in 1960–61; forced a reversal of liberalization in Czechoslovakia in 1968–69; and brought pressure to bear against Poland in 1980–81.

trolled military power in Europe. Yet, as we shall see, even before the outbreak of the Polish crisis in 1980 there were operational, institutional, and socioeconomic reasons that made Moscow unable to count on even a continuation of the East European military effort of the 1970s.

THE EVOLVING ROLE OF EAST EUROPEAN FORCES IN SOVIET STRATEGY

The East European military establishments first became important to Moscow as international tension mounted in the early 1950s. The post-1949 expansion of the Soviet armed forces stationed in East Germany, Poland, Hungary, Romania, and the USSR itself was soon extended to the fledgling East European Communist military establishments as well. Conscription was introduced in all the East European armed forces (except in the GDR, where conscription occurred only in 1962), and by 1953 the resulting buildup had brought about 1½ million men under arms and created 65 East European divisions. Soviet equipment flowed in to replace obsolete World War II armaments.[6]

Harnessed to Stalin's foreign policy in the early 1950s, the East European military establishments were internally Stalinized as well. Military command positions were filled with Communist and pro-Communist officers, usually of "low" social origin and with little or no prior military experience but with postwar training in Communist military institutions. The internal organization, training patterns, military doctrine, tactics, and even the uniforms of the East European armed forces were modified to conform to the Soviet model. Each Communist party established triple channels of political control over the national armed forces: the command channel, secured through the replacement of prewar officers by party loyalists, was complemented by extending the networks of the Central Committee-directed Political Administration and the security service, each with its own chain of command, to the regimental level or below.

Dependency of the East European Communist parties on Moscow notwithstanding, consolidation of national party control over the respective East European armed forces was for Stalin an inadequate guarantee that those forces would be fully responsive to Soviet directives. Direct Soviet channels of control were required. Thus, the newly appointed, Communist-trained East European commanders were subordinated to Soviet officers of respective national origins who had served, sometimes for years, in the Red Army as Soviet citizens and who now formally resumed their original citizenship. This was most evident in Poland,[7] but

6. See Johnson, Dean, and Alexiev, *East European Military Establishments,* chap. 2, and the references and documentation therein.

7. In the early 1950s the posts of defense minister, chief of the general staff, commander of the ground forces, heads of all the service branches, and commander of all four military districts were held by former Soviet officers.

the practice was almost as widespread in the Hungarian army and was followed to a lesser extent in the other East European armed forces. Equally important, thousands of Soviet "advisers" were placed within the East European armies, constituting a separate chain of command. An informal but unified Soviet command-and-control system over "integrated" East European armed forces was in effect established. By means of the senior Soviet officers and the Soviet "advisers" in each East European army, the Soviet High Command was, in practice, able to administer the East European armed forces as branches of the Red Army.

Following Stalin's death and with a partial easing of tensions in Europe, the Soviet leadership sought to relax the most extreme forms of forced mobilization and subservience to Soviet control in Eastern Europe—essentials of the Stalinist interstate system that became Soviet liabilities with the removal of the system's personal linchpin. Economic considerations were cardinal in the Soviet effort to rationalize what was now viewed as Stalin's misallocation of military-related resources in Eastern Europe. Because it so overstretched the East European economies, the military burden in Eastern Europe had seriously destabilizing political ramifications. So in an atmosphere of relaxing East-West tensions, defense spending was reduced and military manpower cut in Eastern Europe, just as in the USSR, and the Stalinist approach to military mobilization was condemned by East European leaders as primitive and wasteful.

As Soviet military thought was freed from Stalin's dogmas, East European military doctrine was modified in turn. Stalin had resisted the technical advantages of greater mechanization and concentration of ground forces; these were now accepted, and motorized divisions replaced infantry divisions in the East European armed forces. Soviet military doctrine now embraced the realities of the nuclear age; a decade before they were to acquire systems capable of delivering nuclear warheads, the East European armed forces received instruction from their Soviet mentors on nuclear warfare.[8]

The founding in 1955 of the Warsaw Treaty Organization (or Warsaw Pact) as the formal multilateral security alliance of the states within the Soviet orbit was not principally a consequence of this process of rationalizing the Soviet and East European military establishments. The creation of the Warsaw Pact was, rather, explained in political terms. Externally, it was a political response to the incorporation of West Germany in NATO. In intrabloc terms, it was an effort to establish a multinational political organization that, together with the Council for Mutual Economic Assistance (CMEA/COMECON) and other specialized bloc organizations, could provide an institutionalized substitute for the personalized Stalinist system of Soviet hegemony in Eastern Europe.

8. Johnson, *Soviet-East European Military Relations*, p. 5.

Article 5 of the Warsaw Treaty did provide for a joint military command, which was formally established in Moscow in early 1956. Yet in military terms, the Warsaw Pact remained a paper organization until the 1960s.[9] At the outset, it served one concrete Soviet military purpose: It offered an alternate source of legitimization for deployment of Soviet forces in Hungary and Romania after ratification of the Austrian State Treaty in 1955. It also supplied the Soviets with a mechanism to contain the renationalization of the East European military establishments that began after Stalin's death. A multilateral alliance framework, no matter how devoid of substance, could serve to formally recognize an East European voice in alliance matters and thus promised to help defuse potentially explosive national feelings and to legitimize Soviet control.

The crises of 1956 in Eastern Europe greatly enhanced the role of the Warsaw Pact as a multilateral institution that could channel and limit East European nationalism. One consequence of Soviet military pressure on Poland and Soviet military suppression of the 1956 Hungarian Revolution was the increased sensitivity of East European leaderships to the forms of national sovereignty, in the military as in other realms. Formal renationalization of the East European armed forces, begun in 1953, was completed after 1956. Most of the former Soviet officers who had commanded the East European military establishments in the early 1950s returned to the USSR, and national military uniforms were rehabilitated. More important, the USSR professed willingness (in the Soviet government declaration of October 1956) to review the issue of Soviet troops stationed in Eastern Europe. Despite Soviet military suppression of the Hungarian Revolution, the USSR concluded a status-of-forces agreement with Poland in December 1956 specifying the terms of the stationing of Soviet forces on Polish territory and pledging their noninterference in Polish affairs. Status-of-forces agreements were also concluded with Hungary, Romania, and East Germany early in 1957. In what might be interpreted as a final Soviet gesture to East European national sentiments, perhaps as a specific result of Romanian economic concessions and Chinese support, Moscow acceded to a Romanian request, advanced even before 1956, and withdrew all Soviet forces from Romania early in 1958.

After 1956 Khrushchev sought to construct a viable "socialist commonwealth" that would ensure Soviet control over the broad outlines of domestic and foreign policies of the East European states. The USSR sought to utilize the Warsaw Pact and CMEA as institutional mechanisms

9. In common Western usage, *Warsaw Pact* refers to any military entities or activities of the USSR and its East European client-states. Here and elsewhere throughout this chapter, discussion of the Warsaw Pact pertains to the formal pact structure, embracing a number of multinational bodies.

for ensuring Soviet hegemony in the region, while dismantling or mitigating the more onerous forms of direct Soviet control and (in contrast to the Stalinist period) permitting room for some domestic autonomy. But little headway was made in translating wish into policy. Indeed, in the military sphere, Khrushchev's initial presumptive effort to use the Warsaw Pact as an organization for Soviet-dominated institution building in Eastern Europe was not pursued vigorously. Until 1961 the Warsaw Pact as such lacked political and especially military substance. The supreme Warsaw Pact organ, the Political Consultative Committee (PCC), met only four times between 1955 and the spring of 1961, even though its statute called for two meetings per year. The fact that the PCC failed to meet at all between January 1956 and May 1958, a very turbulent period, testifies that the Warsaw Pact was not invested with crisis-management prerogatives. There was no visible attempt to promote military integration in a Warsaw Pact framework.

Imperatives of Soviet military strategy, rather than Soviet alliance politics, were responsible for greater Soviet attention to East European armed forces in the early 1960s. Beginning in 1960, Khrushchev sought to modify Soviet military organization and doctrine by emphasizing nuclear missile forces at the expense of the traditional Soviet military strength, ground forces in Europe, and by recasting ground forces doctrine to emphasize blitzkrieg offensives of mobile forces at the expense of Soviet mobilization capabilities. Khrushchev's concept evidently postulated that Soviet ground forces could be further reduced if East European armed forces could be made to assume a more substantial role in Soviet military planning for Europe. Part of the Khrushchevian vision was implemented: The Strategic Rocket Forces were organized in 1960, and the goal of strategic equality with the United States was vigorously pursued. But while overall Soviet military forces for conventional conflicts were reduced after 1960, the combination of heightened East-West tension in Europe associated with the Berlin crisis of 1961 and traditionalist institutional opposition within the Soviet military establishment resulted in a practically undiminished level of Soviet ground forces in Eastern Europe.

Nonetheless, apparently as a direct consequence of the original Khrushchev vision, the USSR began to place more emphasis on an East European military contribution to Soviet power. The Soviet military developed in the early 1960s the concept of *coalition warfare*, which redefined and expanded the role of East European national forces in Soviet military planning. The post-1956 quiescence in Eastern Europe made this possible, and heightened East-West tensions and the emerging Soviet security problem portended by the worsening Sino-Soviet split made it urgent. The Warsaw Pact provided a suitable multilateral framework.

Emphasis on the military as well as the political functions of the Warsaw Pact was first apparent at the March 1961 meeting of the PCC, where the member states evidently agreed on regular consultative meetings of national defense ministers, joint multinational military maneuvers, and Soviet-assisted modernization of East European forces. The first of these multilateral exercises, Brotherhood in Arms, was held in the fall of 1961 in connection with the Berlin crisis of that year. Symptomatic of Soviet priorities in building up the East European military establishments in the 1960s, the exercise involved the USSR, on the one hand, and the GDR, Poland, and Czechoslovakia (the Northern Tier) on the other. Whereas the initial exercises of the early 1960s could be interpreted as largely political demonstrations intended to display Soviet-East European military fraternity, by the mid-1960s they had become serious combat training activities. Moreover, the East European armed forces were now supplied by the USSR with modern T-54 and T-55 tanks, MiG-21 and SU-7 aircraft, and other new weapons. Some East European armed forces were also being supplied with nuclear-capable delivery vehicles (beginning with surface-to-surface missiles, although the warheads themselves presumably remained under sole Soviet control) and were being trained in their use. Standardization of armaments within the Warsaw Pact was enhanced as East European states abandoned some indigenous arms-production capabilities; a nascent East German military aircraft industry was dismantled in 1961, while Poland renounced further development of advanced combat aircraft in 1969.

The doctrine of *coalition warfare* called for the participation of the East European armed forces, in conjunction with Soviet forces, in rapid offensive mobile military operations against NATO. This joint combat training, modernization, specialization, and doctrine suggested that in the mid-1960s the USSR had come to view the East European armed forces as a significant contribution to Soviet military power. Not only did the East European forces extend the Soviet air defense system and constitute a buffer (as they had since Stalin's day), but they were now earmarked for an active mechanized ground-and-air combat role in military operations in Europe.

This Soviet emphasis on the military capabilities of the East European military establishments in the 1960s notwithstanding, there was little indication of military integration through military institutions of the Warsaw Pact itself. The only integrated armed forces branch in the Soviet bloc was air defense, and that was created not under Warsaw Pact auspices but by incorporating East European air defense systems in the command system of the Soviet air defense system, *PVO Strany*. Despite its elaborate formal structure, the Warsaw Pact lacked functional operational military organs. It lacked integrated command and control and logistics systems such as NATO had created. Even the Joint Command's staff lacked continuity. In the 1960s, Soviet military planning for a European war envisaged East European armed forces, like the Groups of Soviet Forces stationed in Eastern Europe, incorporated in Fronts commanded by the Soviet General Staff via theater or field headquarters rather than subordinated to the Warsaw Pact Joint Command. As Malcolm Macintosh suggested, the Warsaw Pact seemed to function as a multinational analogue of a traditional European war office, with administrative duties for mobilization, training, and equipment, but without direct responsibility for the conduct of military operations.[10]

In the mid-1960s the Warsaw Pact military institutions came under attack from some quarters in Eastern Europe for being excessively Soviet dominated. Such criticism emanated primarily from Romania, which under Ceauşescu had launched an autonomous national course that brought it—within clear limits—into conflict with Soviet interests on a broad range of issues. In late 1964, Romania, acting alone, reduced its term of military conscription from 24 to 16 months; this resulted in a cut of 40,000 men in the Romanian armed forces. Romania sought to reduce what it viewed as an excessive contribution to the collective military strength of the Warsaw Pact and to turn to a smaller, more domestically oriented military establishment. Simultaneously, however, Romania sought to increase its national voice in Warsaw Pact military affairs and hence reduce the degree of Soviet control over Romanian defense. In 1966 Ceauşescu obliquely called for the withdrawal of Soviet forces from Eastern Europe. Bucharest proposed that the position of Warsaw Pact commander-in-chief (always occupied by a marshal of the Soviet armed forces) rotate and may have succeeded thereby in forcing a delay in the naming of Ivan Yakubovskii to replace Andrei Grechko as Warsaw Pact commander-in-chief in 1967. Further, Romania argued that East European military expenditures in general were excessive, brought about a dramatic reduction in the size of the Soviet Military Liaison Mission in Bucharest, claimed at least a consultative voice in matters related to nuclear weapons in the Warsaw Pact, expressed concerns about the Non-Proliferation Treaty derived from these sensitivities, refused to permit Warsaw Pact troop maneuvers on Romanian soil, and generally abstained from joint maneuvers involving combat forces in other countries as well.

Unambiguous as it was, the Romanian military deviation alone[11] does not account satisfactorily for the evident lack of progress after 1965 toward the Soviet goal of creating a permanent political coordinating mechanism within the Warsaw Pact, or for the lack of progress in upgrading

---

10. Malcolm Macintosh, *The Evolution of the Warsaw Pact*, Adelphi Papers, no. 58, June 1969, pp. 11–15.

11. Discussed further later in this chapter and in chap. 5.

Warsaw Pact military institutions in a manner strengthening Soviet control. That lack of progress also seems to indicate uncertainty or division in Moscow and neutrality or support for the Romanian position in other East European states. The controversy over the role of the Warsaw Pact evidently strengthened aspirations on the part of elites in other East European countries to achieve a more equal position in Warsaw Pact military affairs as well. Nationalist tendencies appeared in the Polish military. Czechoslovak support for some of the Romanian grievances can be documented as early as 1966, both from the Czech press and from the testimony of former Czechoslovak military officers. In 1968, as the reformist political movement headed by Alexander Dubček gained ground in Czechoslovakia, dissatisfaction with Soviet domination of the Czechoslovak armed forces and Warsaw Pact military institutions was voiced more openly (as will be described below). These military grievances, especially the bluntness with which they were expressed, were doubtless one factor in the Soviet decision to intervene militarily in Czechoslovakia in August 1968.

SOVIET MILITARY POLICY IN EASTERN EUROPE SINCE 1968

The occupation of Czechoslovakia was a watershed in the development of bilateral and multilateral military relationships in the Soviet bloc. The Soviets demonstrated that they were able to mobilize their loyalist allies (Romania abstained) to use military force to impose obedience on a deviant client-state. This was not a Warsaw Pact operation; the Soviet, Polish, Hungarian, East German, and Bulgarian units that constituted the invasion force were mobilized and deployed by various specialized Soviet commands, and the invasion of August 21, 1968, was directed by General Ivan Pavlovskii (commander of Soviet ground forces) from a forward headquarters of the Soviet High Command. Although the invasion was not opposed by the Czechoslovak armed forces and thus revealed nothing about the utility or reliability of the East European armed forces in combat, the USSR did pay a price in terms of the effect of the operation on the East European military establishments. That price included the complete demoralization of the Czechoslovak armed forces and considerable soul-searching in the Polish, East German, and Hungarian militaries as well. One consequence was more relative emphasis by the USSR on Soviet, rather than East European, forces in the area. This implied a recognition that there were limits to the reliance the USSR could place on East European forces to supplement Soviet military power in Europe—limits that could be increased suddenly by developments in Eastern Europe itself.

Five Soviet divisions remained in Czechoslovakia after the 1968 invasion although none had been stationed there previously. A general buildup and modernization of Soviet forces elsewhere in Eastern Europe occurred in the 1970s, with Soviet ground-forces personnel being increased by one-third, to 590,000, in 1977. T-72 tanks, BMP combat vehicles, MiG-25s and other aircraft, new artillery pieces, rocket launchers, mobile air defense weapons, and other new weapons systems were acquired by Soviet operational units.[12] With the deployment of the SS-21 by Soviet forces in the GDR, a new generation of theater nuclear missiles was located in Eastern Europe, underlining the value of the area to the USSR as a forward staging ground.[13]

This increase in Soviet military strength in Europe occurred during a decade when the major emphasis of Soviet conventional-forces development was the military buildup on the Chinese border.[14] Simultaneously, the Soviet leadership emphasized the expansion of Soviet presence in the Third World. In 1979 the Soviet Union invaded Afghanistan, deploying five to eight Soviet divisions in that country. While the stationing (and even the positioning) of Soviet divisions in Czechoslovakia after 1968 could be explained in terms of internal policing, the buildup of Soviet forces elsewhere in Eastern Europe in the 1970s could not. Given the competing claims on Soviet manpower and economic resources, both domestically and in other parts of the world, the Soviet military buildup in Europe in the 1970s is testimony to both the continued centrality of Europe in Soviet geopolitical concerns and the key role the Soviet leadership imputes to military capabilities in advancing Soviet interests.

In the 1970s the Soviet leadership evidently continued to ascribe to East European military forces an important role in the supplementing of Soviet military capabilities for use in a war in Europe. Defense spending increased significantly in Eastern Europe, as the East European armed forces were modernized with Soviet-supplied tanks, advanced MiG-23 and Sukhoi aircraft, SA-4, SA-6, and SA-7 surface-to-air missiles, and other weapons. These efforts were concentrated in Czechoslovakia, East Germany, and Poland to such an extent that this region (the Northern Tier) became almost synonymous with Warsaw Pact. Hungarian and Bulgarian armed forces constitute a much more limited increment to Soviet military capabilities, while the Romanian armed forces serve to counter Soviet capabilities more than to reinforce them. Yet, after the expansion of the 1960s, East European armed forces remained relatively constant in

12. CIA and DIA testimony, *Allocation of Resources in the Soviet Union and China—1978,* Hearings before the Subcommittee on Priorities and Economy in Government, of the Joint Economic Committee, Congress of the United States, 95th Cong., 2d sess., Part 4—Soviet Union (Washington, D.C.: U.S. Government Printing Office, 1978).

13. *Frankfurter Allgemeine Zeitung,* Apr. 21, 1979.

14. The 15 Soviet divisions in the Far East in 1968 had increased to 46 by 1980, while the number of divisions in the interior of the USSR declined (IISS data).

the 1970s at about 1 million regulars. Compared to the late 1960s, the balance sheet of the 1970s is one of less, instead of more, relative Soviet reliance on East European military forces.

The Warsaw Pact Northern Tier: A Soviet Priority

The East German, Polish, and Czechoslovak armed forces continued to be developed during the 1970s for the primary military mission defined for them in the early 1960s: participation in a Soviet-led, rapid, massive, offensive strike into NATO territory in the event of a European war. The doctrine of the Northern Tier armies assumes such a "coalition warfare" role. As Polish doctrine (the most highly developed) stipulates, "Defense must be viewed in coalition dimensions, [Poland having the] obligation to subordinate the national defense system to the fundamental principles and strategic assumptions of the [Soviet] camp as a whole." The doctrine postulates an "external front," on enemy territory, to which the entire operational army is dedicated. Its task, which generally assumes a nuclear battlefield environment, is to destroy enemy forces at home and "thwart their invasion of the territory of the socialist countries."[15] This doctrine assumes that Polish forces will fight abroad in support of a primarily Soviet military offensive, in contrast to Romanian doctrine (discussed below), which envisages reliance primarily on national armed forces fighting within national borders. East German and Czechoslovak doctrines contain postulates similar to Polish doctrine. (In the late 1960s, however, Czechoslovak reformers attempted to counterpose to *coalition warfare* a concept of *national* defense that would have confined operations of the Czechoslovak armed forces to Czechoslovak territory.) Modernization and training have buttressed this offensive orientation of the Northern Tier armed forces.

Given the competing claims on their own military resources, the Soviet leadership may nonetheless have wished for an even larger Northern Tier contribution to Warsaw Pact military capabilities in the 1970s than in fact existed.[16] The obstacles to such a greater East European contribution, however, were both socioeconomic and institutional. East Germany, in spite of a declining population, made the largest proportional contribution to coalition defense. Its total military forces were increased from 190,000 to 230,000 between 1967 and 1978, resulting in the largest number of soldiers per capita in the Warsaw Pact (43 per 1,000). At the same time, its overt military expenditures increased from 3.9 to 5.1% of national income in 1975 (the last year for which data were computed), the

15. Johnson, Dean, and Alexiev, *East European Military Establishments*, pp. 24–27.
16. See n. 4.

highest absolute level in Eastern Europe, and the only case in Eastern Europe of a relatively increasing defense burden in the 1970s. Poland's armed forces increased in the same period from 315,000 to 401,500, but most of this growth was in the home defense forces intended for operations on Polish territory; overt military spending in Poland declined from 4.4 to 3.5% of national income and official Polish sources admitted that Poland's economic problems in the late 1970s precluded any dramatic increase in military expenditures. In Czechoslovakia the post-1968 demoralization of the armed forces (and the Soviets' lack of confidence in them) was reflected in overall military capabilities: Total military forces declined from 265,000 to 195,000, while overt military expenditures fell from 4.5 to 3.7% of national income.[17]

Soviet control over the Northern Tier (and other East European) military establishments is now, by and large, exercised indirectly, via the East European military elites, rather than directly, via Soviet commanders or "advisers," as was the case in the 1950s. Direct controls were totally absent in the 1970s in Poland, the last Soviet-Polish general having retired in the late 1960s. Although two Soviet divisions remained stationed in Poland, the direct Soviet military representation in Warsaw itself was reportedly limited to about a dozen Soviet officers (formally, representatives of the Warsaw Pact High Command).[18] Moreover, there has not been evidence of direct Soviet influence on military promotions since the early 1960s (when at Soviet insistence a number of officers of Jewish origin were removed from their positions). This pattern of indirect Soviet influence applies to Hungarian and Bulgarian forces as well.

In Czechoslovakia, however, the Soviet-led invasion of 1968 and the subsequent disintegration of the Czechoslovak armed forces led to a reestablishment of direct Soviet supervision, which in the early 1970s reportedly included a shadow General Staff at the headquarters of the newly established Central Group of Forces. In the GDR, Soviet influence, while more direct than in Poland, is more institutionalized than in Czechoslovakia. Because of the German past, the GDR's National People's Army is the only element of the Warsaw Pact armed forces formally subordinated to the Warsaw Pact Joint Command in peacetime. There are Soviet representatives in many GDR military bodies, and the senior Soviet general, nominally the Warsaw Pact representative, is reportedly located in the GDR Defense Ministry, along with 80 other Soviet officers.[19] GDR regimental and division commanders evidently have more

17. Johnson, Dean, and Alexiev, *East European Military Establishments*, appendexes B and C.

18. Interview with a former Polish officer, 1978.

19. Johnson, Dean, and Alexiev, *East European Military Establishments*, p. 71.

contact with their Soviet counterparts from the 19 Soviet divisions stationed in the GDR than do other East European commanders.

While there are thus important vestiges of direct Soviet control over East European armed forces, in the region as a whole and vertically within each national military establishment Soviet influence is principally exerted via the East European military elites. These elites are the key to the utility and reliability of the East European armed forces for Soviet purposes—both in Soviet calculations and in our own. These elites have, since the mid-1950s, been composed of nationals of the respective East European countries and are subordinated directly to national military and political leaderships. But they are linked to the Soviet military through a network of professional relationships stronger than analogous links between other East European elites and their respective Soviet counterparts. This system of Soviet-East European military relationships includes East European participation in the institutions of the Warsaw Pact, bilateral military agreements, and a variety of informal ties: training of senior officers at the Voroshilov General Staff Academy in Moscow, joint meetings of senior officers and experts, joint command-staff exercises, and innumerable exchanges of military visits at lower levels. These ties, carefully cultivated in the 1970s, keep East European officers closely attuned to Soviet military doctrine and practice.

Overall, the Soviet leadership probably has more confidence in the East German military establishment than in any other in Eastern Europe. It is a "young" organization, established first in the late 1950s and developed in the 1960s after the Berlin Wall enabled the GDR to halt its manpower drain and begin internal consolidation. It has not experienced the internal conflicts that weakened the Czechoslovak and Polish military establishments but rather has exhibited stability, continuity, and consistent responsiveness to the GDR party leadership. Developed by the USSR after the Stalinist era—and thus without the national resentment against the USSR generated by the blatant disregard of national sensitivities that occurred in Poland and elsewhere in Eastern Europe in the early 1950s—the East German military elite has been subordinated consistently, relatively directly, and apparently without friction to the USSR.[20]

After the mid-1960s, the Czechoslovak military establishment proved to be the most troublesome for Moscow. Nationalist sentiments emerged in the Czechoslovak army in the mid-1960s, as part of the officer corps became a cutting edge of the reform movement that brought Alexander Dubček to power. Indeed, in 1968 a majority of officers appeared to support the Dubček reforms, with a (vocal) minority opposed. The Soviet

20. Ibid., chap. 4.

invasion—which the armed forces, following orders from the Dubček leadership, did not resist—resulted in a demoralization and disintegration of the officer corps on a scale comparable to that experienced by the Hungarian military in the wake of the Soviet military suppression of 1956. Perhaps half the officer corps either was purged or resigned in the wake of the invasion. Since 1975 there has apparently been some progress in rebuilding an officer corps loyal to the leadership of Gustáv Husák and to the USSR, but this recent history and the obvious professional deficiencies of the Czechoslovak military (which in the mid-1970s was accepting officers with only two years of education past high school) must make it highly suspect in Soviet eyes.[21]

The Soviet attitude toward the Polish military establishment was perhaps most ambivalent in the 1970s. As noted earlier, Soviet domination of the Polish armed forces in the early 1950s was particularly heavy-handed, and the nationalist reaction in 1956 was therefore intensified. This reaction confronted both Gomułka and the Soviet leadership with the complicated task of rebuilding the Polish armed forces as an integral part of both the Polish communist system and the Soviet-led military coalition. Tensions in the military elite throughout the 1960s that derived from continuing nationalist sentiments and from internecine party conflict probably lowered Soviet estimates of the success of this rebuilding effort. Consolidation of a homogeneous, stable, professional military elite in the 1970s doubtless reduced some Soviet concerns about the Polish military, but it gave rise to others, which were magnified enormously by the post-1980 Polish crisis. In the 1970s the Polish military, reacting to its "Soviet" past and its use (albeit on a limited scale and reluctantly) for internal repression during the December 1970 unrest, partly revived its traditional ethos as the guardian of national values. Without overtly challenging party supremacy—indeed, in part by default—it achieved a degree of institutional integrity and even autonomy that challenged the traditional Soviet-Leninist forms of party control of the military that the USSR originally imposed throughout Eastern Europe after 1945. Both the national and institutional aspects of this development must have given the USSR pause in the 1970s,[22] well before the emergence of the Polish military as a key, institutionally distinct, political force in 1980–81.

None of the East European military elites, or elements thereof, has served the USSR as a reliable "pro-Soviet instrument" within an East European Communist party leadership since the early 1950s (when Marshal Rokossovskii played something of this role in Poland). Even if a group of officers within a military establishment was inclined to such a

21. Ibid., chap. 5.
22. Ibid., chap. 3.

role (as appeared to be the case in Czechoslovakia in late 1968 and early 1969), this would be a mixed blessing to the Soviet leadership: Such a role would foster military autonomy of party leadership that might serve Soviet purposes in some circumstances but—with subsequent changes in the military elite or if emulated by other groups—could raise the specter of Bonapartism, or undue military influence, and call into question the party's "leading role." It was perhaps this consideration that led Moscow to ignore the blatantly "pro-Soviet" hard-line element of the reconstituted Czechoslovak General Staff in 1969, which appealed to Soviet backing it failed to have or win in calling for a more rapid and radical reestablishment of political orthodoxy in Czechoslovakia after the Soviet invasion. And this concern with party supremacy doubtless colored Soviet appraisals of the imposition by the Polish military command of martial law in Poland in December 1981.

Hungary and Bulgaria: Secondary Concerns

In contrast to the emphasis the USSR has placed on the Northern Tier since the early 1960s, significantly less attention has been paid to the armed forces of Hungary and Bulgaria. This relative neglect of the Southern Tier is understandable, given the priority of Western Europe in Soviet foreign policy and the Central Front in Soviet military planning. As an illustration of this emphasis, only 9 of 50 multilateral Warsaw Pact exercises observed between 1955 and 1976 occurred in the Southern Tier.[23] Throughout this period, Hungary and Bulgaria devoted lower percentages of their national income to defense spending than did the Northern Tier states.[24]

Hungary has figured more prominently than Bulgaria in Soviet military policy. Since the military suppression of the Hungarian Revolution by 8 Soviet divisions in 1956, the USSR has maintained the Southern Group of Forces, numbering 4 divisions, in Hungary. These troops have a clear domestic function, and in addition, they would contribute to a Soviet offensive in Central Europe or could be used for contingencies in Southern Europe, for example, intervention in Yugoslavia.

Complementing these Soviet divisions are the Hungarian armed forces, numbering 93,000 regulars. Although Hungary is not a Northern Tier country, since the mid-1970s its armed forces have joined frequently with Northern Tier forces in Warsaw Pact exercises. Soviet military planners may ascribe to Hungarian forces a combat role in support of Soviet forces in some Central Front conflict contingencies.[25]

23. Johnson, Dean, and Alexiev, *East European Military Establishments*, p. 14.

24. Johnson, *Soviet-East European Military Relations*, pp. 13–14.

25. Graham H. Turbiville, Jr., "Warsaw Pact Forces in Hungary: A Key Element in Pact Contingency Planning," *Rusi*, Dec. 1976, pp. 47–51.

Yet the utility and reliability of Hungarian forces (compared to other East European armies) in support of Soviet military objectives in a European conflict appear to be diminished substantially by lasting scars of the 1956 revolution, when the Hungarian armed forces virtually collapsed. Soviet control of the upper echelons of the military, similar to that exercised through Marshal Rokossovskii in Poland, prevented the Hungarian military from supporting the revolution. But while Moscow could neutralize the army, it could not use it to suppress the revolution; the army disintegrated, and many officers as well as conscripts joined the uprising. Once Soviet forces had suppressed the revolution, the Hungarian army had to be rebuilt almost from nothing. The near decimation of the Hungarian officer corps in 1956–57 was a harbinger of what would occur in Czechoslovakia in 1968.

In the 1960s and 1970s a new Hungarian officer corps took shape— like its counterparts elsewhere in Eastern Europe, increasingly professional.[26] But recovery from the trauma of 1956 was slow; Hungarian forces were evidently the last to receive new generations of Soviet weapons, and today the Hungarian armed forces are still less than half of their 1956 size. Since the early 1960s the Soviet Union has forced the Hungarian military elite to embrace the concept of *coalition warfare*, whereby Hungarian forces would join a massive, rapid offensive onto enemy territory in the event of a European conflict. In terms of national interests, this defense concept is even less viable in Hungary for strategic/geographic reasons than in Czechoslovakia, and there is some evidence that even Hungarian officers view this mission with skepticism. A 1968 Hungarian military publication criticized viewpoints within the Hungarian army that held, in effect:

that the Soviet army should fight the battles instead of us . . . , that we cannot be engaged in main front-line operations, but will only secure the communications and base areas of the Soviet army, or that the Soviets will in any case deal with the problems.[27]

Given the history of the Hungarian army and the morale problems created in 1968 by its participation in the occupation of Czechoslovakia, its use in quelling domestic repression also seems questionable, as does its utility in military suppression of unrest elsewhere in Eastern Europe or as part of a Soviet-led invasion of Yugoslavia.

The Bulgarian armed forces, although larger than those of Hungary, are even less central to the USSR: Bulgaria, with regular armed forces numbering 149,000, has been only a marginal participant in multilateral

26. See Iván Völgyes, "The Political and Professional Perspectives of the Hungarian Armed Forces," *Journal of Political and Military Sociology*, 5 (Fall 1977), 279–94.

27. As quoted in R. Rubin, "The Hungarian People's Army," *Rusi*, Sept. 1976, pp. 59–66, n. 36.

Warsaw Pact exercises. Its geographic isolation has been compounded since the mid-1960s by Romania's deviant position within the Warsaw Pact. This has hindered the large-scale transfer of Soviet troops to Bulgaria for exercises or for a military buildup—a seldom-appreciated cost for Moscow of Romania's independent policies. It also inhibits use of Bulgarian troops in Central Europe, as demonstrated in 1968, when no Bulgarian ground forces (and only token airborne forces) participated in the occupation of Czechoslovakia. This constraint has been only partly overcome by the initiation of large-capacity ferry service between Bulgaria and the USSR in 1978.

By necessity more than by choice, the USSR has favored bilateral military relations with Bulgaria over multilateral relations in the context of the Warsaw Pact. The extent of top-level military exchanges and the introduction of new weapons systems in Bulgaria sooner than in some other Warsaw Pact countries suggest Soviet confidence in the Bulgarian military, as a potential complement to Soviet military power, for any military contingencies in southern Europe involving Turkey, Greece, or Yugoslavia.[28] The anomaly of the absence of stationed Soviet forces in Bulgaria may perhaps be explained by both Bulgaria's secondary geographic position and its political and military reliability. Given Bulgarian-Yugoslav national animosities, the Soviet leadership may view the Bulgarian army as the one East European army that might contribute significantly to Soviet military intervention in Yugoslavia. Between 1971 and 1982, in line with its policy of wooing rather than threatening Yugoslavia, the USSR refrained from holding joint Bulgarian-Soviet maneuvers that would be intended—or interpreted in the West as intended—to exert pressure on Yugoslavia.[29] But large-scale joint maneuvers, involving troops from all Warsaw Pact countries except Romania, did take place in Bulgaria in September 1982, perhaps a harbinger of greater Soviet attention to the Southern Tier.[30]

The Romanian Military Deviation

While Hungary and Bulgaria have been of secondary military importance for the USSR in the past decade, Romania has continued to be an irritant in military as well as political terms, detracting from the concept of Warsaw Pact unity espoused by the USSR, setting a "bad example" for other

28. In 1978, Bulgarian forces reportedly received MiG-27s (*Aviation Week and Space Technology*, 108 [Apr. 3, 1978]).

29. Such maneuvers were falsely reported (and interpreted as pressure on Romania and Yugoslavia) in early 1979. See *Neue Zürcher Zeitung*, Feb. 28, 1979.

30. Ibid., Oct. 1, 1982. Yugoslav commentators voiced concern that the maneuvers might be directed against Yugoslavia (e.g., Bajalski dispatch, *Politika*, Sept. 13, 1982).

East European military establishments, and, for some purposes, diminishing overall Soviet military capabilities in Europe.

Romania's "deviation" in the military sphere was initiated shortly after conflict between Romania and the USSR on developmental policy within CMEA came to a head in the early 1960s and Romania began to define for itself an autonomous position within the Soviet orbit. Early manifestations of the Romanian military deviation have been traced in the preceding pages. Romania's autonomous stance on military affairs was probably the catalyst for Soviet acceptance in the late 1960s of the formal Warsaw Pact bodies (such as the Joint Staff of the Warsaw Pact Joint Command) that provided at least the semblance of greater East European representation and participation. Romanian policy was also a source of encouragement for nationally inclined elements in the military establishments of other East European countries—demonstrably so in the case of Czechoslovakia, and perhaps in Poland and even Hungary as well. Romania's independent course in military affairs was clearly demonstrated in 1968, when it abstained from participating in the Soviet-led military occupation of Czechoslovakia. Thereafter, Romania further widened, rather than limited, its sphere of autonomy. This was one sign, among many others, that the Soviet-imposed "normalization" in Czechoslovakia after 1968 was not accompanied by a successful, wide-ranging reimposition of political orthodoxy throughout the Soviet bloc.

While the other East European military establishments copied or refined the Soviet coalition warfare doctrine in the 1970s and adapted their forces and weaponry to this end, the Romanian military developed a nationally based concept which maintained that defense was solely the prerogative of the nation-state and was valid only within national territory. The doctrine thus explicitly rejected the concept of *coalition warfare* and a strategy of rapid massive offensives into enemy territory. According to Romanian doctrine, any aggression against Romania will be turned into a "people's war"—a concept similar to, and clearly in part inspired by, the Yugoslav doctrine of "total national defense." This concept is unprecedented in the Warsaw Pact, although Czechoslovak military theoreticians began to espouse such notions in the mid-1960s. Emulating the Yugoslavs to some degree in practice as well as in theory, Romania reorganized its defense system in the 1970s to stress a smaller but well-trained regular army and compulsory civilian involvement in defense, including a network of Patriotic Guard and other paramilitary organizations.

Romania has also decreased its dependence on the USSR for armaments. It has entered into agreements with a number of non-Warsaw Pact countries to coproduce weapons—some of them rather sophisticated—including jet fighters (Yugoslavia), helicopters (France), jet engines

(Great Britain), and missile boats (China). It has also developed an extensive program of exchanging military visits with a variety of non-Warsaw Pact countries, including NATO countries.[31]

At the same time, Romania has remained active in Warsaw Pact affairs on issues and occasions of its own choosing. It has sought to have the best of both worlds: to minimize its obligations yet maximize its influence on Soviet blocwide military affairs. Romania continues to abstain from Warsaw Pact maneuvers and has allowed no such maneuvers (except for limited staff exercises) on its own territory since 1962. Furthermore, it has not agreed to Soviet troops transiting Romania (as noted, an important constraint on Moscow's ability to deploy Soviet forces in Bulgaria, or Bulgarian forces in Central Europe). Its presence in pact councils has prevented the USSR from achieving the unanimity it has sought on military-related issues. This was demonstrated best in November 1978, when Romania evidently resisted (and publicized) Soviet demands that the East European states increase their defense expenditures. On that occasion, just as earlier, its actions reportedly encouraged other East European representatives to speak out in a similar vein.

Party leader Nicolae Ceauşescu led Romania to embark on an autonomous course in matters of defense. But refinement and implementation of that course have been the responsibility of the Romanian military elite. In Romania, even more than was the case in Czechoslovakia in the mid-1960s, an outwardly uniformly loyal pro-Soviet officer corps was harnessed to the cause of a national military deviation without internal conflicts.[32] Today, Moscow lacks any substantial influence over the Romanian military elite. Soviet forces have been absent from Romania since 1958, while the Soviet military representation in Bucharest (formally, the Warsaw Pact representation) was reduced to a minimum at Romanian insistence in the mid-1960s. Romanian officers have evidently ceased attending Soviet military schools, while formal military exchanges with the USSR are now outnumbered by those with NATO countries. The top military leadership has remained loyal to Ceauşescu in his defiance of Moscow; there has been no evidence in Romania of pro-Soviet generals (like those in Czechoslovakia in 1969) who could have served as a potential counterelite for Soviet purposes.

The Romanian military deviation has constituted an important challenge to Soviet concepts of how the Warsaw Pact should organize military affairs throughout Eastern Europe. It has contradicted Soviet claims to unanimity within the pact on numerous occasions, detracted from Soviet

31. See Alexiev, *Romania and the Warsaw Pact*, pp. 18–21.
32. See Alex Alexiev, *Party-Military Relations in Romania* (Santa Monica: The Rand Corporation, P-6059, Dec. 1977).

military capabilities in southern Europe, contributed to the isolation of Bulgaria, created a basis for Romanian military resistance in the event of Soviet military invasion, and shown both the USSR and the West how quickly an apparently reliable military elite can become "unreliable" (from the Soviet perspective) in response to changes in national policies.

Soviet toleration of the Romanian military deviation for more than fifteen years is part and parcel of Soviet toleration of Romania's autonomous course generally. That toleration is usually assumed to be based on Romanian respect for certain limits—especially domestic political and economic orthodoxy and continued formal membership in the Warsaw Pact—and on a lesser Soviet stake in Romania, given its location, than in the Eastern Central European countries. It should also be remarked that the Romanian deviation developed gradually, and so presented the Soviets with no clear-cut, dramatic challenge that could catalyze a Soviet decision to intervene. In military terms, Romania is far less significant to the USSR than are the Northern Tier countries. And yet when all the "logic of the situation" arguments are marshaled, it must be said that the Soviet leadership has tolerated in Romania a remarkable degree of departure from Soviet preferences for the organization of military affairs in Eastern Europe.

RELIANCE ON THE UNRELIABLE: KEY ISSUES FOR THE 1980s

In the 1980s the USSR will evidently continue to rely in its planning for European military contingencies on a significant contribution from East European military forces that, on many counts, appears to be unreliable. The East European armed forces are manned by conscripts who are a rough sample of their societies. However good their military training and discipline, East European soldiers lack commitment to Communist party values and Soviet interests. Anti-Soviet attitudes are perhaps strongest among Czechoslovak and Polish conscripts but they evidently exist among other East European conscripts as well. In the wake of Pope John Paul's triumphant return to his native Poland in 1979, Stalin's query, "How many divisions has the Pope?" assumed a new relevance. Is this apparent paradox of Soviet reliance on unreliable East Europeans the consequence of Soviet illusions? Or does it signify a Western failure to appreciate the dynamics of the Soviet-East European military relationship?

Soviet military planning takes into account the partial coincidence of the state and national interests of the East European communist states with those of the USSR. GDR and Soviet interests coincide most closely, given the geographic situation of the GDR and its continued political insecurity as the smaller and weaker part of a divided nation. Poland's national rationale for fidelity to the USSR, which was strong in the early postwar period, declined with the fading of German irredentism. Yet Poland's geopolitical position perforce would involve it in any European war. Poland's numerous regional disarmament proposals, beginning with the Rapacki Plan, served Soviet policy interests but originated from this Polish security imperative. Czechoslovakia's geopolitical incentives to minimize involvement in a Warsaw Pact-related conflict, so prominent in the late 1960s, are presently suppressed, and Bulgaria's historic conflict with Yugoslavia reinforces its ties with Moscow. Throughout the region, the Communist party-dominated political systems rest fundamentally on Soviet support. For all the party leaderships in Eastern Europe (with the exception of the Romanian), adherence to the Warsaw Pact and fulfill-ment of the ensuing military tasks stipulated by Moscow is a fundamental alliance obligation. The same is true of loyal adherence to Soviet view-points in East-West negotiations such as the Mutual and Balanced Force Reductions talks. Indeed, it was understood in Poland and Hungary after 1956 and in Poland again in 1980 (but was not understood in Czechoslo-vakia in 1968) that loyalist fulfillment of alliance military obligations is a precondition for achieving any degree of internal autonomy.

On the other hand, the East European countries have not shared Soviet global security concerns and have sought with considerable success to limit their involvement in Soviet military activities outside Europe. They have successfully resisted the Soviet desire to expand the Warsaw Pact to include extra-European members and to reply to military con-tingencies outside Europe. They have not responded to the Soviet wish to station at least token East European contingents on the Sino-Soviet border.[33] While all the East European countries have been involved in some fashion in Soviet policy toward the Third World, their contribution to Soviet military activities in the developing countries has been (in terms of total Soviet-sponsored efforts) limited, consisting mainly of Czechoslo-vak arms sales (a traditional Czechoslovak export) and East German se-curity advisers. In Europe the more distant an East European country is from the Central Front, the more nationally based defense concepts have come to the fore, most dramatically in Romania but also at times in Czecho-slovakia and Hungary.

Soviet military planning is also premised on the character of the East European military elites and officer corps, generally well-trained profes-sionals who—both because of the directives of their national political leaderships and through their links to the Soviet military—are imbued with and evidently committed to Soviet-defined concepts of warfare. They command well-trained and well-disciplined armies.

Given these premises, Soviet military strategy is designed to optimize

33. See Robin Remington, *The Warsaw Pact* (Cambridge, Mass.: MIT Press, 1971), pp. 116, 142–45.

the possibilities for utilizing East European armed forces to serve Soviet military purposes in a Warsaw Pact-NATO conflict. As described above, the Soviets first placed greater emphasis on non-Soviet Warsaw Pact forces in the early 1960s, as Soviet military thought and strategy were transformed. The resultant emphasis on rapid advance of quantitatively superior Warsaw Pact forces onto enemy territory at the outset of a European war, along with a concept of *coalition warfare* that provided for East European forces to fight in conjunction with Soviet forces rather than autonomously, served to increase the utility of the East European forces. Indeed, Soviet lightning-war offensive strategy may constitute the strongest Soviet lever for ensuring substantial and reliable East European military participation in support of Soviet objectives in a European war. In such circumstances it would be to Soviet advantage to achieve quick multinational involvement of forces and early battlefield success.

It would also be in the Soviet interest to minimize consultation with the East European leaderships. In such a contingency, one could hardly expect a repetition of Khrushchev's diligent personal consultation with the East European leaderships in their own capitals prior to Soviet suppression of the Hungarian Revolution. Still less likely is multilateral consultation, such as in the Čierná and Bratislava meetings prior to the occupation of Czechoslovakia. Given Warsaw Pact offensive strategy and a high state of readiness, there may even be some circumstances when operational considerations would require East European military commands to undertake action on Moscow's directive, before national political decisions were made. But more fundamentally, the Soviet leadership can calculate, probably realistically, that the motivations and opportunities for political and military leaders in Eastern Europe to "opt out" of a Soviet war would be quite limited. For whatever the likely horrors of a NATO-Warsaw Pact conflict for any East European country, East European leaders may conclude (not without cause) that these would only be magnified by any attempt to opt out or participate less than wholeheartedly in a Soviet campaign. In such an event the Soviets can also calculate, again possibly realistically, that nothing would succeed like success. East European military units advancing in Western Europe would probably fight—if they continued to advance, and because Soviet forces would be behind and around them.

It is in these terms that we should probably view the substantial reliance that Soviet political and military leaders evidently place on East European armed forces in planning for European military contingencies. This strategic calculus is likely to hold in the 1980s. Because the Soviet leadership will undoubtedly find itself faced with more competing claims for scarcer military resources, both at home and in other parts of the world, it will be motivated to rely even more on East European military forces as a supplement to Soviet military capabilities. Yet in fact the USSR is unlikely to command a greater relative East European contribution to Warsaw Pact military capabilities in the 1980s, and it would not be comfortable with such an enhanced East European role. For the considerations that led the USSR to increase its own relative share of European-oriented Warsaw Pact military capabilities after 1968 are likely to be compounded in the 1980s.

Operational considerations alone argue against an enhanced East European role. The Soviet concept of *coalition warfare* assumes that Soviet military forces must play the primary role in all military operations, with no primary military task entrusted to any East European army on its own. East European units cannot replace Soviet military units. To diminish significantly the relative Soviet contribution to Warsaw Pact capabilities—even assuming a greater East European contribution could be forthcoming—would mean a more important operational role for East European forces, a situation that Soviet generals would find intolerable.

Rising professional military consciousness in Eastern Europe may reinforce such Soviet concerns. Military professionalism is a two-edged sword for the USSR. It has increased the combat effectiveness of the East European armies but it has spawned a new set of grievances against the USSR. As the East European military establishments became more modern and professional, their military elites expected the USSR to grant them the status of junior partners in Warsaw Pact affairs. But the evidence is that the Soviet Union has yet to do this: It continues to dominate the operations of Warsaw Pact military institutions; new weapons systems are often made available to the East European armed forces only after they have been supplied to Soviet client-states in the Third World; and Soviet officers openly display a patronizing attitude toward their East European counterparts. Moscow must be particularly concerned by the fact that professional grievances of the East European countries are likely to be linked to national feelings, as has been the case in Czechoslovakia, Romania, and—at least incipiently—Poland. Barring a fundamental change in Soviet behavior, the issue of rising professional military expectations in Eastern Europe is likely to be increasingly troublesome for the USSR in the 1980s.

Nor can the Soviet leadership fail to be concerned with the domestic political role of some East European military establishments. It has seen first in Yugoslavia and then in Czechoslovakia how the Soviet concept of the proper *leading role of the party* in the armed forces was undermined.[34] By the turn of the 1980s the military establishment in Poland had become master of its own house to a degree inconsistent with Soviet-defined,

34. For the Yugoslav experience, see A. Ross Johnson, "The Role of the Military in Yugoslavia," in Andrzej Korbonski and Roman Kolkowicz, eds., *Soldiers, Politicians, and Bureaucrats* (London: Allen & Unwin, 1981).

Leninist notions of the proper party-army nexus. This raised the possibility of a Bonapartist challenge to party rule from the military—which in fact occurred in Poland in December 1981, as the military in effect superseded the party apparatus as the primary instrument of rule.

Domestic socioeconomic resource constraints on increased defense spending in Eastern Europe are likely to be more severe than those in the USSR itself in the 1980s. Only the GDR increased its defense burden in the 1970s. Socioeconomic constraints were especially pronounced in Poland in the late 1970s and were then multiplied manyfold after 1980. One consequence of the course of developments in Poland is that both Soviet and East European leaderships will be forced to pay closer attention to potential disruptive social consequences of economic policies, and in turn will have to reconsider the extent to which the military burden is compatible with social stability and economic viability in individual East European countries. In Poland itself, and perhaps elsewhere in Eastern Europe, economic problems might become severe enough to cause Soviet leaders to consider a neo-New Course in economic policy necessitating, as in 1954–55, a partial reduction in the military burden. It is difficult to imagine that even under optimistic assumptions the USSR can count on any significant increase.

Moreover, East European political stability is a prerequisite for Soviet reliance on East European military forces in its military planning. It was in a period of East European political quiescence in the early 1960s that Khrushchev and Marshal Grechko first promoted an enhanced military role for East European forces within the Warsaw Pact. Today no Soviet leader anticipating the course of the 1980s can count on such stability.

As events in Poland unfolded after 1980, Soviet concerns about the consequences for the role of the Polish armed forces in the Warsaw Pact must have mounted. After the imposition of martial law in December 1981 the involvement of the Polish military in running the country surely increased those concerns. For the Polish army—the key East European army in Soviet coalition warfare doctrine—turned inward: its senior officer corps attempted to rule Poland and salvage its economy; the loyalty of its conscript regulars (many former Solidarity members) was more suspect; the military economy and mobilization base declined rapidly; and regular military units were redeployed to back up the internal security forces that actively enforced martial law. In these circumstances, it was doubtful that the Polish army could carry out its assigned missions within the Warsaw Pact and that the Soviet General Staff would rely on the Polish army in any European conflict.[35]

---

35. See A. Ross Johnson, *Poland in Crisis* (Santa Monica: The Rand Corporation, N-1891-AF, July 1982), p. 55.

Domestic and Intrabloc Considerations

The East European military establishments—originally alien, Soviet-dominated entities—were integrated into their respective national political systems after 1956. This meant that for all practical purposes they could no longer be employed by the Soviet leadership for domestic political purposes in Eastern Europe, either to serve as a pro-Soviet faction within a party elite or as a coercive military force in the direct pursuit of Soviet aims. In 1956 Khrushchev could command Marshal Rokossovskii to move his divisions toward Warsaw in an attempt to intimidate the new Gomułka leadership. Thereafter, such Soviet use of East European military forces became unlikely. The East European armed forces—the regular units, as opposed to elite internal security forces generally under the command of the Interior Ministry—are also by and large unsuited for domestic repression. This has evidently been well understood in Eastern Europe and the USSR alike. Imposition of martial law in Poland notwithstanding, there has in fact only been one instance in which regulars were used successfully in such a mode: in Poland in 1970 to suppress worker unrest, and that on a very limited scale and with a demoralizing impact on the Polish officer corps.

Policies are often choices among unsatisfactory alternatives, and Soviet military policy toward Eastern Europe is no exception. In fostering the development of East European armed forces since the early 1960s, as a supplement to Soviet military capabilities that could be used in coalition warfare against NATO, the USSR accepted their renationalization. While it is true that the East European military elites have closer ties with the Soviet military than do other elites with their respective Soviet counterparts, these ties have their limits. East European military establishments today are components of their respective domestic political systems: they are not alien, Soviet-imposed bodies. As a consequence the Soviet Union is less able than in the 1950s to use the East European armies for surrogate domestic influence or repression. The Brezhnev leadership could not use the Czechoslovak army as a coercive political presence in 1968. Soviet and not Eastern European military forces are likely to be required in the future for political coercion or repression in Eastern Europe—the imposition of martial law in Poland in December 1981 notwithstanding.

In August 1980 and for a year thereafter, the Polish military leadership under General Wojciech Jaruzelski sought to counter by political means the challenge to the communist system posed by Solidarity. It abjured the prompt resort to force urged on it by party hard-liners, evidently because it anticipated that a crackdown would involve such a degree of internal resistance as to require Soviet troops, not just Polish troops, to suppress it. But in December 1981, as internal tension and Soviet pressure mounted, the Polish army in effect assumed supreme political leadership in Poland and imposed martial law, suppressing Solidarity yet failing to revive the party—a stalemate that continued even after the ending of martial law in July 1983.

To enforce martial law, the military high command did not rely principally on the regular armed forces. Instead it turned to elite internal security units—in particular militarized police units (ZOMO)—subordinated to the Interior Ministry that had been prepared for this purpose. These units, reinforced by military units, were able to suppress Solidarity without direct Soviet assistance by the sudden and effective imposition of martial law (with a general absence of active resistance). Yet until the Jaruzelski leadership showed itself capable of "normalizing" Poland, as Czechoslovak party leader Husák was able to reconsolidate party rule in Czechoslovakia after 1968, the repression imposed in Poland by the military leadership in 1981 was hardly a model. Moreover, active violent popular protest remained a very real possibility. Limited resistance could probably not be put down as easily a second time by internal security forces alone. And following martial law just as prior to it, it was unlikely that domestic violence that the security organs were unable to handle could be put down by the Polish army on its own.[36]

The Soviets appear to have little grounds for optimism that the East European armies could be utilized effectively for repression elsewhere in the region. In any intra-Soviet bloc policing operation, the Soviet leadership would have to weigh the benefits of utilizing other East European forces to provide an "internationalist" cover against the risks that those forces might not only prove useless in military terms but could, in some circumstances, end up siding with the invaded country. Should the USSR consider using military force in Yugoslavia, where protracted resistance is a near certainty, it would have cause to be even more concerned about the utility and reliability of East European contingents. These conclusions are not contradicted by the participation of Polish, East German, Hungarian, and Bulgarian contingents in the Soviet-led invasion of Czechoslovakia in 1968. That invasion was predicated on the near-certain knowledge that there would be no organized Czechoslovak resistance. Even so, there is evidence that the operation gave rise to severe morale problems in the Polish, Hungarian, and even the East German armed forces; the GDR contingent, moreover, was small and kept well away from population centers.

The post-1980 Polish crisis raised anew the prospect of yet another

36. See ibid. and Johnson, Dean, and Alexiev, *East European Military Establishments*, pp. xi–xiii.

role for East European military forces: that of defending their country against Soviet military invasion. This role, unthinkable in normal times, has become thinkable in past crises, and corresponding military preparations have been made. Some Czechoslovak politicians and officers proposed (but did not implement) such resistance in 1968. This possibility was very real in Poland in 1956, when internal security forces loyal to Gomułka were prepared to forcibly resist Rokossovskii's troops marching on Warsaw, and major navy and air force units were prepared to fight Soviet forces. As Khrushchev recounted,

Marshal Konev and I held consultations with [Polish Defense Minister] Rokossovsky, who was more obedient to us [than the Polish political leadership]. . . . He told us that . . . if it were necessary to arrest the growth of these counterrevolutionary elements by force of arms, he was at our disposal. . . . That was all very well and good, but as we began to . . . calculate which Polish regiments we could count on to obey Rokossovsky, the situation began to look somewhat bleak.[37]

This history arguably affected the perceptions of the Soviet leadership, as it affected all elements in Poland, in 1980–1981 and was a major reason for Moscow's decision not to invade Poland in the initial stages of the crisis. Throughout Eastern Europe, Soviet influence over and access to military institutions are probably sufficient to enable the USSR to neutralize any unified military resistance commanded by the General Staff.[38] Yet in the case of Poland after 1980, many observers inside Poland and abroad felt that any Soviet military occupation would be met with lower level military resistance—even after the imposition of martial law.

CONCLUSIONS

In the 1980s, Europe is certain to remain a central preoccupation of Soviet foreign and military policy. Central Europe will remain the key area of interest to the USSR, even though southern Europe may become increasingly important, in view of Soviet involvement in the Middle East and Persian Gulf. Developments in Turkey, Yugoslavia, and perhaps other southern European countries may also present Moscow with opportunities or challenges.

The USSR may wish it could rely more in the 1980s on East European military forces to maintain or raise the present level of Soviet-controlled military power in Europe while minimizing the commitment of additional

37. *Khrushchev Remembers: The Last Testament*, Strobe Talbott, ed. (Boston: Little, Brown, 1974), p. 203.

38. This and other internal control functions of the Warsaw Pact are stressed (but the primary external war-fighting missions neglected) in Christopher D. Jones, *Soviet Influence in Eastern Europe: Political Autonomy and the Warsaw Pact* (New York: Praeger Special Studies, 1981).

Soviet military resources to this region. Soviet military forces are being subjected to increased and competing demands in the Far East, Central Asia, and other areas; at the same time, domestic Soviet economic trade-offs between military and civilian production are being posed more sharply. Demographic changes in the USSR involving the relative increase of the non-Slavic populations at the expense of the Slavs portends a much greater proportion of Asiatics in the Soviet armed forces that is yet another constraint.

Yet the USSR will have to rely less, rather than more, on East European military forces. No significant increase in the East European military contribution to Soviet military power is to be expected in the 1980s. Moreover, it will be difficult for the USSR to maintain the current level of East European military preparations. Operational, institutional, and socioeconomic factors that make a greater or even undiminished East European military contribution unlikely have been discussed above. The post-1980 Polish crisis has dramatized, for the Soviet leadership just as for the rest of the world, the vulnerabilities inherent in the present level of Soviet reliance on East European military forces. Development of East European armies for coalition warfare, emphasized by Khrushchev at the turn of the 1960s as a "quick fix," has reached the point of diminishing returns. In its military policy toward Eastern Europe in the 1980s, as in so many other policy areas, the Soviet leadership will have to make hard choices: It must either dedicate relatively more of its own increasingly scarce military resources to Europe or permit a relative decline in Soviet-controlled military power in the region.

10

Soviet Policy in Western Europe: The East European Factor

PIERRE HASSNER

Can the Soviet Union have its cake in Europe and eat it too? Can it preserve its control over Eastern Europe and at the same time preserve its ability to influence Western Europe? That is the main question of this chapter. Answering it involves a study in the management of contradictions and in the art of escaping hard choices and of using one's weaknesses to obtain further concessions from adversaries. The Soviet Union, I shall argue, has practiced this art altogether successfully in its triangular relationship with Eastern and Western Europe, albeit with costs and setbacks. As the interdependence of Eastern and Western Europe has grown along with their dependence on the rest of the world, both the Soviet Union's difficulties (particularly in Eastern Europe) and its opportunities (particularly in Western Europe) in playing this game have increased.

My principal intention is to go beyond a simple categorization of Soviet policy as defensive or offensive, aimed at keeping Eastern Europe or dominating Western Europe. My interest is in the trade-offs and in the influences on Soviet relations with the two halves of Europe. The guiding thread will be the duality of Soviet policy, which uses both indirect encouragement and direct control to affect various situations and processes. This creates a basic dilemma between influence and control, both in target areas (Eastern Europe and Western Europe, Germany, and the United States) and in policy instruments (multilateral institutions, interstate diplomacy, Communist parties, and social movements). Through all this, however, the question remains whether the changes in setting produce changes in the actors themselves, including the Soviet Union, and in their relations with one another.

For instance, at times it has seemed easier for the Soviet Union to influence Western Europe than to control Eastern Europe. Compare, for example, the early successes of Moscow's campaign against the deployment of NATO's medium-range missiles in Western Europe with the fruitlessness of its campaign against the Polish renewal from the summer of 1980 to the winter of 1981. In the one case, the sophisticated exploitation of the fear of war and of differences within the Atlantic alliance by means of peace initiatives and veiled threats seemed to find a powerful echo among ever wider segments of the West European public. In the other, all Moscow's huffing and puffing, all its ideological name-calling and military maneuvering seemed powerless to change a situation that the Soviets were apparently unable even to grasp, let alone to control.

Were the two phenomena linked? Was an agonizing reappraisal of Soviet priorities involved? Was Moscow tolerating a highly unwelcome situation in Poland in order not to jeopardize favorable trends in Western Europe, especially in Germany? Or, to use Richard Löwenthal's formulation at the time of the invasion of Prague,[1] did it still prefer a sparrow (whether Polish or Czechoslovak) in the East European cage to two birds (whether French or West German) in the bush of détente? Or, as a result of the Soviet-encouraged repression in Poland in December 1981, has the Soviet Union once again succeeded in having its cake and eating it? Has it retained control of a key East European country and in the process added to the disunity of the West and confirmed the unconditional attachment of many Europeans, particularly the Germans, to détente?

Obviously, as Zhou Enlai is supposed to have said when asked about the impact of the French Revolution, it is too early to tell. Caution is particularly called for in the present case because the short-run and long-range effects of the December 13, 1981, coup may well go in opposite directions. In other words, the Soviet Union has certainly won a victory in the short run, but it may well yet turn out to be a Pyrrhic one in the long run.

Before December 13, the Soviet Union seemed caught in the dilemma of tolerating an evolution that endangered its rule, or at least the legitimacy of its rule, in Eastern Europe, or of resorting to a military intervention that would threaten its influence upon Western Europe, or at least its latest and most promising campaign—the encouragement of the antinuclear movement.

It has evaded this dilemma more elegantly than almost anybody expected. Although in East Berlin (1953) and Hungary (1956) Soviet tanks had to open fire and although in Czechoslovakia (1968) they still had to be present, in Poland they did not have to intervene directly. This was crucial for the first reaction of the Polish church and population and even more, perhaps, for that of the West. The semifiction of a national military coup played the same role in providing legitimation for the continuation of European détente as distance had done in the case of Afghanistan. In fact, with few exceptions, the Western actors went only one step further in their reaction to Poland than to Afghanistan: the gap between the stronger American and the weaker German reactions, as between the stronger

1. Cf. Richard Löwenthal, "A Sparrow in the Cage," *Problems of Communism,* 17 (Nov.–Dec. 1968), 2–28.

reaction of the Italian Communist Party (PCI) and the weaker reaction of the French Communist Party (PCF), was the same as in the Afghan case. Only the attitude of the French government was considerably different. Not only were the costs to the Soviets relatively limited (a further assertion of PCI independence and a certain division within the European peace movement) and the major risks (the canceling of the pipeline and of the Intermediate-Range Nuclear Force [INF] negotiations and Strategic Arms Reduction Talks [START]) avoided, but also the U.S.-European rift arising over the sanctions issue provided an additional bonus.

The other side of the coin, however, is no less striking. A year after the coup, a comparison of the Polish situation with the East German in 1954, the Hungarian in 1957, and the Czechoslovak in 1969 shows it to be at least as worrisome to the Soviets as the earlier ones were reassuring. There are no signs of a successful normalization, whether political or economic. The Polish people did not put up the immediate and active resistance, whether armed or not, that their predecessors did, but neither had they fallen into line a year later. With the survival of autonomous centers of power on the Polish side, and with new inhibitions on the use of military force (because of the international context) and of economic means (because of the general crisis of the system) on the Soviet side, the stalemate seems to continue. Although no one knows whether it will lead to explosions or to sullen resignation, two things seem clear: First, two peoples, the Afghans and the Poles, continue to resist and to constitute a drain on the Soviet Union—a source of worry for the Soviet leaders and of unease for Western proponents of détente. Second, the entire empire is in crisis, its own resources are more and more taxed, and, with the admittedly major exceptions of the European pipeline and the American grain sales, it cannot count on the West to bail it out.

The Soviet Union can afford neither real Stalinism and autarky nor real reform and détente. And it cannot hope that muddling through from case to case offers much chance of either containing the Polish virus or shaking off the progressive paralysis of the system. No unified pattern of either reform or repression within the empire, or of accommodation or confrontation with the West, seems to be emerging. But if the Polish and Afghan cases are any guide, the difficulties seem more likely to come from Eastern societies than from Western governments.

The only safe assertions from which to start are that Europe, both West and East, is a more immediate and essential priority for the Soviet Union than before; that a crucial link between Soviet policies toward the two halves of Europe exists; but that the nature of this link is uncertain and the Soviet ability to manipulate it is running into additional obstacles. During the cold war, Eastern and Western Europe were separated by the iron curtain, and Soviet policy seemed to give an absolute priority to the former while having little means of affecting the latter. With détente and the idea of the European security process, Moscow thought that the same pan-European policies could extend its influence in Western Europe and, ipso facto, consolidate its authority in Eastern Europe. Today, it just does not know, and nobody else does either.

The uncertainty is compounded by the fact that Western Europe seems both more central and more derivative as a target of Soviet policy. There was a time when Soviet policy was directed predominantly at Europe, as the big stake in the conflict with the United States, while Moscow had little means of influencing the rest of the world. Later, Europe appeared as the continent of stability or stalemate while the Third World was the big target of opportunity in the global contest. Today, after the invasion of Afghanistan and the election of Ronald Reagan, we may be in a phase where expansion in the Third World is temporarily too costly or dangerous, while Western Europe appears more vulnerable to Soviet blackmail and more detachable from an adventurous or maladroit American policy. But, in turn, these new West European opportunities may be jeopardized by the revived dilemma imposed by the renewed dangers lurking in Eastern Europe.

While it may be more promising, for the time being, to direct efforts at Western Europe than at the United States or Eastern Europe, policy-makers may see the former, more than ever before, primarily in light of the latter two. The crisis in relations with the United States pushes the Soviet Union toward increased détente with Western Europe in order to divide the Atlantic alliance or to enlist West European help in modifying American policy. But the crisis in relations with Eastern Europe, particularly Poland, pushes the Soviet Union toward a harder policy in Western Europe, or at least the threat of such, in order to counter the latter's influence in Eastern Europe.

THE ACTORS AND THE SETTING

Let us begin with the question of the extent to which Western and Eastern Europe are coherent and identifiable targets of Soviet concerns and policies.[2] In one sense, they are increasingly so. Soviet efforts toward promoting the integration of CMEA, the Warsaw Pact, and the socialist community intensified after the Czechoslovak events and, again, during the Polish crisis. Similarly the Soviet Union has since the 1960s recognized an autonomous and possibly even positive West European role. But after the Afghanistan crisis, this recognition took on the quality of a conscious strategy, as the Soviets were seeking to exploit France's and Germany's

2. See Jean Laloy, "Western Europe in the Soviet Perspective," *Adelphi Papers*, no. 85 (London: International Institute for Strategic Studies, 1972), p. 22.

more favorable attitude toward détente against a more critical American one. On the other hand, Soviet policy must also take into account the increasing differentiation occurring within both Western and Eastern Europe themselves, with Germany in a special position in the West, and Poland in a special position in the East.

As important, and possibly newer, are the consequences of the broadening horizon tending to blur the qualitative distinction between Eastern Europe as part of the Soviet bloc and Western Europe as part of the Atlantic one. This broadening of the horizon takes a double form: that of the globalization of East-West relations and that of growing pan-European interdependence. As Soviet power becomes global so does the "world socialist system" and even the "socialist community." The globalization of the Council for Mutual Economic Assistance (CMEA), through the inclusion of Mongolia, Cuba, Vietnam, and an increasing number of associates, is a long-standing phenomenon that makes this world economic organization of communist states more the counterpart of OECD than of the European Economic Community (EEC). More recent and highly significant are the attempts at globalizing the Warsaw Pact, giving it a potential anti-Chinese role, a step resisted not only by Romania but, less overtly, by other East European nations as well. They have not, however, been able or willing to resist involvement in the Third World—especially in Africa and the Middle East—with the East Germans playing a proxy role as important as that of the Cubans.

On the pan-European side, the progress of East-West trade, of intra-German travel and contacts, of transnational communication and of intergovernmental negotiations has created a genuine, if imperfect and uneven, network of human and economic ties. The Soviet peace policy, with its themes of a European system of security and cooperation and of an irreversible European political—and military—détente, can be seen as aiming at consolidating, formalizing, and exploiting this de facto network in order to create an "organic" relationship with Western Europe that would increasingly separate it from the United States.[3]

This goal is very far from being reached: From almost every point of view, Western Europe has more ties of interdependence and interpenetration with the United States than with Eastern Europe. But it remains true that the Kissingerian goal of a "stable structure of peace," which has completely failed at the global level and in Soviet-American relations, does have a certain reality in Europe. This accounts for the greater attachment of Europeans to détente but also for their greater sensitivity, encouraged by the Helsinki process, to what happens within the societies in the other half of Europe.

3. See John Van Oudenaren, *The "Leninist Peace Policy" and Western Europe* (Cambridge: MIT Center for International Studies, 1980).

Thus, at the theoretical level, the very success of Soviet expansion elsewhere makes Eastern Europe look more like the Soviet Union's most important, rather than its only, sphere. Brezhnev's authoritative statement at the 26th Congress of the Communist Party of the Soviet Union (CPSU) included 11 states in the socialist community (the Soviet Union, the East European satellites, plus Cuba, Mongolia, Vietnam, and Laos). With Cambodia, and now Afghanistan, a Soviet-dominated communist subsystem seems (at least to some observers) almost as solidly in place in Asia as in Eastern Europe. Indeed, Soviet control has seemed less directly assured in Eastern Europe, when confronted by an unstable and complex society such as Poland's, than in some states of socialist orientation in the Third World. The justification for the Afghan invasion as a duty to protect the conquests of socialism everywhere—and not to allow another Chile—confirms the notion that the Brezhnev doctrine is not limited to Eastern Europe but is open-ended, applying to socialist states in the Third World as well.[4]

In general, the fact that the Soviet Union has shown more patience in Poland and more readiness to use the Soviet army in Afghanistan than was commonly expected does suggest that the distinction between a zone of domination in Eastern Europe and zones of influence in the Third World is blurring. Countries like South Yemen or Ethiopia appear increasingly to belong to a new, intermediate zone in which the Soviet presence may be less heavy and irreversible than in Eastern Europe but less fragile than was earlier the case in the Third World.

Instead of the three worlds of the socialist community, the capitalist world, and the Third World, there emerges then a potential Soviet-centered system under various degrees of control, in which Eastern and Western Europe represent different shades within a wider spectrum rather than two contrasting positions. In 1975, Avigdor Haselkorn noted the emergence of a "Soviet collective security system," a way of representing the operational and logistical links among the different Soviet regional alliance systems, in particular among the Warsaw Pact, the Indian subcontinent, and Moscow's allies in the Middle East.[5] Since then, such relationships have become more precise and important with, for instance, East Germans and Cubans being flown back and forth between Ethiopia and Yemen.[6] At a more general diplomatic and ideological level, one is tempted to link Khrushchev's earlier notion of a *zone of peace* (uniting the

4. See Peer H. Lange, "Afghanistan—World Power Politics Without Sensitivity," *Aussenpolitik* (English language ed.), 32, no. 1 (1981), 73–85.
5. Avigdor Haselkorn, "The Soviet Collective Security System," *Orbis*, 19 (Spring 1975), 231–54.
6. Avigdor Haselkorn, "The Expanding Soviet Collective Security Network," *Strategic Review*, 6 (Summer 1978), 62–71.

socialist system and the anti-imperialist countries in the Third World)
with the renewed insistence at the 26th Party Congress on *peace zones* in
the narrow sense of denuclearized or demilitarized zones, and then to
relate these ideas to Brezhnev's statement that "the resolutions of the
European [Helsinki] Conference are, in effect, aimed at making all Europe a zone of [peace]."[7]

This *zone of peace,* in the Soviet conception, is destined to become a
sphere of co-prosperity in the Japanese sense. In other words, the Soviet
regional policy of relating these various subsystems that it controls or
influences, of making them reinforce one another or of mediating among
them, may reflect a particularly fertile combination of military and economic geopolitics. There are tenuous signs of the emergence of a kind of
triangular or quadrangular Soviet thinking about relations among the
Soviet Union, Europe (East and West), and the Middle East. From the
long-standing Soviet idea of a European energy conference within the
framework of the Conference on Security and Cooperation in Europe
(CSCE), through a much noted TASS commentary suggesting a community of interests between the Soviet Union and Western Europe in the
security of oil supplies troubled only by American militaristic interference,[8] to the Brezhnev proposals on the Indian Ocean and his overtures at the 26th Party Congress, one can infer a line of thinking according to which the Soviet Union, by guaranteeing Western Europe's energy
supplies, would induce Western Europe to underwrite Eastern Europe's
economic development. Certainly the famous—or infamous—gas deal
seems a strong step in this direction. Western authors have developed
various versions of this scheme. Steven Burg has based it on Soviet financial needs for the development of Central Asia, while the French economic analyst Jean Denizet sees Western Europe, vulnerable through the
fragility of its oil supplies, being compelled to save Eastern Europe from
economic collapse.[9]

There is no hard evidence for this line of Soviet thinking but there are
precedents for it in other earlier Soviet policies, like the encouragement
of the special intra-German trade relationship or of East European oil
imports from the Middle East. Accordingly the Soviets well may calculate
that a certain dilution of their control over Eastern Europe as a result of
this area's increasing economic contacts with Western Europe and the

7. Leonid Brezhnev, Report to the 26th Party Congress of the CPSU, as published in
New Times, no. 9 (Feb. 1981), p. 28.

8. Moscow TASS International Service in Russian, 1010 GMT Feb. 29, 1980, in Foreign
Broadcast Information Service (FBIS) *Daily Report* (Soviet Union), Mar. 3, 1980.

9. Steven L. Burg, "Soviet Policy and the Central Asian Problem," *Survey,* 24 (Summer
1979), 81–82; Jean Denizet, "La guerre froide aura-t-elle lieu?" *L'Expansion,* Feb. 8, 1980,
pp. 50–51.

Middle East is an acceptable trade-off for their increased influence over the other two partners. Western Europe's role as supplier of technology and credits to its big neighbor and its allies, while under the threat of Soviet military power, has been aptly labeled "hongkongization" by the Polish writer Alecsander Smolar. Whether or not the Soviets think along these precise lines, the important point is that they do seem to distinguish between (and integrate) the subregional level (East European and West European) and the regional (pan-European) level, as well as between the subglobal level (the "peace camp," including the "socialist common-wealth," plus the "peace zone") and the global one.

PERMANENT DILEMMAS AND CHANGING SOLUTIONS

In this moving and contradictory setting the basic dilemmas of Soviet policy have not really changed. Except in terms of short-run priorities, they are not between the offensive and the defensive, between an expansionist and a status quo-oriented foreign policy, or between an ideological and a pragmatic one. All basic Soviet notions, like Khrushchev's "dynamic status quo" (by which he defined Third World revolution as the status quo), or "peaceful coexistence," transcend such static distinctions. All suggest a relationship more dynamic and more conflictual than their Western counterparts, such as détente or the balance of power. Like the Soviet tradition itself (whether its Russian or its Marxist side), they all cut across the distinction between offensive and defensive in the direction of an imperial conception of security. By its very nature this conception leads to wanting control over the environment (or at least a *droit de regard* or veto power) in order to prevent negative influences over the more exposed parts of the empire.

Moves such as the building of the Berlin Wall and the invasion of Czechoslovakia were defensive in the sense that they were essentially reactions meant to counteract a dangerous trend. But, after an initial deterioration in relations with the West, these moves were eventually beneficial to the Soviet Union in showing Soviet resolve and the West's inability to respond. This led, in the first case, to the beginning of Brandt's *Ostpolitik* and, in the second, to the success of the Soviet campaign for a European security conference. In both cases, the result was greater Western acceptance of the status quo in the East, which in turn had consequences for intra-Western relations since the actions ultimately led to the differences between Europe and the United States over détente. The same dialectical ambiguity between defensive and offensive, however, exists in policies directed to the world outside the empire, in particular to Western Europe. Opposition to a strong and united Western Europe or to an independent Eurocommunism can be seen in the first instance as an effort to protect Eastern Europe from its attraction. Yet, in a competition for comparative strength, unity, or resistance to crisis and disintegration, what is defensive for the Soviet Union is necessarily offensive to its neighbors, and vice versa.

This does not mean, however, that the Soviet Union does not face genuine dilemmas over priorities if not in policy. But, precisely because Soviet policies, unlike Western ones, are never either purely status quo oriented (the status quo itself being conceived in asymmetrical, conflictual, and dynamic terms) or purely radical (their aim being more to encourage and exploit favorable trends and to discourage and contain unfavorable ones), these real dilemmas are between *process* and *control:* that is, between (1) an emphasis on encouraging processes favorable to the Soviet Union because they help to alleviate its economic problems, or to enhance its influence, or to weaken the West; and (2) an emphasis on controlling these same processes for fear that they may get out of hand by provoking a Western counterreaction or by producing an uncontrolled contagion within the Soviet empire itself.

Contradictory phenomena, ranging from détente and East-West economic cooperation, through Eurocommunism and the increasing role of the Socialist International, to international terrorism and the economic crisis of the West, are both encouraged and feared by the Soviet Union. It tries to influence and to exploit them while protecting itself and Eastern Europe against their fallout. Of course, for the reasons I have already touched on, its chances of success in this balancing act vary from case to case but are less and less guaranteed in a world whose general confusion makes people, forces, and events more tempting to manipulate but also more difficult to control.

In policy terms, the dilemma is between *influence* and *control.* In general, in the choice between gambling on long-range processes reinforced by patient and sometimes indirect influence and pursuing direct and short-range control, the Soviet Union has chosen the former in dealing with the international environment and the latter within its own empire. There is, of course, an element of inevitability about this: the Soviet Union is structurally bound by the nature of its power to insist on influencing its environment and on controlling its own empire.

But, as already indicated, this division is becoming slightly blurred. The invasion of Afghanistan would seem to be an attempt at direct control over a country that was outside the socialist community, but under considerable Soviet influence. On the other hand, in Poland it tried harder and longer than many would have thought to influence events through pressure and manipulation—rather than controlling them by the use of military force. This raises the question of whether the increase in Soviet military power gives Moscow opportunities for extending the sphere of its direct control while, conversely, the evolution of societies at home makes direct control costlier, even within the empire itself.

In Europe the dilemma of choosing between control and influence is both more and less acute than elsewhere. The Soviet Union has no fore-seeable prospect of controlling Western Europe, at least directly, or of preserving its rule over Eastern Europe only through influence. One may wonder, though, whether in both cases the implicit or explicit threat of using force, rather than its actual use, is not becoming the central element of a more direct form of influence in Western Europe and of a less direct form of control in Eastern Europe. The real question, however, remains that asked at the beginning: Are the degree of influence over Western Europe and the degree of control over Eastern Europe related and, if so, is the correlation positive or negative?

The two may enhance each other: control over Eastern Europe, by increasing Western perception of Soviet power, may bring West Euro-peans to make concessions. This happened after the building of the Berlin Wall in 1961 and the invasion of Czechoslovakia in 1968. Similarly, the West Germans reacted to harsh East German measures, like the in-crease in the mandatory currency exchange for visitors, introduced after the October 1980 elections in the Federal Republic and the August events in Poland, by giving ground to the GDR's position on representation and on the concept of a German nation. (This is the position of the former Bonn representative in East Germany and close associate of Willy Brandt, Günter Gaus.) In turn, Western acceptance of these "realities" may facili-tate Soviet control over Eastern Europe. This is certainly one of the main considerations behind the original Soviet advocacy of the European se-curity conference.

More often than not, however, they have to be balanced. The brutality of Soviet control over Eastern Europe can detract from Soviet influence over Western Europe. This happened under Stalin, who, as Jean Laloy has frequently pointed out, may have jeopardized his original hopes for an all-German policy by the harshness of his direct domination over East Germany.[10] A Soviet invasion of Poland might have the same effect. Conversely, the search for influence over Western Europe through dé-tente can bring instability to Eastern Europe. This is a fear particularly felt by East German rulers but not only by them, as shown by the re-sistance to various past Soviet leaders when they, as Beria and Malenkov in 1953 and Khrushchev in 1964, have tried to move too far or too fast in easing Soviet-West German tensions. This fear also explains Soviet am-bivalence on pan-European institutions that could provide an instrument for influencing Western Europe but might also threaten Soviet control in

10. Jean Laloy, *Entre Guerres et Paix* (Paris: Plon, 1966), p. 118.

Eastern Europe, as happened for example with the dissidents' use of the Helsinki charter. Developments in Poland, which though certainly not caused by détente have been greatly facilitated by it, show that this fear is well-founded.

Indeed, there is a special irony at work here. The Khrushchevian formula of the "dynamic status quo" has two aspects. The first concerns the dialectical relationship between stability and change; for, as Willy Brandt, too, recognized in designing his *Ostpolitik,* the very recognition of the status quo encourages forces that challenge it, and actions to check instability at one point of the system may have a destabilizing effect elsewhere. This is certainly a valid insight. It focuses precisely on a point usually missed by both proponents and opponents of détente: The former see détente as a harmonious process leading to stability and cooperation, the latter as a Machiavellian device for weakening or manipulating the enemy. Both views are too static, because they neglect the unpredictable character of social and political change.

But the Soviets also insist on an important asymmetry, on the notion that the dialectics of stability and change should stop at the borders of the Soviet empire; that the "dynamic status quo" should be all dynamism outside and all status quo inside—or, as formulated by John F. Kennedy: "What's mine is mine, and what's yours is negotiable."

The critical view of détente, too, has some validity, given the real asymmetry of the two systems and the greater ability of the Soviet Union to control change within its own camp through the instruments of the party, the police, and ultimately, military force. Yet the fact is that the socialist states are not immune to the winds of change and Soviet moves have their own countervailing effects. Thus, actions taken to stop change within the empire, such as the building of the Berlin Wall or the intervention in Czechoslovakia, promoted a Western acceptance of détente on the basis of the status quo, which in turn created divisions, particularly between Europeans and Americans. Yet, the same détente on the basis of the status quo also had its effect on Eastern Europe, especially in the German Democratic Republic (GDR) and Poland. In both cases a defensive move led to offensive results that later may have contributed to instability within the very empire originally protected by aggressive Soviet steps.

We have, then, a double paradox: First, a defensive repression favors détente and then détente favors destabilization both in the West and in the East, although in different degrees and in different ways. And the same dialectics of defensive intervention, offensive détente, and mutual destabilization can be found in the case of the invasion of Afghanistan.

In order to understand how the Soviet Union has attempted to manage these contradictions, it may be useful to break them down into a series of dilemmas while hastening to warn that the usefulness of these categories lies precisely in showing that, whatever the shifts in its priorities, the Soviet Union has never totally chosen one side of a dilemma over another; it has always tried to eat its West European influence and to have its East European control too.

A first series of dilemmas concerns the priorities among the regional targets of Soviet policy. Going from East to West, they concern first the priority of control over Eastern Europe or of influence over Western Europe; second the choice between an anti-German or a pro-German policy, which at first was a choice between favoring the division of Germany or its unity and then became a choice between isolating the Federal Republic of Germany (FRG) or seducing it; and third, the choice between a policy of superpower bilateralism aiming at an agreement with the United States over the division of Europe (or its joint control) and a regional policy aiming at eliminating the American presence from Europe (or at making it irrelevant).

A second series of dilemmas concerns less the particular targets than the general character of Soviet policy, its strategy, its instruments, and its specific nature. Here again, even more than with the first series, the dilemmas are not clear-cut but involve dimensions that Soviet policy tries to combine, in the process often raising questions of priority and sometimes forcing Soviet leaders to contemplate hard choices they would rather avoid. The first is a question faced by any foreign policy: that of an emphasis on acrobatics or architectonics, to use Zbigniew Brzezinski's expressions, that is, on bilateral diplomacy within the existing framework or on multilateral institutions, with a view to systemic change.

The second one is more specific to an ideological, particularly a communist, power. It is the classical distinction between state-to-state and party-to-party relations, an emphasis on the first being indicative of a more settled diplomacy and one on the second of a more revolutionary orientation.

Finally, the last distinction goes to the root of the problem of an imperial system that puts a premium on authoritarian control of social developments and hence on insulation from the outside world, yet that needs this outside world both for political expansion and for economic cooperation and wants to rely abroad on the very trends it fears at home. Whether formulated in terms of state and society or of process and control, this is the ultimate dilemma and the key to the priority of Eastern or Western Europe.

THE DILEMMAS IN CHOOSING OBJECTIVES

In terms of regional targets, the precise dilemmas concern Eastern versus Western Europe, policies toward the central problem of Germany, and the triangular game with Western Europe and the United States.

Controlling Eastern Europe or Influencing Western Europe

Here Soviet policies have followed an almost cyclical character. Stalin gave absolute primacy to control. The logic of his policy, as expressed in conversations with Milovan Djilas, could be summarized as: "No Red Army without communism, no communism without the Red Army." Khrushchev was more confident in the dynamics of history and, as a result, readier to take risks both abroad and in what Brzezinski has called a policy of "premature globalism," which included the 1958–61 Berlin crisis, and in Eastern Europe through a more flexible and reformist policy. In neither case could he control the processes he set in motion.

Brezhnev represented a blending of Stalin and Khrushchev: He pursued the latter's global ambitions but with the former's emphasis on caution and direct control. During his 18 years in power, however, one can observe definite shifts of emphasis, particularly in European policy. Between 1964 and 1968 the emphasis was on influencing Western Europe—what Marshall Shulman at the time called "a more open game of political maneuver across the entire continent" replacing "the previous Soviet emphasis on the status quo (meaning American acceptance of the Soviet position in Eastern Europe)."[11] This took the form of the campaign for the dissolution of NATO by 1969, of the Karlovy Vary proposals, of the abortive attempt to revive the peace movement, which was to meet with more success 10 to 15 years later. All this was matched on the Western side by a proliferation of schemes such as de Gaulle's "Europe from the Atlantic to the Urals" and Brzezinski's "alternative to partition," the title of his 1965 book. During the same period, in Eastern Europe, the Soviets were showing relative passivity—one of the reasons for the Prague Spring.

However, 1968 brought about an awakening for both sides and moved the West to accept the status quo and the East to stress its consolidation. The Soviet Union shelved the theme of the dissolution of the blocs, accepted the presence of the United States and Canada at the CSCE, and, as the latter was progressing, became less and less enthusiastic about its institutionalization—all for the sake of improving stability in Eastern Europe. The same priority inspired the attempts at integration at every level, from CMEA's Comprehensive Program to efforts at ideological, cultural, and political integration, called *sblizhenie* in Russian, a word for the process of integration taking place among the Soviet republics. Conversely, the West, in particular the Federal Republic of Germany, was abandoning earlier attempts at "peaceful engagement" and accepting Soviet primacy in the region.

After 1975, a third period began, shaped above all by such extra-European factors as America's post-Vietnam, post-Watergate paralysis

---

11. Marshall D. Shulman, "'Europe' versus 'Détente'?" *Foreign Affairs*, 45 (Apr. 1967), 389–402.

and the Soviet Union's increasing military strength. It is not too far-fetched to say that Moscow was returning to a kind of neo-Khrushchev-ism, marked by greater globalism and activism abroad, especially in the Third World, and greater passivity in Eastern Europe. In Eastern Europe integration was no longer being pursued actively, and an element, if not of "benign neglect" at least of political complacency, crept into Soviet policy, perhaps, as in the case of Czechoslovakia, contributing to the 1980 events in Poland. This may also explain the discrepancy in Soviet handling of the Afghan and Polish challenges.

Both crises, however, ushered in a fourth cycle in Soviet behavior. Immediately after the Afghan invasion, the Soviet Union seemed less interested in seducing the West Europeans. Instead, counting the faithful, stopping the rot, and, as a bonus, intimidating the West Europeans appeared to be the priority. At the party level, the rallying of PCF Secretary-General Georges Marchais to the most bellicose version of the Soviet line and the April 1980 Paris meeting of European Communist parties, boycotted by the Italians and the Spaniards, are cases in point. At the state level, in January 1980 Chancellor Helmut Schmidt was disinvited from his planned February meeting with Erich Honecker in East Berlin, and a general suspension of East-West meetings was apparently imposed on reluctant East Europeans. As we shall see, this very reluctance can also be interpreted as serving Soviet interests in fact if not in intention by maintaining a source of influence over Western Europe while Moscow itself was concentrating on putting its own house in order.

In the late spring of 1980, as 11 years earlier after the suppression of the Czech experiment, the Soviet Union launched its own peace offensive, culminating in Brezhnev's report to the 26th Party Congress in February 1981. The aim was to split Western Europe from the United States by encouraging the idea of a separate European détente. For this Western Europe's special links with Eastern Europe, particularly West Germany's ties with East Germany, were quite useful, if not carried too far. But they could be dangerous if the Polish crisis were to escalate or were it (or the reaction to an eventual repression) to have a contagious effect. The retrenchment provoked by the Polish crisis was already in evidence, especially in East Germany. But it was partly counteracted by two other important priorities: the battle to encourage pacifism and neutralism in Western Europe and to cancel NATO's decision to deploy long-range theater nuclear missiles, without at the same time sacrificing Western economic assistance to the faltering economies of the whole Eastern bloc.

With or against Germany: The Soviet-German Love-Hate Relationship

The future of Germany has, of course, always been at the center of Moscow's European policy. Does it want to divide Germany or to reunify it? To seduce it or to encircle it? In other words, does European security, as seen from Moscow, ultimately rely on a bilateral Soviet-German rapprochement or on a multilateral system aimed at isolating Germany (or controlling it with the help of its neighbors)?

At the cost of some simplification, Soviet policy toward Germany can be divided into three periods. Before 1954–55, while consolidating its hold over Eastern Europe, the Soviet Union played with German aspirations for reunification, holding open the idea of a neutralized Germany. Between 1955 and 1969, policy started from the fait accompli of German rearmament and the solidity of the division of Germany and was primarily dedicated to isolating the Federal Republic. Since 1969 the Soviet Union has tried primarily to use the Federal Republic's ties with the East, encouraged by détente, and with the West, expressed in the Common Market and NATO, in order to draw special benefits at the bilateral level while gaining some leverage over Western policies, both within Western organizations and toward the East.

Whatever the dominant priority of the period, the Soviet Union has never completely given up on the possibility of drawing the other Germany away from its allies. Even when Khrushchev was declaring to a delegation of French socialists in 1956: "You keep your Germans and we keep ours," he was also predicting that one day the time would come for a new Rapallo. Even at the height of his successors' dialogue with Willy Brandt in 1970, they were pursuing a policy aimed at singling out the Federal Republic for special constraints in the Mutual and Balanced Force Reductions (MBFR) negotiations.

In the present period, two features are particularly interesting. One, the culmination of a long-standing trend, is the growing importance of the GDR within Soviet policy. More than ever, the Soviet Union's German policy is based on the triangular politics of its relationship with the two Germanys. The complexities of this triangle are analyzed elsewhere in this volume.[12] Suffice it to say here that, with the passing of time, the idea of the Soviet Union sacrificing the GDR for the sake of a grand deal with the FRG, trading reunification for neutralization, is growing more unthinkable. Simultaneously Soviet and East German interests are becoming less similar. In the last analysis, of course, the GDR's policy toward the FRG still moves with the prevailing wind from Moscow: Normalization between the two Germanys followed the Soviet-German treaty, the Soviet hardening after Afghanistan was followed by an East German one after the Polish Summer of 1980, and the Soviet peace offensive was dutifully joined by the East Germans, who insisted on the importance of including arms control in the intra-German dialogue. Meanwhile, for a limited

12. See chap. 2 and Renato Frisch, *L'URSS et les Deux Allemagnes* (Paris: Presses de la Fondation Nationale des Sciences Politiques, 1980).

period, East German policy toward the Federal Republic also served as a brake or counterweight to the prevailing trend of East-West relations and even of Soviet policy. This was the case in 1970–71, with Ulbricht's resistance to the Berlin agreement (reminiscent of his resistance to the New Course of 1953) and to some extent, later in the 1970s, with Honecker's policy of *Abgrenzung* (demarcation). It was again the case, but in the opposite direction, at the beginning of 1980, when the GDR signed an important agreement with the FRG in January, at the time of maximum Soviet post-Afghanistan hardening, and reluctantly canceled the Schmidt–Honecker meeting. But it is difficult to ascertain whether the discrepancy between the attitudes of the GDR and the Soviet Union was due to conflicting interests, to a division of labor, to a difference in emphasis, or to imperfect coordination within a basically common strategy.

At any rate, the special links between the GDR and the FRG, and the idea of a separate intra-German détente decoupled from the vagaries of East-West relations, are certainly encouraged and used by the Soviet Union, which sees in the GDR an instrument for affecting the behavior of the FRG, levering it in the direction of détente and negotiation. This allows the Soviet Union to use the FRG indirectly, in turn, to influence Western Europe, NATO, and the United States to move in the same direction.[13]

At the same time, the GDR constitutes a brake on Moscow's own dialogue with the FRG. On the one hand, being more vulnerable than other East European states, it demands more protection from the fallout of contacts with the West; on the other hand, when seeking rather than shunning the intra-German dialogue, the GDR arouses Soviet suspicions that it may go too far and that the two Germanys may be tempted to break loose from their respective groupings, perhaps even presenting a common front to the superpowers. Intra-German détente is useful to the Soviet Union but only if it feels it can control the relationship.

This leads us to the second feature of the current period, which concerns West Germany's ties not so much with East Germany and Eastern Europe but with France and Western Europe. The Soviet Union has always encouraged divisions between Germany and its allies during the past phases of bilateral dialogue almost as much as during the phases of hostility. In particular it has always tried to use historical rivalries to revive mutual suspicions between France and Germany. After the Soviet invasion of Afghanistan, when Helmut Schmidt and Valéry Giscard d'Estaing expressed views distinctly more favorable to the continuation of détente

13. See F. Oldenburg and G. Wettig, *Der Sonderstatus der DDR in Europäischen Ost-West Beziehungen* (Cologne: Bundesinstitut für ostwissenschaftliche und internationale Studien, May 1979).

than the Americans did, Moscow started for the first time to see Franco-German cooperation in a favorable light. An important but admittedly somewhat idiosyncratic commentator like A. Bovin went so far as to write that "without a common position between France and Germany on the great world problems, it is difficult to think of Europe as a continent of peace and cooperation."[14]

Very rapidly, however, it fell to N. Portugalov to mark the limits of this benevolent attitude toward Franco-German collaboration. He strongly criticized any prospect of its extension to the military field and argued that Franco-German collaboration and independence from the United States could play a positive role for peace only as long as they did not lead to an independent center of military power, did not exclude Eastern Europe and the Soviet Union, and took the road of "military détente" leading to a pan-European system of security and cooperation "which would deprive by definition the American military guarantees to Western Europe, which condition its permanent dependence upon the United States, of any utility and point."[15] In other words, Europe should become more independent of the United States, but only as long as it becomes more dependent upon the Soviet Union. NATO should be weakened, but only as long as it is not replaced by an independent European defense.

With or against the United States: The Soviet-European-American Triangle

Should Moscow play off the West European countries against the United States in the hope of dominating the whole continent, or the United States against the West Europeans in the hope of maintaining a bipolar and bilateral status quo?

Again, it is obvious that Moscow has never clearly chosen one way or the other. Its ideal has been to combine a dialogue with the United States and one with the West Europeans. However, there have been periods when one or the other track has predominated (largely because of the opportunities or reactions coming from the various Western interlocutors). Even then the other alternative has always been kept in reserve. The ultimate goal, however, to the extent that it involves a choice and that this choice is consciously envisaged by the Soviet rulers, remains unclear to the Western observer.

The periods that corresponded best to Soviet preferences were probably between 1965 and 1968, and, even more, the early 1970s, when they were able to conduct a dialogue with the United States—first on non-

14. A. Bovin, *Izvestiya*, June 9, 1980. See the commentary by D. Vernet in *Le Monde*, July 11, 1980.

15. N. Portugalov, "Behind the looking glass," *Literaturnaya Gazeta*, Aug. 6, 1980.

proliferation and then on SALT—raising European fears of condomini-
um, and at the same time one with the Europeans—first de Gaulle, then
Willy Brandt—raising American fears of European neutralism or reversal of alliances. In the earlier period, under Khrushchev, there was an
almost exclusive preoccupation with the United States and a neglect of
European opportunities. Today, after Afghanistan and the breaking
down of the dialogue with the United States, there is an emphasis on the
divisibility of détente and a courting of the Europeans. Throughout all
this the element of short-run tactics ultimately directed at the United
States and those of a more long-range strategy or regional dominance are
hard to disentangle.

A third subject on which the Soviet rulers themselves probably have a
difficult time deciding is closer to the theme of this book: the impact of the
East European dimension. Ideally, as we have seen, the Soviets hope that
making Europe a "zone of peace" will both increase their influence in
Western Europe and help legitimize their authority in Eastern Europe.
This, however, goes for their optimistic moments, when they are most
inclined to trust the process of détente and the instruments of influence.
When their control in Eastern Europe seems threatened, as in 1968, they
emphasize instead the status quo side of the "dynamic status quo." This
leads them, at least in the short run, to place a greater stress on the bipolar
partition of Europe, whether in the version of confrontation against or of
collusion with the United States.

As at the time of Brezhnev's Tbilisi speech in 1971 when, by touting
the notion of MBFR the Soviet leader lent the Nixon administration a
powerful argument with which to kill the Mansfield amendment (demanding a withdrawal of American troops from Europe), the Soviets
have occasionally given signs that they would find a *precipitate* unilateral
withdrawal of American troops from Europe destabilizing. But that does
not prevent them from trying to reduce American presence and influence in Europe, and, more generally, to make NATO weaker and more
divided than the Warsaw Pact.

There is no inconsistency here but rather one more proof that a policy
that is both dynamic and patient, like the Soviet one, cannot easily fit the
static frameworks suggested by abstract Western thinking. The USSR's
view of the Soviet-European-American triangle cannot be based on the
acceptance of symmetry between its own relations with Eastern Europe
and those of the United States with Western Europe.

In terms of the general concept for relations between the two superpowers and the two halves of Europe, one can distinguish four simple
formulas that were, at various times, either advocated in the West or
attributed by Western sources to the Soviets. These are (1) the acceptance
of the status quo based on partition; (2) the mutual disengagement of the

superpowers; (3) the incorporation of Western Europe (or at least of West Germany) into the Soviet sphere; and (4) the abandonment of Eastern Europe by the Soviets and their acceptance of its incorporation (or at least that of East Germany) into the Western sphere. None alone has ever satisfactorily explained the goals of Soviet policy. The Soviets have always pursued a "status-quo-plus" policy of keeping Eastern Europe as a first priority, while also seeking some combination of the second and third options, that is, detaching Western Europe from the United States and attaching it to the Soviet bloc, at least in the milder form of making its ties with the United States more precarious and marginal and its ties with the Soviet Union and Eastern Europe more central and irreversible.

This is the essence of the Soviet policy on European security. It does not, as in earlier periods, demand the cutting of ties between West Berlin and West Germany, the neutralization of NATO, or the departure of American troops from the European continent. But it does involve, through a mixture of pressure, of diplomacy, and of reliance on long-range processes, a West Berlin as separated as possible from the Federal Republic, with increasing ties to the GDR; a Federal Republic in as special a position as possible within the West, with improving Eastern relations; and a Western Europe as autonomous as possible in relations with the United States, with growing links to the Soviet bloc to the degree these do not bring instability to Eastern Europe.

For this the preferred solution is détente in conditions of clear Soviet military superiority. Soviet superiority or military pressure without détente is likely to encourage Atlantic unity or, if the Atlantic connection is seen as unreliable by the West Europeans, drive them toward unity and an autonomous defense; détente without Soviet superiority is likely to encourage instability in Eastern Europe by raising East European expectations and West European influence in the area. It is only the combination of both that maximizes Soviet interests. This interest is expressed with marked clarity in the current campaign for military détente as well as in the idea Andrei Sakharov heard voiced as early as 1955 of ensuring Europe's cooperation by controlling its energy supplies.[16]

Again, this double campaign probably has both a minimum short-range goal and a maximum, longer range one, and both are probably directed at the same time to the United States and to Western Europe. The ambition to play a central role in European security and to push the United States into a marginal role is probably the longer range goal, a goal toward which present Soviet actions and proposals point more directly than at other times; but the dialogue with the United States maintains its parallel importance. In the short run, playing the peace issue by juxtapos-

16. Andrei D. Sakharov, *My Country and the World* (New York: Knopf, 1975).

ing European to American attitudes on détente fulfills a double function: either helping to change the American position through West European influence or alternatively driving a wedge between the West Europeans and the Americans if the latter do not change.

THE DILEMMAS OF GOVERNMENT, PARTY, AND SOCIETY IN THE EUROPEAN INTERSTATE SYSTEM

In terms of both goals and strategies, Soviet views on the future of Europe cannot be understood by simply exploring the dilemma the Soviet Union faces in selecting among its three targets: Europe (East and West), Germany, and the United States. One has to deal with the specific character of Soviet policy, with its tendency toward short-term maneuvering and long-term strategies, and with its use of specific policy instruments.

This can be expressed in another series of three dilemmas: (1) between "acrobatics" and "architectonics" (including the choice between bilateral diplomacy and multilateral institutions); (2) between interstate and interparty diplomacy or between *Realpolitik* and "proletarian internationalism"; and (3) more broadly, between state and society or between the dynamics of social and economic change and the challenge of maintaining regime and empire in Eastern Europe, bringing us back to the original dilemma of process and control. It is these three dilemmas that underscore what is *Soviet* about Soviet foreign policy.

Diplomacy and Institutions

The Soviet Union has a great tradition of playing off its adversaries against each other but also of advocating multilateral conferences like the CSCE and, now, a conference on European disarmament. At the time of the campaign for the CSCE, the Soviet Union, Romania, and Yugoslavia supported the idea, but for opposite reasons: the Soviet Union, in part, to bring its allies into line, Romania and Yugoslavia to give small states more freedom of action. The results were mixed. At Helsinki, Romania made a great show of independence but was not followed by other Warsaw Pact countries. At Belgrade, it played a less active and spectacular role, but other East European countries, particularly Poland, began to show more originality in style, though perhaps with Soviet connivance. The behavior of the two German states also bore the signs of this special relationship. But the more striking phenomenon in Helsinki was the cohesion of the nine members of the European Economic Community, and in Madrid that of NATO as a whole, often with the support of the group of neutrals and nonaligned. Thus, while for each camp the ideal is to display a maximum of cohesion, simultaneously encouraging a maximum of division on the other side, in the CSCE the Soviets have done better at the first than at the second.

On the sensitive Basket III issues having to do with culture, information, and human contacts, multilateralization may serve a useful function for the Soviets to the extent that it reduces the range of the satellites' bilateral cultural contacts with the West. Still, by legitimizing the whole issue and making it a subject of diplomatic negotiation, it has certainly created more problems for the Soviet Union than it has solved—hence Moscow's reduced enthusiasm for the whole adventure save for the use that it may be in reinforcing the Soviet campaign for "military détente."

On the economic side, however, things are more ambiguous. Despite the fact that Basket II is mostly empty precisely because the reality of East-West economic relations is essentially bilateral, the Soviets seem attached to multilateral frameworks and declarations of principle. On the other hand, the only issue on which Karl Birnbaum has found a distinct difference of attitude in Madrid within the Western camp was on Brezhnev's proposal for a European energy conference—the United States being more opposed. Although for the time being this aspect has remained marginal, it does give support to John Van Oudenaren's view of the CSCE process as one aspect of a general Soviet strategy meant to make the Atlantic connection appear marginal or anachronistic in relation to the new realities of irreversible détente present in pan-European ties.[17]

Do not such ties also dilute East European integration and Soviet control over it? From an economic point of view, the results are mixed and the Soviet view is almost certainly ambivalent, for, as Morris Bornstein has shown, East-West economic relations have in some cases helped to promote, and in others to detract from, CMEA integration.[18] In general, however, it seems that since the 1970s the Soviets have chosen to accept not only economic interdependence but West European economic integration and are eager for some form of mutual recognition between the CMEA and EEC, hoping to derive from it an increased legitimation for the former.

It is not clear whether the same calculation applies in the security sphere, and, indeed, beyond current tactics, whether the Soviets actually would toy with the idea of substituting for a military détente (proceeding from a nonaggression pact through a no-first-use agreement to a nuclear-free Europe) that preserves NATO and the Warsaw Pact, a pan-Euro-

17. Van Oudenaren, *"Leninist Peace Policy,"* pp. 39–61.

18. Morris Bornstein, "East-West Economic Relations and Soviet-East European Economic Relations," in *Soviet Economy in a Time of Change,* compendium of papers submitted to the Joint Economic Committee, Congress of the United States, 96th Cong., 1st sess., Oct. 10, 1979, vol. 1 (Washington, D.C.: U.S. Government Printing Office, 1979), p. 368.

pean security system based on the dissolution of the NATO and Warsaw Pact military organizations.

Here, again, one may tentatively see a dialectical tension between the East and West European dimensions. For the long run, the Soviets still advocate the dissolution of the blocs—a meaningless step, the Western powers contend, because of the social and ideological divisions between the two camps and because of Moscow's bilateral treaties with its East European allies, which are more permanent than the Warsaw Pact and have no equivalent in the West. In recent years, however, the Warsaw Pact seems to have become more of a genuine military organization and to have acquired, in addition, a political and police function as an instrument of control and, if need be, of intervention in Eastern Europe that cannot easily be duplicated by purely bilateral arrangements.

On the other hand, if Soviet political strategy toward Western Europe is going to rely increasingly on the peace issue and on finding a common ground with Socialist parties, the theme of dissolving the blocs and of developing an alternative security system may, at the propaganda level at least, be refurbished rather than abandoned.

Governments and Parties

This leads us to the second dilemma of Soviet strategy, and one central to a communist power: the dilemma between interstate and interparty diplomacy, between relying on Communist parties or, more broadly, on left-wing movements or, even more broadly, on social forces in the West, and, on the other hand, relying on established bourgeois or conservative governments.

Of course, the Soviet Union has always combined all these levels. Even in its earliest, most revolutionary period it sometimes sacrificed Communist parties to Soviet state interests; at times even when the clear priority was the foreign policy of existing governments rather than the future of revolution, it has never been oblivious to the role of Communist parties as instruments for influencing these foreign parties. The triangular game between the Soviet Union, all the governments of the Fifth Republic from de Gaulle to Giscard d'Estaing, and the French Communist party is eloquent enough.

The two relevant questions are, first, what role has the East European factor played in influencing Soviet priorities on this issue and, second, have recent changes in the East and the West changed these priorities? The way in which the East European question has arisen most prominently in interparty politics concerns, of course, the evolution of Western Communist parties, or what for a time was called Eurocommunism. The Soviets are certainly aware that the two major landmark years in the drifting away of Western parties from the CPSU were 1956 and 1968.

Every testimony indicates the contempt with which Soviet leaders regarded these reactions and their absolute priority on keeping control over Eastern Europe rather than respecting the feelings and fortunes of West European Communist parties.[19]

On the other hand, contempt for and willingness to sacrifice these parties as a last resort does not mean indifference either to the opportunities or to the dangers they represent. Here, again, the Soviet Union faces the dilemma of influence and control. Eurocommunism represents a channel for influencing Western Europe, particularly the foreign policies of its governments (whether through Communist participation in government or through their role in opposition); but it also represents a threat to Soviet control over Eastern Europe by legitimizing revisionism. (This was always truer of East Germany, where dissidents were still Marxists, than of Poland, where the influence of Eurocommunism was much overrated.)

Hence the dual attitude of the Soviet Union, especially toward the Italian Communist party with which, in a way, it pursues both state-to-state, that is, virtually diplomatic relations, and party-to-party, that is, ideological relations. The state-to-state relations represent an important political force with great potential influence on the future of its country, and the party-to-party relations are with a bad pupil or a dangerous heretic whose influence in Eastern Europe must be checked both by restatements of the true line and by preventive hardening within the empire.[20]

This dual policy produces, in turn, a dual policy among the Western Communists, which, in turn, is exploited by the Soviet Union. For many years, a party like the PCI has justified avoiding a break with the Soviet Union by its influence in Eastern Europe. Its strong reaction to the December 13, 1981, coup in Poland, and its charge that East European societies have lost their capacity for reform and the October Revolution its capacity for inspiration, do amount to a recognition of defeat. However, a subsequent mellowing and the maintenance of contacts not only with Moscow but also with the Jaruzelski leadership, which takes great care to explain its moves to the PCI, have been justified as the only hope for altering Eastern Europe's misguided course. To the extent that this is more than an alibi, Eastern Europe is useful to the Soviet Union as a bridge to the Eurocommunists and a constraint on their rebelliousness.

At any rate one can distinguish at least three categories: the autono-

19. In particular that of E. Weit, Gomułka's interpreter, and that of Z. Mlynář. See Zdeněk Mlynář, *Nightfrost in Prague: The End of Humane Socialism* (New York: Karz Publishers, 1980).

20. See my "The Left in Europe: Security Implications and International Dimensions," California Seminar on Arms Control and Foreign Policy, Discussion Paper no. 83 (Santa Monica: California Seminar on Arms Control and Foreign Policy, Apr. 1979).

mists, that is, the Yugoslavs and the Romanians, who were allied to the
Italians and the Spanish in fighting the Moscow line during the preparation of the Berlin Conference of 1976; the pro-Soviet dogmatists, like the
Bulgarians and the Czechoslovaks, who have specialized in attacks on
Eurocommunism; and the diplomats or soft-liners, like the Hungarians
and the Poles, who have been much more restrained in their condemnation, have tried to build bridges and, at times, to make use of special
bilateral relations (such as those of the Hungarian party with the PCI) to
play a mediating role.

A special and intriguing case is that of the East German party, which,
on ideological and on East European matters, is an extreme hard-liner
(witness its attitude toward the Prague Spring and the Polish Summer)
but, in relations with Western parties, has been rather moderate and
discreet. The fact of having hosted the June 1976 Conference of European Communist Parties is obviously not a sufficient explanation. The
fact of competing with the Social Democratic Party (SPD) for influence
over the Eurocommunists or, conversely, of occasionally using them as a
bridge to West Germany may be more decisive (witness the role played by
the PCI at the beginning of *Ostpolitik*).

Here as elsewhere, the German case is both sui generis and a micro-
cosm of the more general problem, and it leads us to the second question,
that of the evolution of priorities. Today, the real issue in the eyes of
Moscow is not the challenge of Eurocommunism as such, if it ever was;
more and more, Moscow's attitudes toward Western Communist parties
should probably be seen less in terms of the world communist movement
as such and more in connection with the political evolution both in Eastern and in Western Europe.[21] This situation is bounded, on the one side,
by the crisis in Poland and, on the other, by the evolution of West European Socialist and Social Democratic parties and of Soviet attitudes toward them.

The most spectacular aspect of recent Soviet West European policy
has been its peace campaign, aimed primarily at fighting the NATO
decision on long-range theater nuclear forces but also, more broadly, at
promoting a separate détente with the Europeans (though perhaps it is
also intended to soften the reaction to an intervention in Poland, should
one have been or become necessary). The peace offensive has been pursued at every possible level: Governments have been bombarded with
letters and initiatives; use has been made of Communist parties; but the
most striking dimension is the priority given to peace movement activities,

21. Although this latter dimension acquires a new relevance in the context of Sino-Soviet
relations and of the hope of reintegrating the Chinese into a looser version of the world
communist movement, it is significant that Marchais should have used the Italian theme of a
"new internationalism" in his October 1982 trip to Beijing.

that is, to encouraging all potentially pacifist or neutralist forces, particularly the Christians, the environmentalists, and, last but not least, the Social Democratic parties, to oppose NATO—or at least the deployment of nuclear weapons, together with related issues, such as civilian nuclear energy.

Several questions arise: Is the goal of these campaigns limited to influencing Western policies on these specific points? Or, beyond that, are they designed to help bring the left to power, counting on its greater tendency toward pacifism or neutralism? Or, finally, do they pursue the destabilization of West European societies themselves in order either to create a revolutionary situation or, more modestly, to jeopardize the capacity of these societies for acting in foreign affairs, for progressing toward integration, and for influencing Eastern Europe by their attractiveness as models?

On the preference for conservative or for Social Democratic governments, the two principles of (a) the priority of foreign policy and (b) repugnance for the unknown seem to be the only clear and constant keys to Soviet attitudes. Earlier, before the elections of Helmut Kohl and François Mitterrand, they led the Soviets to support the Social Democrats, including Helmut Schmidt (although preferring Willy Brandt), in the Federal Republic, and the conservatives, including Giscard d'Estaing (although preferring the Gaullists), in France.

But in the long run real dilemmas exist: a Social Democratic Europe would offer less military resistance to Soviet policy in Western Europe but more of an ideological challenge in Eastern Europe.[22] In a period of détente the latter may be more dangerous. In a period of a renewed cold war and an arms race, with the Reagan administration in Washington and the missile decision at the top of the political agenda, Social Democratic governments become more attractive—although in some cases, like that of France, they may present the Soviet Union with both sets of problems by their ideological challenge and antipacifist stand.

On the ideological level, the Soviets continue to insist on a clear separation between communism and Social Democracy and to criticize notions like the Euro-Left, the Third Way, and the new internationalism promoted by the Italian Communists.[23] But on the international level, particularly on questions of peace and security, their relations with the Socialist International, with certain Social Democratic parties, and with the left wing of Social Democracy everywhere are more and more cordial.

After Boris Ponomarev's presence at a meeting of the Socialist Inter-

22. See my "Western European Perceptions of the USSR," *Daedalus*, 108 (Winter 1979), 147–49.

23. See "Mosca riapre la polemica con l'eurocommunismo. Bersaglio, 'Il nuovo internazionalismo' con l'argumento: non esiste terza via," *L'Unità*, May 9, 1981.

national in 1978, its leaders were received by Brezhnev in Moscow in 1979, and a whole paragraph of his report to the 26th Party Congress is addressed—in favorable terms—to this organization. In the same report, as in the preceding one to the 25th Party Congress, he presents a score-card of improving Soviet relations with various Social Democratic parties. (For some reason, the Belgians figure prominently, while the French dropped in their standing from the previous congress.) In May 1981 they all received letters from Brezhnev about his peace proposals. Most strik-ing is the third element, the distinction between the bad (Atlanticist) and the good (peace loving) forces within Social Democracy and the open attempt at playing the latter against the former: Willy Brandt's trip to Moscow in June 1981 is the most spectacular illustration.

In general the common initiatives on disarmament with nonparlia-mentary forces (such as the German environmentalists), which are openly encouraged and sometimes financed by Moscow, are more and more frequent. At times, there has seemed to exist a conflict, more than a mere division of labor, between initiatives of the Euro-Left type (such as the conference held in Madrid in February 1981, based on a dialogue be-tween Eurocommunists and Social Democrats) and initiatives of the World Peace Movement type denouncing the Western rearmament effort and denying the problem of imbalance created by the Soviet Union (like the Sofia meeting of September 1980 that launched the mass cam-paign against the deployment of NATO's intermediate missiles).[24] After summer 1981, however, the two types of initiatives tended to converge. On the one hand, the Soviet Union incorporated proposals made earlier by the PCI (like the notion of a moratorium on deployments) and the campaigns it inspired paid lip service to the need for controlling the SS-20s. On the other hand the PCI began riding the wave of the peace movement by hardening its position against the NATO decision. As a result, the Soviets strongly emphasized that whatever their differences on Poland, the Italian Communists were their allies in the struggle against the deployment of cruise missiles in Italy, and more generally on the peace issue. In this respect they included them in their general dialogue with the European left on peace and disarmament.

So far, at least, the goal of these campaigns and of Soviet policy in general seems to have been to influence, rather than to replace, West European governments. The opening to Social Democracy is less an opening to popular fronts than an opening to all the forces capable of influencing governments of the left or the right, so that they, in turn, may

---

24. See the polemic between *L'Unità* and the pro-Soviet General N. Pasti, in "Che pro-getto ha il senatore Pasti? Iniziative che non servono alla pace," *L'Unità*, Apr. 19, 1981, and "Una lettera del senatore Pasti. Non cerca una discussione," *L'Unità*, Apr. 23, 1981.

influence the United States in the direction of military détente. It is this leverage through a chain of proxies that seems the immediate priority.

The East Europeans play a variety of roles within this chain of proxies. In line with the contrast between the global theater of conflict and the European structure of peace, one can distinguish their role as intervention-proxies, mostly in the Third World (e.g., East Germany), and as détente-proxies, mostly in Europe (e.g., Hungary and pre-1982 Poland).[25]

Other cases involve interesting complexities: Bulgaria has been considered by the Yugoslavs as a potential intervention-proxy against them but also seems to serve as a détente-proxy for the Soviet Union toward Romania and Albania. Romania has a genuine conflict with the Soviet Union, partly based upon its relations with the West, in which, as in the recent agreement with the European Economic Community, it goes far beyond Soviet desires, but it also serves Soviet interests by using anti-Soviet arguments in advocating causes favored by the Soviet Union. This was the case for the convocation of the CSCE, in the campaign against INF modernization, and on contacts with the Karmal government in Afghanistan.

The problem with the chain of proxies is threefold: the chain is not quite a chain, the proxies are not quite proxies, and, above all, both the chain and the proxies themselves can break. At one level, the Soviets have been quite effective in the manipulation of ambiguity. They have used whatever autonomy (however limited) East European governments and parties retain in order to encourage the autonomy of Western Europe from the United States. But at another level this very strategy may be threatened by what happens in East European societies and, indeed, in Western ones, even when the course of events has been encouraged by Moscow.

Conservative Governments and Unstable Societies

This raises the last dilemma involving Soviet strategy: that between the interstate system and the dynamics, domestic and transnational, of social, economic, cultural, and political forces. This dilemma has a permanent aspect, which is symbolized by the three Baskets of the CSCE. It concerns the management of East-West communication by the Soviet Union, or the dilemma between the acceptance of interdependence for the sake of economic benefit and the insulation of Eastern Europe for the sake of

25. See, for instance, the debate between G. Gaus and government spokesman L. Rühl on including arms control in the intra-German dialogue, in "Die Kritik des Regierungssprechers Rühl an Gaus stösst auf den Widerstand der SPD," *Frankfurter Allgemeine Zeitung*, May 2, 1981.

political control. Trying to have it both ways, reaping the economic, diplomatic, and perhaps arms control benefits while limiting the cultural, ideological, social, and ultimately political fallout within the empire, presupposes a certain stability and predictability of regimes, in both Eastern and Western Europe. It is the calling into question of this stability that gives a new form and acuteness to the old dilemma.

As late as 1980 the joint attempts of Schmidt and Giscard to save first European détente, in spite of the invasion of Afghanistan, and then their favorite East European interlocutor, Edward Gierek, in the face of the Gdansk strikes, and the high priority apparently given by both German states to maintaining their contacts against unfavorable winds, seemed to underline the advantages of dialogue with Western Europe. Or to put the point in terms of the six dilemmas I have been exploring, they underline the advantages of influencing Western Europe, though at the risk of diluting their control over Eastern Europe; of seducing West Germany rather than isolating it; of making the United States appear irrelevant to European security rather than basing the latter on superpower bilateralism; of encouraging the CSCE and pushing for a European Conference on disarmament; of emphasizing good relations with conservative West European governments rather than with Communist parties; and finally, of pushing for economic interdependence, at least with Western Europe, rather than for autarky, whether at the national or the bloc level.

The Franco-German entente, on the one side, and the paternalistic, more or less managerial and consumer-oriented regimes in Poland, Hungary, and, in some ways, East Germany, on the other, seemed to constitute poles both of stability and of détente. Between them a dialogue could be encouraged or discouraged but at any rate managed if not manipulated, contained if not controlled, by the Soviet Union.

With a fragmented Europe, where France is going to the left, as are the SPD and the Labour Party, but where, in the French case, a Socialist government gives greater priority to supporting NATO decisions, while the German government shifts to the right with the return of the Christian Democratic Union; where Spain both enters NATO and becomes less Atlanticist under a Socialist government; where Papandreou's neutralist Greece makes a unanimous European or NATO policy impossible; where Turkey is under military rule and Yugoslavia threatened by civil strife, the Soviet Union may well be tempted to reassess the situation.

In the future the Soviet Union may be less interested in tolerating some degree of European unity for the sake of a separate European détente, and more interested in exploring European fragmentation and weakness—less interested in supposedly stable and predictable bourgeois governments and more interested in increasingly anti-American and pacifist left-wing parties and movements, even though it knows they are even

harder to control. Within the empire it may practice economic retrenchment, with a corresponding increase in authoritarian controls, rather
than cooperation with the West and economic decentralization.

One hesitates to go further in speculating about Soviet interest in the
destabilization of some West European countries, given the inordinate
amount of unproved sensationalism associated with the notion of Soviet
support for European terrorism.[26] But there is enough solid testimony
on the importance attached by the Soviet Union to preventing Spain's
integration into Western organizations, enough plausible speculation
about its interest in changing Italy's decision on Euromissiles, enough
publicly expressed suspicions by the Italian president and the Spanish
prime minister about the link between terrorists in Turkey, Italy, and
Spain and foreign interests seeking the destabilization of NATO's southern flank, and enough talk of a Cominformist role in Yugoslav Kosovo to
force or at least to envisage a more aggressive and more dangerous, if not
revolutionary, Soviet option.

It remains hard to believe that under any circumstances the Soviet
Union would really give away the diplomatic and economic cards associated with its search for political influence and diplomatic recognition in
the West, in favor of a deliberately and uniformly sectarian policy at home
and abroad. Even during the Reagan administration, it will never re-
nounce using the GDR to influence the FRG, and using the FRG and the
other West Europeans to influence the United States. And it is not likely
to abandon pragmatic tolerance within the empire where it seems to be
working, as in Hungary. One may even imagine, under the new Soviet
leadership, bolder attempts at détente abroad and reform within. But one
may safely predict that these attempts will, once again, find their limits in
the primacy of control. For the time being at any rate, it is the latter, and
the various options associated with it, that seem likely to prevail. Efforts
at turning Europe into a "peace zone," as free as possible of American
nuclear weapons, and at redressing the performance of the Soviet and
East European economies, will not be abandoned, but the former may
rely more on intimidation than on seduction and the latter more on
discipline than on devolution.

Of course, the most crucial factor of all will be the evolution in Eastern
Europe, especially in Poland, and reactions elsewhere to it. In this case as
in all the others, the Soviet success in managing the contradictions and
dilemmas I described cannot be separated from the way other actors—
East European societies, West European political forces and governments, and, last but not least, the United States—overcome the strains of

26. See the balanced appraisal by Brian Jenkins in his review of Claire Sterling's "The
Terror Network," *International Herald Tribune*, May 28, 1981.

economic dependence, social turmoil, and political fatigue. While the long-range prediction is the familiar one of "competitive decadence" between East and West, nothing can be said for the short run which is not certain to be soon superseded—nothing, except that Europe risks becoming a zone of turbulence as much as a zone of peace and that whatever accommodation may be reached between Eastern and Western Europe may look less like a "stable structure of peace" than like a delicate balance of instability.

11

Eastern Europe in the Context of U.S.-Soviet Relations

RAYMOND L. GARTHOFF

Soviet hegemony in Eastern Europe is considered by Soviet leaders to be a vital interest, primarily as a touchstone of the national security of the USSR, but also as the one significant sign of a historically expanding "socialist commonwealth," and as a foundation for efforts to extend Soviet influence in Western Europe and more generally in the world. The Soviet stake in Eastern Europe and continuing unease as to its security, stability, and durability make the Soviet leadership highly sensitive to any external or internal challenge. The United States, as a dominant world power and principal rival and competitor to the Soviet Union, has been seen ever since the end of World War II as the potential source of greatest danger to this core interest of the Soviet Union. And the Soviet Union has had abiding suspicions of American designs to weaken East European ties to the Soviet Union, even though in practice the United States has not directly challenged Soviet hegemony. Still and all, Soviet policy toward Eastern Europe has (as we have seen) a number of focuses much more significant than East European relations with the United States.

American interest in Eastern Europe and the U.S. approach to the countries of Eastern Europe, on the other hand, are predominantly influenced by considerations of the Soviet relationship to the area and to particular countries in the area. Though the United States does not "accept," as a political right, Soviet hegemony in Eastern Europe, in practice it does of course accept it as the prevailing political condition. Confusion over this point has occasionally erupted in relatively minor domestic political controversy in the United States (for example, in the brouhaha over the so-called Sonnenfeldt doctrine in 1976, with distorted interpretations of American support for an "organic relationship" between the Soviet Union and Eastern Europe,[1] and in caricature in President Ford's notorious incidental misstatement on Polish independence from Soviet domina-

---

1. The main part of the text of the presentation, by Counselor Helmut Sonnenfeldt of the Department of State, originally made privately to a conference of American ambassadors, was released to the press following a distorted leak that seemed to imply positive U.S. support for Soviet hegemony in Eastern Europe (see David Binder, "A Modified Bloc Is Avowed as U.S. Policy," and "State Department Summary of Remarks by Sonnenfeldt," *New York Times*, Apr. 6, 1976, pp. 1, 14).

tion in an election debate later that same year). But not since the quiet abandonment of the rhetorical policy of "rollback" of communism in the 1950s has the question been posed in terms of possible active American attempts to upset Soviet primacy in Eastern Europe. During the 1960s the United States came to establish its relationship with the countries of Eastern Europe on the basis of the existing political situation. During the 1970s the United States developed these relations on a more normal basis—and, paradoxically, by striving for less, achieved more in terms of actual American involvement and influence in the area. Now, however, in the early 1980s, the United States is again seeking to pursue a more activist forward policy.

The American interest in the Warsaw Pact countries of Eastern Europe focuses on the area as an extension of Soviet military and political power. Eastern Europe is recognized to serve as a strategic defensive glacis for the Soviet Union, but given widespread American concerns over Soviet expansion it is more widely seen as an offensive *place d'armes* vis-à-vis Western and southern Europe. East European ties with Western Europe—political and economic—are viewed either with satisfaction or with concern, but in both cases principally in terms of East-West and ultimately Soviet-American competition and conflict. American (and Western) strategies for conducting the relationship are conceived either in terms of Western initiative in peacefully penetrating the Soviet sphere (culturally, economically, and even politically and ideologically) or of countering Soviet-manipulated penetration and disarming of the West by these same indirect means.

There is another important dimension to American policy that reflects both ideological and domestic political aspects (often, unhappily, intertwined). Apart from identifiable—and limited—American strategic, political, and economic "national interests" in Eastern Europe, there has been a long-standing American attention to the area stemming in part from a Wilsonian heritage and in part from large-scale past immigration to the United States from Eastern and Central Europe. Thus the United States has displayed a particular interest in self-determination and freedom for the peoples of this region, and this attention has been sustained and has entered the internal American political arena due to the continuing concerns of millions of Americans of East-Central European descent.

Yugoslavia, as a nonaligned state not subject to Soviet hegemony, stands in a situation very different from that of the other communist states in Eastern Europe. Also, American relationships with Yugoslavia— and Soviet consideration of that fact—are accordingly on a different basis from U.S. relations with members of the Warsaw Pact.[2] But again, Ameri-

2. In 1982, in deference to this distinction the name of the Office of Eastern European Affairs in the U.S. Department of State was formally changed to the Office of Eastern European and Yugoslav Affairs.

can interests and relations with Yugoslavia are also keyed primarily to the Soviet factor—in this case, because of Soviet nondomination and Yugoslavia's strategic position and world role as an active nonaligned power, rather than because of other intrinsic bilateral interests. (Albania, the other nonaligned communist state in Eastern Europe, can be set aside from consideration since, by Albanian choice, it has virtually no relations with either the Soviet Union or the United States.)[3]

Thus Soviet policy toward Eastern Europe includes American-East European relations as one important, although not predominant, consideration. The United States, in contrast, makes relationships with the Soviet Union central to its policy toward Eastern Europe. Nonetheless, the American role has tended to increase, affecting both the relative significance of American relations with the countries of Eastern Europe and American and Soviet perceptions.

HISTORICAL BACKGROUND

American policy toward Eastern Europe has been influenced by the traditional American support for national self-determination. Five of President Wilson's Fourteen Points in 1918 concerned self-determination in Eastern and Central Europe. So did President Roosevelt's Atlantic Charter in 1941. But although the Fourteen Points, surprisingly and under unusual circumstances, did affect the redrawing of the political map of Europe after World War I, this may only have fostered the illusion in the United States that national self-determination (and American advocacy of it) was feasible under other circumstances. In any event, as World War II drew to a close, from Yalta through Potsdam and beyond, the United States found its ability to resist the Soviet drive for a dominant position in Eastern Europe sharply circumscribed. Without reviewing here the arguments over the respective roles of misunderstandings and perfidies, entangled aims of security and expansion, and differing Soviet and Western concepts of democracy, it may suffice to remark that in practice the Soviet Union reluctantly settled for giving the United States and Great Britain a freer hand in Japan, Italy, the western half of Germany, and Greece, while the United States reluctantly settled for Soviet hegemony in most of Eastern and Central Europe. (The unsuccessful efforts of the United States to mitigate Soviet imposition of control, especially in the former Axis countries Romania, Bulgaria, and Hungary, were counterposed to

3. An illustration of the extremes of Albanian diplomatic distancing from the United States and the Soviet Union occurred in Sofia in 1978, when the Albanian chargé d'affaires promptly departed from a dinner hosted by the Pakistani ambassador immediately after his arrival upon learning that an American was present; his chancery had specifically checked on whether the *Soviet* ambassador would be present and the invitation was accepted when told he would not, but they had neglected to inquire about an American presence.

the U.S. rebuff of the Soviet attempt to participate in the control of West Germany, Italy, and Japan; the connection was often specifically cited by the Soviet side.) Whether this was the only or the best arrangement that could have emerged, it is the one that did. And accordingly, while the United States may not have accepted the result as definitive, it had to recognize it as a reality.[4]

American policy toward "the Soviet satellite states in Eastern Europe" was in fact established in NSC 58/2 in December 1949 (a top secret policy guidance that has recently been declassified). The National Security Council paper noted that the United States had made "substantial strides in developing Western Europe as a counterforce to communism," and concluded: "The time is now ripe for us to place greater emphasis on the offensive to consider whether we cannot do more to cause the elimination or at least the reduction of predominant Soviet influence in the satellite states of Eastern Europe" (identified as Albania, Bulgaria, Czechoslovakia, Hungary, Poland, and Romania; East Germany was not yet a state, and Yugoslavia and Finland were specifically excluded). The report made clear that the American "ultimate aim" was the establishment of noncommunist states to participate in "the free world community," but as an interim more practical immediate objective sought "to foster a heretical drifting away process" leading to what were termed "schismatic communist regimes" such as Tito's Yugoslavia, although without publicly acknowledging this more limited aim. Finally, the policy report made clear that "the satellite question is a function of our main problem—relations with the USSR."[5]

In the 1950s the gap between illusion and reality grew, as the United States publicly championed, at least rhetorically, a "rollback" of communism and "liberation" of the "captive nations" of Eastern Europe. The

4. Among the many studies of American-Soviet relations with respect to Eastern Europe in the period at the end of World War II, see especially Geir Lundestad, *The American Non-Policy Towards Eastern Europe, 1943–1947* (Oslo: Universitetsforlaget, 1978), esp. pp. 435–65; Lynn Davis, *The Cold War Begins: Soviet-American Conflict Over Eastern Europe* (Princeton: Princeton University Press, 1974); and for the entire period from the late 1940s through the 1960s, see Bennett Kovrig, *The Myth of Liberation: East-Central Europe in U.S. Diplomacy and Politics Since 1941* (Baltimore: Johns Hopkins University Press, 1973).

5. NSC 58/2, A Report to the President by the National Security Council on *United States Policy Toward the Soviet Satellite States in Eastern Europe,* Dec. 8, 1949, 14 pp., Top Secret (Declassified). Quotations cited above are from pp. 1, 2, 9, and 12 of the original document. The major part of the report, not including the conclusions, was declassified in 1976 and appears in *Foreign Relations of the United States, 1949,* vol. 5, *Eastern Europe: The Soviet Union* (Washington, D.C.: U.S. Government Printing Office [hereafter GPO], 1976), pp. 42–54, with the passages quoted from pp. 43, 44, 51, and 54. The conclusions, with some paragraphs deleted for security, were subsequently also declassified. The report, as adopted by the NSC on December 8, was approved by President Harry S Truman on December 12, 1949, and became official U.S. policy.

United States mounted a major propaganda effort, including the establishment of Radio Free Europe. Moreover, in some cases covert action went beyond rhetoric and propaganda.[6] But American nonintervention at the time of the Soviet suppression of the Hungarian Revolution in 1956 decisively showed the limits of American action to oppose Soviet predominance (as foreshadowed by inaction at the time of suppression of the spontaneous uprisings in East Berlin and East Germany in 1953 and as confirmed again at the time of the Soviet-led Warsaw Pact occupation of Czechoslovakia in 1968).

The one special exception was, of course, Yugoslavia. There, after the initial break between Tito's "national communist" Yugoslavia and the Soviet bloc of communist states, once Yugoslavia had on its own established its independence, the United States accepted and supported this defection from Moscow's East European empire for both political and strategic reasons (and despite residual qualms by some on ideological grounds). American support included the sale of arms.

In the 1960s the hollow rhetoric of the cold war was largely abandoned,[7] and the United States sought to develop relations with the countries of Eastern Europe and to foster greater independence by "peaceful engagement," by "building bridges" between West and East.[8] The Soviet Union was highly suspicious of what appeared to be an American strategy of weaning these countries away from the Soviet Union. In any event, this policy of the mid-1960s was stillborn, as the Prague Spring of 1968 resulted in the Soviet occupation of Czechoslovakia, suspending for a time

6. In recent years it has been authoritatively disclosed that from the summer of 1950 to the end of 1952 the United States airdropped agents and military equipment to an anticommunist opposition movement in Poland—which, it later was learned, had all along been controlled by the UB, the Polish security police. See Harry Rositzke, *The CIA's Secret Operations* (New York: Readers Digest, 1977), pp. 169–71. Similarly, an American and British attempt to "liberate" Albania was mounted from 1950 to 1952, infiltrating many agents and arms. It failed; only later did it become known that the British Secret Intelligence Service control, Kim Philby, had been a Soviet agent (Rositzke, pp. 171–72). Agents had also been infiltrated by the CIA into the USSR, including liaison with resistance forces in Lithuania until 1952 and in the Ukraine until 1953 (Rositzke, pp. 168–69). Finally, in the summer of 1956, after the Poznan uprising, the CIA reportedly dispatched trained agents into Hungary (and had prepared others for Czechoslovakia and Romania) with the aim of destabilizing Communist rule in those countries. See William R. Corson, *The Armies of Ignorance: The Rise of the American Intelligence Empire* (New York: Dial, 1977), pp. 366–72.

7. One exception is the annual presidential proclamation of Captive Nations Week, ever since it was unanimously mandated by the Congress on July 17, 1959. In the 1970s consideration was given within the executive branch of at least two administrations to seeking its repeal but did not proceed far because of the judgment that such a move would stimulate strong domestic political objection and would probably fail.

8. These slogans were launched in two pronouncements on American policy toward Eastern Europe by President Lyndon Johnson in May 1964 and October 1966. See Lyndon B. Johnson, *The Vantage Point: Perspectives on the Presidency, 1963–1969* (New York: Holt, Rinehart & Winston, 1971), pp. 471–75.

both the budding movement toward East-West détente in Europe and the American variant of "bridge building" to Eastern Europe, with its more activist thrust.

American policy in the 1950s, and to a declining extent in the 1960s, condemned not only the Soviet role in Eastern Europe but also the "satellite" Communist regimes in power there. During the 1960s there was gradual but uneven movement toward more normal relations.[9] But on the whole American policy toward the countries of Eastern Europe was derivative of American policy toward the Soviet Union. Only gradually in the 1960s was distinction given to differences in relations among these countries and between them and the Soviet Union—in part belated but in part reflecting the gradual emergence of differences, such as the growing independence of Romanian foreign policy and fluctuations in internal repression and liberalization in various countries.

American domestic political considerations have intermittently come to the fore, sometimes supporting closer relations with and support for countries in Eastern Europe (as in Poland), sometimes militating against closer relations (as in the domestic political constituency supporting an annual presidential proclamation of Captive Nations Week despite the negative impact this has on efforts to develop improved relations).

In general, American policy moved along with or followed West European relations with the countries of Eastern Europe during the 1960s. The United States did not assume a leading role; indeed it sometimes restrained its European allies. But there were no serious differences, and the United States did not attempt to harness the alliance into its pattern of minimal bilateral relations. While France had taken a leading position on détente and European-centered policies, the initially cautious but eventually forward German *Ostpolitik* was the most significant Western development of that decade.

U.S. POLICY IN THE 1970s

American policy toward the communist states of Eastern Europe, and differentiation in our policy and posture toward each state, has been

9. See Congressional Research Service, *U.S. Relations with the Countries of Central and Eastern Europe*, Report prepared for the Subcommittee on Europe and the Middle East of the Committee on Foreign Affairs, U.S. House of Representatives (Washington, D.C.: GPO, 1979). This report, while it contains some errors of fact, provides a useful summary of U.S. policy and relations and a compilation of related data. In addition, see the observations of several academic specialists in United States Senate, Committee on Foreign Relations, *Perceptions: Relations Between the United States and the Soviet Union* (Washington, D.C.: GPO, 1978), pp. 137–70, and the historical review in the chapter by Bennett Kovrig, "The United States: Peaceful Engagement Revisited," in Charles Gati, ed., *The International Politics of Eastern Europe* (New York: Praeger, 1976), pp. 131–53.

based to a significant extent on the relations of each country to the Soviet Union. Official statements of American policy during the 1970s stressed three general areas of American interest: a security interest, a humanitarian interest (with particular attention to ethnic ties of Americans descended from peoples of Eastern Europe), and economic interests.[10] The security interest is paramount, and it is directly related to East European-Soviet relations (and less directly but also importantly to East European and Soviet relations with Western Europe).

As the United States, under the first Nixon administration, launched a general policy of seeking "an era of negotiations" to replace an era of confrontation, the basis for American policy toward Eastern Europe was articulated in 1970 with two themes, which were to continue. The president stated:

We are aware that the Soviet Union sees its own security as directly affected by developments in this region. . . . It is not the intention of the United States to undermine the legitimate security interests of the Soviet Union. . . . Our pursuit of negotiation and détente is meant to reduce existing tensions, not to stir up new ones. By the same token, the United States views the countries of Eastern Europe as sovereign, not as parts of a monolith. And we can accept no doctrine that abridges their right to seek reciprocal improvement of relations with us or others.[11]

In more concrete terms, the Nixon administration sought demonstratively to encourage the greater independence shown by Romania and to bolster Yugoslav independence by the unprecedented personal visits of the president to those two countries in 1969 and 1970, respectively. (For mixed reasons, primarily to stress close American ties, President Nixon also visited Poland in 1972, an election year.)[12]

Improved terms for trade and economic relations were seen to be the principal "incentive" the U.S. government could provide to countries of Eastern Europe. The Nixon administration, in 1973, established internal policy guidelines relating such economic measures to desired conduct by the countries of Eastern Europe, seeking not only improved resolution of

10. See Robert L. Barry, *U.S. Policy and Eastern Europe,* U.S. Department of State, Current Policy no. 169 (Apr. 22, 1980), p. 2.

11. *U.S. Foreign Policy for the 1970's: A New Strategy for Peace,* A Report to the Congress by Richard Nixon, President of the United States (Washington, D.C.: Feb. 18, 1970), pp. 138–39. See also the other three volumes of this series, *U.S. Foreign Policy for the 1970's: Building for Peace,* vol. 2, Feb. 25, 1971, pp. 42–44; *U.S. Foreign Policy for the 1970's: The Emerging Structure of Peace,* vol. 3, Feb. 9, 1972, pp. 49–51; and *U.S. Foreign Policy for the 1970's: Shaping a Durable Peace,* vol. 4, May 3, 1973, pp. 91–92. Treatment in this series incidentally reflects the subordinate—and diminishing—significance assigned to U.S. relations with Eastern Europe in the early 1970s.

12. The U.S. aim is candidly avowed by Henry Kissinger, *White House Years* (Boston: Little, Brown, 1979), pp. 155–58, 928–30, 1265–66.

bilateral issues (e.g., settlement of the claims of private American holders of prewar government bonds as a prerequisite to consideration of possible most-favored-nation [MFN] status and Export-Import Bank loans) but also "satisfactory" political conduct on international issues in which the United States had particular interest.[13] The connection between American policy and relations of these countries with the Soviet Union was left implicit. The guidance did, however, establish a rank order of each East European Warsaw Pact member (except the German Democratic Republic [GDR], with which the United States did not yet have diplomatic relations) specifying relative priority for commercial, cultural, and scientific agreements. Those countries considered to hew most closely to the Soviet foreign political line and internal political model were at the bottom of the list. Thus, for example, the United States would not conclude a commercial or cultural agreement with, say, Bulgaria until it had done so with Romania and Czechoslovakia, and indeed all states "above" Bulgaria on the scale of priority.[14]

The Nixon and Ford administrations expanded economic and cultural relations and normalization (for example, consular agreements) with various countries of Eastern Europe. The powers to liberalize trade granted by Congress in December 1974 were far less than President Johnson had sought (without success) in 1965, or than President Nixon could have gotten in 1969, and imposed conditions on emigration policy despite opposition of the Nixon and Ford administrations. These conditions sharply reduced possibilities for foreign policy use of MFN or credits as leverage in dealings with the countries of Eastern Europe (and the Soviet Union). The Ford administration did obtain MFN status for Romania in 1975 despite the need to "bend" the rules on liberalized emigration. American trade with the countries of Eastern Europe continued to grow, but only modestly.

13. These policy guidelines were laid down in a National Security Decision Memorandum, NSDM 212, on May 2, 1973, the text of which remains classified. For a public statement of policy, see Deputy Secretary of State Kenneth Rush, "U.S. Policy Toward Eastern Europe: Affirmative Steps," *Department of State Bulletin*, 68 (Apr. 30, 1973), 533–38.

14. A few anecdotes can illustrate the sensitivity of the East Europeans to questions of "rank order" in relations with the United States. Once the Czech foreign minister, while I was serving as ambassador to Bulgaria, jocularly inquired of me whether American relations with Bulgaria or Czechoslovakia were at the bottom of United States priorities in Eastern Europe. Similarly, the Bulgarians were only too conscious of the fact that, by 1979, Secretary of State Cyrus Vance had met at least in brief sessions in New York on the fringes of the annual UN General Assembly meetings with every foreign minister from Eastern Europe except the Bulgarian—the result, incidentally, of unplanned and uncalculated spot decisions in the cases of the meetings with the foreign ministers of Czechoslovakia and the GDR, not representing any intention to place American relations with Bulgaria in a lower priority position.

The main political development in this period was American recognition of the German Democratic Republic (or East Germany) in September 1974, following the lead of the Federal Republic of Germany (FRG). Generally, both before and after establishing relations with the GDR, in deference to the position held by the Federal Republic on the existence of a single German nation, the United States has generally followed the lead of the FRG on matters specifically relating to the GDR.[15]

It is sometimes suggested that the Nixon administration subordinated policy toward Eastern Europe to policy toward the Soviet Union. In the sense that American policy toward Eastern Europe was subordinate in importance, this was of course true (as indeed it has been with preceding and subsequent administrations). To contend, however, that American policy toward Eastern Europe was fashioned to fit American-Soviet détente in some way differently from what it would otherwise have been, and to sacrifice Eastern European interests, would be difficult to sustain.

State Department Counselor Helmut Sonnenfeldt, in voicing the so-called Sonnenfeldt doctrine earlier noted, did say the United States should "strive for an evolution that makes the relationship between the East Europeans and the Soviet Union an organic one." It was an obscure formulation, subject to the initial misinterpretation it swiftly earned in a leaked form, namely, that the United States endorsed and supported Soviet hegemony in Eastern Europe. In fact, what he had also said was that the existing relationship was "unnatural" and that "our policy must be a policy of responding to the clearly visible aspirations in Eastern Europe for a more autonomous existence within the context of a strong Soviet geopolitical influence."[16] Although a far cry from public statements of American preference in the 1950s or even the 1960s, this was (after all, in a statement given to a conference of American ambassadors and not intended for publication) essentially a restatement of the actual position underlying American policy since the 1950s under all administrations, with or without an American détente with the Soviet Union. (Incidentally, this franker acceptance in the mid-1970s of the status quo in Eastern Europe, albeit as a base for peaceful change, paralleled a vigorous opposition even to peaceful change in Western Europe, exhibited by an American offensive against Eurocommunism and the pos-

15. Incidentally, for both political and geographic reasons, the GDR alone of the European communist states west of the USSR is not included in the area of responsibility of the Office of Eastern European and Yugoslav Affairs in the U.S. Department of State, but in the Office of Central European Affairs, along with the FRG, Austria, and Switzerland.

16. See the reference in n. 1 above. In addition see "United States Security Policy Vis-à-Vis Eastern Europe (The 'Sonnenfeldt Doctrine')," *Hearings Before the Subcommittee on International Security and Scientific Affairs of the Committee on International Relations, House of Representatives*, 94th Cong., 2d sess., Apr. 12, 1976 (Washington, D.C.: GPO, 1976), 67 pp.

sibility that Communist parties might accede to power by parliamentary means in Portugal and possibly other countries in Southern and Western Europe. Implicitly, while cautiously supporting the possibility of change in Eastern Europe, the United States may reasonably have seemed to accept predominant Soviet interest in its sphere, while forcefully reasserting predominant American interest in Western Europe.)

Policy toward Eastern Europe has not been a prominent feature of overall American foreign policy, or an issue within the official foreign policymaking elements in the government, since the 1950s. Some aspects of Soviet-American relations have impinged fairly directly on our relations with Eastern Europe. For example, the congressional refusal to support the Nixon administration's trade relations policy in 1973–74, while aimed against the Soviet Union, also directly affected our relations with East European countries. If the negotiated agreement with the Soviet Union had been supported without crippling amendments, MFN would undoubtedly have been extended to the countries of Eastern Europe as well as to the Soviet Union. Indirectly, Soviet-American relations under all administrations have impinged fairly routinely on relations with Eastern Europe.

All the countries of Eastern Europe support European détente[17] (with some reservations in the GDR), and also the American-Soviet détente that developed rapidly in the early 1970s and continued, with strains and deterioration, until the end of the decade. Indeed, given the particular symbolic importance of the United States in Eastern Europe and the sensitivity of Soviet reactions to American influence, the American-Soviet détente permitted development of a much more forthcoming American relationship with countries of Eastern Europe than would otherwise have been possible. Moreover, it reinforced the promise of the European détente for reduced East-West tensions and lower arms burdens, as well as for increased economic and other ties. Eastern and Western Europe would like to see improvement in American-Soviet relations.

All the countries of Eastern Europe have welcomed the opportunity to expand their contacts in the world and to establish their identity on the world scene, to "spread their wings," as it were, even if pursuing more or

17. The single most important element in this process was West Germany's *Ostpolitik*, which led directly to the establishment of relations between the Federal Republic and all the Warsaw Pact countries of Eastern Europe, including the GDR, in the early 1970s. This opened the way for the United States and other Western countries also to establish relations with the GDR. Indirectly, *Ostpolitik* also helped pave the way for the parallel quadripartite negotiations leading in September 1971 to the successful conclusion of a Four-Power Agreement on Berlin. The culminating development was the Helsinki Final Act of the Conference on Security and Cooperation in Europe (CSCE) in July 1975, including the United States (and Canada) in this détente "charter" for Europe and establishing a continuing CSCE process.

less disciplined alignment (more in the cases of all except Romania, and of course excluding nonaligned Yugoslavia). Détente has also established new forums such as CSCE and MBFR, in addition to opening greater opportunities to participate in existing ones and to develop wider bilateral ties with Western countries. The United States has sought quietly to encourage this increased presence and activity by the countries of Eastern Europe, to the extent that they have more opportunity and experience in autonomous roles.[18]

One key aspect of the development of East-West détente in Europe has been the revival of a conception of *Europe* rather than an exclusive distinction between *Western Europe* and *Eastern Europe*. Countries of Eastern and Western Europe—within, to be sure, the continuing constraints of adversarial alliances—again see and deal with one another as countries sharing the geography and history of a great continent. The Soviet Union, as a European power, has shared this perspective to a certain extent in a way that the United States has not. The United States, even during its détente phase, saw Europe primarily as a theater of U.S.-Soviet political engagement—of preeminent importance to many, but still as one of several global theaters of economic, political, and military involvement. Thus even when an American-Soviet détente coincided with a détente in Europe, during most of the 1970s, they remained separate. And as American-Soviet détente declined and dissolved at the end of the decade, an American estrangement from the East-West détente occurred, which has come to affect American relations with countries of Western as well as of Eastern Europe. Moreover, the tendency in the United States in the early 1980s is to see Europe again as a theater of U.S.-Soviet political engagement—this time, again in confrontation.

The Carter administration in 1977 in Presidential Directive 21 (PD-21) essentially continued the overall approach of the Nixon and Ford administrations, modifying it in two respects.[19] First, the stated criterion for favorable American attention was shifted from satisfactory general international "conduct" to the twin aims of enhancing the international

18. For example, during 1979 the United States consulted individually in bilateral meetings with each of the countries of Eastern Europe (except Albania), just as with non-Communist governments, in exchanges of views in preparation for the CSCE meeting in Madrid in 1980—something it had not done prior to Helsinki in 1975 or before the Belgrade meeting in 1977. Incidentally, as another example of the attention paid by East European governments to "precedence," they showed keen interest in the order of such consultations, in relation to U.S. consultations with Western and neutral countries—and, of course, with the Soviet Union.

19. The text of Presidential Directive 21 (PD-21), issued in September 1977, remains classified and has not been released; a generally accurate account of the main provisions was, however, given in an officially inspired article unhappily titled "'Mischief' in Moscow's Front Yard," *Time,* 111 (June 12, 1978), 19.

independence of action of the countries of Eastern Europe, and of increasing their internal liberalization. The second change was to discard the rigid rank order of individual countries. There remained, however, a general rank distinction of the six East European Warsaw Pact members into two groups, based on a judgment as to amalgamated standing in terms of either relative international independence *or* relative internal liberalization, as seen in Washington. Bilateral American-East European relations, including in particular but not limited to favorable economic treatment, while not differing greatly in practice from the past and while slightly more flexible, were tied more explicitly than before to the perceived relationships of each country with the Soviet Union.[20] As Assistant Secretary of State George Vest stated in congressional testimony: "Our approach is designed to recognize and support the sovereignty and individuality of each Eastern European nation in its domestic and foreign affairs." And, "We intend neither to leave our relations with Eastern Europe hostage to relations with the Soviet Union, nor to conduct a policy that is reckless and destabilizing."[21]

In this same testimony Secretary Vest indicated the differentiation among East European states in American eyes by stressing that U.S. relations were "particularly active and fruitful" with Romania, Poland, and Hungary; these three are also the only Warsaw Pact and CMEA members to which the United States has accorded MFN tariff benefits and access to Export-Import Bank credits. In practice, what the Carter administration did was to "raise" Hungary to join Poland and Romania in the ranks of those East European countries favored by the United States, as evidenced in the return of the crown of St. Stephen and the granting of MFN in 1978. Czechoslovakia, Bulgaria, and the GDR were left in the less favored category.

In one case that deserves note, the sentimental (and domestic political) influence of the existence of a large American population of Polish descent has led American administrations since the 1940s to give special and favorable attention to Poland, buttressing signs of internal liberalization

20. The principal statements under the Carter administration were those by Deputy Assistant Secretary of State William H. Luers to the Subcommittee on Europe and the Middle East of the House International Relations Committee on September 7, 1978, republished as *Eastern Europe: An Overview* (Washington, D.C.: Department of State, 1978), esp. pp. 20–30; Statement by Assistant Secretary of State George S. Vest to the same subcommittee on July 12, 1979; and Deputy Assistant Secretary of State Robert L. Barry, Address before the Cleveland Council on World Affairs, Apr. 22, 1980, *U.S. Policy and Eastern Europe*, Current Policy no. 169 (Washington, D.C.: Department of State, 1980).

21. Statement of George S. Vest, Assistant Secretary of State for European Affairs, in *Hearings Before the Subcommittee on Europe and the Middle East of the Committee on Foreign Affairs, House of Representatives*, 96th Cong., 1st sess., July 12, 1979 (Washington, D.C.: GPO, 1979), p. 12.

and national pride in that country and cultivating a Polish-American tie implicitly competing with Soviet-Polish ties. The wave of Polish workers' strikes in the latter half of 1980 (an American election year), leading to Gierek's fall and the unprecedented grant of "free" trade unions, posed in particular the question of a possibly more active American political stance. Wisely, in my judgment, the Carter administration scrupulously avoided intervention in the tense situation in Poland.[22]

The Presidential Directive (PD-21) had been drafted by the NSC staff, under the personal direction of Zbigniew Brzezinski. Brzezinski saw the main difference between the conception of détente held by Kissinger in the Nixon and Ford administrations, and that which he wished the Carter administration to pursue, as involving precisely the attitude toward change within the communist world. Whereas Kissinger had stressed involving the Soviet Union in a web of ties increasing their stake in the status quo, thus reducing temptations to disrupt the status quo, Brzezinski placed more emphasis on prompting positive change in the Soviet Union, especially through encouraging peaceful change in Eastern Europe. But Secretary Vance and the Department of State were less inclined to define our détente policy toward the Soviet Union and Eastern Europe in terms of pressing for internal change, although internal liberalization was seen as a desirable ultimate fruit of détente.

Brzezinski clearly played the primary role in charting the new—or, more correctly, modified—policy toward Eastern Europe established in 1977. While consistent with his earlier views and his long-standing interest in the area, the new policy was considerably more low key than the "bridge-building" concept enunciated by President Johnson in 1966 in a speech drafted by Brzezinski during his previous tour of duty in the U.S. government (as a member of the Policy Planning Council of the Department of State). Brzezinski characterized the change in policy, in an interview, as follows: "We wanted to show that the road to Eastern Europe did not necessarily lead through Moscow."[23] In practice, U.S. relations with the East European countries prior to that time had not been so "channeled," and the United States did not reduce its attention to the relations of these countries with the Soviet Union. The change was at most in explicitness and emphasis rather than in direction.

22. Although the Carter administration did refrain from intervention, Brzezinski came perilously close to exceeding prudence in personal actions that he has disclosed in his memoirs, including—at a tense time of expected Soviet military intervention in December 1980—in his words "through my own channels, I arranged for telephone calls to alert the Solidarity leaders in Warsaw." (He also, with the president's approval, "called the Pope and briefed him on the situation" in Polish.) See Zbigniew Brzezinski, *Power and Principle: Memoirs of the National Security Adviser, 1977–1981* (New York: Farrar, Strauss, & Giroux, 1983), pp. 466–67.

23. See *Time*, 111 (June 12, 1978), 19.

Many involved with East European policy in the Department of State had been unhappy with the priority ranking of countries and rigid hierarchy of steps in developing bilateral relations under the Nixon and Ford administrations. When the Carter administration provided greater flexibility in this respect the change was welcomed, but again many in the Departments of State and Commerce believed that the remaining categorization was unduly constraining. And, indeed, in his most notable (but rare) comment on relations with the countries of Eastern Europe, Secretary of State Cyrus Vance was clearly more flexible. At a news conference in Budapest, on January 7, 1978, Secretary Vance was asked if there was any difference between the policy of the Carter administration and its predecessor in policy toward Eastern Europe. He replied that the administration was seeking to improve relations with the countries of Eastern Europe on the basis of our respective national interests and declared: "We shall pursue these [interests] on the basis of dealing on a case-by-case basis, country by country, on the various issues and common concerns which we have."[24] Such an approach was not, in fact, what was specified in PD-21.

The differences in approach within the Carter administration never became a real issue, because in practice no issues requiring the articulation and choice between these approaches were ever presented for high-level decision. Differences were not regarded as sufficiently weighty, and indeed policy toward Eastern Europe was not considered sufficiently central, to justify a challenge by those who would have formulated it differently. Moreover, there was a general consensus on the *aims* of policy: to encourage prudently greater external independence and internal liberalization of the Warsaw Pact countries of Eastern Europe. The potential unjoined issue has been whether it was more efficacious to maintain a formal American differentiation among the countries of Eastern Europe, and to withhold "rewards" until "earned," or alternatively to proceed with economic and general normalization and let the *effects* of such developments influence East European practices and policies.

American development of relations with individual countries has, in practice, reflected a range of common interests in each case. To note but one example with which I am particularly familiar, during the latter half of the 1970s the United States concluded a series of bilateral agreements with Bulgaria: a consular agreement (1975), a fisheries agreement (1976), a cultural exchange agreement (1977), reciprocal elimination of travel restrictions on accredited diplomats (1977), a scientific exchange agree-

24. Secretary of State Cyrus Vance, *Transcript of News Conference*, Budapest, Hungary, Jan. 7, 1978. Vance was in Budapest for the ceremony of returning the crown of St. Stephen to Hungary, a move that evoked fleeting conservative and ethnic political objection in the United States.

ment (1978), an agricultural information agreement (1979), and a settlement of claims of private American holders of prewar Bulgarian bonds (1979). In addition there is close bilateral cooperation (including American training) in interdiction of international narcotics trafficking, and in 1979 Bulgaria and the United States jointly hosted an international conference of customs officials on this subject—at which, incidentally, the Soviet Union was not even represented.

The Carter administration's strong emphasis on human rights, although entirely compatible with its desire to encourage greater national autonomy and internal liberalization, caused problems. Romania, for example, continued on its course of a more independent foreign policy than the other Eastern European members of the Warsaw Pact but was not internally so liberal as some of the others that remained more closely aligned with the Soviet Union. Moreover, stress on evaluating human rights on a worldwide basis tended to group all the communist countries of Eastern Europe with the Soviet Union rather than to accentuate differences among them. Similarly, the stress on Basket III (humanitarian rights) in evaluating conformity with the Helsinki Final Act tended to emphasize the division between Eastern and Western Europe rather than the distinction between Eastern Europe and the Soviet Union.

No American administration has considered drawing the line between the Warsaw Pact countries of Eastern Europe, on the one hand, and the Soviet Union itself, on the other, as a basis for our relations. It would, for example, be possible (with congressional concurrence) to grant MFN status and access to credits from the Export-Import Bank and the Commodity Credit Corporation to all the countries of Eastern Europe while withholding those benefits from the Soviet Union. After the Soviet occupation of Afghanistan, the Carter administration did apply a differential on some products in trade licensing to the countries of Eastern Europe and to the Soviet Union while requiring and monitoring nontransfer of the goods from those countries to the USSR. Also, in the 1970s reciprocal bilateral limitations on travel of assigned diplomatic personnel were dropped, after country-by-country negotiation, until such restrictions remain in effect only between the United States and the Soviet Union.[25] Similarly, official United States government claims have now been settled with all the countries of Eastern Europe (tentative settlements negotiated

25. It may be useful to recall that it was the United States that first levied these restrictions on East European diplomatic personnel in the United States, as a corollary to imposing such restraints on Soviet personnel; the process had been initiated by the Soviet Union, but the United States decided for reasons of practical effectiveness to retaliate by restricting representatives of other Warsaw Pact countries as well, and these countries then responded in kind. The last negotiation removing these reciprocal restrictions was concluded in 1977, with Bulgaria.

with Czechoslovakia in 1964 and 1974 were not accepted by the U.S. Congress, but a new settlement was concluded in early 1982). None of these, however, were elements of a policy program specifically designed to differentiate between American relations with the countries of Eastern Europe on the one hand, and relations with the Soviet Union on the other. Rather, American policy continued throughout the 1970s to distinguish two or more categories of East European states depending upon a kind of litmus test of degree of national autonomy, measured in departures either from Soviet foreign policies or from the Soviet system in domestic structure and programs.

The most significant and extensive contacts of the Western countries, including the United States, with Eastern Europe occur in the economic sphere. These economic ties are of growing importance and indirectly affect the political as well as the economic life of the countries of Eastern Europe. Economic relations are based chiefly on trade and financial credits for trade but have also extended to coproduction ventures in third countries and within the East European countries themselves. While each country determines its own foreign trade and economic development needs, it does so in the context of extensive integration under the CMEA Comprehensive Plan and also under conditions of varying but always substantial dependence on economic ties with the Soviet Union.

United States trade with Eastern Europe doubled in the second half of the 1970s (after an even larger percentage increase from very low initial levels in the first half of the decade). In absolute terms, this meant an increase from about $1.5 billion in 1974 to more than $3 billion in 1979. But it remained much lower than the absolute levels or increases of a number of West European countries. Also, there was little growth in the very modest share of overall U.S. foreign trade, or even in the U.S. share of the trade of those countries. Thus although economically worthwhile, the role of American trade was not really economically significant. The very process of developing trade was, however, politically significant.

American policy toward the countries of Eastern Europe is also influenced by the relations these countries have with other nations, and their international activities in general. In the case of Yugoslavia, the United States applauds its vigorous support for genuine nonalignment in the Nonaligned Movement despite Yugoslav support for a number of positions opposed by the United States. Romania is also praised for "strengthening its ties with the nonaligned as an extension of its independent foreign policy."[26] Romanian diplomatic ties with Israel and Egypt and support for both their efforts to work toward a solution to the Arab-Israeli-Palestinian issue not only differentiate its position from that of the

26. Barry, *U.S. Policy and Eastern Europe*, p. 2.

other members of the Warsaw Pact, but also lead it to pursue a course generally parallel to American policy. Romania has also adopted an independent line on a number of arms control proposals.[27] On the other hand, the role of the German Democratic Republic in active involvement in military and policy security assistance and training in such countries as Angola, Ethiopia, and the People's Democratic Republic of Yemen is seen as support of the Soviet Union in activities that do not contribute to international stability.

Relations of the countries of Eastern Europe with the People's Republic of China have been a long-standing concern of the Soviet leaders, and with the rapprochement between the United States and China in the 1970s this aspect of Soviet-East European relations has also acquired a relevance to American relations with Eastern Europe. The United States has not sought to align itself with China in the attempts by the latter to increase its standing and influence in the region.[28] Nonetheless, it is a fact that Yugoslavia and Romania, the two countries that the United States has praised and rewarded for greater international independence, have been most receptive to Chinese overtures. Both hosted high-level Chinese visits in the late 1970s and have developed cordial if not close ties. Despite Soviet concerns, American policy toward countries of Eastern Europe has not been affected by the continued coolness of these countries (except only Romania and Yugoslavia) toward China, and it is not likely to be. But the American-Chinese rapprochement in the late 1970s did feed Soviet suspicions of American policy toward Eastern Europe.

The United States has also taken into account the differing attitudes shown by East European governments toward Eurocommunism and the more independent course chosen by some Western Communist parties, notably the Italian. Czechoslovakia, the GDR, and Bulgaria have been most hostile to Eurocommunism and most vocal in support of the Soviet concept of *real socialism,* and this fact along with others contributes to their lower standing in American favor.

In sum, in terms of relations with third countries, the touchstone of American evaluation is in terms of the extent to which each country of Eastern Europe serves Soviet bloc aims, or pursues a less aligned course. There is an unarticulated assumption—undoubtedly sometimes justified but probably often not—that the aims any of these countries choose in pursuit of their own individual, national objectives would not coincide

27. See David S. Mason, "Romanian Autonomy and Arms Control Policies," *Arms Control,* 3 (May 1982), 13–36.

28. Incidentally, improving Chinese-Yugoslav relations, and perhaps even more the Chinese-American rapprochement, contributed greatly to Chinese-Albanian estrangement at this time but did not lead Albania to seek better relations with the Soviet Union or other East European countries.

with aims of the Soviet Union and the Soviet bloc (essentially, the Warsaw Pact alliance).[29] Also, there is a hope that greater external autonomy will lead to greater internal freedom. In the meantime, however, the United States has had to recognize that in some cases, notably Romania, the policy of rewarding relative independence in external relations not only has involved overlooking internal rigidity and repression but indirectly has even supported such policies by supporting such a regime.

SOVIET POLICY IN INTERACTIONS WITH U.S. POLICY

Earlier chapters in this volume have surveyed and analyzed the many dimensions of Soviet policy toward Eastern Europe. Evidently, the Soviet leaders are highly attentive to American policy aims and actions that could impede or negate achievement of their own. For this reason, Soviet policy toward and relations with the countries of Eastern Europe are also affected by the relations of the United States with those countries (in addition to possible effects on Soviet-American relations). To a great extent, this is encompassed in Soviet reaction to the relationship between the West and East European countries in general, but there are also some aspects especially or even uniquely stemming from American relations.

American (and other Western) political and cultural relations with Eastern Europe are closely monitored by the Soviet Union—as well as by the East European governments themselves. The East European states vary in their specific concerns and constraints on Western contact, but all must balance desired effects of détente with those that are not favored. American policy has combined a firm stand on the principles of free contact and movement of ideas and people with a flexible and nonaggressive use of available opportunities to contribute to this process. American official propagation of ideas and conduct in cultural, informational, and political contacts has been measured and essentially held to the limits set by the countries of Eastern Europe themselves (the only partial exception is broadcasting by Radio Free Europe, which is objected to and jammed in several East European countries). American cultural-political influences are, nonetheless, considerable. As has been observed, apart from Soviet and Eastern European concerns over American and other Western export of ideas, there is also well-founded concern over import of such influences by the peoples of those countries.[30]

29. One category of third-country relationships of especial sensitivity both for the United States and for the Soviet Union concerns disputes and tensions between East European countries—notably the Romanian-Hungarian tensions over the ethnic Hungarian minority in Romanian Transylvania, and recurring Yugoslav-Bulgarian tensions over the Macedonian question. The United States has wisely sought to avoid involvement and has favored peaceful bilateral resolution of such disputes.

30. A point first noted by Vernon Aspaturian, "Has Eastern Europe Become a Liability to the Soviet Union? (1) The Political-Ideological Aspects," in Gati, ed., *International Politics*, p. 26.

The Soviet attitude toward American (and other Western) relations with countries of Eastern Europe is guarded and ambivalent. On the one hand, they have welcomed acceptance of the legitimacy of the Communist governments of these countries and their borders, both through bilateral diplomatic recognition and dealings and through such multilateral instruments as the CSCE Final Act. Moreover, to the extent that Western countries build a stake in development of détente relations, this is seen as moderating confrontational situations. Also, to the extent that the legitimacy conveyed by such ties discourages popular belief within the Eastern European countries in Western support for alternative policies or political systems, it is welcomed. Finally, the Soviet Union and East European countries among themselves simply cannot provide all the economic resources needed to ensure economic viability and progress. On the other hand, to the extent that contacts of various kinds with Western society, its people, products, and above all ideas build awareness and encourage desire for things that are not or cannot be provided by the communist system, they are feared, and efforts are constantly made to curtail or counter such influences. Also, on the economic side, the Soviet leaders are concerned about dilution of ties within the Eastern bloc and about undue East European dependence on or preference for Western ties.

The most dramatic American political demonstrations at the official level have been the visits of three successive American presidents to countries of Eastern Europe (Yugoslavia, Romania, and Poland, each receiving two or three presidents) and to a lesser extent visits by cabinet officers, especially when timed for political effect (such as the sudden visit by Secretary of the Treasury W. Michael Blumenthal to Romania in December 1978, just after the widely reported Romanian balking at efforts to increase Warsaw Pact military expenditures). In particular, the visit by President Nixon to Romania in August 1969, the first ever to an East European communist country by an American president, was not welcomed by the Soviet leaders. One reason that this visit particularly rankled Soviet sensibilities was its timing, just as Soviet-Chinese tensions were at a height. In addition it showed clearly that despite the beginnings of movement toward a Soviet-American détente, the United States was not going to relinquish to that endeavor its interests in the East European communist countries. Selection of Romania accented American encouragement to all the countries of Eastern Europe to follow a more independent foreign policy line.

The increasing Western, including American, trade and other economic ties with the countries of Eastern Europe interact both directly and indirectly with Soviet economic relations with those countries. Although the United States is not the foremost Western economic partner of the East European countries, its leading political and symbolic role makes its relations with them of special significance to the Soviet Union, and often to the countries of Eastern Europe as well, even though these economic relations are minor to the United States.

The countries of Eastern Europe must compromise conflicting policy desiderata, and the Soviet Union must take this into account in evaluating East European economic ties with the West. Trade with the West is necessary to reach some desired economic goals and advantageous in many other cases; at the same time, there are economic and political reasons for restricting the scale of such trade. The desire to reinforce ties among members of the CMEA-Warsaw Pact bloc and to limit political ties with the West pull in the direction of limiting East European-Western (including U.S.) economic ties. These considerations must, however, be weighed by East European leaders (and recognized by Soviet leaders) in terms of limits on the ability of CMEA and the Soviet Union to meet economic requirements. Moreover, while the Soviet Union seeks to encourage integration within CMEA, it does not wish unduly to subsidize it. Furthermore, the Soviet Union, as well as the countries of Eastern Europe themselves, have a strong stake in assuring the continued economic viability of these countries as an end in itself, as a visible indication of their progress, and as the foundation for their political stability. The Soviet leaders must, perforce, countenance increasing East European economic ties to the West as long as these relations do not weaken ties within the socialist community or result in vulnerable dependence on the West.[31]

The Soviet leaders also do not wish any East European country to overextend itself so much that the Soviet Union would have to face the decision either to bail out that country or to see a loss in credit-worthiness harmful to the entire CMEA community. Also, of course, the Communist leaderships of the countries of Eastern Europe, and of the Soviet Union, do not wish to see economic dislocation lead to political instability, as occurred in Poland in 1970 and dramatically since 1980.

The Polish case represents the most extensive instance of overindebtedness, but not the only one. Paradoxically, the other countries of Eastern Europe in the most precarious and overextended position of indebtedness to the West are those that politically have been most independent: Yugoslavia and Romania. Thus encouragement of less economic dependence on the East has also in practice involved more economic imbalance and vulnerability. This presents dilemmas for the countries of the region, the Soviet Union, and the West. The Soviet economic weaknesses that were responsible for permitting this increased East European turn to the West remain to plague Soviet efforts to curb it. It also illustrates the

31. For an example of Soviet expression of some of these concerns, see Yu. Kormnov and I. Petrov, "Détente and Economic Cooperation," *Voprosy ekonomiki* (Problems of Economics), no. 2 (Feb. 1976), pp. 57–67.

hazards for these countries of overeagerness both on their part and by Western banks to extend credit without adequate economic basis, a practice indulged in during the 1970s.

There are also specific political issues concerning U.S. and Soviet relations with Eastern Europe involved in dealing with some essentially economic matters. For example, since the Trade Reform Act of 1974, East European countries wishing MFN status from the United States (as they all do) must take into consideration Soviet rejection of that American legislation (requiring assurances concerning freedom of emigration) as applied to the USSR. The circumstances and qualifying requirements differ in degree, but only in part, for the various East European aspirants. Romania (in 1975) and Hungary (in 1978) qualified for MFN by "assurances" on freedom of emigration accepted by the United States (with tongue in cheek), but for these countries (this would also be true for Czechoslovakia, Bulgaria, and the GDR) this means "acceptance" of American legislation that Moscow has found not acceptable. Decisions may still be made and justified by East European countries concerned, but each must decide not only what compliance would amount to in its case,[32] and whether they wish MFN sufficiently to comply, but also how negotiations with the United States would proceed, how strongly the USSR would object and how strongly they should press for it, whether to consult in advance with Moscow or to advise it during or after negotiations with the United States, and what the political effects would be.

THE POST-DÉTENTE PERIOD: ENTERING THE 1980s

The virtual collapse of the American-Soviet détente at the beginning of 1980, in the wake of the Soviet occupation of Afghanistan and American countermeasures, posed a question as to the continued American-East European détente (and, to some extent, as to East-West détente in general). The United States took the position that this development need not impair its relations, since the East European Warsaw Pact allies of the Soviet Union did not participate in the occupation of Afghanistan (and were not even consulted in advance by the Soviet Union; indeed, at least some were not even advised of the Soviet rationale for the action by Moscow until *after* the United States had been). This American stance was made known not only in private diplomatic contact but also publicly.

---

32. Each year, the MFN waiver under the Jackson–Vanik amendment has required reconsideration and, in practice, quiet negotiation again between the United States and Romania. The hazards of this continuing American condition became clear when, in March 1983, the Reagan administration announced plans to suspend MFN for Romania after that country instituted a tax on emigrants. Negotiations finally resulted in an agreement that averted suspension, but the recurring uncertainty was demonstrated.

Deputy Assistant Secretary of State Robert Barry stated in an address on American policy toward Eastern Europe in April 1980:

Soviet pressure on Eastern Europe for foreign policy unity and domestic ortho-doxy has heightened in the face of the international outcry against Soviet aggres-sion in Afghanistan. What remains to be seen is whether U.S. relations with East-ern Europe are doomed to decline in step with U.S.-Soviet relations. From our perspective, the answer is clearly "no." . . . We are determined that the Soviets must pay a real and lasting cost for their brutal aggression in Afghanistan. . . . But it would make little sense for us to apply the same measures to the countries of Eastern Europe, since that would give them no incentive to conduct policies re-flecting their own national interests. Indeed, in the wake of Afghanistan we should—and will—try harder to maintain and build on the progress we have made with the countries of the region, confident this is in our best interest and theirs.[33]

This statement laid out American policy objectives with almost embar-rassing clarity. It was intended both to explain our policy to, and to elicit support from, the American people. While the policy was welcomed by the East Europeans, they do not wish too tight an embrace.

Though the Soviets do not call upon the East Europeans to retaliate against the United States and more generally have avowed continuing full support for East-West détente, they have reacted against the sharp Amer-ican differentiation and what they see as an attempt to drive a wedge between Eastern Europe and the Soviet Union. For example, a Soviet political observer noted in a broadcast on Radio Moscow that "the White House, having announced the introduction of trade and economic sanc-tions against the Soviet Union [after the Soviet occupation of Afghani-stan] was in a rush to issue an assurance that they did not apply to the other socialist countries." He described this as "a provocative tactic aimed at weakening the unity of all the forces working for peace and progress."[34]

The United States also applied a new criterion or litmus test to the policies of the countries of Eastern Europe in the period following the Soviet occupation of Afghanistan. Thus in 1980 American relations to-ward individual countries of the area were to be modulated to reflect American dissatisfaction with those countries most vocally supporting the Soviet actions in Afghanistan and to reward those not doing so or at least most restrained in support. In practice this did not make any noticeable difference except to restrain further possible American moves to improve

33. *U.S. Policy and Eastern Europe*, p. 3. The speech also candidly includes reference to "convincing private disclaimers" that the United States had received from unspecified East European governments contradicting their "enforced" public support for the Soviet posi-tion on Afghanistan.

34. Vladimir B. Lomeyko, on "International Observers' Roundtable," *Radio Moscow*, Domestic Service (Mar. 30, 1980).

relations with the GDR, Czechoslovakia, and Bulgaria—all of which had promptly voiced support for the Soviet move (the GDR most vociferously). Hungary and Poland were clearly reluctant to declare direct support for the Soviet move but did so within the first two weeks of the action. All supported the Soviet Union in the UN General Assembly. Romania, on the other hand, demonstratively reaffirmed its independent stand by not participating in the UN General Assembly meeting that voted condemnation. Yugoslavia condemned the action from the outset.

The first major domestic development in Eastern Europe in 1980 was the death of Marshal Tito. For many years, as Tito outlived putative successors and assumptions as to his longevity, speculation thrived as to what changes the post-Tito era might bring not only to Yugoslavia but to the whole of Eastern Europe as well. The initial transition, at least, has been made with relative ease.

As for American policy, apart from public and private reassurances to Yugoslavia and the demonstration of American support conveyed by the visit of President Carter in June 1980, the aforecited general restatement of United States policy toward Eastern Europe in the spring of 1980 stated that "Yugoslavia will be much more central to our foreign policy. . . . An independent, united and nonaligned Yugoslavia is crucial to the stability of Europe and the world, and support for that country's territorial integrity, independence, and unity is central to U.S. policy." Moreover, while disclaiming any specific security commitment to that nonaligned country, the American statement warned: "To Moscow and its allies, it should be clear that attempts to undermine Yugoslavia's unity, territorial integrity, and independence would be a matter of grave concern to the United States."[35] A leading TASS news analyst commented on the very next day that the deputy assistant secretary of state, "having obviously lost any idea of what should and what should not be stated by an official spokesman of the U.S. foreign policy department, not only cast aspersions on the policy of the USSR, but nearly went as far as threats against the land of the Soviets."[36]

As long as the situation in Yugoslavia remains stable, it is quite unlikely that the Soviet Union will attempt to intervene, even indirectly. It is also not likely that Yugoslav policy will shift greatly away from the long-standing balance of relationships among the West, the East, and the nonaligned Third World (although its role in the latter may well be diminished). The existing situation does not correspond to the first preferences either of the Soviet Union or of the United States, but it continues to represent a situation with which both are satisfied and that does not pose a threat to

35. Barry, *U.S. Policy and Eastern Europe,* pp. 3, 4.
36. Yuri Kornilov, TASS political news analyst, *Radio Moscow (Apr. 23, 1980).*

either. Yet Yugoslavia remains potentially one of the most critical clashing points in Europe between Soviet and American political and security interests, in the event of internal disruption and a Soviet attempt to capitalize on that situation.

The Reagan administration has continued basically unchanged the policy of its predecessors toward Eastern Europe. The Department of State, in congressional testimony in June 1981, again stated that the primary American interests were security, humanitarian, and economic-trade interests. The policy of the United States was said to be "tailored to our interests and to the situation prevailing in each country. We differentiate between these countries and the USSR to the degree that they pursue independent foreign policies and/or more liberal domestic policies." While no clear hierarchy has been indicated, the priority of listing in the most authoritative statement to date is not surprising: Poland, Romania, Hungary, Bulgaria, Czechoslovakia, and the GDR. Yugoslavia is said to continue to have "special importance to the United States."[37]

The Reagan administration did not, in fact, establish its own policy toward Eastern Europe until August 1982, when a secret National Security Decision Directive (NSDD-54) was issued. The framework of policy remained basically unchanged: it continues to stress differentiation, without a rigid rank order, based on the traditional criteria of independence in foreign policy *or* more liberal internal policies.[38]

The first major public statement of this policy was not made until September 1983, when Vice-President George Bush visited Hungary, Romania, and Yugoslavia and climaxed his tour of the area with a strident speech in Vienna. He frankly stated: "Our policy is one of differentiation—that is, we look to what degree countries [of Eastern Europe] pursue autonomous foreign policies, independent of Moscow's direction, and to what degree they foster domestic liberalization—politically, economically and in their respect for human rights." He went on to specify that "the United States will engage in closer political, economic and cultural relations with those countries such as Hungary and Romania which assert greater openness or independence. We will strengthen our di-

37. Statement by Assistant Secretary of State for European Affairs Lawrence S. Eagleburger to the Subcommittee on Europe and the Middle East of the House Foreign Affairs Committee on June 10, 1981, *U.S. Policy Toward the USSR, Eastern Europe, and Yugoslavia,* Current Policy no. 184 (Washington, D.C.: U.S. Department of State, 1981), pp. 4–5.

38. Authoritative administration sources privately confirmed these central elements of policy and endorsed the main points essentially as set forth in the Eagleburger testimony, while stating that his testimony had represented a Department of State position on policy not reviewed and approved by the White House. During the interagency review and preparation of NSDD-54, consideration was given to adopting a more stringent criterion of both greater independence *and* internal liberalization, but this idea was rejected. The NSDD also did not set a rank order of Eastern European states.

alogue and cooperation with such countries." And, he went on, "We will not, however, reward closed societies and belligerent foreign policies— countries such as Bulgaria and Czechoslovakia, which continue to flagrantly violate the most fundamental human rights; and countries such as East Germany and, again, Bulgaria which act as proxies to the Soviets in the training, funding and arming of terrorists, and which supply advisors and military and technical assistance to armed movements seeking to destabilize governments in the developing world." Bush drew a line, albeit ambiguously, when he further said: "The United States does not seek to destabilize or undermine any government, but . . . we support and will encourage all movement toward the social, humanitarian and democratic ideals," without even saying such "movement" itself must be peaceful. Finally, Vice-President Bush made clear that the United States did not regard the wartime Yalta agreement as dividing Europe into spheres of influence, and said that in that accord the Soviet Union had "pledged itself to grant full independence" to the countries of Eastern Europe, and that "the Soviet violation of these obligations is the primary root of East-West tensions today."[39]

The Polish Crisis

The most momentous development in Eastern Europe since 1980 has been the extended tension within Poland caused by the emergence of the non-Communist popular labor union Solidarity and the inability of the Communist authorities to find a way to contain it short of forceful repression. In the period prior to imposition of martial law and suppression of Solidarity on December 13, 1981, the United States, under both the Carter and Reagan administrations, (and other NATO powers) sought to express sympathy for Solidarity without interfering with Polish internal affairs and to deter Soviet intervention by stressing the need for an internal Polish resolution of the question and the serious adverse effects any direct Soviet intervention would have on East-West relations. Thus, in the Department of State's policy statement on Eastern Europe in mid-1981, it was said that the United States would "continue to refrain from words or actions which would complicate the resolution of Poland's problems by the Poles themselves."[40] This position was outflanked when the Polish

39. Address by Vice-President George Bush to the Austrian Foreign Policy Association, Vienna, Sept. 21, 1983 (press release by the office of the press secretary to the vice-president, pp. 4, 5). Bush also couched his speech in a directly anti-Soviet and anti-Russian direction, contending that the countries of Eastern and Central Europe were European while the Russians were not, and that our aim was to see "our neighbors to the East once more become a full part of Europe" (p. 7). The principal Soviet response was a bitingly sarcastic article by Melor Sturua, "Rejoinder: Blazing Bush," *Izvestiya*, Sept. 23, 1983.

40. Eagleburger, in *U.S. Policy Toward the USSR, Eastern Europe, and Yugoslavia*, p. 4. This position, in retrospect, is one the administration may wish it had not taken.

authorities themselves, rather than the Soviet army, acted under martial law to suppress Solidarity.

The American reaction to the Polish suppression of the liberalization reluctantly granted in 1980–81 was to respond with punitive sanctions against both Poland and, especially, the Soviet Union. (A widespread American assumption of Soviet instigation of the imposition of martial law is unproved; General Jaruzelski and his Military Council of National Salvation may well have seen no alternative. Soviet pressure for and support of the action is, however, evident.)

American leverage on Soviet policy in such a situation may have been weakened by the earlier dismantling of the Soviet-American détente of the 1970s after the Soviet intervention in Afghanistan, but it had never been great. The continuing East-West détente in Europe and Soviet interest in its continuation provide some—but, again, very limited—Western leverage. Sanctions hardly provide a substitute. The $27 billion Polish debt to Western banks and governments (80% to West Europeans) has proved a two-edged sword. American suspension of most-favored-nation trade status for Poland in 1982 when Solidarity was formally abolished had little economic effect, given the Polish economic and trade slowdown, and no impact on Polish political decisions. Confrontational tactics and sanctions, as applied most extensively by the United States, would not have been effective with Poland or the Soviet Union, even if the West Europeans had adopted a tougher position. On the other hand, unimpaired détente would not have changed the outcome.

The main conclusion that emerges from a study of the situation is that neither Western inducements and pressures based on use of "linkage" as to future assistance nor punitive sanctions have had (or even had the prospect of having) much impact. The Soviet, as well as Polish, leaders have never wanted to react with more force than necessary to preserve their political control. But when the leaders of the Soviet Union, and of Poland, concluded that there was a clear and present danger to their political control and the viability of their political system, they moved to deal with that danger, notwithstanding political and economic costs in East-West relations or longer term risks to reestablishing Polish economic viability. Indeed, to the extent Western (in particular, American) threats of economic warfare or political interference have been made or perceived, this has only had the effect of making the need for stringent internal measures in Poland seem all the more necessary.

Recognition of the limitations on American (and in general Western) ability to influence such Soviet and Polish decisions does not, of course, obviate the need for Western policy decisions. There has, however, been a tendency to assume greater Western leverage, and a wider range of policy choices, than in retrospect can be supported. Moreover, beyond difficult immediate choices, such as how to handle overdue Polish debt payments, even more difficult and potentially significant policy issues lie just below the surface. Thus, as we shall discuss presently, basic issues of American policy toward Eastern Europe and the Soviet Union in the 1980s have been posed as a consequence of the Polish crisis.[41]

Prospects for the 1980s

The Soviet Union has not been pleased by the continuing American policy objective of encouraging greater international independence of action by its East European allies. The generally indirect nature of its application, however, has mitigated the effect in most cases from their standpoint. For example, the fact that the United States has deliberately moved slowly in developing ties with Czechoslovakia, Bulgaria, and the GDR, regardless of the American rationale, has probably not been unwelcome to Moscow. On the other hand, the more dramatic indications of American encouragement for independence, such as demonstrative visits to Romania (especially at times of Romanian opposition to Soviet positions), are seen as hostile moves.

As we enter the 1980s, the Polish upheaval has dramatized the new challenges presented by the stirrings within Eastern Europe. These developments are, of course, occurring in a new international context, with its mixture of a continuing if less ebullient East-West European détente coupled with heightened tension in relations between the United States and the Soviet Union.

Relations with the countries of Eastern Europe have certainly been in the shadow of American relations with the Soviet Union. They should stand more on their own. Perhaps one incidental favorable development accompanying the unfavorable turn in American-Soviet relations will be a greater readiness to conduct our relations with the countries of Eastern Europe more on their own merits. More weight should be given to matters of direct concern to the United States relating to bilateral relations. For example, should even such important questions as support for the Soviet position on Afghanistan, or UN General Assembly votes on Kampuchea, Israel, or South Africa be made a touchstone of American bilateral relations with countries of Eastern Europe—while not applied to relations with many other countries? Also, many other countries in the world that have notoriously bad records on human rights, and on voting against American-favored positions in the United Nations, nonetheless continue to enjoy MFN and sometimes American economic assistance.

41. For a thoughtful and provocative analysis of the Polish crisis and American policy options and dilemmas, see Jerry F. Hough, *The Polish Crisis: American Policy Options* (Washington, D.C.: The Brookings Institution, 1982), 80 pp.

Has American policy been too cautious? Could the United States have served its interests, and furthered its objectives of greater East European liberalization, by bolder action? These questions open two areas for speculation: bolder action in pursuit of détente, or in confrontation?

Has America been too cautious in pursuing peaceful engagement and détente? Should it have considered European security and arms control negotiations—frequently proposed by the other side—earlier and pursued them with a broader political vision rather than more militarily anchored security conceptions? Considerations of impact on Eastern Europe, including relationships between Eastern Europe and the Soviet Union, have been notably absent from American arms control and security policy. The Polish Rapacki Plan in the late 1950s may have been an early case in point. It would not have been useful for the United States and NATO to have threatened or bluffed military counterintervention to deter Soviet armed intervention in Hungary in 1956 or Czechoslovakia in 1968 (indeed, an overt stance posing a threat of NATO's move eastward might well have made such Soviet intervention seem even more obviously necessary in Moscow). But did the United States in 1968 have to virtually assure the Soviet leaders of no counteraction? A combination of warnings *and* reassurances, privately delivered, might be both prudent and more effective. An attempt to do this, of undetermined effect, was made in December 1980 with respect to Poland. Beyond such last-minute actions, let us consider the situation if a mutual force reduction and limitation agreement had been reached in the 1960s: might it not at least have inhibited Soviet military intervention in Czechoslovakia in 1968 by making massive troop movements for maneuvers, and later in an invasion, violations of a multilateral compact with the West?

The Polish crisis has, for the time being, dramatically increased the salience of Eastern Europe in American and West European thinking. As earlier noted, it has posed anew the question of the relationship between American policy toward the countries of Eastern Europe and U.S. policy toward the Soviet Union. It also raises other latent policy questions such as how to deal with American-West European divergencies over policy toward Eastern Europe. Most fundamentally, it poses the issue of whether the United States should continue to seek to further peaceful change in the area (aside from thorny questions of what course best serves that objective), or whether the United States should in fact seek to saddle the Soviet Union with economic and political burdens in the region. Most starkly put, does the United States seek stability and political evolution in Eastern Europe, or destabilizing turmoil and political revolution?

Only in the early 1980s has any significant element within the United States government again, after a span of twenty-five years, been ideologically and psychologically receptive to the idea that instability and conflict,

and Soviet repression within Eastern Europe, might be in the interests of the United States. Although that approach has not been formally adopted as American policy, it has found expression in authoritative American pronouncements, in particular in the aforecited speech by Vice-President Bush in September 1983. Moreover, that line of thinking has been reflected in some policy actions as well as in rhetoric. For example, some in the Reagan administration, notably Secretary of Defense Caspar Weinberger, have advocated economic warfare with the Soviet Union and see political and propaganda advantages for the United States, as well as economic drain from the military potential of the USSR, in Soviet entanglement in suppression of political evolution in Eastern Europe. Some express the hope that such developments will strengthen the Western alliance in the face of a more militant Soviet threat; others, seeing a different European reaction, are nonetheless willing to accept even serious frictions with America's West European allies in order to press the Soviet Union, as the controversy over American efforts to enforce its sanctions against Western firms assisting the Soviet pipeline demonstrated. The imposition of those sanctions was in part, but only in part, related to the internal political repression in Poland. It also was justified on the ground of economic warfare. The sanctions thus represented an effort adopted by this American administration, but not by the West Europeans, to substitute a policy of confrontation for one of détente.

While the interests of East European countries may once have seemed to some to be slighted in the interests of American-Soviet détente, East (and even West) European interests could be sacrificed with a vengeance in the interests of American-Soviet confrontation.

While questions as to American policy toward Eastern Europe have been precipitated by the Polish crisis, the fundamental issue remains American policy toward the Soviet Union. Even a policy of confrontation ostensibly seen as "freeing" American policy toward Eastern Europe from deference to Soviet interests would only end by reaffirming the necessity for consideration of the Soviet role (even apart from the fact that its real purpose also would probably have been to weaken the Soviet Union).

The root of the problem lies in Eastern Europe itself. After more than a decade of détente, the continued fragility and brittleness of Communist rule in Eastern Europe has again been demonstrated by the events in Poland. The situation differs from country to country, and it is unwise to generalize. Moreover, things do change over time. Nonetheless, the differing eruptions of widespread dissatisfaction in East Germany in 1953, Hungary in 1956, Czechoslovakia in 1968, and Poland in 1980–81 (after earlier rumblings there in 1956, 1970, and 1976) do suggest widespread and persistent weakness of a system initially imposed from above and from without. While this poses dilemmas for American and West European policymakers, it poses even more critical dilemmas for the peoples and governments of the countries of Eastern Europe, and for the Soviet leaders.

American (and other Western) policies do not, and cannot, play a central role in Eastern Europe. Indeed, the question arises whether the influence of the United States, and indeed of the West, is so limited that they should not even try to affect events. Are Western efforts to ameliorate the situation in Poland and to assist gradual political liberalization not only unproductive but doomed to be counterproductive? Alternatively, can Western efforts to encourage challenges to the Soviet Union and the East European governments allied to it do nothing more than prompt repression that the West is unable to deter or to counter? Is the best Western reaction to stand aside and not rock the boat by, in effect, colluding in either raising or quieting eruptions of tension?

In practical political terms, the fact of limited Western influence is recognized (if not always adequately), but it is not taken as the basis for a judgment that the West should stand completely aside. Capability as well as intention to influence events cannot, however, be dismissed from consideration as we face the basic policy dilemma: Should the United States seek to support by the modest measures at its disposal the long-term political evolution of Eastern Europe *and the Soviet Union,* as the two are inextricably bound together, or should it seek to promote the disintegration of the Soviet bloc and the collapse of the Soviet Union by exacerbating internal East European, and East European-Soviet, problems in order to encourage radical or revolutionary change in the Soviet system?

American interests, and therefore policies, toward Eastern Europe and the Soviet Union cannot of course be addressed in isolation. American policy toward the East European countries cannot be made without impact on its fundamental relationship with its West European allies (again, as the pipeline sanctions showed, American policy may be made without coordination or consideration of this relationship, but not without impact on it). It is also evident that Western Europe does not intend to join a crusade in the 1980s to escalate tensions in the name of an offensive against Communist rule in Eastern Europe.

American interests in Europe are many but certainly paramount among them is our security interest. Although, as we have seen, a U.S. security interest in Eastern Europe has been regularly, one might almost say routinely, reaffirmed by a succession of administrations, it has rarely figured in concrete policy save in terms of rather obvious application such as coordinating Western positions on East-West arms control negotiations relating to Europe. A change in basic policy would, however, require a very different approach. National security is of course the bedrock of U.S.

foreign policies, and it is difficult to imagine any American policy that would *choose* to court unlimited confrontation and conflict with the Soviet Union. American defense of Western Europe against a Soviet or Warsaw Pact assault is a fundamental American security interest. An American offensive against the Soviet Union and the Warsaw Pact, even a political-ideological-propaganda-economic offensive, cannot be considered a comparable security interest.

Adoption of a policy of an offensive against the Soviet political (and security) system in Eastern Europe would surely divide the American people and would alienate the United States from its West European allies. It also predictably could have only two alternative outcomes. First, the policy might be ineffective in its challenge to the viability of the Soviet system in Eastern Europe. Alternatively, a revolutionary situation might in fact unfold in Eastern Europe, undoubtedly prompting forceful Soviet suppression, in which the United States again (as in 1953, 1956, 1968, and 1981) could not militarily intervene, but carrying serious risks of spilling over into an East-West military conflict in Europe. In either case, it would surely prompt a vigorous Soviet counteroffensive against American interests around the globe, thus generating further risks. In short, prospects for achieving the desired result would be low, but the risks of war would be perceptibly increased—imperiling the central American security interest because it would have challenged a central Soviet security interest, as well as possibly precipitating unpredictable clashes elsewhere. Moreover, neither alternative outcome would serve any other American interest—including sympathy for East European aspirations.

On balance, American policy toward Eastern Europe—and the Soviet Union—is not likely to change dramatically. Despite sympathy for more militant alternatives, it is unlikely that the Reagan administration or any successor would in practice (as distinguished from rhetoric) change the basic policy of coexistence and containment. There is a greater emphasis on building military power, and on competition and containment, and decidedly less on cooperation—to say nothing of détente. Moreover, while American policy toward Eastern Europe is affected by this general atmosphere, and the Polish crisis has caused some sanctions to be levied in its name, it is not central to the administration's concerns. (Recall that it was twenty months before the Reagan administration formally established its own policy, and then—eight months after the Polish imposition of martial law—it did not make any significant departure or announce its policy.)

Assuming no drastic recasting of policy objectives, what, if any, refinement or improvement can be introduced into the continuing American policy toward Eastern Europe? Let us consider again the position of the East European countries.

Each country of Eastern Europe develops its relations with the United States—and with the Soviet Union—on the basis of its own interests. These interests are framed within a context of geopolitical realities. The East European allies of the Soviet Union must (and in most cases, for most purposes, wish to) maintain and develop relations with the United States and other Western powers on the basis of consistency between these bilateral ties and their allegiance to the socialist community and alliance headed by the Soviet Union. They conduct their relations with the United States with an eye on how Moscow would regard any new departure (sometimes, but not always, consulting Moscow directly). Romania alone among them has established a number of distinctive, independent foreign policy positions. Yugoslavia has a positive interest in continued acceptance of its nonaligned status by both superpowers; it sees strong support by the United States, on the basis of its neutral status, as reinforcing Moscow's continued acceptance of this status. Albania will probably continue to prefer to minimize absolutely its relations with both powers.

American policies toward Eastern Europe, through all their variations, have sought to encourage greater external independence and internal liberalization—that is, to weaken Soviet influence in the area. To be sure, it does make a difference whether the aim is to expel Soviet presence, or to mitigate it; whether the means include active efforts to "destabilize" the situation and dislodge Communist control, or broadened cooperation with local Communist governments.

Paradoxically, American (and other Western) contact and influence became greater, and internal dynamics involving greater autonomy and liberalization developed, under a détente championed by the Soviet Union at least as much as by the West, rather than under Western policies of overt confrontation or penetration. Détente opened new channels of involvement and offered new forms of potential leverage—for both sides (relating to Western as well as to Eastern Europe). While posing a less direct and blatant challenge to Moscow, more *active* if less *activist* American involvement in Eastern Europe provided at least potentially greater American leverage and influence in the area. Moreover, the American objective clearly remains diminution of Soviet control. Thus, to the extent that the American approach itself is less objectionable, but the consequences more serious, the Soviet task of combating the American influence is seen as more difficult but, from their standpoint, also as more necessary.

On balance, the West has gained greater (though still circumscribed) leverage through economic ties with Eastern Europe, but such leverage is at least in part hostage to Western continuation of economic concessions to the Soviet Union, and increasingly also in some cases to Soviet economic ties with Western Europe. The United States, while a participant in these activities (as well as in Western multilateral policymaking and consulting forums), has not chosen to engage in economic relations with Eastern Europe (or with the Soviet Union) to an extent even remotely reflecting its potential or its economic weight in the West. This fact cushions, but also limits, American leverage on East European and Soviet developments. It also means that for the Soviet Union and Eastern Europe it is feasible to separate punitive curtailment of American détente relations from the economically more significant West European ties. And to the extent that the United States attempts to force the West Europeans into sanctions, as we have seen, the principal effect is to weaken Western alliance ties, not the Soviet Union.

Above all, the Polish crisis has reminded us of the limits of Western leverage in any situation in Eastern Europe where the Soviet leaders believe their vital security interests are endangered.

The American definition of its interests and subordination of its relations with the countries of Eastern Europe to its relations with the Soviet Union ultimately reduce its margin of influence in Eastern Europe (and arguably to some extent in Western Europe as well). The ultimate relationship between policies toward Eastern Europe and the Soviet Union must of course be recognized. But the United States can still frame its relations with the countries of Eastern Europe more on their own merits.

The policy of détente in Europe pursued by both the East Europeans and Soviets and by the West Europeans (and, formerly, by the United States) must face a troublesome fact. The Polish crisis was, after all, in several ways a product of East-West détente. Without détente, it is unlikely that the limited internal Polish liberalization of the late 1970s would have occurred. More significantly, the distorted economic development and overindebtedness of Poland could not have occurred without Soviet permissiveness and Western business and banking cupidity under détente, as well as laxity by the Polish leadership and uneconomic popular consumerism not adequately supported by an inefficient economic system. Thus détente, as well as confrontation, carries risks of destabilizing developments. And although American policy cannot fail to be an element in the equation, it also cannot be central.

American-Soviet relations have an important effect on American-East European relations; they help to establish the context and directly or indirectly impinge in various ways. The United States has chosen to make the relations of these countries with Moscow an important consideration in its policy position. Still, American relations with individual countries of Eastern Europe also depend on other factors, in particular on bilateral interests, to which the United States could give greater attention.

The Soviet Union, for its part, must balance advantages and disadvantages of varying levels and kinds of East European relations with the West, including the United States. It must consider the limitations on its own economic ability in helping these countries to progress and to maintain their economic and political viability. The events in Poland at the beginning of the 1980s, with their very wide potential impact, have posed this task as a critical challenge to the Soviet Union and the countries of Eastern Europe. Finally, the Soviet leaders must evaluate the increasingly complex nature of the overall relationship of the Soviet Union to the East European members of the socialist commonwealth, and the potential impact of developments in Eastern Europe on the Soviet Union itself. The initial Soviet response to this challenge was (during the 1970s) to permit increased East European-Western contact within the context of détente. As economic difficulties prompted an uncontrolled political response in Poland that came to challenge Communist political control, all other countervailing considerations of restraint were overridden by what was perceived in Moscow—and Warsaw—as a vital security need to suppress a popular movement out of control and posing increasingly blatant political challenges.

For the longer run, the Soviet dilemma remains. Paradoxically, it is not entirely unlike the parallel dilemma for the United States, although the Soviet involvement, and stakes, are immeasurably greater. The Soviet dilemma is this: how to permit and channel necessary economic and even political evolution and change in Eastern Europe without undermining vital security, political, and economic interests of the Soviet Union. And for the United States: how to contribute to political evolution and change without stimulating challenges to Soviet security interests that would provoke suppression. Finally, to the extent the governments of the countries of Eastern Europe can influence or control events, they must share both dilemmas.

12

Soviet Policy in Eastern Europe: The Challenge of the 1980s

SARAH MEIKLEJOHN TERRY

In the thirty years since the death of Stalin, successive Soviet leaderships have tried with a singular lack of success to find a formula for stability in Eastern Europe: the proper mix of "viability and cohesion" that would both protect Moscow's perceived security, political, and economic interests and, at the same time, ensure an adequate level of well-being and popular acceptance of the local regimes. Twice—first in the 1950s and again in the 1960s—relaxation of Stalinist-style controls led to miscalculations on the part of one or another East European party, in the end necessitating Soviet military intervention to restore the obligatory order and followed in each case by a search for a stabler foundation for bloc relations. In the first instance, the invasion of Hungary led to Khrushchev's effort to reintegrate the bloc through the hitherto moribund mechanisms of CMEA. Foiled in that attempt by the recalcitrant Romanians, Khrushchev unwittingly compounded Moscow's problems of control with the renewal of de-Stalinization in the early 1960s.

Similarly, Soviet policy toward Eastern Europe in the wake of the 1968 invasion of Czechoslovakia grew in large part out of the challenge of the Prague Spring, which once again forced Moscow to redefine its strategy of alliance management—this time in a way that would permit the East Europeans to address their mounting economic problems but without the unacceptable political risks of the Czech reforms. At the same time, the Soviets' new approach to alliance problems was also shaped by evolving perceptions of their own needs and interests, reflecting both the USSR's enhanced global capabilities and ambitions and a desire to tap the resources of their CMEA partners in the pursuit of "common" goals. Hence Brezhnev's three-pronged strategy for the 1970s: (1) East-West détente with attendant increases in credit-financed trade and technology transfer to both Eastern Europe and the USSR; (2) a reassertion of Soviet ideological initiative, in a negative rather than positive sense—less in order to impose rigid orthodoxy or conformity (what must be) than to place limits on systemic diversity (what must not be); and (3) renewed emphasis on economic integration within CMEA, soon expanded to include a growing number of Moscow's Third World clients.

In a superficial sense the latter two elements (stressing economic and ideological cohesion) may have appeared incompatible with the atmosphere of détente. Indeed, the apparent permissiveness of détente, combined with Soviet activism in other parts of the world, has led some to suggest that Kremlin policy toward Eastern Europe in the 1970s was essentially a repetition of the benign neglect of the mid-1960s. In the Soviet mind, however, the three elements were not only compatible but each was the necessary complement of the others, the long-term goal being a strengthening of bloc cohesion rather than its dissipation. Specifically, in the absence of comprehensive Czech-type reforms, the essential improvements in economic performance, whether in Eastern Europe or the Soviet Union, could be had only at the price of substantial increases in trade and technology transfer from the West. On the other hand, if Moscow were going to allow Eastern Europe's participation in détente, prophylactic measures to forestall ideological erosion were necessary. The third element, the tightening of CMEA ties through the 1971 Comprehensive Program and subsequent joint investment plans, was intended to ensure that expanded trade links with world markets would not be at the expense of Moscow's long-term development plans or Eastern Europe's support of its Third World activities.

The first half of the decade augured well for the new policy. Escalating levels of East-West trade and credits sustained growth rates and boosted living standards throughout the bloc, without the need for destabilizing reforms; even global economic developments, in particular the quadrupling of oil prices in 1973–74, initially seemed to favor Moscow's hand, providing it with a flexible but effective form of leverage over those East Europeans who might be tempted to stray too far from the fold or to neglect their obligations to "international socialism." Yet by the early 1980s Brezhnev's strategy, like Khrushchev's before it, lay in shambles—a failure of which the Polish crisis provided the most dramatic but by no means the only example. Across the board, with the partial exceptions of only Hungary and the GDR, failure to carry out basic reforms left the East bloc regimes unable to take advantage of imported technology; growth rates had fallen markedly from the levels of a decade earlier; living standards were stagnant or declining, food shortages and debt burdens rising. In brief, most of the political and economic tensions that Brezhnev hoped he was laying to rest after Czechoslovakia were threatening to reemerge in even more acute form—and at a time when the international and domestic economic climates alike offered fewer options for dealing with them.

The situation is not without its quotient of poetic justice—what one might call Marx's revenge against Lenin: to wit, that the crisis in Poland (and potentially throughout Eastern Europe) presents Moscow with a quintessentially Marxian dilemma—that of a maturing socioeconomic base rebelling against (or at best stagnating under the weight of) an obsolete and ossified political superstructure fashioned for an earlier stage of development (if it was ever suited to Eastern Europe's needs at all). One suspects, however, that, given their peculiarly Leninist outlook with its fixation on the controlling influence of the political factor, the Kremlin leaders are more perplexed and frustrated by, than comprehending of, such ironies. Indeed, the message of the Brezhnev strategy, undoubtedly drawn from the experiences of the Prague Spring and now Poland, appears to be that the key to stability in Eastern Europe lies in supporting leaderships capable of maintaining order in their own houses rather than those inclined to adapt to changing realities. One can well imagine that Soviet disappointment with the now-deposed Gierek focused less on his sins of economic mismanagement than on his failure to quash the intellectual and working-class opposition in 1976 and 1977 before it snowballed into the nationwide Solidarity movement in 1980.

Whatever the precise mix of causative factors or misperceptions behind the present crisis, Eastern Europe's new "time of troubles" could hardly have come at a less opportune moment. Brezhnev's death in November 1982, although not unanticipated, has set in motion what in all probability will be a lengthy two-stage succession process. Combined with the Soviet Union's own multiple economic ills, this process will heighten the risks and narrow the options available to Moscow for maintaining stability in the region.

Soviet succession politics have traditionally had a destabilizing effect on Eastern Europe. The political uncertainties and personal rivalries that typically characterize a change of leadership in the Kremlin tend to be accompanied by a preoccupation with domestic Soviet affairs and, consequently, by an absence of consistent policy guidance in relations with the regional parties. While only those parties that are already experiencing domestic dislocations and turmoil are likely to be so destabilized, neither the record of past succession periods nor the present situation in Eastern Europe can offer much comfort to Brezhnev's heirs.

The Soviet invasion of Hungary occurred three years and eight months after Stalin's death in March 1953, the Warsaw Pact invasion of Czechoslovakia three years and ten months after Khrushchev's removal in October 1964. In neither case was the timing coincidental. In the first instance, the rapid-fire shifts in Soviet policy in the three years after Stalin's death—the Moscow-initiated New Course, Malenkov's defeat in the "second industrialization debate," followed by the beginnings of de-Stalinization with Khrushchev's secret speech to the 20th Congress of the CPSU—had a whipsaw effect on the more vulnerable East European regimes. In Hungary, in particular, Malenkov's defeat left the hapless

Nagy at the none-too-tender mercies of Rákosi. By the time the Kremlin leadership had recognized its mistake, the frustrated aspirations of Nagy's countrymen for a more humane form of socialism had boiled over into unacceptable demands and open revolt. Similarly, the vaguely populist or reformist signals emanating from Moscow during the late Khrushchev period and the early stages of the 1965 economic reform, together with the apparent quiescence of the "re-Stalinizers" in the immediate post-Khrushchev period, ultimately contributed to the excesses of the Prague Spring.

The present Kremlin leadership is assuredly aware of this past pattern of misperception and miscalculation. Indeed, inasmuch as Brezhnev's strategy toward Eastern Europe throughout the 1970s was specifically aimed at averting a repetition of the miscalculations that had led to the Czechoslovak crisis (with Poland as a blunt and continuing reminder of the potential for instability in the region), his former colleagues and immediate heirs are likely to be highly sensitive to the problem. Nonetheless, there are several reasons why, despite whatever precautions the post-Brezhnev leadership may take, the succession factor is likely once again to play an unsettling role in the region. For one thing, while a succession period in the Soviet Union is perforce characterized by greater preoccupation with internal issues, its destabilizing effects on Eastern Europe are due less to such inattention or benign neglect on Moscow's part than to the dynamics of the process itself: the inevitable jockeying for position among competing factions in the absence of institutionalized mechanisms for the transfer of power, the equally inevitable policy shifts as one group encroaches on or edges out its rivals, and the pervasive opaqueness of Soviet political discourse temporarily masking or distorting those shifts. It is these features of the Soviet succession process that tend to have ripple effects on the East European regimes, disorienting their leaderships or shifting the balance of power among factions within their parties.

Second, the remarkable stability of the Brezhnev leadership between 1964 and 1982 has now become an element of instability in the post-Brezhnev period; moreover, the high rate of natural attrition that will affect several layers of Soviet power during the remainder of the decade will be complicated by parallel successions in several of the East European countries. Third, the acute nature of the economic problems afflicting both the Soviet Union and most of its East European allies will accentuate the competition for available resources, and therefore for political power, both within the individual countries and on a blocwide basis. These last two factors—the multistage, multidimensional nature of the ongoing succession process and the acuteness of the blocwide economic crisis—merit more extended comment.

By now it is conventional wisdom that the Soviet succession will be a

two-stage affair, stage one involving the emergence of an interim caretaker government made up largely of Brezhnev's aging colleagues and
committed essentially to a policy of Brezhnevism without Brezhnev, but
unlikely to last more than five to six years at most. By contrast, stage two
beginning later in the decade will witness a wholesale generational turnover, affecting not only top party and governmental posts but reaching
down into the second and third layers of the Soviet power structure, and
will bring to the fore groups whose political attitudes are largely unknown
and untested and whose exposure to the outside world (including Eastern
Europe) has been minimal.

Adding to the potential for instability in Soviet-East European relations will be the parallel succession processes that we can expect to see by
the mid-to-late 1980s in several of Moscow's regional dependencies. Four
of the party leaders in question are 70 years of age or older (Zhivkov in
Bulgaria, Kádár in Hungary, Husák in Czechoslovakia, and Honecker in
the GDR), the first two having held their positions for more than a quarter
of a century; only in Hungary has there been a concerted attempt to bring
a new generation of leaders into positions of genuine responsibility. In
Poland and Romania, the other two full members of the bloc, the leaderships are somewhat younger but, for different reasons, are also vulnerable to rapid change: in Poland because of the ongoing political and economic turmoil in the wake of the crushing of Solidarity; in Romania
because of the dismal economic performance and political oppressiveness
of the Ceauşescu regime. On the fringes of the bloc both the Yugoslav and
Albanian leaderships are subject to destabilization: in the former, the
precarious ethnic balance bequeathed by Tito on his death in 1980 could
be upset by a combination of intractable economic problems and national
tensions; in the latter, the aging Hoxha leadership, in power now for close
to 40 years, has already begun to crumble. Thus, the legacy of leadership
continuity that has characterized both the East European and Soviet
scenes for well over a decade will in all probability be rapid leadership
turnover in the next decade, with unpredictable consequences for the
political stability of the bloc.

The emergence in November 1982 of Yuri Andropov as the apparent
primus inter pares for the first or caretaker stage of the succession suggested the possibility of a less wrenching transition to stage two. The fact
that he was "only" 68 years of age at the time he assumed the general
secretaryship, and therefore that he might remain at the helm for five
years or more, together with his reputation as one of the more pragmatic
and efficiency-minded members of the Brezhnev collegium (as evidenced
by the flurry of personnel changes that followed his appointment), could
portend a more gradual generational changeover than if the interim
successor had been Kirilenko or Chernenko.

Moreover, insofar as Soviet-East European relations were concerned, Andropov's appointment brought to power the only remaining member of the Brezhnev team (after Suslov) with lengthy exposure to the problems of the region. Indeed, in view of the seriousness of those problems, this may well have been a factor in his selection. And while most Western observers chose to focus on his role as Soviet ambassador to Hungary during the 1956 invasion or as head of the KGB for 15 years, it is also relevant that Andropov was the Central Committee secretary responsible for supervising relations with the East European parties between 1957 and 1966, a decade that witnessed a gradual relaxation of Soviet policy toward the region and an unprecedented degree of experimentation in several of the countries. The fact that the Czechoslovak experiment was brought to an abrupt end in August 1968 does not obscure the equally important fact that the Hungarian New Economic Mechanism (NEM) was not and that the new Soviet leader may take some personal satisfaction in Kádár's relative success.

Whether Andropov's tenure in office will better reflect his image as a guardian of orthodoxy or as a pragmatic manager—indeed, whether he remains general secretary long enough to leave a distinctive stamp on Soviet policy—only the future will tell. What *is* predictable is that the Soviet-East European relationship will loom large on his or any future leader's agenda of problems in the volatile period that lies ahead, and that economics—both the precarious state of the East European economies and the declining ability or willingness of the Soviet Union to prop them up in time of crisis—will be the major constraint not only on the management of those relations but also on Soviet policy generally.

According to one estimate, the aggregate annual growth rate of the six East European members of CMEA in the 1981–85 period will be on the order of 1.4%, or less than one-fifth the rate achieved in the 1971–75 plan period and barely more than one-third that of the 1976–80 period. Even excluding the data for Poland (where national income is expected to drop by an average of 3.3% over the five years), growth rates in the remaining countries will show a marked deterioration from the levels of a decade earlier.[1] In view of the importance attached in recent years to the gradual betterment of the lot of the consumer as a major underpinning of the system's legitimacy—in view also of the unbalanced growth that typifies most of Eastern Europe and the fact that living standards tend to grow more slowly than the economies as a whole—such trends may well lead to serious dislocations and a rising level of social and political tensions throughout the region.

1. Jan Vanous, "East European Slowdown," *Problems of Communism*, 31 (July–Aug. 1982), 1–19.

In the past, Moscow's management of crises in its East European dependencies has been facilitated by two factors: first, that at any one time the crisis has been limited to a single country (even in 1956 the climax of the Polish events had passed before the Hungarian situation got out of control); second, that despite the shortcomings of their own economy the Soviets have always had sufficient resources to tide over the faltering regime, and by so doing to avert unwanted political change. In the foreseeable future, neither of these conditions seems likely to hold. On the one hand, the pervasiveness of the region's economic malaise increases the probability either that crises may erupt spontaneously and more or less simultaneously in two or more countries, or that the ripple effects of a crisis in one of these economies may be enough to tip the balance in others. (Already we have seen how the collapse of Polish coal exports in 1981 caused serious dislocations in energy supplies and industrial production in the GDR and Czechoslovakia.)

On the other hand, Moscow's capacity (not to mention willingness) to mediate future political crises with timely infusions of economic largesse, either as a supplement to or substitute for the use of military force, is open to serious question on several grounds. Like its East European counterparts, the Soviet economy is experiencing a long-term secular slowdown. With annual growth rates for 1981–85 not expected to exceed the 2.5–2.8% level, if that—and with multiple and intersecting bottlenecks in such critical sectors as agriculture, transportation, metallurgy, resource development, and technological innovation—any future Soviet leadership will be hard pressed to find the resources necessary to rescue future Polands. Indeed, the Soviet economy, which has long acted as a buffer between Eastern Europe and the harsh realities of the world market, is rapidly becoming part of the region's problem. As we have seen, Eastern Europe's terms of trade with the Soviet Union will continue to deteriorate at least through 1985 as intra-CMEA prices (especially for energy) chase world levels; as a result, the East Europeans will be forced to export a rising volume of manufactures to pay for stable or declining deliveries of energy and other raw materials, thus further straining domestic markets.[2]

Moreover, the cost to the Kremlin of its periodic rescue efforts has escalated sharply over the years. Here the example of Poland's three most recent crises is instructive. After the December 1970 crisis, a Soviet hard-currency loan of $100 million was apparently sufficient to overcome the immediate difficulties (in part because it was soon supplemented by the influx of Western credits). In the wake of the June 1976 food price riots, Soviet aid was reportedly on the order of $1.3 billion in ruble and hard-

2. Ibid.; see also chaps. 6 and 7.

currency loans, plus an increase in oil deliveries at the subsidized intra-CMEA price; by then, $100 million would have been enough to cover a mere two months' interest on Poland's Western debt. Soviet aid to Poland since August 1980 has so far eluded even a rough official calculation; unofficially, when trade credits, increased deliveries of energy and raw materials, and (at least in the early months of the crisis) help in meeting debt service are all added up, the total through 1982 almost certainly exceeded $5 billion. Trade credits alone for 1981 and 1982 were approximately $3.9 billion, although the Poles were apparently told that they had to balance their trade account for 1983.[3]

Such largesse, apart from the burden it places on Soviet resources, clearly poses the danger that other East European countries will try to use their economic weakness as leverage. The fact that Moscow was largely unsuccessful in inducing others to share the Polish burden may have been part of the rationale for the 10% cut in 1982 oil deliveries to all of East European CMEA as a means of forcing the rest to absorb some of the cost and, perhaps, of impressing on them that there are finite limits to the resources Moscow is willing to pour into the region.

What, then, are the options open to the post-Brezhnev leadership in reordering its relationship with Eastern Europe? Perhaps the only thing that can be said with fair certainty is that the new Kremlin leaders will at last have to *choose*. The Brezhnev-era expectation that they could have their cake and eat it too—that they could demand of their regional clients both economic viability and systemic orthodoxy, as well as tangible support for Soviet interests abroad—has proved both illusory and costly, and now dangerously destabilizing.

From a purely theoretical point of view, the options appear to be three. First, the Soviets might tell the East Europeans that henceforth they must fend for themselves, politically as well as economically, on the ground that, in light of both Soviet domestic needs and broader global interests and capabilities, they represent a net liability—that is, the economic burden these dependencies impose is no longer sufficiently offset by the political and strategic benefits to Moscow. Second, and at the other extreme, the Soviets could opt for retrenchment and the reimposition on the bloc of Stalinist-style orthodoxy, austerity, and isolation, on the ground that the dangers of political erosion accompanying the more open policy of recent years far outweigh the putative (and all too temporary) economic gains. Or, third, they could encourage limited reform, largely of the economic variety, to make the East European systems more efficient and self-supporting within the context of existing bloc institutions

3. See chap. 3. n. 38.

and relationships, but with somewhat greater autonomy and flexibility for member countries in setting domestic policies and priorities.

Of the three options, the first two appear to be the less realistic in present circumstances: the first because it seriously understates the continuing centrality of Eastern Europe's strategic and legitimizing functions in Kremlin calculations and because it fails to take into account the constituency-building characteristics of a succession period, which would make such an unprecedented departure from previous policy well nigh impossible. The second option, although less improbable in the sense that there is ample precedent for it (and no doubt potential support within both the Soviet and East European bureaucracies), also offers no long-term solutions. The need for food imports alone makes any notion of Stalinist-style autarky for the bloc as a whole unthinkable, while the selective isolation of the East European economies (even if it were possible) would merely increase the burden they represent for the USSR without addressing the underlying causes of their inefficiency and instability.

That seems to leave option three, or some degree of in-system reform, as the logical choice. The possible variants are several, ranging from the partial, incremental approach characteristic of most "reforms" adopted in the past, in both the USSR and Eastern Europe, to the comprehensive decentralization attempted by the Hungarians after 1968. The sobering lesson of past reform efforts, however, is that incrementalism, or muddling through, simply has not worked—that it invariably falls victim to the bureaucratic inertia of the existing system and that only the more comprehensive approach is likely to produce measurable improvements in performance. At the same time, the facile assumption that the Hungarian experience (itself none too easy or free from contradictions) can be replicated elsewhere in the bloc may prove unfounded. The potential pitfalls include the difficulty of the transition process, the coincidence (once again) of East European reform efforts with a Soviet succession, and the likelihood that such reforms will have costly side effects for Kremlin interests elsewhere.

Even under the most favorable circumstances, reform of the East European economies will be a lengthy and delicate process, economically and politically, and will require a high degree of policy consistency both at home and in Moscow. From the economic point of view, the establishment of some degree of equilibrium seems to be a prerequisite to implementation of genuine reforms (including an end to rigid price controls and central allocation of key commodities and, in most countries, a restructuring of investment priorities), if the reforms are not to bring unacceptable levels of inflation and (at least temporarily) unemployment; it is worth remembering that in pre-NEM Hungary this preparatory period extended over more than half a decade. From the political point of view as well, effective reform will require both a gradual weeding out of party and government officials who have opposed past reform efforts as well as the neutralization of those elements who might be tempted to push the reforms beyond acceptable limits; in the Hungarian case, the total collapse of the Stalinist party in 1956, the simultaneous defeat (and emigration) of the forces of liberalism, and the subsequent support that Kádár enjoyed vis-à-vis his domestic hard-liners from both Khrushchev and (at least until 1971) Brezhnev were all essential ingredients in the successful (if still not total) implementation of the NEM.

In brief, then, meaningful economic reform in Eastern Europe is not a quick fix but a complex process that can easily be derailed—whether by the domestic balance of power, by policy and/or leadership changes in Moscow (with the inevitable spillover into East European politics), by the absence of slack in the economy to ease the dislocations of transition, or (most commonly) by a combination of the above. Yet, as the post-Brezhnev era began, none of the East European regimes (including potentially a post-Kádár regime in Hungary) enjoyed the constellation of favorable political and economic conditions, both domestic and external, that facilitated the NEM in the 1960s.

The implications for Soviet policy toward the region—indeed, at least indirectly, for Soviet policy in general—appear to be several. First, on the assumption that additional Western credits to Eastern Europe in the foreseeable future will do little more than refinance existing debt (if that), the Soviet Union remains the only source of the financial resources essential to the successful introduction of reforms. Although Moscow seems determined to phase out subsidies on its energy exports, a continuing net flow of Soviet resources into the region could take other forms: direct trade credits (such as those extended to Poland since 1980 and, in lesser amounts, to the others); elimination or severe curtailment of East European "aid" to Soviet Third World clients (a difficult item to calculate but possibly far more significant than available data suggest);[4] or a similar curtailment of CMEA's "long-term target programs," which are primarily oriented toward meeting Soviet development needs, often at the expense of balanced development of the East European economies.

Although any of these policy shifts would in one sense represent merely a continuation of a long-standing policy of subsidizing its East European clients, the fundamental shift in the rationale for such a policy should not be overlooked: Heretofore Soviet economic assistance (and leverage) has been used almost exclusively as a counterweight to reform. What we are suggesting is that, if Moscow is serious in its desire to foster stable and prosperous societies in a region long regarded as indispensable

4. For an example, see ibid., n. 17.

to its own security and legitimacy, it will now have to use its assistance to *facilitate* reform—moreover, it will have to do so at the expense of urgent domestic needs, as well as larger ambitions elsewhere. Such a course will demand of the new leaders uncharacteristic foresight and decisiveness.

Yet as of this writing, nearly a year after Brezhnev's death, signals out of the Kremlin remain contradictory. Although initially it looked as if an Andropov leadership might favor a combination of Hungarian economics and political orthodoxy, by the spring of 1983 the momentum behind economic reform in the Soviet Union was already flagging, having brought little more than a flurry of personnel changes and a brief campaign against corruption and lax labor discipline. It is too soon to say whether the shift was due to Andropov's inability to consolidate his position as fully or rapidly as anticipated, to his uncertain health, or simply to a misperception of his policy preferences. What is certain is he has been unable to translate his injunctions concerning the urgency of "improving the economic mechanism" into a concrete program for change. Moreover, subtle warning flags began going up in Eastern Europe as well: to the bloc as a whole that it was time to close ranks, economically as well as politically; and in particular to the Hungarians, to the effect that, while Moscow still found their economic experiments "very interesting," they should be careful not to get too far out of step with the others (and especially with Soviet policy).[5]

Nowhere has the indecision and disarray over future policy been more evident than in preparations for a full-dress CMEA summit, the first since 1971. Since the idea was broached by Brezhnev at the 26th Soviet Party Congress in early 1981, and despite numerous preparatory meetings, the members have been totally unable to work out an agenda or even to agree on the merits of holding a summit at all. Indeed, at the time of the most recent postponement, in May 1983, the parties seemed as far apart as ever, each nursing its own set of expectations and anxieties. Not surprisingly the Poles were seeking a comprehensive aid package to put their economy back on its feet, something the others have been resisting for several years; they were no more receptive to Romania's pleas for increased food and raw material imports at concessionary prices, lest its economy go the way of Poland's. The Hungarians, understandably concerned that renewed emphasis on integration and joint planning would undercut their plans for expanding ties with world markets, continued to press for blocwide price reform and currency convertibility. Even the Czechs, who together with the Hungarians have been pushing for a summit, were critical of existing mechanisms of integration. The East Ger-

5. Reported by John F. Burns, in the *New York Times*, May 5, June 17, 1983, and "Soviet Signals on Economic Management Picked Up In Hungary," *Radio Free Europe Research* [*RFER*], RAD Background Report/68 (Mar. 31, 1983).

mans and Bulgarians seemed least interested of all, perhaps because, in view of the relative strength of their economies, they feared they would end up footing the bill for any concessions to others.

Despite the special interests dividing them, however, the most serious sources of disagreement appeared to be those uniting the East Europeans against Moscow: first, the sharp increases in prices for Soviet energy and raw materials and hints that the Soviets might press for further cutbacks in oil deliveries or part payment in dollars; and second, fears that Moscow's proposals for "rationalizing" CMEA through closer plan coordination, stepped-up specialization, and the establishment of "joint enterprises" would further compromise their economic autonomy. Ironically, the strains within the bloc seem to have increased since Brezhnev's death. For, despite Andropov's reputed sensitivity to Eastern Europe's concerns, he is apparently more insistent than his predecessor on putting real teeth into CMEA's integrating functions. Moreover, with the example of Poland as a useful object lesson, the Soviets reportedly hope to use the summit "to curb members' financial and technological dependence on the West and force them to do more business with Moscow."[6] Yet, to the extent they succeed in integrating the East Europeans more closely into their own unreformed economy, they will put out of reach the improvements in technology and productivity they are demanding.

As British philosopher Edmund Burke once wrote, "Most political decisions are a choice between the disagreeable and the intolerable." The choice that Moscow faces in Eastern Europe today is either to continue propping up inefficient and sullen (and with growing frequency, unstable) dependencies or to allow them sufficient latitude (economic as well as ideological) to put their own houses in order. Both courses carry risks to the Soviets' most vital interests in the region. What is not yet clear, perhaps even to them, is which alternative they view as intolerable and which merely disagreeable. Whether the new men in the Kremlin will exhibit the necessary quotient of determination, imagination, and policy consistency to make a clear-cut choice—and, if so, whether they will be able to impose that choice on special interests at home (not to mention the East European parties)—remains to be seen. In the meantime, they may have reason to recall another time-honored saying: the old Chinese curse, "May you live in interesting times!" In Soviet-East European relations, the coming times should be interesting indeed.

6. *The Economist* (London), May 7, 1983, pp. 33–34. For other reports on preparations for the summit, see John F. Burns in the *New York Times*, May 10, 1983, and *RFER*, Czechoslovak Situation Report/9 (May 19, 1983).

Contributors

John C. Campbell served for a dozen years in the Department of State, mainly in the Office of Eastern European Affairs and on the Policy Planning Staff. From 1955 to 1978 he was senior research fellow and then director of studies at the Council on Foreign Relations. He has written extensively on American foreign policy, Soviet foreign policy, and the affairs of Eastern Europe. Among his works are *American Policy Toward Communist Eastern Europe, Tito's Separate Road: America and Yugoslavia in World Politics,* and *Successful Negotiation: Trieste 1954.*

Raymond L. Garthoff is a senior fellow in Foreign Policy Studies at the Brookings Institution. He served as Ambassador to Bulgaria from 1977 through 1979 and is a retired Foreign Service officer specializing in Soviet and East European affairs. He is also the author of a number of books and studies on Soviet policy and international affairs, including *Soviet Military Policy* (1966) and a forthcoming study on American-Soviet relations in the 1970s and 1980s.

John P. Hardt is associate director for senior specialists and senior specialist in Soviet economics of the Congressional Research Service. He is also adjunct professor of economics at both George Washington and Georgetown universities. His doctoral degrees in economics and Soviet area training were received at Columbia University. Dr. Hardt is a frequent traveler to Eastern Europe and the Soviet Union.

Pierre Hassner is a senior research associate at the Centre d'Etudes et de Recherches Internationales, Fondation Nationale des Sciences Politiques in Paris. He is the author of *Change and Security in Europe; Europe in the Age of Negotiation; The Left in Europe: Security Implications and International Dimensions;* and of many contributions to symposia, including *Eurocommunism and Détente* (Rudolf L. Tőkés, editor) and, most recently, *The Atlantic Alliance and Its Critics* (Robert W. Tucker, editor). He has also written many articles on international relations, particularly on East-West relations in Europe, including "Moscow and the Western Alliance" (*Problems of Communism,* May–June 1981).

A. Ross Johnson is a senior staff member of The Rand Corporation in Santa

Monica, California. He has engaged in research on international political and security issues, with special attention to East European affairs. He has led projects on Soviet-East European relations, East European military establishments, Yugoslavia, Poland, and communist media. Dr. Johnson lectures frequently on East European affairs and is the principal author of *East European Military Establishments: The Warsaw Pact Northern Tier* (1982).

Andrzej Korbonski is professor of political science and the Director of the Center for Russian and East European Studies at the University of California, Los Angeles. He has written extensively on various aspects of Soviet and East European politics and economics.

Paul Marer is professor and chairperson of international business at the School of Business, Indiana University. He is the author of *Soviet and East European Foreign Trade*, editor of *U.S. Financing of East-West Trade*, coeditor (with J. M. Montias) of *East European Integration and East-West Trade* and (with E. Tabaczynski) of *Polish-U.S. Industrial Cooperation*. Professor Marer is the author of more than fifty articles and chapters on the economies of Eastern Europe, East-West trade and finance, and intra-CMEA relations. He has served as consultant to the World Bank on centrally planned economies, to the International Monetary Fund on Hungary, to the OECD on East-West technology transfer, and to various congressional committees on Eastern Europe.

Angela E. Stent is associate professor of government at Georgetown University. She is also an associate of the Georgetown Center for Strategic and International Studies and a member of its Soviet Project. She has published extensively on Soviet-West European relations and East-West trade and technology transfer and is the author of *From Embargo to Ostpolitik: The Political Economy of West German-Soviet Relations, 1955–1980* (1981) and *Soviet Energy and Western Europe* (1982).

Sarah Meiklejohn Terry is assistant professor of political science, and a former associate dean, at Tufts University. She is also a fellow of the Russian Research Center of Harvard University. Her publications include *Poland's Place in Europe: General Sikorski and the Origin of the Oder–Neisse Line, 1939–1943* (1983), awarded the 1983 George Lewis Beer Prize in European International Affairs by the American Historical Association, and numerous articles on contemporary East European affairs.

Jiri Valenta is associate professor and coordinator of Soviet and East European Studies at the Naval Postgraduate School, Monterey, California, and a Woodrow Wilson Fellow in the International Security Studies Program. He is the author of *Soviet Intervention in Czechoslovakia, 1968:*

Anatomy of a Decision (1979), coauthor of *The Soviet Invasion of Afghanistan: Three Perspectives* (1980), and coeditor of and contributor to *Eurocommunism between East and West* (1980) and *Soviet Decisionmaking for National Security* (1983).

William Zimmerman is professor of political science and a research scientist at the Center for Russian and European Studies, University of Michigan. His most recent articles have appeared in the *American Political Science Review, World Politics,* and the *British Journal of Political Science.* He is a coeditor, with Morris Bornstein and Zvi Gitelman, of *East-West Relations and the Future of Eastern Europe* (1981).

Index

365